Science, Faith, and Revelation

An Approach to Christian Philosophy

SCIENCE, FAITH, AND REVELATION

An Approach to Christian Philosophy

Edited by
BOB E. PATTERSON

BROADMAN PRESS
Nashville, Tennessee

© Copyright 1979 • Broadman Press

4218-09
ISBN: 0-8054-1809-1

Dewey Decimal Classification: 200.1
Subject heading: RELIGION—PHILOSOPHY

Library of Congress Catalog Card Number: 79-50751
Printed in the United States of America

Contributors

ROBERT M. BAIRD — Professor of Philosophy, Baylor University, Waco, Texas

G. R. BEASLEY-MURRAY — Professor of New Testament, Southern Baptist Theological Seminary, Louisville, Kentucky

JOHN POWELL CLAYTON — Professor of Religious Studies, Furness College, University of Lancaster, Lancaster, England

R. E. CLEMENTS — Professor of Religion, Fitzwilliams College, Cambridge, England

RICHARD B. CUNNINGHAM — Professor of Christian Philosophy, Southern Baptist Theological Seminary, Louisville, Kentucky

ROGER HAZELTON — Professor of Christian Theology, Andover-Newton Theological School, Newton Centre, Massachusetts

W. L. HENDRICKS — Professor of Theology and Philosophy, Golden Gate Baptist Theological Seminary, Mill Valley, California

E. GLENN HINSON — Professor of Church History, Southern Baptist Theological Seminary, Louisville, Kentucky

OSADOLOR IMASOGIE — Professor of Religion, Nigerian Baptist Theological Seminary, Ogbomosho, Nigeria

DORAN MCCARTY	Professor of Christian Theology, Midwestern Baptist Theological Seminary, Kansas City, Missouri
JOHN MACQUARRIE	Emeritus Professor, Union Theological Seminary, New York. Lecturer, Oxford University, England
PAUL S. MINEAR	Emeritus Professor of New Testament, Yale Divinity School, New Haven, Connecticut
DAVID L. MUELLER	Professor of Theology, Southern Baptist Theological Seminary, Louisville, Kentucky
BOB E. PATTERSON	Professor of Theology, Baylor University, Waco, Texas
WILLIAM G. POLLARD	Physicist, clergyman, and author; executive director, Oak Ridge Associated Universities, Oak Ridge, Tennessee
MAX E. POLLEY	Professor of Religion, Davidson College, Davidson, North Carolina
LEROY SEAT	Professor of Religion, Hirao, Chuo-ku, Fukuoka, Japan
STUART SPRAGUE	Professor of Religion, Anderson College, Anderson, South Carolina
FRANK STAGG	Professor of New Testament, Southern Baptist Theological Seminary, Louisville, Kentucky
AL STUDDARD	Professor of Philosophy and Religion, Pembroke State University, Pembroke, North Carolina

Contents

PREFACE

To me, Eric C. Rust will always be the "Great Reconciler." He did for me what I had been unable to do for myself—reconcile the worlds of science, philosophy, Christian doctrine, and the Bible in a wholesome and winsome way. Like most American youth, I grew up in a completely secular atmosphere, i.e., I assumed that God did not exist (or if he did, he didn't make much difference). And like a fish in the sea, I unthinkingly gulped in the credo of secular naturalism—the provisional character of all reality, the temporal process is the only process, the relativity of all values, and my own self-sufficiency. I never dreamed during those formative years that soon, as a young person in a Baptist college, God would place his arresting hand on me, that I would be soundly converted ("born again") to a personal faith in Jesus Christ as Savior and Lord, that I would turn to the Bible as a full authority in matters of faith and practice, or that I would urgently seek to lead my secular friends to a faith in Christ.

Since God's call to Christian vocation was as imperative to me as his call to conversion, I began to prepare while in college for a Christian ministry. Soren Kierkegaard said that there are two types of people: those who are inert, and those who are alert. As a Christian I was suddenly thrown, wide-awake and gawking, into a new cosmos of meaning that I had not known to exist a short time before. But I could neither forget nor ignore the world of my "spiritually inert" years. I read the words of Charles Darwin long before I read the words of Jesus. My studies in the hard sciences had been naturalistically slanted (deterministic, reductionistic, and naively realistic), and this mentality had unfortunately carried over into my studies in psychology, sociology, and history. As a new Christian I knew that God was the center of cosmos and life, but I was unnerved by some of the dilemmas posed in technology and science. I sensed that biblical theism should be the intellectual context in which all my future studies should

ix

find illumination and moral norms, but I was puzzled over how this happy blend was to come about. My hopes for a dialogue between Christian values and scientific commitments was becoming urgent.

I completed my college work and then took a year of graduate program in philosophy. In this discipline I struggled with the impossible—trying to bring together in a meaningful harmony the thought worlds of logical positivism and existentialism while the world of science and the world of the Bible constantly clamored to get into the arena of action. By the time I walked into the classroom of Eric C. Rust and took my seat, I needed help. I could see, recognize, and even talk about many of the trees in the forest, but I could not discover how the root systems intertwined. I needed someone to paint for me on a broad canvas a picture of the whole forest. As Professor Rust painted, I started seeing how individual trees fitted into the larger cluster. With a healthy balance of piety and scholarship, Rust was beginning to show me how God's divine revelation could be in dialogue with the arts and sciences. He was leading me to see that my personal faith in Jesus Christ could coalesce rather than conflict with my modern world.

I was not the only one for whom Professor Rust was the "Reconciler." He helped "put it together" for scores of my fellow students. What the psychologists call the "pregnant moment" came for a host of us young theologs in Rust's classroom when we said, "Ah, yes! Now I see." This British Baptist who came to the "colonies" to teach was a providential gift to many of us. Southern Seminary remains one of the most exciting schools in America for young people preparing for a Christian ministry, and Eric Rust is one of the reasons for that excitement. For three years in graduate school I was his assistant Teaching Fellow. Although I never developed an Oxford accent, I did profit immeasurably from this intellectually stimulating and spiritually warm relationship. Through his students Rust's influence has penetrated American religious life for more than a quarter of a century, and through our students his influence will go marching on.

Editing this work has been a distinct privilege for me, and certainly a labor of joy. I have divided the volume into four parts to correspond to the four major emphases of Professor Rust's writings. The general theme of the work is the perspective of faith, and the four parts are: faith and transcendence, faith and the historical process, faith and the biblical revelation, and faith and the natural order. I have asked three groups to contribute chapters to the book: colleagues of Rust, other international scholars, and former students of Rust. Each writer is a gifted and respected scholar with expertise in his professional field. This book is the disciplined reflection of good minds on the implications of the Christian faith in four areas.

In editing this volume I am indebted to others. My thanks go to my secretaries Virginia Ann Cooley and Cathy Walling for their skills at the typewriter, and to my graduate assistant, David Trantham, for his library skills. I am grateful to Baylor University for its generous sabbatical program in giving me a leave of absence to complete this project. I am grateful to Southern Baptists for nurturing me, for educating me, for allowing me to study with a man such as Dr. Rust, and for giving me a place to serve. Finally, I am pleased that Broadman Press is publishing this book, because Broadman Press honors itself as it honors a distinguished son, Eric C. Rust.

BOB E. PATTERSON

Baylor University

1.

Eric Charles Rust
Apostle to an Age of Science and Technology

E. Glenn Hinson

Those who are familiar with the classroom teaching, writings, and lecture circuits of Eric Rust will understand readily why I have labeled him an "apostle to an age of science and technology." In most of his career as minister, teacher, and scholar, he has wrestled with and addressed himself to the relationship of Christian faith to modern science, an issue which has increasingly taken a central place in Christianity.

Rust's work is appraised most accurately as an attempt to make the central verities of Christian faith come alive in the modern context, not for eye-catching novelties. Rust would see himself in the lineage of Paul, Augustine, Calvin, Pascal, Kierkegaard, and other interpreters of biblical faith in changing times and circumstances. He has never sought a priori, Hegel-like, to formulate a grand design which would encompass all truth. Quite the contrary, he has labored hard to awaken his contemporaries, embued with science and technology as he himself has been, to the truths which Christians have believed God gave by divine revelation.

For this reason it is futile to try to thrust Eric Rust into modern theological pigeonholes—Barthian, Neoorthodox, Tillichian, Existentialist, Process, Theology of Hope. Many of these influences can be seen in his teaching and writing, to be sure, and Rust will readily admit his indebtedness to them. Knowing the way certain great books sometimes seem to "fall from heaven" at pivotal moments when we are most amenable to their influence, I would judge that William Temple's *Nature, Man and God,* first published in 1934, had the most visible influence on Eric Rust's philosophical and theological outlook. It was the book which "put it all together," as it were, in an area of intense concern at that moment.

But behind Temple and all the others one could mention we must see the Bible and the biblical revelation as the axle around which

13

Rust's mind has revolved. Eric Rust, no more than the rest of us, could scarcely escape the formative influence of his family's faith. It was no surprise really that, though setting his course in science and mathematics, he ended up in the study of theology under H. Wheeler Robinson. Students of Rust know how often he alludes to Robinson and, more significantly, how much the realism of the Old Testament intrudes upon his view of reality. In the last analysis, Rust weighs and judges modern questions in light of "salvation history," the heart of biblical faith, *veritas Hebraica,* to borrow a phrase from Jerome. He couples an empiricism drawn from science with a biblical realism. -

Here is where we must give Eric Rust himself full credit. Working in a conservative theological context, he has fed through his own mind and heart a multiplicity of issues posed for Christian faith by modern science and technology. He has sorted out and tested the issues by channeling them through a complex computer program set up by intensive study of the Scriptures and great theologians. At the end he has come out with a sane and balanced perspective on Christian faith in the modern world. Some would criticize the absence of startling and innovative thoughts as a lack of originality. Whether this criticism is fair will depend on how we define originality. If it means uniqueness or novelty, then Eric Rust, like many of the rest of us, would not qualify. If it means freshness in understanding old truths, then he would qualify in an unusual way. He has "Rusticized" Christian faith in its central tenets, and in this he has rendered a service which will benefit future generations as much as his own.

The Shaping of a Scientist

From the beginning Eric Rust must have felt the tension of the two poles of a modern Christian—faith and science. Until about age twenty-two he was drawn more strongly toward a scientific career, though, like his father, he maintained an active involvement in the life of Baptist churches near his home, doing some lay preaching.

Eric Charles Rust was born at Gravesend, England, June 6, 1910 to Charles Henry Rust and Ruth Wiles. His father was a master barge builder. The family were members of Sittingbourne Baptist Church, in which Eric's grandfather was an elder and his father a deacon "lay preacher." Eric was baptized into this church fellowship at age fourteen.

Rust grew up in Sheerness, where his father was transferred at the outbreak of World War I and made responsible for the construction of smaller naval craft by the British Admiralty. Until age eight he attended a private school, then shifted to Borden Grammar School, a public and private school at Sittingbourne. He remained at Borden for all of his secondary education with the exception of two years (age 12-14) in the Junior Technical School, where he studied calculus at age twelve. Taking his 0-level exams at age sixteen, he demonstrated his intellectual gifts by receiving "distinctions" on ten out of twelve exams. Meanwhile, he began preaching in small Baptist churches near his home.

A scientific vocation, however, kept opening out before him. In 1928 he began to specialize in mathematics, physics, and chemistry. On the basis of his excellent performance on A-level exams he received a Royal Scholarship at the Royal College of Science, the MIT of England, where, among others, H. G. Wells had studied. Rust obtained first class honors in two years of mathematics and physics. Then, at age twenty he became a "demonstrator" or instructor in math and began doing research at the Royal College of Science. In 1930 he received the Bachelor of Science with first class honors and the ARCS at the Royal College.

At the same time a vocational conundrum began to arise. In 1928 the family moved to Bexley Heath, where they joined Trinity Baptist Church. Eric entered as a lay preacher, and during his two years at the Royal College of Science preached regularly as a member of the London Baptist Preachers Association. In this context he began wrestling with what has been his predominant interest throughout his academic career, how to reconcile faith and science. Many Baptists took a fundamentalist stance that alienated them from science. Given his scientific training, Eric Rust could not countenance such thinking. Little by little he began to see that his real calling lay not in science but in service of the church. He could be a bridge builder between faith and science.

He remained at the Royal College of Science until 1932, when he received both the Master of Science of the University of London and the DIC of the Imperial College of Science. By this time, however, his sense of vocation had shifted strongly enough to encourage him to look for theological training. The Secretary of the Baptist Union in London, M. E. Aubrey, directed him to Wheeler Robinson, principal of Regent's Park College, Oxford. Shaped as a scientist, he was now to be shaped as a minister and theologian.

The Shaping of a Minister and Theologian

When he entered Oxford University in the fall of 1932, Eric Rust was ripe for theological formation. He had resolved the vocational polarities, but the intellectual ones remained, sharpened by doing battle with fundamentalists in London. Fortunately Oxford was alive with intellectual stimulants. His tutors included H. Wheeler Robinson, a distinguished Old Testament savant; T. W. Manson, eminent in New Testament studies; John S. Whale, a young Congregationalist theologian later to distinguish himself by his exposition of Protestant theology; C. J. Cadoux, an already established authority in church history; and Nathaniel Micklem, principal of Mansfield College. He attended lectures by such notables as Austin Farrer, R. G. Collingwood, B. H. Streeter, Kenneth Kirk, C. J. Stone, and R. H. Lightfoot. All of these doubtless added something to the fertile field in which Rust's mind grew and flourished, but none quite as much as H. Wheeler Robinson.

Robinson (1872-1945) combined piety and scholarship in a remarkable way. Educated for the Baptist ministry at Edinburgh and Oxford, he held brief pastorates at Pitlochry and Coventry. In 1906 he joined the staff of Rawdon Baptist College, where he distinguished himself as a teacher and scholar and where Eric Rust later taught. From 1920 to 1942 he served as principal of Regent's Park College and was largely responsible for its moving from London to Oxford. His chief interests were in Old Testament theology and the doctrines of the Holy Spirit and redemption. Among other things Robinson had published *The Christian Doctrine of Man* (1911), *The Religious Ideas of the Old Testament* (1913), and *The Christian Experience of the Holy Spirit* (1928). The last was a writing which grew out of an experience of illness. From Robinson, Rust doubtless obtained reinforcement of an already deep and abiding love for the Old Testament, a hermeneutical method, insights into the Hebrew approach to history, and a push toward the "salvation history" school and away from the "history of religions" school.

Further nudging in the same direction came from Rust's New Testament tutor, T. W. Manson, whose significant study of *The Teaching of Jesus* first appeared in 1931. Like Manson, Rust has tenaciously insisted upon the full significance of the Jesus of history. In his first published writing he criticized even Emil Brunner, then a mentor, for seeming to "understate the historical element" while emphasizing the "supra-historical." [1]

While Robinson and Manson were steering Rust toward the "salvation history" school, R. G. Collingwood, whose lectures he attended at Oxford, supplied him with a crucial insight for relating faith to history. In lectures given while Rust was at Oxford but published posthumously in 1946, entitled *The Idea of History,* Collingwood took issue with those who wanted to treat history as a science. While he admitted that evolution supplied a model for history as for nature to some degree, he contended at the same time that the historian's task differs from the scientist's. The historian distinguished between what Collingwood called "the outside" and "the inside" of events, something which the scientist cannot do. History, he contended, is not "a story of successive events or an account of change" but "knowledge of mind" and the historian's task is to rethink the thoughts of history.[2]

In 1935, having taken first class honors in the honors school at Oxford, Eric Rust took his first pastorate at Bath. As war clouds gathered on the horizon, his theological interests increased. In the meantime, the writings of both Barth and Brunner began to appear in English translations. Barth's commentary on *The Epistle to the Romans* was translated by Edwyn C. Hoskyns and published in 1932. Brunner's trilogy—*The Mediator, The Divine Imperative,* and *Man in Revolt*—appeared serially in English translations in 1934, 1937, and 1939. Despite the towering influence of Barth in European theology, it was Brunner, especially in *Man in Revolt,* who added most to Rust's theological perspective at this time. Rust sided with Brunner against Barth, for instance, in accepting natural revelation. "The injunction of Karl Barth is salutary, that 'we cannot speak of God simply by speaking of man in a loud voice'," he wrote in *The Christian Understanding of History,* "although we cannot follow him in denying any point of contact whereby we may grasp something of the ultimate Truth. Our conscience and our reason alike may be vitiated by sin but we must not deny that they provide us with signposts to reality, albeit paradoxical." [3] He found Brunner compatible with his own thought in many ways, but interest in John Baillie's writings kept him from a complete identification with neo-orthodoxy. Baillie directed his attention also to Paul Tillich, whose publications were just beginning to appear in English.

In December, 1939 Rust moved to Oxford Road Baptist Church in Birmingham. There he continued to sustain academic contacts. He served as extension lecturer for the University of Birmingham and taught sixth form mathematics at King Edward High School, a school which counted J. B. Lightfoot and B. F. Westcott among its distinguished alumni. Meantime, he was writing *The Christian Understanding of History,* a book which earned him an Oxford B. D. in 1946. In this book one may see the maturation of the minister and scholar. Not surprisingly, in December, 1942 he received an invitation to become pastor of a large Baptist congregation, the New North Road Church, in Huddersfield. He also became extension lecturer at the University of Leeds. Then, in 1946, he was asked to become senior tutor at Rawdon College.

Teacher and Theologian

At Rawdon Rust taught biblical theology, ethics, philosophy of religion, and Old Testament. When A. C. Underwood, principal of Rawdon, died in 1948, Rust added world religions and systematic theology. His academic reputation grew. In 1947 he gave an academic address on "Science and Religion" at the Seventh Baptist World Congress held in Copenhagen. In 1952 he was invited to Crozer Theological Seminary as visiting professor of biblical theology and, while there, to give the Norton Lectures at the Southern Baptist Theological Seminary. In May, 1953 he joined the faculty of the latter and continued there until his retirement.

A study of Rust's teaching and writing during this period of his life will reveal little shift in its basic salvation history thrust. He has addressed himself to new questions as they have arisen and interacted with new philosophical and theological currents. The usually reflective way in which he evaluates the thought of others will sometimes give the appearance of a shift, for Rust can speak appreciatively of views as far removed from his own as "God is dead" theology. Moreover, we must remember that his active career has spanned a generation prolific in theological currents: neo-orthodoxy, existentialism, radical or secular theology, process theology, and the theology of hope. He has not missed the fact that all of these have struck gold sometimes in their quest to enrich the Christian understanding of faith.

At the same time Eric Rust has shifted and weighed each of these currents in the apparatus he devised early. He is interpreted most accurately as a representative of the "salvation history" school who has spiraled outward from this traditional base in response to questions of faith in relation to the modern world. As he has proceeded to trace a path farther and farther outward from the center, he has registered little discernible change of position, but he has assimilated much that coalesces with the center. The center has always been biblical faith, not according to the fundamentalists' proof-texting method but according to conservative critical historical interpretation.

This hypothesis can be established rather easily by looking at Rust's publications in chronological order. First of all, the subjects of his writings, the fact that he has taught chiefly in the field of philosophy of religion notwithstanding, show an abiding and dominant interest in biblical and especially Old Testament theology, a subject he has taught most of his career. Of ten major publications, four have been devoted specifically to commentary on biblical theology: *Nature and Man in Biblical Thought* (1953); a commentary on "Judges, Ruth, I and II Samuel," in *The Laymen's Bible Commentary* (c. 1961); *Salvation History* (1962); and *Covenant and Hope: A Study in the Theology of the Prophets* (1972). In addition, numerous brief articles have dealt with such topics as "The Theology of the Old Testament" [4] and "The Theology of the Prophets." [5] His competence in biblical theology has remained high even as he has relinquished a formal teaching responsibility in the area.

The same point is confirmed, secondly, by observing the content of the remaining writings, which have dealt chiefly with two topics—faith and history, and faith and science. In looking at Rust's views, as a matter of fact, one must be careful not to distinguish even these two topics sharply, for Rust has, as it were, reversed the secular trend in approaching both nature and history. Whereas secularists from Comte on have insisted on using the model of science to interpret history, i.e. as cause and effect, Rust, perhaps taking a cue from Collingwood, uses the model of salvation history to interpret nature. Even nature has an "inside" as well as an "outside." Thus, salvation history everywhere dominates his theology, apologetics, or whichever term is most accurate to describe his work.

The dominance of salvation history is evident in *The Christian Understanding of History*, a modern version of Augustine's classic philosophy of history, *The City of God*. The thesis which Rust argues is that "the true meaning of historical existence is disclosed by God only to faith, for this meaning is concerned with the sovereign purpose of a personal God, to a knowledge of whom reason of itself is powerless to attain. Hence the Christian finds the truth about history in a series of historic events in which God himself acts in order to disclose and actualize His purpose in the lives of men." [6] In demonstration of his thesis Rust wrote essentially two books, one constructing a philosophy of history and the other summarizing salvation history.[7] It is revealing that subsequently he expanded and updated *The Christian Understanding of History* by producing two separate volumes, one entitled *Salvation History* (1962) and the other *Towards a Theological Understanding of History* (1963).[8] In the sixteen or seventeen intervening years Rust did not perceptibly modify his earlier position about faith and history. To be sure, he interacted with writings which had appeared in the interim and smoothed the rough edges off his own views. But his essential thesis remained the same. Christians take evil seriously and affirm that God, "a living and personal reality," acts redemptively "by disclosing himself and his purpose in history in such a way that his purpose becomes actualized and dynamically redemptive in historical existence. Hence God reveals himself in a special stream of historical events which thereby bears the central meaning of all history and becomes the focal point for the actualization of that meaning." [9]

The dominance of the salvation history model is equally evident in Rust's handling of the faith-science issue. He is, of course, an empiricist, but not of the philosophical stripe. He has argued rather for "a wider empiricism" in which there is room for divine disclosure. In his initial venture into this arena he admitted quite readily that he would not hold on to the biblical world view as literalists do. "The Biblical world-view must be corrected by the discoveries of modern science," he conceded, "and a rational critique of it should have complete freedom. . . . The Biblical science is not ours, and it needs to be corrected by our more exact knowledge." [10] He proceeded to argue, however, that nature, like history, possessed an "inside" as well as an "outside." God "is directly behind every event of the natural order, and in some way He is especially present for the redemption of men and the fulfillment of His purpose." [11] The scientist, *qua* scientist, cannot enter into an interpretation of the "inside" of nature's processes, but the person of faith can. In interpreting nature and man, then, Rust insisted that "Christian thinkers will lean to the Biblical rather than to alien modes of interpretation" and that "They will, of course, be prepared to emend these in so far as they do not adequately express the basic presupposition that God was in Christ." On the periphery biblical modes may not affect interpretation so much. "The nearer we get to the centre, however, the more the Biblical categories and concepts will condition our thinking." [12]

In its application this approach results in the rejection of "natural theology," for example, that of Thomas Aquinas, which would begin with the "analogy of being" and reason from that to faith. Rust has consistently followed the Augustinian line with Pascal, Kierkegaard, and others: *credo ut intellegam,* "I believe so that I may understand." Here Rust comes very close to the early Barth. We cannot understand God the Creator unless we first know him as the Redeemer, that is, in Christ. "In the Bible we do not start from metaphysical being but from the revealed character of God; not from speculation but from personal disclosure." [13] What the Bible reveals about nature is its utter dependence and, conversely, God's complete sovereignty. "He can stand alone, the self-sufficient free and sovereign Lord, perfect in Himself. Apart from Him, on the other hand, the world could not exist." [14] At the same time Rust finds a consonance between the Christian doctrine of "continuous creation" and modern scientific thought. Fortunately, he notes, the old mechanical theory is giving way to a view of the universe which is more amenable to faith.

In what is undoubtedly his most erudite and sophisticated publication, *Science and Faith: Towards a Theological Understanding of Nature* (1967), Rust spiraled out a considerable distance from *Nature and Man in Biblical Thought* in grappling with the science-faith issue. He undertakes in this work to give a solid grounding for a Christian epistemology which would stand firm against rationalism. In the process he relies heavily upon Michael Polanyi's theory of the personal nature of all knowledge and the use of analogies by I. T. Ramsey, and he interacts with data from many scientific and technological fields in a significant way. Nevertheless, he remains firmly anchored in the salvation history stream. The Incarnation, God's redemptive activity, unlocks the mystery of nature and man, viz. the nature of God's creatorhood.

So behind the observable realm that science studies, faith sees the transcendent presence, immanently active, the personal depth who sustains and redeems his creatures, who called them into being out of "not being," and who will ultimately bring them into the perfect actualization of his creative intention. He stands above our spaces and beyond our times, and yet is present in and through all spaces and times, for they are his creative work. Creation and consummation, providential activity and miraculous disclosure, man in nature and yet in his personal transcendence controlling nature—here faith illuminates science as science may illuminate faith. The models of science and the analogues of faith may become complementary.[15]

In the body of this important book Rust argues that these two ways of knowing, that of science and that of faith, coalesce rather than conflict with one another. He deftly, even if critically, reconciles the biblical doctrine of creation with the scientific theory of evolution, the biblical understanding of human beings as psychomatic wholes with modern physiological and psychological interpretations, and the biblical doctrine of incarnation with the "sacramental universe" model of modern science. It is never the scientific answer that is normative, however. Rust leaves no room for doubt here. However much we may learn externally from science about the nature of things, he insists, it is from God's self-disclosure—above all, that self-disclosure in Christ—that we gain true and reliable insight into reality. In the conclusion of *Science and Faith,* denying that any physio-chemical explanation ever suffices to explain life, he lays out clearly his own perspective:

Man does have an inner being which is more than a bundle of reflex actions. Human personality has an inward freedom and a sense of moral obligation which no causal scheme can finally explain. There is a beauty and harmony in the universe for which mere mechanical notions of material particles can never satisfactorily account. There is cooperation and directiveness in the process of living things to which random mutations in genes and natural selection do not hold the key. The universe points towards the incarnate Christ, in whom the principle of order and meaning has tabernacled in our midst. He is still disclosing himself to us in all his redemptive glory. Wherever men seek for meaning they are encountering him, and his immanent Spirit, present creatively and sustainingly throughout the created order, still opens our blind eyes that we may behold his glory, who holds all things together.[16]

The dominance of the salvation history model is also evident in two recent works by Rust which have not been mentioned thus far—one an evaluation of evolutionary or process philosophy, the other an evaluation of secular or radical theology. In the first, *Evolutionary Philosophies and Contemporary Theology* (1969), he reflected his growing sentiment that no intelligent person could avoid evolutionary thought. What he sought to do was to examine "how far evolutionary categories may be taken from the biological level in which they originated and applied to the understanding of the whole creative process of the universe, of the movement of human history, and of the nature of the God whom Christians worship." [17] He reviewed appreciatively such diverse contributors to process thought as Hegel, Temple, Harts-horne, Collingwood, Darwin, Bergson, Whitehead, Cobb, and Teil-hard. To some degree, he could position himself among followers of Whitehead or Teilhard, but never comfortably. He has greater affinity for Teilhard than for others because Teilhard's understanding of God comes closest to Christian theism, and it is "theistic faith," *viz.,* salvation history, by which Rust weighs the insights of evolutionary theories. In this book, he may have backpedaled a little ways from a less critical acceptance of evolutionary thought toward a more critical position. It is interesting, at any rate, to observe how many times he quotes or alludes to his old mentor, H. Wheeler Robinson, along with William Temple and H. H. Farmer.

In his evaluation of secular theology, *Positive Religion in a Revolutionary Time* (1970), Rust has again come forth with a balanced appraisal of the movement which resulted from Dietrich Bonhoeffer's call for "religionless Christianity." Defining "religion" in the narrow sense in which Bonhoeffer employed it, to use God as a *deus ex machina,* Rust can agree with this summons. He can also applaud the challenge to this-worldy concern which radical theology issued. However, he does not define religion in the narrow sense in which Bonhoeffer did; consequently, he argues for a more "religionish" interpretation of Bonhoeffer himself than the latter's most zealous followers allowed. Not unexpectedly, he does so from the background of traditional emphases of salvation history—worship of the transcendent God, the incarnation, and the Christian hope. Christianity can see itself as a religion which has continuity with all religious history and yet as unique in that the *eschaton* has become incarnate in Christ.

The Contribution of Eric Rust

It may be premature to assess the contribution of Eric Rust to us, for he is still teaching and writing as senior professor of Christian philosophy at Southern Seminary. However, he has already left a substantial legacy through his preparation of scholars and ministers, his sermons and lectures, and his writings which may allow some room for judgment even now.

Rust himself, I suspect, would prefer to be judged first as a minister and teacher of ministers, and in both of these tasks he has excelled, as his career testifies. It is difficult to measure impact on other persons, but there can be no question that he has etched his perceptions about Christian faith deeply upon the minds of many. A scintillating and stimulating preacher and teacher, he has compelled a generation of students to scratch below the surface and to come up with more profound solutions to questions than they would have sought by themselves. Many students have groaned and moaned under the load he placed on them, but none has come through his classes with the same outlook he or she entered with.

Laboring within a conservative context both in England and America, he has done as much if not more than any Baptist scholar to demonstrate the way in which a serious Christian can relate his or her faith to the modern world. To be sure, he has not converted all or even most conservatives to his point of view. Among Southern Baptists, for example, the majority are still biblical literalists or near-literalists. Indeed, a small but vociferous group called the Baptist Faith and Message Fellowship is intent on halting the critical-historical interpretation of the Bible in the seminaries and Convention agencies. Such people as these have not heard and perhaps will never hear Eric Rust.

Some may fault Rust himself for this fact. The truth of the matter is, he has not written for a popular audience. Instead, he has addressed himself to scholars, ministers, and students. In this, I think he has acted wisely. The time was not right for wholesaling his approach. Consequently, he has constructed a bridge which some, especially of the present generation, are ready to cross. He has equipped others to lead the next generation across. We must remember that historical critical interpretation had barely gotten started even in Southern Baptist seminaries when Eric Rust first began teaching at Southern in 1953. What he has done in his teaching, writing, and lecturing has been to show that we today need not fear stepping across the stream of biblical faith to the modern world. Quite consistently, he has demonstrated how we may scrutinize the perceptions of the modern day about history and science under the searchlight of salvation history.

The specific judgments he has made for his day will not be his enduring legacy, and he would not expect it to be so. He has revised his own writings several times in a span of three decades. New data which are hurled at us in a dizzying whirl call for continuous assessment and reconstruction. His enduring legacy, therefore, consists precisely in revealing how we go about looking at our contemporary existence through spectacles supplied by revelation, God's disclosure of himself and his purpose in history. Many persons with less love for the Scriptures than Eric Rust may dismiss this approach with a wave of the hand as too traditional. In the last analysis, however, we have to ask whether the church has ever laid hold on another method. The perennial issue for Christian believers is whether they have anything to say to persons of their age and time beyond that which the latter already know. If they have nothing further, no "word of the Lord," then they may as well go out of business. It is precisely because they are convinced they have this word about the inner meaning of things that they have a sure calling. It is this which has constituted and validated the apostolate of Eric Charles Rust.

NOTES

[1] E. C. Rust, *The Christian Understanding of History* (London & Redhill: Lutterworth Press, 1947), pp. 82-83.

[2] See R. G. Collingwood, *The Idea of History* (New York: Oxford University Press, 1946), pp. 205ff.

[3] Rust, *op. cit.*, p. 47.

[4] *Broadman Bible Commentary* (Nashville: Broadman Press, 1969), Vol. 1, pp. 71-86.

[5] *Review and Expositor,* LXXIV (Summer, 1977).

[6] *The Christian Understanding of History,* p. 21.

[7] Observe especially that Part II (pp. 87-188) dealt with "The Course of Salvation History and Its Eschatological Framework."

[8] The latter covers the same ground as Part I and III of *The Christian Understanding of History.*

[9] *Towards a Theological Understanding of History* (New York: Oxford University Press, 1963), pp. 14f.

[10] *Nature and Man in Biblical Thought* (London: Lutterworth Press, 1953), p. 17.

[11] *Ibid.,* p. 18.

[12] *Ibid.,* p. 19.

[13] *Ibid.,* p. 253.

[14] *Ibid.,* p. 258.

[15] *Science and Faith* (New York: Oxford University Press, 1967), p. 141.

[16] *Ibid.,* p. 316.

[17] *Evolutionary Philosophies and Contemporary Theology* (Philadelphia: Westminster Press, 1969), p. 15.

PART I
FAITH AND TRANSCENDENCE

2.

Karl Heim and Teilhard de Chardin
Christian and Scientific Responses
to the Problem of Transcendence

Doran McCarty

People of faith have characteristically believed in something (or someone) which is beyond them; this is the transcendence of God. Also the people of faith have believed in their human ability to relate to this Beyond. This is the transcendence of man in his freedom above the natural order and above animal nature.[1] Without a belief in a transcendent God, few persons find satisfying religious experiences or an adequate religious system. It is unusual to find a person who does not believe in human transcendence even if it is borne out of a purely humanistic framework and does not affirm any type of immortality.

While it has been characteristic of the human race to believe in transcendence of persons and that which is beyond humans, these ideas have been severely challenged with increasing intensity over the last 500 years. New, deterministic, physical sciences challenged the idea of the transcendence of God and won in many intellectual circles. The debate went on, however, because of the belief in the transcendence of man; there had to be a way to explain the human phenomenon. Darwinianism challenged the transcendence of man and the debate ended. From that point on scientists talked to scientists about science. They talked about those who believe in transcendence more than they talked to them. It seemed as if science and religion started with apparent mutually exclusive epistemologies and metaphysics. The theologians talked to theologians about theology, but there was no room for them to stand on the unholy ground of the scientific method.

Two twentieth-century religious savants found ways to stand in the world of science and develop ideas of transcendence. These two persons were Karl Heim and Pierre Teilhard de Chardin. In the main, science did not hear Karl Heim and his theology. The church was too busy with Barthianism to listen very carefully. Science has been listening more keenly to Teilhard de Chardin, and while the verdict is still out, he may cause conversations to begin again between theologians and other disciplines.

Transcendence in Historical Perspective

Belief in transcendence has not been the only human religious response. Animism has been more immanent than transcendent, identifying an indistinct, diffuse, and impersonal power with objects. However, from time to time animistic people spoke of a special agent, often referred to as man, invading the objects thereby creating the kind of dichotomy needed in the conceptualization of transcendence.

Early cultures had difficulty verbalizing transcendence. While Greek polytheism had gods who were external to humans, the gods were projections of what humans experienced (beauty, love, war, etc.) more than a transcendent reality. However, this was a new stage because they were able to conceptualize experience and project the conceptualizations rather than just responding to the unknown and novel.

The religions of "the fertile crescent" struggled toward belief in transcendence but often not in a self-conscious way. While Re was spoken of as a transcendent God, still the king was divine. While Baal could be suspected of going away on a trip, he was identified with the natural processes, especially fertility. Belief in transcendence appeared in the fertile crescent, and it can be seen in the religious belief in the Genesis account of Abraham. The vehicle of transcendence in the Genesis account is highly anthropomorphic, but it shows a transcendent God. Abraham's God was not so highly transcendent that he did not affect the affairs of the world; but when he did, God's immanence was seen as an intrusion into the world rather than a condition of immanence.

The classical religion of the Hebrews and ancient Israel was a transcendent religion although there were groups within these who were deeply influenced by fertility religions. Nevertheless, it was the religion of transcendence which won out in Israel. In fact, the question changed from "is God transcendent?" to "how transcendent is God?" Many Hebrews had a strong sense of transcendence and believed that only special people communicated with God such as Moses on Sinai. God spoke to special persons—the prophets. God resided at a special place which was progressively defined as more removed: Zion, the temple and the holy of holies. They believed that "no man has seen God." The belief in transcendence affected the cultic rites of Israel, keeping them from using the most holy name of God and from making any icons representing God.

Transcendence was not complete in Israel's religion, for while they had the law by which the people could live without having direct access to God, there was also the word of God which came directly to the prophets. Through the word of God, the transcendent God of Israel broke into the affairs of the human race. However, the intrusion of the transcendent was neither a common phenomenon nor at man's disposal and initiation. The Law of God and the word of God existed side by side in Israel's religion although not without causing some tension. Following the Babylonian captivity, the Law became the expression of Israel's religion and the idea of the word of God diminished. The result was a modified deism. The supremacy of the Law replaced the need for new revelation. Deuteronomic justice meant that justice was programmed, mechanical, and impersonal rather than God's personal intrusion into the world to reward or punish. Another signal of the new deism was the new angelology in Judaism which served as a buffer between God and humans so that God was not directly involved with humans (and remained highly transcendent) since the intermediaries (angels) cared for divine things.

The practical deism of first-century Judaism created the climate into which John the Baptist and Jesus appeared. The Baptist was a prophet who did not appeal to the Law but claimed to have a message directly and contemporarily from God. However far Jesus went in claiming messiahship, he surpassed the audacity of the Baptist. Jesus promised that the Spirit of God rather than the Law of God would be with them. The early Christian church experienced the presence of the Spirit for several decades. The Baptist and Jesus broke the silence of God, brought God into human experience, and with the presence of the Spirit, the early Christians experienced the immanent presence of the transcendent God.

Apocalyptic literature usually signals an exaggerated transcendence and a loss of the experience of the presence of God. The book of Revelation is apocalyptic literature which sounds as if it were describing the final round of Deuteronomic justice by a "push-button" God who does not get directly and immanently involved with persons. New Testament apocalypticism reflected the beginning of a new period of high transcendence. When this was threatened by the enthusiasm of the Montanists, the church suppressed the Montanist movement.

The institutionalization of Christianity continued to heighten the notion of transcendence. Just as Judaism in the postexilic period, the Christian church developed means to mediate God and accentuate his transcendence. These means were the clergy, tradition, sacraments, the development of the Stoic idea of nature and the church itself. Also the church developed a system of Mariology and sainthood which did the same thing that angelology had done in the postexilic period. During the first fifteen centuries, the view developed that God is in heaven, but men have the church as his representative.

The idea of transcendence had been simple enough in ancient cosmology. The earth, the ancient people believed, was flat with a vaulted roof above it and a chamber in the dome of the vault. God's transcendent place was in that chamber.

The Ptolemaic view of the universe did not bring bitter opposition from the religious world because there was still room for God somewhere "out there" and that went without serious challenge. While the Copernican idea of the universe drew great opposition from the church, it was not because of protecting God's transcendence but because Copernicus replaced man as being in the geographical center of the solar system as well as theologian's commitment to biblical literalism. As far as the theologians could see, God was still "out there" and he could still influence the affairs of men. However, it was not long until transcendence became a problem. The new physical sciences were mechanistic in theory and empirical in practice. The "new" universe empirically examined had no "out there" place for God and if he existed, he could not influence the affairs of man anyway in a mechanical and deterministic world. Christian thinkers resorted to formal deism asserting that God made the mechanical and deterministic world and left it to operate without him. Deism was not satisfactory to most Christians and to few scientists. There was just no place "out there" for God. The dualism of Descartes and Kant excited philosophers, but their language was strange to theologians and not useful to the empirical sciences.

It was Friedrich Schleiermacher who found a way to deal with the problem of where to put a transcendent God. Everyone[2] still believed in the soul of man which transcends the body of man so that was the place to put God. Schleiermacher saw God in the "absolute dependence" and "god consciousness" with man. To be sure, this meant an identity of transcendence and immanence but it preserved a place for God. Schleiermacher was the father of liberalism exactly at this point. Edward Farley observed: "Generally speaking however, the total mood of liberalism was one of continuity rather than discontinuity, and one dominated by immanence rather than transcendence. 'Within' was the direction in which liberalism attempted to locate God rather than 'without'." [3] Later theologians, especially Barth and his followers, reacted negatively to Schleiermacher's identity of transcendence and immanence.

However, the nemesis of Schleiermacher was not a theologian but a divinity student turned naturalist—Charles Darwin. It was he who projected the theory which the empirical scientists accepted enthusiastically and as a result they did away with the idea of the transcendence of man and the last resting place for a transcendent God. While Darwinianism explained man biologically in a nontranscendent way, Sigmund Freud explained man psychologically in a nontranscendent way. Now there was no place for God geographically and no place for God psychologically. Darwin and Freud destroyed the transcendence of both God and man. Scientists no longer needed to speak to theologians about theology, and theologians could speak with one another only about the world of science and often in pejorative terms. This left theologians to talk among themselves about transcendence (the Barthians); to interpret all transcendent language as mythological (Bultmannians); or to interpret transcendence as being whatever the next evolutionary step is that the world is headed toward (S. Alexander and the theological futurists).[4]

There have been two Christian scholars, Karl Heim and Teilhard de Chardin, who have taken upon themselves the apologetic task of building a bridge between religion and science with a special interest in the issue of the transcendence and immanence of God and providing a "space" for God to be. Heim has had the misfortune of being overshadowed theologically by Barth and not being able to create attention in the scientific community. Teilhard is being heard both among the theologians and scientists. We have yet to find out whether his hearing is faddish or substantive and whether it is because of his power of intellect or because he was a martyred hero.

The Response of Karl Heim to the Problem of Transcendence

Karl Heim's life and thought touched on many movements and philosophies: phenomenology, existentialism, ontology, and hermeneutical principles, as well as science and Barthianism.[5] Heim was one of the early Barthian theologians, and although he never accepted some of Barth's theological positions, Heim carried with him the importance of the transcendence of God. Heim's emphasis was not Barth's. Whereas Barth's interest was to make the distance between the transcendent God and earthbound man a very great distance, Heim wanted to show that there was a place or space where a transcendent God could reside consistent with the modern world view.

Heim believes that the idea of God's transcendence of the world and universe is basic to the Christian faith and the loss of pre-Copernican astronomy has made the question of the nature of God's transcendence a critical question for the Christian faith. Heim's analysis is that the post-Copernican astronomy, which speaks of the boundlessness of the universe, destroys the idea of God as "above" or "beyond" the universe. Therefore theologians must make intelligible what they mean when they speak of God's transcendence for the Christian message to be understood in the modern world.

Heim addresses the problem of transcendence utilizing Albert Einstein's "new physics" and Martin Buber's concepts and *I and Thou*.[6] Einstein did away with absolute time and space. He saw latitude, longitude, and altitude as dimensions which help to locate objects; but in order for people to have adequate knowledge of location, they must also know time; therefore time is the fourth dimension. According to the "new physics," there is no necessity to limit the universe to four dimensions.

This is the starting point of Heim's defense of the transcendence of God. Heim writes:

There are two ways in which two given objects may be differentiated from one another. The first is exemplified by two adjacent squares on a chessboard. . . . The differentiation lies in the fact that two things occupy parts of a common space, and that within this space one of the things restricts the space which is available for the other. We shall call this relation the *boundary of content*. . . .
We see a wholly different kind of boundary-line in the case of two infinite planes intersecting at an angle. Neither plane taken by itself is bounded. Even when one intersects and passes through the other, it does not stop at the intersection to make room for the other. . . . Both retain, after as before, their character of content, we give this type of delimitation the name of *boundary of dimension* since it is in spatial dimensions that it is most clearly seen.[7]

Graphically, the boundary of content should be portrayed as on the next page: There are two objects, i.e., (1) and (2) which occupy two exclusive, limiting spaces, i.e., (A) and (B).

(1) (A)	(2) (B)

Below is the graphic picture of the boundary of dimension: In the boundary of dimension (1) occupies the space (dimension) of (A) and (2) occupies the space (dimension) of (B). Since we are dealing with two infinite planes, when they cross (C), they are in neither (A) space (dimension) nor (B) space (dimension). They share a space and do not place limitations on one another.

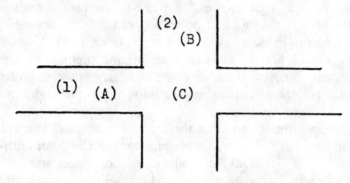

Heim relates the ideas of Buber to his interpretation of boundaries. Buber spoke of I-It relationships as being the relationships of objects or things; this corresponds to the boundary of content. Buber puts the I-Thou relation over against the I-It relation. The I-Thou relationship is a relationship of "Thous" (persons), and it is therefore a subjective relationship. If one person in the relationship treats the other person as an object rather than as a person, the relationship moves from an I-Thou relationship to an I-It relationship even though persons are involved.

As Heim sees the world, there are dimensions where we identify the objectifiable (boundaries of content) but there are also dimensions where there can be non-objectifiable egos (boundaries of dimension). Whereas Einstein saw no reason for there not to be multiple dimensions beyond the four dimensions, Heim makes multiple dimensions essential to his system.

Man is non-objectifiable ego grounded in the three (now four) dimensional world according to Heim. Man always experiences this polarity. However God is the Supreme Thou who has his own dimension and is not subject to polarity; God is supra-polar and has his supra-polar space. Where there is polarity (four dimensional), one moment follows another moment and every moment is different, but suprapolar space escapes this polarity of time.

God exists in his own supra-polar space while we are limited by our polarity. We experience the presence of God when he opens the supra-polar space to us. Jesus was the one who opened the possibility of supra-polar space to us. This is where Heim's concept of "Jesus as Leader" becomes so important to this whole system.[8] Man is unable to make a bridge from himself to God. Heim called it a "Schnee-brucke"—a bridge of snow. God in his grace (in Jesus) opens the bridge to himself. Heim writes, "if there is any possibility at all of breaking through the curse of polarity it can only be one which we cannot think out in view of our form of existence, but only accept." [9]

Tillich speaks of man's sin of transforming preliminary concern into Ultimate Concern. Heim sees man's idolatry as worship of something in the polar world, changing God into polarity rather than accepting God's supra-polarity.

Karl Heim attempts to open the modern concept of the universe for an ancient but indispensible concept for the Christian faith—the transcendence of God. Did Heim offer us science fiction, an interesting analogy of reality, or a glimpse of reality itself? [10] Heim started on the basis of the second answer and proceeded on the basis of the third. Regardless of the answer, the savant's scientific world did not take Heim seriously. They were too busy talking among themselves about their dramatic discoveries acting much as though they were the intellectual *nouveau riche*. Theologians also talked among themselves; but too many of them, defeated in previous attempts, retreated from believing that sense could be made out of both the world and God. Heim was overshadowed by towering personalities, i.e., Barth, Brunner, Tillich. Heim's intellectual defense weapons of the faith remain largely untested waiting for someone to bring them out of oblivion, even if out of season, the way Kierkegaard was belatedly discovered.

The Response of Teilhard de Chardin to the Problem of Transcendence

Teilhard de Chardin was a Jesuit and a scientist, a philosopher and a mystic. His appraoch is wholistic so that he tries to integrate all data, sacred and secular, into a single system of thought. He accuses scientists of refusing to look at all of the data and therefore not being scientific. He believes that science must be more than analytic; it must also be integrative. Specifically, Teilhard observes that scientists analyze the external, empirical data but never deal with the "within" of reality. Since science is supposed to deal with all of reality, if the "within" is real and they ignore it, they are not being scientific.

The usual interpretation of transcendence has been to talk about what is "above" and "beyond" but Teilhard speaks of the "within" of matter. Teilhard differentiates between tangential and radial energy. Tangential energy is the outward, physical energy which scientists work with. Radial energy is the "withinness" which is not subject to the physical limitations as tangential energy is (e.g. entropy). He refers to radial energy at times as love and spirit and occasionally infers that it is divine. Purpose in the universe (orthogenesis) flows from radial energy. Whereas Schleiermacher escaped the loss of "outthereness" by internalizing transcendence within the psyche of man, Teilhard seems to internalize transcendence into the heart of matter itself. There seems to be a transcendent power at work within matter when Teilhard speaks of the unity of matter. Concerning the particles of matter, "It is not possible to say that one particle is here and completely isolated from another particle that is over there. While a particle's sphere of influence may be greater at one point than another, it is coextensive with the entire universe." [11] Unless Teilhard means to provide a new definition of time and space, he infers that every particle of matter has transcendence which relates each particle to every other particle. In Teilhard's little book, *What I Believe,* he elevates the Spirit and indicates that Spirit is the "Withinness" of things.[12] The Spirit seems to be for Teilhard the reality behind even all primordial stuff. This raises the question as to whether Teilhard responds to the problem of transcendence by finding a place for a transcendent God or whether Teilhard answers with a pantheism or panentheism.

Transcendence has a larger place, however, in Teilhard's system. Teilhard believes that a particular level of reality ramifies for a period until the principle of centrism can adequately operate upon that level to cause convergence. When the intensity and convergence is great enough, it passes through a peduncle, and a new phylum appears. Teilhard traces this process of transformism through several phyla including biosphere [13] and noosphere.[14] This means that transcendence is real in Teilhard's thought, and it is dynamic rather than static. There is one more stage of transcendence in Teilhard's system: the

Christosphere.[15] Christ was the firstfruits of this stage which will finally reach the ultimate end: the Omega Point. Therefore, the main thrust of transcendence in Teilhard is not a static concept of space but a dynamic concept of the future. Transcendence has *happened* and will be completed in the Omega Point.

Whereas Heim seeks God's transcendence in a new interpretation of the world order, Teilhard seeks God's transcendence in a new interpretation of world history—although this world history certainly has changed the world order. There are interpreters who have taken this to mean that Teilhard denied transcendence. Martin Marty and Dean Peerman have said:

> To many half-thoughtful followers and to most Catholic detractors, Teilhard seemed to lead Christians to an embrace of the world, to the neglect of even a vestigial quest for the transcendent.
> Teilhard vehemently put down such followers and attackers in his lifetime. Like many men in the subsequent decade, he wanted not to deny transcendence but to reformulate the concept of it.[16]

Did Teilhard pull it off? Did he escape submerging God in a panpsychism or a pantheism? The emphases of the future and of hope have gathered theological momentum since Teilhard's writings were published. There are theologians expressing transcendence more in terms of the future than geography since Teilhard. However, there is one special area in which Teilhard's contribution exceeds that of Heim: Teilhard has attracted the attention of the scientists in a way Heim was never able to do.

The transcendence of God began as geographical and moved to the human soul when it was deposed from the universe. When the transcendence of God was exiled from the human soul, Heim found a refuge for it in the new Einsteinian world. Teilhard found the transcendent God in the "within" (not totally unlike Heim) and in the dynamic of the future.

The question is: While these "places" satisfy some as they seek a place for God, will they be adequate answers? Or, as John the Baptist asked, "Do we look for another?"

NOTES

[1] See Reinhold Niebuhr's book *The Self and the Dramas of History* (New York: Charles Scribners Sons, 1955).

[2] I do not mean that the notion of the soul had not been challenged and denied. Certainly empiricists such as Hobbes and Hume had done so, but other empiricists such as Locke and Berkeley maintained their belief in the soul of man. Apparently most men of science believed in the soul of man whether they could square it with their scientism or not.

[3] Edward Farley, *The Transcendence of God* (Philadelphia, Pa.: The Westminster Press, 1960), pp. 21-22.

[4] David Cairns, *God Up There?* (Philadelphia, Pa.: The Westminster Press, 1967), p. 36.

[5] Dean G. Peerman and Martin E. Marty, editors, *A Handbook of Christian Theologians* (New York, N. Y.: The World Publishing Company, 1965), p. 277.

[6] Martin Buber, *I and Thou,* trans. Ronald Gregor Smith (Edinburgh: T & T Clark, 1952).

[7] Karl Heim, *God Transcendent* (London: Nisbet & Co., 1935).

[8] See Karl Heim's books *Jesus the Lord* and *Jesus the World's Perfector* (Edinburgh: Oliver & Boyd, 1959).

[9] Heim, *Jesus the Lord,* p. 142.

[10] John Dillenberger, *God Hidden and Revealed* (Philadelphia, Pa.: Muhlenberg Press, 1953), p. 174.

[11] Doran McCarty, *Teilhard de Chardin,* ed. Bob E. Patterson (Waco, Texas: Word Books, 1976), p. 38.

[12] Pierre Teilhard de Chardin, *What I Believe.*

[13] "Biosphere. The realm, envelope or layer of living things which now forms a covering over the earth." McCarty, *Teilhard de Chardin,* p. 145.

[14] "Noosphere. The stage of evolution where there is an envelope or realm of thought embracing reality. . . ." *Ibid.,* p. 146.

[15] "Christogenesis, the beginning of the Christosphere is described as the term coined by Teilhard to describe the final phase of evolution (after cosmogenesis, biogenesis, anthropogenesis). This stage is the great synthesis of mankind into the 'mystical body of Christ'." *Ibid.,* p. 145.

[16] Martin E. Marty and Dean G. Peerman, editors, *New Theology No. 7* (London: The Macmillan Company, 1970), p. 16.

3.

Transcendent Beliefs
John MacQuarrie

To many people it has seemed very much of a scandal that the most important questions of life (or what have usually been taken as the most important) belong to the realm of belief rather than of assured knowledge. Some have reacted to this situation by taking the view that since they cannot *know* the answers to such questions, they will suspend any judgment on them. For instance, Bertrand Russell mentioned in his autobiography that from the time when he was a young man, he was resolved not to accept any theological proposition unless it could be substantiated in the same way as a piece of scientific knowledge.[1] This is actually an impossible demand, and it means in practice that no proposition of a theological kind could ever be accepted. On the other hand, there have also been religious thinkers who have been very unhappy that their fundamental doctrines were matters of belief and felt as much as Russell that we ought to *know* the answers to questions before giving our assent. So they have tried hard to convert belief into knowledge, and the most obvious illustration of this is the long series of attempts to prove beyond doubt the existence of God. It is generally agreed that these attempts have failed to provide demonstration, and that we still have to do with a matter of belief, not knowledge. But what is interesting is that those who have attempted to construct such proofs had the same attitude toward belief as the agnostics who suspended judgment. Both sides regarded belief as somehow unworthy and unsatisfactory, at best a makeshift that could only be made respectable through being converted into knowledge.

When I believe a proposition, a story, a body of doctrine, or whatever it may be, I accept it as true, I have confidence in it, I am even prepared to act on it, although I lack conclusive evidence that it is in fact true. We all live much of the time by our beliefs, and perhaps there are relatively few matters on which we can claim to have knowledge, in the strictest sense of the word. For a large part of the time, we move in the realm of belief, and have to accept with Bishop Butler that "probability is the guide of life." [2]

Of course, many of our beliefs relate only to some passing state of affairs, and are quite trivial. I believe that the car that has just passed me on the motorway must have been traveling at eighty miles an hour. I believe that it will be fine today, so I shall take a trip to the coast. Other beliefs are much more serious and lasting, and may be acquired, elaborated, and deepened over a long period. Such are a person's political opinions or his beliefs about his work. But people also have a core of what I may call "transcendent beliefs." In using this expression, "transcendent beliefs," I do not mean that they imply belief in a transcendent reality, though in many cases they may do so. I mean beliefs that transcend the level at which empirical evidences could, at least in principle, be decisive for establishing the truth or falsity of the beliefs or even for establishing a high degree of probability or improbability. Such would be beliefs about the nature and destiny of man, his place in the universe, about good and evil and the conduct of life, about God or the absence of God. These transcendent beliefs could equally well be called "ultimate" beliefs. It is when we come to matters of this kind that we are made very much aware of the limitations of human knowledge and of the problematic nature of belief. It is here that persons of strongly empirical temperament find themselves very uncomfortable, and may even tell us that we must not assent to beliefs that transcend the limits of what can be empirically decided. But the ultimate questions do not go away, and the problems are not solved by the vanishing of the problems. They seem to be built into our humanity, and even if only implicitly we find ourselves giving answers. The problems call for answers, and even to refuse to give an answer is in fact to give an answer of sorts. "Skepticism," as William James wrote, "is not avoidance of option; it is option of a certain particular kind of risk. Better risk loss of truth than chance of error—that is your faith-vetoer's exact position. He is actively playing his stake as much as the believer is." [3]

Let us come back to the attempts to turn belief into knowledge, to reach assured conclusions on all questions, and in particular to the many attempts that have been made to prove the existence of God. As far as our everyday beliefs are concerned, it is of course both legitimate and desirable to convert them into knowledge. A scientific hypothesis, for instance, is subjected to every kind of testing, all relevant evidence is brought to bear upon it, questions are raised about its verifiability and its falsifiability; and if it stands up to all these tests, then it becomes part of current scientific knowledge, though we recognize that the word "knowledge" is used here in something less than its strictest sense. But transcendent beliefs are not scientific hypotheses, and are therefore not amenable to the same kinds of testing and cannot be verified or falsified by the same kind of evidence. Scientific hypotheses always refer to some limited state of affairs and therefore have a context which supplies evidence relevant to the truth or falsity of the hypothesis. A transcendent belief is more like a vision of the whole, and the whole has no context.

Concerning the many attempts to prove the existence of God, Kierkegaard wrote: "With what industrious zeal, with what expenditure of time, of diligence, of writing material, the speculative philosophers have laboured to get a strong and complete proof of the existence of God! But in the same degree that the excellence of the proof increases, certitude seems to decrease." [4] This may seem a strange thing to say, but I think that reflection will show us several reasons for it.

In the first place, Kierkegaard was acutely aware that our human experience is finite. As much as any agnostic, he denied that we can ever attain to a demonstrated knowledge of the answers to transcendent or ultimate questions. These questions, as we have noted, ask about the world as a whole, but the human being is inserted into the world as one item in it, and he can never step out of it, so to speak, so that he could view reality as a whole. He may (and in fact he does) entertain beliefs about the whole or have some vision of the whole, but it is absurd either to demand or to offer the kind of demonstrable knowledge concerning the whole that we may have about limited facts or sets of fact within the whole—the facts or sets of facts with which science is concerned and about which empirical evidences may be decisive.

But Kierkegaard went further than this, in his claim that the more excellent the proof, the less sure we seem to be! Can this be the case? Well, I suppose that if the very attempt to prove God's existence is fundamentally in error, because it rests on a failure to distinguish transcendent beliefs from everyday and scientific beliefs, then it can in the long run only produce confusion and bewilderment, so that it shakes rather than establishes belief in God's reality. But there is more to it than this, and I think that Kierkegaard was pointing to something very profound in human experience when he taught that belief is not a form of knowledge (and we must remember here that he was thinking of what we are calling "transcendent" belief, not everyday beliefs or scientific beliefs). Transcendent belief is not, as it were, an inferior or provisional form of knowledge, and it could not be. Therefore we are wasting our time and misunderstanding the situation when we seek to convert this kind of belief into knowledge. Belief has an essential role to play in human existence, and it plays that role in its own right. Belief stretches the human being beyond himself; it sets before him visions that do not let him settle down in this comfortable assurance of the familiar and the well known. To go back to William James for a moment, belief assumes the risk of losing truth to be a more serious danger than the risk of embracing error. Kierkegaard conceived human existence in a surprisingly modern way, as something dynamic and as yet unfinished, always on the move, always reaching out for a completion that lies ahead. Many contemporary philosophers, from existentialists to neo-Marxists, use the word "transcendence" for this dynamic quality of man's life, and transcendent beliefs have their part to play in an existence which can itself be called "transcendence," as we shall see. For such an existence has to be lived in risk, as it is constantly projecting itself into the region of the new and untested. In such an existence, belief rather than knowledge must be our guide. To use another Kierkegaardian expression, there has to be a "leap" beyond the secure region of proofs and evidences. Perhaps it is even like leaping into Kierkegaard's "seventy thousand fathoms" of water—a procedure no doubt risky, but also exhilarating to those who have the nerve. Transcendent or ultimate beliefs, understood in this way, are not static metaphysical prejudices, inherited from the past and inhibiting further thought. The opposite is the case. These transcendent beliefs are themselves aids to transcendence. We could call them thought experiments or—to borrow a term from space exploration—"probes" out beyond the familiar and the well known, searching for the vision that will make sense of human life and give it the dignity that we feel belongs to it.

But does not this talk of dignity and feeling give the show away? Are we not confessing that these beliefs are without any cognitive significance or any link with reality? Are they not just subjective imaginings?

I have made several mentions of Kierkegaard, and many people believe that he did make belief a purely arbitrary matter, a leap of faith having no regard to the evidence. One can find passages in his writings where belief is closely linked to passion, and one could argue that he quite separates belief from knowledge and that these two lie side by side with no relation to each other. William James, too, associates belief with the will and the passions, and visualizes the possibility that these may have to be our guide when evidence is lacking or is even balanced on either side.

Admittedly, Kierkegaard in his conflict with the rationalist philosophers of his time and James in his critique of the neo-Hegelians of his time, sometimes give the impression of advocating an irrational type of faith. But it is not so simple as that. William James's pragmatic test of truth, for instance, when fully developed, is seen to be not so very different from the coherence theory of truth held by his philosophical opponents. The case is not so clear with Kierkegaard, but he does explicitly say that the believer must use his understanding and that he cannot believe nonsense.[5] If one eventually comes to believe the paradox, it is not because it is absurd *(quia absurdum)* but because reason itself has brought the thinker to a limit and impels him to go beyond the reach of reason.[6]

For my own part, I would wish to go much further than Kierkegaard in recognizing the role of critical understanding in belief. In particular, I find his scorning of probability unacceptable. He is of course right in claiming that no weight of empirical probability will ever establish a transcendent belief, because inevitably one is going to come to the critical leap *eis allo genos,* as he is fond of saying. But does he do justice to the negative significance of probability? For instance, there is no accumulation of probability derived from observation that would establish belief in God's beneficence, for this is not an empirical generalization but a transcendent belief. On the other hand, an accumulation of evidence that the universe is full of suffering, waste, and evils of various kinds, might be so impressive that one would be deterred from making the leap to belief in divine goodness. One can agree that there are important questions where one must go beyond the evidence and commit oneself to a belief—and, as we have seen, even the refusal to commit oneself is to take up an option. But we can only commit ourselves responsibly if we have reflected as deeply as possible on the situation and taken account of whatever evidence may be relevant. If our beliefs are relevant at all to our lives, then some evidence must be relevant. To assert this is quite compatible with holding that the multiplication of evidence will never demonstrate a transcendent belief. To give an illustration related to Kierkegaard's work, we may agree with him that if we had the most minute historical details concerning the life of Jesus Christ, this would bring us no nearer to establishing faith's assertion that he is God incarnate, for that is not an assertion of the same order. But if the evidence made it seem highly probable (and Kierkegaard rightly holds that it can never attain to certainty) that Jesus was a hypocrite or that he was a mythical invention, then this would surely deter us from embracing the church's transcendent beliefs about him. It is probability rather than improbability that must be our guide. There are beliefs that cannot be converted through demonstration into knowledge, but whatever beliefs we hold—and the more ultimate the beliefs, the more strongly this applies—we must hold them responsibly, and that means reasonably. We have to take account of what is compatible with the belief or even indirectly supportive of it, but also of what counts against it, and to weigh them against one another. Some of our transcendent beliefs will stand up to this kind of testing. They will remain beliefs and they will include a leap beyond the evidence, but we shall be able to hold them without any *sacrificium intellectus.* On the other hand, it may come about that a belief has so much arrayed against it that finally we are driven to abandon it.

At this point, however, it is worth noting that a belief should not be abandoned as soon as it strikes against difficulties. I have said that transcendent beliefs are not the same as the hypotheses of the scientist, but there are some analogies. Thus some philosophers of science recognize a principle of tenacity in scientific method, by which is meant that only by adhering to a line of inquiry and by not giving it up too quickly will an investigator exploit its full potentialities. To be sure, it may be necessary to discriminate the point at which a principle of tenacity can become an unreasonable stubbornness, but this does not invalidate the principle itself. Even more in the case of an ultimate or transcendent belief is it necessary to stay with it through times when it may look highly implausible if its validity is to be tested and even its very meaning deepened.

But does not this talk about a principle of tenacity and a deepening of meaning amount again to a veiled confession that there is no foundation for transcendent beliefs? For are these expressions not simply rather evasive ways of saying that we are going to stick to these beliefs whatever the evidences, and that we are going to change the meaning and shift the ground of evidence when we find it convenient? And does not this just mean that we are going to believe what we want to believe, and that these ultimate beliefs are no more than the expression of our deepest wishes?

Certainly, these ultimate beliefs involve us emotionally in a way which our beliefs about indifferent matters of fact do not. The question whether God is in his heaven is for most people a much more exciting question and one that touches their personal interests more than the question whether there is water vapor in the atmosphere of Jupiter. We are ready, almost anxious, to believe some things, reluctant to believe others, and indifferent about a great many others. Still, there has surely been a marked tendency in recent years to exaggerate the extent to which our beliefs are determined by our desires and by other psychological factors—the extent to which we engage, usually unconsciously, in "wishful thinking." Clearly, psychological and sociological skepticism can be carried only to a certain length. If all our beliefs were determined by our secret wishes, our psychological histories, our responsiveness to social pressures, then there would be no point at all in debating the claims of rival beliefs; for each person would believe only what these factors operating on him determined him to believe. In such a case, the question of truth and falsehood could scarcely arise. But the question does arise. The psychological or sociological skeptic believes that his own analysis of the situation is true. So this kind of skepticism is possible only if some beliefs are products of psychological and sociological factors, while others are judged to be true on rational grounds. The skeptic then would have to explain why his own position is a privileged one, freed from the distorting influences affecting those whom he criticizes. It is certainly not clear that he can do this.

If, for instance, there is an accusation of "wishful thinking," this entails that some beliefs fall under this description but others do not. Then we have to ask, "Which ones?" It is often supposed that belief in God is a candidate for the category of wishful thinking, but that would depend on what kind of God one was thinking about. Let us agree that the indulgent God of much popular belief might well be considered a product of human imagination. But the God of the Bible, with his demand for obedience, justice, love, self-sacrifice is a thoroughly inconvenient God. It is hard to believe that he could ever have been invented to satisfy human desires (even unconscious ones), and in the Bible itself we read about those who tried to evade this God and shut him out of their lives. On the other hand, many people might wish that such an uncomfortable God did *not* exist, so unbelief too may be the result of wishful thinking. Certainly, it would often seem to be influenced by the history of the person concerned and his relation to his parents.

Similar considerations arise if we consider the question of belief in a continuing personal existence beyond death. As H. H. Price has remarked, there are wishful thinkers on both sides. While there are no doubt many people who want to survive death, others do not, for the religions have never taught that happiness is the only possible destiny that awaits human beings. Indeed, the traditional Christian view was that the majority of people would end up in hell, and this provided, as Price says, "a very strong motive for *not* wanting to survive death." [7]

But *ad hominem* arguments of this sort really get us nowhere. Every belief has a psychological history, but this does not determine its truth or falsity. Most beliefs too have both emotional and cognitive aspects. To recognize these nonrational factors and to analyze them is useful, but it never delivers us from responsible consideration of whether the particular beliefs are likely to be true or false.

But now a further question arises. We have been talking about ultimate or transcendent beliefs as if they were matters of high importance, but are they really so? Are there not many people in the world who apparently get along very well leading happy, balanced, interesting, and useful lives without ever raising questions about man's place in the universe, his ultimate destiny, and whether or not God exists? Some of them might even say that they are too busy with the duties, challenges, adventures, and enjoyments of life to spend time speculating, perhaps fruitlessly, on transcendent questions.

It is surely true that many people do not give a thought to such questions, at least, for most of the time. Yet it can be argued that even if they never make their beliefs explicit to themselves, yet some beliefs there are at the back of their minds, and these are expressed in the values they pursue and in the priorities they set up.

Even the agnostic or the positivist who tries to suspend belief about matters where a scientific approach to the question is impossible can hardly avoid having some creed, some ultimate or transcendent beliefs by which he orients his life. At an earlier stage, I quoted Bertrand Russell's defense on the assured ways of scientific thought as opposed to what he took to be the ill-founded assertions of religious faith. But later in his autobiography, we find him saying: "I have a very simple creed—that life and joy and beauty are better than dusty death." [8] I doubt very much whether this creed is as simple as Russell would have us believe, for there is a lot to unpack from it. I doubt very much too whether any scientific considerations are relevant to the question of its truth or falsity, or could be used to commend it. But it certainly is an affirmative creed, and the religious believer would have no problem about going along with it. However, he might feel that this was only a beginning, and that in his own creed he would want to go much further. A Christian believer would say, "I believe in one God," and proceed to fill out this creed with the basic doctrines of his faith. Russell's creed may be, in the eyes of the religious believer, very much reduced and attenuated, but so far as it goes, it still stands in some recognizable connection with the traditional creed of the Christian world and promotes some of the same basic values. Russell's creed, as I have said, is an affirmative creed, unlike some negative creeds or anti-creeds that today seem to have broken almost entirely with the tradition and promote a kind of nihilism. Transcendent beliefs present us with a whole spectrum of contents, ranging from the "I believe in one God" as one limiting case to something like nihilism at the other.

But not only is there this spectrum of different contents, there is also a whole range of degrees of intensity with which beliefs are held. Kierkegaard is a striking example of a man for whom belief was a matter of passionate intensity—indeed, he sometimes suggests that the intensity of a belief is more important even to its truth than its content. We have noted, however, that there are many people at the opposite extreme. They never trouble to work out their ultimate beliefs, and the questions with which these beliefs deal do not seem to bother them. Between the extremes of intensity and indifference, there is what may be called half-belief. We have all heard of the agnostic's prayer: "O God (if there be a God), save my soul (if I have a soul)." This is usually taken in a humorous way, as an illustration of extreme intellectual scrupulosity. However, it does represent the not uncommon frame of mind of the person who is torn between belief and disbelief. It has its serious counterpart in the New Testament story of the man who said to Jesus: "I believe; help thou mine unbelief" (Mark 9:24). No doubt most people who try seriously to clarify and explicate their ultimate beliefs experience something of this oscillation.

These remarks have led us into something of a digression, and it is time for us to come back to the question which gave rise to them and which they were intended to help us answer. Are ultimate or transcendent beliefs really important? Does it matter what people believe? I want to answer these questions by saying, "Yes, it is important for people to have some deep affirmative beliefs about life, even if they cannot go so far as the traditional affirmation, 'I believe in one God.' And it is also important that, as far as they are able, people should clarify their beliefs and hold them in responsible awareness."

The reasons for making these judgments can be quite briefly stated, for they follow from points that have been made earlier. If it is true that man is a being who is incomplete and on the move, reaching out for a realization that lies ahead, a being with a certain plasticity to his nature so that he may become either one thing or another, then to some extent man becomes what he believes he is, his society becomes what he believes a human society is, even his world is shaped by his beliefs. If beliefs are as influential as I am claiming, then obviously too they have to be made explicit, and it is in the interests of responsible living that the deep convictions which many people act upon but never make explicit, should be brought into the open.

If a person has affirmative beliefs about himself, then these tend to shape his life in an affirmative way; and if he has negative beliefs about himself or others, then these too come to be reflected in his life and society. For instance, if we believe along with one popular zoologist that man is to be understood fundamentally as a naked ape, a rather unfortunate development among the primates, differing from other apes not only in the lack of a hairy covering but also in being more aggressive and more lustful, then it is hard to see how one could have much respect or hope for humanity, how one could be trustful toward other people or how one could avoid feelings of misanthropy, for inevitably we would tend to conform our behavior to the image of humanity promoted by the belief. Again, if one supposes as another widely read scientist who ventures into philosophy and theology tells us, that man has come into existence purely by chance, that we are here (in his vivid way of putting it) because our number came up in the Monte Carlo game, then it is hard to see how one could face the problems of humanity with any hope or even any seriousness, such as would come from believing that there is some purpose in the creation of man and some meaning and goal to his history.

Belief at any level carries an element of risk and adventure, but in the case of belief at the transcendent level, the stakes are high indeed. But I do not think any of us can avoid taking the risk of committing ourselves, even implicitly, to one belief or another at that level. We dare not be uncritical in our beliefs, for history is full of examples of people and even whole nations who were destroyed by false—and sometimes cruel—beliefs. Yet we dare not despise belief, for if men had never allowed their minds to be seized by visions and commitments beyond what they could prove or guarantee to themselves at the time, they would have made little progress. And we cannot say that we shall wait until belief has been converted into knowledge, for transcendent beliefs never will. They belong inalienably to the finite human condition and every important action we do implies some such belief.

Perhaps it is harder for some to believe than for others. There are skeptical natures, and we need them, for without their criticisms and questions, human beings of a more credulous type might be swamped by false beliefs. Perhaps it is possible for some people to get along on a more reduced basis of belief than others. Perhaps there will always be only a minority who believe with passion and intensity, though these may turn out to be the shapers of human destiny. But life itself seems to call for some affirmative belief commitment, for at least some degree of participation in the belief that found classic expression in the words: *Credo in unum Deum*—I believe in one God.

NOTES

[1] Bertrand Russell, *Autobiography* (London: Allen & Unwin, 1967) vol. I, p. 41.

[2] Joseph Butler, *The Analogy of Religion* (Oxford: The Clarendon Press, 1896), p. 5.

[3] William James, "The Will to Believe" in *Selected Papers on Philosophy* (London: J. M. Dent, 1917), p. 120.

[4] S. Kierkegaard, *The Concept of Dread,* trans. W. Lowrie (Princeton: Princeton University Press, 1957), p. 125.

[5] S. Kierkegaard, *Concluding Unscientific Postscript,* trans. David F. Swenson (London: Oxford University Press, 1945), p. 504.

[6] S. Kierkegaard, *Philosophical Fragments,* trans. David F. Swenson (Princeton: Princeton University Press, 1936), p. 29.

[7] H. H. Price, *Essays in the Philosophy of Religion* (Oxford: The Clarendon Press, 1972), p. 98.

[8] Russell, *Autobiography,* vol. III, p. 124.

4.

Transcendence and Theological Method

Roger Hazelton

The current preoccupation with method in theology is something of a mixed blessing. While such attention is timely and profitable in the long run, it does tend to deflect our energies from more pressing tasks like doctrinal restatement or cultural analysis. A time of unprecedented theological pluralism, when theologians "diverge on urgent voluntary errands," may not be opportune for raising questions of basic method. Some have even scored such a concern as a betrayal of theology's main purpose—that of getting on with imperative human issues such as liberation, justice from oppression, or survival on the planet Earth. Without doubting for a moment that theologians must try to understand and contribute to the "life-world" in which they work, it may be useful to recall that knowing what one is doing is by no means peripheral to doing it. If theology is for the sake of praxis, then the praxis of theology assumes increased importance. No one is excused from self-examination regarding his or her procedures in the light of freely chosen purposes. Tools are sharpened only in order to be used; but a too-functional view of what theology intends to be about may only cheapen and blunt the tools which are in fact being used.

Then, too, it is pertinent to point out that questions of method cannot be divided from questions of content without doing violence to both. Neither kind of question can be asked apart from the other. A technics-dominated age easily becomes fascinated with method abstracted from content and has to be reminded that the *how* of any activity is developed only in attending to its *what*. If the choice of method is instrumental in determining content, it is content that is indispensable in shaping and sharpening method. Anders Nygren has made this especially clear in the case of theology, insisting that "a method without any material to work on will accomplish nothing at all, while material simply as material, unrelated to any method, will

49

be nothing but a chaotic, meaningless agglomerate." [1] All of which is, or should be, elementary; but the clumsiness of language for expressing it, compounded with oversimple theories that have made a wasteland out of lived experience, make this rehearsal of the obvious a kind of moral duty.

Hence there is no way, in theology or anywhere else, to avoid Bernard Lonergan's "three questions: 'What am I doing when I am knowing? Why is doing that knowing? What do I know when I do it?'" No way; if I ask any one of them I am at once involved with the other two as well. Actually they are not separate or separable questions at all; they are distinguished only in order that they may become transparent to each other, in what Hans-Georg Gadamer calls "the belongingness between subject and object" which gives any form of inquiry or action its very *raison d'etre.*

But if no hard-and-fast distinction can be usefully made between what theologians think about and the ways in which they think, what then? Do we not land in the box where Feuerbach tried to put us in claiming that "theology is anthropology"? No, not necessarily, for there are other, better ways of understanding the belongingness between subject and object than mere subjectivism in the mode of psychological projection. Words like "subject" and "object" may have value in marking shifts of attention or intention, but they do not function as mutually exclusive terms defining an either/or situation. That is, they do not serve to divide real from unreal, or true from false. The subject-object way of situating problems of method is itself highly problematic. Applied to Feuerbach's assertion, for example, does it mean that theological statements (those about God, at any rate) have no warrant but the feelings which inspire them? This is the sense in which it is usually taken, and it must be deemed excessively reductionistic. Yet Feuerbach's much-quoted dictum has at least the merit of insisting that God cannot be a matter of fact with properties to be read off and described. That is a lesson which theologians seem to need to learn over and over again; we should be grateful to Feuerbach (or Freud) for teaching it to us.

No theologian, and no anti-theologian, is at liberty to posit a subject-object dichotomy as definitive in his or her work, for the reason that it is always premature and presumptuous. One would have to live on both sides of the distinction to know what belongs to each side. But doing what one knows, like knowing what one does, is not so readily forced into fixed categories. And the built-in requirement of tentativeness in any sort of study that is serious must make us wary of deciding in advance, by a kind of methodological tyranny, the very questions that are to be faced and maybe answered. So far as theological work goes, any dismissal or avoidance of the very predicament that makes doing theology both possible and necessary can only bring the whole enterprise to a grinding halt. At least one demonstrable value of a viable theological method is that it keeps open questions really open. It must be said, so let us say it, that there is a certain skepticism born of Christian faith itself, and underscored by reasonable intelligence, which does not permit theology to prejudice its inquiry into the truth of faith.

Perhaps all that is contended for in this essay is a frank recognition of the requirement that theological method should itself be theological. If such a contention should strike the reader as redundant or gratuitous, let it be remembered how thoroughly modern theology has been influenced by the models and aims of modern science. Apart from scientific method, what other kind of *method* is there? If we are going to talk about method, must we not talk scientifically? My first teacher of theology, Henry N. Wieman, used to make this point most emphatically in the days when process-theology was still called "naturalism." Such an equation dies hard, though it is precisely what is at issue in more recent discussions of method in theology.

Is it possible today to delineate a theological method which does more than duplicate or imitate the method appropriate to work in the natural sciences? Surely no one would sponsor or defend an approach to method that is patently unscientific or prescientific. This would only widen the communication-gap between theology and its neighboring intellectual disciplines; and what is more, it would but deepen the crisis of credibility in which most theologians now find themselves. However, the issue is not chiefly one of strategy at all; what is at stake is whether theologians can accept a "nothing-but" view of the method governing their work, or should insist upon a "more-than" understanding of the ways in which the *why* of their task determines both its *how* and its *what*. At present, a large part of that task consists in doing theology in such a way that it is actually theology which is being done. Spelling out relevant criteria and procedures is assuredly important, but only so long as they proceed from the *opus operatum*, the nature of the work being worked.

A reliable, fruitful method has no existence of its own apart from that which is investigated and interpreted. It is not a bundle of procedures or a set of prescriptions applied externally to what is being studied. One may talk about method in the abstract, to be sure, but this ought not to lead us to suppose that there is no reciprocal relation between the material to which questions are being put and the method which is the right way of putting those questions. The sterility of many discussions of method is due to an unexamined, pseudoscientific notion that the verbal distinction of content from method accurately represents a real separation rather than a useful fiction. Here again words fail us, but we can probably find no better definition of method for our purposes than Lonergan's: "a normative pattern of recurrent and related operations yielding cumulative and progressive results." [2] This has the merit of placing the emphasis where it belongs, namely, upon the way of working itself rather than an arid functionalism or a prescriptive formalism.

II

Speaking of theology as based upon "an undistorted hearing of God's word with a view to salvation," Karl Rahner writes: "In no other science is there such a gulf between the statement and what is stated, between what is expressed and what is implied, between what we lay hold on and the mystery that lays hold on us." [3] It is precisely this "gulf" that situates the theological task and occasions a method, or methods, appropriate to that task. Without presuming to be too precious about theological language, which shares with human speech in general the predicament of difference and distance from that which is spoken about, it does seem clear that theology imposes upon language some added, special burdens of its own.

The gulf to which Rahner refers is usually indicated by the term "transcendence," which has acquired several shades of meaning in our intellectual history. From philosophy, theologians borrowed the meaning of otherness or overagainstness, whether it has to do with moral imperatives, objects of perception and cognition, or the reality of other persons. In Kant's philosophy the term, used as an adjective, designates what lies beyond percept and concept and hence may be called unknowable; this mode of reference often appears in theological discourse. Most frequently theologians employ the term "transcendence" as a synonym for "God." In this usage the word indicates the "infinite qualitative difference" that distinguishes divine Being from all other being as its ground or source; the opposite pole of meaning is conveyed by the word "immanence."

Significantly, contemporary humanistic psychologies have adopted the term "self-transcendence" for referring to the dynamic potentialities of selfhood—for growth, ego control or satisfaction, future intentionality, and the like. It is somewhat curious that this current usage restores the original meaning of transcendence as a crossing over, going beyond or surpassing some obstacle or other—a meaning that seems to have been reversed in technical philosophy-theology where the word has come to mean that which *cannot* be transcended. Such reversals are not rare in the history of language, especially when terms move from common into technical use. At all events, transcendence meaning self-transcending would appear to be the very opposite of what the same word means to theologians and philosophers who stand within the major modern traditions. Whether these two meanings, transcending and being transcended, can be reconciled or placed in mutual, complimentary relationship is a matter of some interest and importance in present-day theology.

There is one meaning of transcendence coming from the past which embraces that of immanence as well. It belongs to the Scholastic view that certain "transcendental" categories such as reality, being, truth, unity, or goodness are characteristic of anything thinkable or possible. Since they cannot be denied without self-contradiction they must be presupposed; hence they transcend all thinking about what is real precisely by being universally present in thinking. Only the transcendent can be genuinely immanent, and immanence is the signal of transcendence.

Christian theology has traditionally affirmed both the transcendence and the immanence of God. So, in Van Harvey's words, "Transcendence suggests the independence or freedom of God to be immanent"; [4] which is the primary and which is the derivative term may be argued interminably (and unprofitably); but both words taken together are required to spell out the full meaning of "God," at any rate as biblical and Christian faith envision and interpret God.

Nevertheless, the habit of polarizing the two terms as logical-conceptual opposites has dogged the course of modern theology. For instance, is it not generally understood that belief in divine immanence encourages a high estimate of secular experience and optimism regarding human possibilities for self-fulfillment, whereas belief in divine transcendence emphasizes by contrast that "before God, man is always in the wrong" (Kierkegaard)? Yet it is not as if we were forced by the theo-logic to choose one over the other. Each term suggests a mode of *relationship* on God's part to whatever is not God. The reference is made by means of spatial metaphors, one of which indicates outsideness, the other insideness. The whole point of either figure is lost if the other figure is forgotten or neglected. Since theology is habitually done in one-thing-at-a-time propositional language, rather than by creating metaphors of evocative and participative power, about all that can be achieved is to maintain a dialectical balance between immanence and transcendence in what we say regarding God.

But even striking such a precarious balance, remembering to say on page 2 what one has omitted on page 1, will not really do. In many ways concepts are clumsier than images, as they tend to be more pretentious and assertive of their truth. What is required of the method-conscious theologian is that he or she will find fresh ways of thinking and saying together and at once what William Temple called "the immanence of the transcendent" and "the transcendence of the immanent." No one pretends that this is easy, but the challenge is there to be taken up and followed through; different styles, new options in method, some of which may turn out to be quite ancient, too, are certainly being tried.

Quite recently Charles Hartshorne has addressed this whole issue in a manner that is strikingly suggestive. He first identifies "the phenomenon of simple transcendence," according to which God is defined as different in principle from every lesser, inferior sort of reality. This "venerable scheme," he holds, destroys the analogy between the eminent, nonsurpassable reality meant by the word "God" and creaturely, finite realities such as things, events, or persons. But this analogy must be logically assumed precisely in order to make sense of any significant difference. He writes:

Why say that God cares about, or cherishes, his creatures and yet insist that what happens to the creatures literally *makes no difference* to him, one way or another? Yet this is the clear, logical implication of putting deity entirely and exclusively on the side of the independent, immutable, necessary pole of the contrasts in question. . . . I think no meaning is left, on that assumption.[5]

He therefore proposes that we think of God as being "on both sides in uniquely excellent ways,"[6] since a God shut up in static godhood—cause but not effect, influencing but not influenced—would be no God at all in any sense worthy of worship or answerable to faith. Only a transcendence capable of transcending itself deserves the name of God.

It follows that whatever is not God participates positively, though "non-eminently," in those qualities which define God uniquely but not absolutely or exclusively. Hartshorne calls this "dual immanence," the obverse of God's "dual transcendence." The difference between Creator and creature must be bridged in order to be noted or respected, for "between eminent and non-eminent mind, however humble, there can be intelligible relations of love, participation, mutual contributions." [7] If not, we had better abandon speaking of the love of God.

Here then is an essay in divinity which takes the concept of love with logical seriousness in thinking about God. One may doubt whether the scheme of out-and-out transcendence taken as utter difference in all respects is actually as "venerable" as Hartshorne says. A transcendence that excludes every trace of immanence could not even be known, or for that matter believed, to be transcendent. Conceptions of grace and Spirit are as much a part of classical Christian theology as those of absoluteness and aseity. Also, since qualities of eminence or unsurpassability are at bottom comparative and relational, the question is left open in Hartshorne's view as to whether God is different in kind, or only in degree, from everything that is not God.

More questionable still, from the standpoint of theological method, is Hartshorne's insistence that "categories are literal, or they are nothing. . . . They are not pictures." [8] As an example, he gives "contingent," meaning "might not have been"; but this is to ignore another meaning, "might have been otherwise," which is as germane as the first. More careful attention to the metaphorical (not literal) character of "contingent" as signifying "touching-with" would have disclosed that its meaning cannot be confined to "conditional" or "non-necessary" without conveying that of "possible" also. What Hartshorne does in this instance is to treat the word as a dead, dried-up metaphor to be construed conceptually with a single "literal" meaning. Thereby he chooses to neglect its live, tensive properties which do not serve his logical purpose. But can we so readily "transform a category into a transcendental" [9] by a process of "literal" abstraction? Not without doing violence to the truth of faith which theology must understand and set forth. Therefore one has to ask whether such a categorizing—and literalizing—of transcendence really answers the problem posed by the "gulf" of which Karl Rahner speaks.

III

Such hesitations aside, Hartshorne's criticism of a simple, hard-and-fast view of divine transcendence is surely well taken. The gulf with which theology must deal is far more interesting than a bare otherness which is tantamount to nothingness. So far so good. An alternative to Hartshorne's rendering is the method of Lonergan, Rahner, and the Roman Catholic "revisionists" who propose to deal with matters of transcendence not categorically but "transcendentally," that is, by recovering "the turn to the subject." This turn, or rather return, is worth studying because it puts contemporary theologians back in touch with premedieval, indeed Augustinian, ways of thought ("God and the soul I wish to know . . . nothing more") by giving up the fruitless effort to locate transcendence in a divine super-object capable of being described in take-it-or-leave-it categorical terms.

For must we not agree with Nathan Scott's judgment? He writes that "now, at the end of the modern age, the word *God* is a dead word that has very largely lost its power to focalize or to name Transcendence." [10] This sobering reflection, this hard truth, marks the place where, for us, Christian theology has to begin. It describes a gulf on the edge of which we all stand, theologians and nontheologians alike. Furthermore, it indicates not only the depth of present-day disaffection but also the demand for doing theology in a new key and with new motivations.

On the surface, at all events, what could be more appropriate and adequate than a "transcendental method" for conveying truth about transcendence? It follows closely the rule that content should determine method, and it seeks to provide ways of working with the content that conform to our "lived experience" of what is being thought and spoken about. Difficult as it may be to indicate by thought or word the gulf indicated by "transcendence," it is made mandatory by the urgent inner need for the transcendent that is alive in all of us today.

In a real and compelling sense, the search for transcendence is taking shape at present as an inquiry into what makes human beings human. This inquiry proceeds on many cultural fronts and follows up clues from a variety of sources. Undoubtedly there is a religious dimension in all this searching, of which current theology becomes increasingly aware and to which intellectual response and evaluation are already being made. What Dietrich Bonhoeffer, years ago now, called "this worldly transcendence" finds its expression in a whole spectrum of

concerns extending from theologies of political, sexual, or racial liberation to theologies of a more privatistic sort which try to recover the
lived reality of human experiencing, with its capacities for intimacy
and ecstasy, as the matrix of reflection upon perennial problems and
doctrines. It is perhaps not sufficiently realized that a shared interest
in what is uniquely, universally human, namely self-transcendence,
inspires all these theological explorations which in some ways seem
to be contradictory, even as they make their various appeals to common
principles of human dignity, worth, or potency.

Yet it is not as if whatever remains of the meaning of transcendence
has been taken back from "God" and given exclusively to "what man
can make of man." The broadening of transcendence to include self-
transcendence represents a significant departure from neo-orthodox
premises, to be sure; this means that the contours of theological work
are drastically changing, so that something of traditional and scriptural
dialectic may now be recovered in speaking about God. Here, one
might say, the hardening process which identified God with paradoxical Otherness is being challenged and reversed, as "interiority" no
less than "exteriority" is seen to belong to the very meaning of transcendence. God is still "the problem" for theology, but as I have written
elsewhere, instead of describing this problem as expounding the *logos*
of *theos,* we are called to explore the *theos* of *logos*— the transcending
and transcendent horizon of all human meaning.[11]

It is right that theologians should be moved by the inward impulsion,
widely and deeply shared by men and women of our epoch, to discover
a mode of truth which will be true to ourselves, yet not out of tune
with Christian witness and mission as these have been handed down
to us. The inhuman concept of "man" which has dominated much
recent theology needs to be resisted and replaced. What Pascal termed
"the greatness of the human soul" needs celebration and rendition
in theology as elsewhere. One has at least the right to hope that the
age of anxiety so thoroughly delineated by poets, philosophers, and
theologians may in the course of human events give way to an age
of creativity, in which a view of human being as "absolutely open
upwards" (in Rahner's phrase) becomes more focal and controlling.
We have been badgered and put down enough by illusions that pretend
to be free of all illusion, by views of life-in-the-world that are not
humanly recognizable, depending as they do upon models provided
by the mechanics of sensation, the emission of behavioral signals, or
the lifeless symbols of monarchical and patriarchal authority which

make subjects of us all, in both the philosophical and the political-cultural senses of that unfortunate term. It is indeed time for a change.

But there is ground-clearing, then constructive work ahead for Christian theologians who care mightily for the human future yet are not prepared to abandon insights and impulsions coming from the long historic past. Christianity was not born yesterday, nor even the day before, but has its roots in ancestral and primeval insights which in myth and parable, doctrine and liturgy, have delineated the human journey as a covenanted pilgrimage, an independence rooted in dependence, a determination to "be at home in the homeland" (Heidegger). Something of the ancient flexibility and amplitude that belongs to the birthright of theology has been missing and is long overdue.

At present, therefore, theologians are quite seriously exploring the connections of their discipline with those modes of inquiry and interpretation traditionally known as the humanities. And this is as it should be, since it has become clear that the case for "God" and humankind must stand or fall together. Far more than conceptual bridge-building is involved, although that may also help. What is required is some sureness of apprehension that theology and the humanities are basically engaged in the same tasks: of rediscovering and then reaffirming the human measure of the world, without succumbing to the idolatrous rationalism of pseudoscientific theologizing on the one hand or to the irrational promptings of a glib polytheism on the other. It remains to be seen how successful theologians can become in treading such a difficult path, but for some of us at least there can be no turning back.

This mandate, which is increasingly forced upon us by what Rico Lebrun calls "the unmanageable design of our condition," may also be stated in less hortatory terms. Indeed, I believe that this is just what Lonergan and Rahner have done, to the great profit of contemporary theologians. Responsive to the cultural situation as they see it, they have adapted traditional modes of theological exploration to the purpose of rethinking the God-humanity relationship in ways consistent with our present experience. Their transcendental method is no novelty or contrivance but a sustained, consistent effort to give voice to Christian wisdom that is both ancient and new. Whatever criticism may be offered of their particular formulations, their provenance in biblically grounded faith and in our own life-world, taken together, must be acknowledged.

There are, to be sure, significant differences in the theory and use of transcendental method in the work of these two theologians. Lonergan employs a careful, cautious interweaving of Kantian with Thomistic meanings of "transcendent"; it is as if Scholastic ontology and Kantian epistemology were being brought into a mutually reinforcing theological overview of method. In Rahner's thought, "to interpret the whole of dogmatic theology as transcendental anthropology" means that neither God nor humanity can be comprehended at all without the other, that it is impossible to say something about God without saying something about humanity, and vice versa, and therefore that the "inextricable interrelation of the 'objective' and 'subjective' side" of every topic in theology needs to be granted even where it is not explicitly discussed.[12] As Lonergan's viewpoint has frequently been explicated and evaluated, our focus here will be chiefly upon Rahner's setting-forth of transcendental method.

It is true that Rahner's work has been done chiefly within the sphere of dogmatics rather than in what has come to be called "fundamental theology." This means that he has developed his thought regarding transcendental method primarily with reference to work on specific doctrinal topics. Nevertheless, such leading concepts as that of "potentiality for obedience," "the supernatural existential," or "horizon" have a comprehensive, foundational importance in his theology. Although David Tracy categorizes him as a neo-orthodox theologian because of his early interest in responding to the Barthian stress upon the Word of God, Rahner's later writings depart from this context and give positive indications that he has become increasingly concerned to work out a "theological anthropology" which is at the same time an "anthropological theology."

Just how does Rahner pursue this course? Put as succinctly as possible, his transcendental method is a sustained effort to do theology without relying on the polarizing and objectivizing formats which have so bedeviled both traditional and recent work in the discipline. In the Chicago lecture from which previous summary citations have been drawn here, Rahner gives three reasons why a change of direction toward transcendental "anthropological" theology is necessary now. He mentions first the general philosophical principle that "every question concerning any object whatever also formally implies the question of the knowing subject," [13] because "the subject must carry with it the limits of the possibility of such knowledge." [14] Hence in theology God can scarcely be said to be the ground of possibility for revealing or saving knowledge unless this possibility, "man's saving receptivity for" the object spoken about, is seen to be "the human spirit's transcendental and limitless horizon as its inner motive and as the precondition of its existence." [15] This is Rahner's answer, despite the Germanic circumlocutions in which it is couched, to Barth's attempt to make theological method out of the proclamatory premise that "God is in heaven while man is on earth."

A second reason for this change in direction, according to Rahner, is that in our time theology can no longer be confused with proclamation, but must take upon itself the burden of reflecting on its own "realization of the realities of faith" as "explicitly included in" its statements about those realities. Such reflection has for Rahner not the status of an afterthought but of a priori presuppositions which alone can get theology off the ground, so to speak. Yet the fact that they are to be presupposed does not mean that they are to be taken merely for granted; on the contrary, they give veracity and authenticity to whatever theologians may say about our human "origin in and orientation towards God."

Rahner's third reason for the necessary change comes from the apologetical situation in which present-day theology stands. He believes that the difficulties of unbelief or disbelief today are at least partly due to the fact that "theological statements are not formulated in such a way that man can see how what is meant by them is connected with his understanding of himself, as witnessed to in his own experience." [16] Clearly, it is hard to fault Rahner on this point. The remedy for theological isolation and irrelevance would seem to lie, not in the simple demythologizing of language about God by translating it into statements about human experience (as in the work of Gregory Baum, for instance), but rather in discovering such connections as in fact hold "between the content of dogma and man's experience of himself" which keep the circuit of meaning open at both ends, as it were, by changing to "a transcendental anthropological method in theology." [17]

Hence Rahner's chosen method, which is by no means exclusively his own or unprecedented in the history of Christian thought, offers itself as an option for doing theology in ways both critical and constructive. It represents a relocating of transcendence so as to include human self-transcendence, rather than confining it conceptually to a causal object called God. It proposes a renewal of theological language by attending to the "correspondences" between experience and revelation, history and salvation, which make it possible to see that the most objective truth of faith is also the most subjective, "an immediacy before the absolute mystery of God." [18] Moreover, it opens up a way of dealing with transcendence questions not dogmatically or descriptively but relationally and experientially—a way of theological flexibility and freedom.

IV

It remains to indicate some of the stresses and styles in theological method which may be employed to convey these more inclusive and authentic meanings of transcendence. Let us say at the outset that the aim of such moves is not to remove or lessen the "gulf" between form and content, expression and implication, in theological discourse. The purpose must be that of keeping just this gulf always in focus, adapting structures and habits of speaking and writing to this end. Obviously, however, some kinds of language-use serve this purpose better than others. Words purporting to signify with objective accuracy qualities of the transcendent that are neither experienced nor experienceable labor under peculiar disadvantages. Phrases that presume to put transcendence in its place, rather than making room for transcendence in discourse itself, can only harden and deaden what needs most of all to be elicited and brought to conscious life.

So long as theological language remains locked into habits and forms of propositional, declarative utterance, the Word that should inform our words will be unspoken and unheard. Talking about transcendence easily becomes a substitute for thinking, feeling, or willing it. "The Beyond that is within" may be finally unstatable, but that does not mean that it cannot be suggested or evoked by theological modes of speech. At least it may be given room by more spacious words and phrases that do not preclude methodically the belongingness of subject and object, the integrity of intimacy and ultimacy, in setting forth the truth of Christian faith.

In Rahner's way of putting it, the gulf between "the mystery we lay hold on and the mystery that lays hold on us" needs not only recognition but rendition in the very method of theology. That these are not two mysteries but one is plainly implied by the existence of the gulf itself; being aware of such a gap involves some recognition of the mystery that constitutes the gap. The kind of "concrete approach" that is prompted by Gabriel Marcel's Gifford Lectures on reflection and mystery is germane to theological work. It can best be carried on perhaps by a theology that is deliberately, rather than unconsciously, metaphorical in tone and texture—a way of working in which analysis and argument yield pride of place to more poetic forms of language such as parable, allegory, or myth. Actually, of course, such elements abound in classical theological writing; they "function" not as illustrations appended to a line of reasoning but as guiding images that "give rise to thought" in Paul Ricoeur's familiar phrase. Since every theologian is a poet *malgré lui/elle,* that is, one engaged in "bodying forth the forms of things unknown," it is, as T. S. Eliot might say, "behovely" that mystery should be made meaningful through metaphor.

That notion that gulfs in thought or speech exist simply in order to be bridged by problem-solving techniques really does not stand up under critical reflection. In theology, at any rate, mystery is not a marginal concept but a constitutive factor in all speaking and writing which deepens the more it is penetrated. Among other things this means that a tenuous yet tensive relation must always hold between what is expressed and what is implied, as between the knowledge of mystery and the mystery of knowledge. Theologians should become more adept, more cognizant of these built-in requirements of their craft. A problematic, so-called "direct" approach to mystery—which is but another name for transcendence as used here—can only result in its transmogrification by dismissal. The theologian's task, in Emily Dickinson's words, is to "tell the truth, but tell it slant." Can there be any other way?

Blaise Pascal proposed in his *Pensées* a distinction between the *esprit de géométrie* and the *esprit de finesse.* Although these terms do not come over easily into English, they may be roughly translated as the analytical and the penetrative mind. Pascal had already made his reputation as a mathematician and physicist to whom the *esprit géométrique* was second nature, but when he turned to "the study of man" he found its methods too blunt and wooden to take in the kind of truth which Kierkegaard was later to call the truth of "subjectivity." Method must be suited to content, Pascal held, and when the content is a human being's "life-world," the mentality and method of analytical construction cannot do the work required. Therefore he expressed the hope that in human situations and evaluations a way could be found to overcome the crudity and sterility of proof by rational progression, through a mentality bent on developing a fineness of perception utterly lacking in the maxims, mother-wit, and fabulation usually brought to bear when "man" is in question. Therefore in the *Pensées* he made a determined, consciously artful effort to articulate a method and style that can "see the thing all at once, with a single glance, and not by rational progression—at least to a certain degree." [19]

Obviously, Pascal was not anticipating here the extension of the methods of natural science which has produced what are called the human sciences. Nor was he suggesting anything like a Ritschlian duality of fact and value as the basis for the *esprit de finesse*. He wished to find and put to work an art of persuasion that could address the will as much as the intellect, follow more flexibly and faithfully the contours of experience, and stimulate self-recognition through sharing humane insights. No single method, he believed, could guarantee such results. The step-by-step solidity of the *esprit géométrique* needs to be corrected and complemented by the subtlety of the *esprit de finesse*. It is not as if we theologians were forced to choose between them. One must, after all, learn to speak and write humanely about human matters; and transcendence is assuredly a matter of this kind.

The language used in theology has for so long been modelled on the paradigms of scientific rationality that this plea may go unheeded. Nevertheless, it ought to be made, considering the state of disarray and discredit in which most theologians find themselves at present, both ecclesiastically and culturally. The reasons are not solely strategic or apologetic; they are also, and even more, foundational to the enterprise of Christian theology itself. Just as method ought to take its cue from content, so style should be responsive to substance—in this case the substance of doctrine regarding the relationship of God with "man." The name of that relationship is transcendence in the double sense of transcending and being transcended, for which the traditional theological terms are spirit and grace. The mystery of this relationship, proclaimed in the gospel and enacted—however hesitantly—in the church, needs always to be conveyed in a style both appropriate and adequate to its substance.

Theology is not and never can be poetry or praise, and yet it cannot be itself or do its work except in close affinity with these modes of discourse. Such affinity may well be more suggestive than definitive for theological language, but for all that it remains imperative if theology is ever to become convictional and persuasive, rather than merely descriptive and "analytical." Giving reasons for the hope that is in us, like knowing in whom we have believed, is very far from being a categorizing of the attributes of deity or a dredging-up of qualities identified with the human psyche.

"The belongingness between subject and object," then, is the matrix where all theologizing must begin. Neither the objectifying of God as external cause or supervening principle, nor the subjectifying of the human as confined within something miscalled "experience," can be permitted to dictate the requirements of sound theological method any longer. There is finer, more demanding work to be done. To that end, the hermeneutical investigations of Paul Ricoeur and Hans-Georg Gadamer have much to contribute, as do the studies of image, metaphor, and meaning in the "new criticism" and the findings of the "humanistic" psychologies.

It may be objected that the recommendations made here simply encourage the abandoning of clarity for vagueness, by a too diffuse and imprecise revision of the norms appropriate to theological method. But there is more than one way of being clear and precise; the way chosen depends quite definitely upon the mode of truth one wishes to communicate. If that truth concerns the God of Christian faith who is "nearer than breathing, and closer than hands or feet," who in Augustine's words is "higher than my topmost part, and more inward than my innermost," the language used to communicate such truth will need to become equal to the task. At least, the forms of theological statement may better suggest what is being stated; and the manner of expression used may resonate more truthfully with what can only be implied. Then theology, in Rahner's words, may refer us "from the apparent clarity of its conceptions to the blinding brilliance of mystery which seems to us to be darkness." [20]

NOTES

[1] Anders Nygren, *Meaning and Method* (Philadelphia: Fortress Press, 1972), p. 3.

[2] Bernard J. F. Lonergan, *Method in Theology* (New York: Herder and Herder, 1972), p. 4.

[3] Karl Rahner and Herbert Vorgrimler, *Theological Dictionary* (New York: Herder and Herder, 1965), pp. 456-457.

[4] Van A. Harvey, *A Handbook of Theological Terms* (New York: Macmillan, 1964), p. 128.

[5] Charles Hartshorne, "Love and Dual Transcendence," in *Union Seminary Quarterly Review,* Winter-Summer, 1975, p. 96.

[6] *Ibid.,* p. 97.   [7] *Ibid.,* p. 100.   [8] *Ibid.,* p. 99.   [9] *Ibid.*

[10] Nathan Scott, *The Poetry of Civic Virtue* (Philadelphia: Fortress Press, 1976), p. 34.

[11] "Relocating Transcendence," in *Union Seminary Quarterly Review,* Winter-Summer, 1975, p. 102.

[12] Karl Rahner, *Theological Investigations,* Volume IX (New York: Herder and Herder, 1972), p. 33.

[13] *Ibid.,* p. 34.   [14] *Ibid.*   [15] *Ibid.,* pp. 35, 34.   [16] *Ibid.,* p. 41.

[17] *Ibid.,* p. 42.   [18] *Ibid.,* p. 37.

[19] Blaise Pascal, *Pensées,* Everyman's Library (London: Dent, 1960), p. 265.

[20] Karl Rahner and Herbert Vorgrimler, *op.cit.,* p. 457.

5.

The Mystic Union
in the Sermons of Meister Eckhart
David L. Mueller

The purpose of this chapter is to indicate what seems to me to represent the *leitmotif* of Meister Eckhart's theology, namely, the mystic union of the soul with God. One's understanding of this emphasis is largely determined by the approach taken to this somewhat enigmatic German Dominican mystic (ca. 1260-1327). Was Eckhart primarily a Scholastic theologian or a mystic? Is the genuine Eckhart to be found in the Latin writings or in his German sermons? Whatever the various answers to these questions may be, no interpreter can deny the significant influence which Eckhart exerted on his own and subsequent ages. This is due, in part, as Otto Karrer has rightly observed, to the fact that Eckhart represented the epitome of the teacher-preacher and the Scholastic-mystic combination. Thus the tradition of medieval Scholasticism served, to a certain degree, as the theological foundation of Eckhart's mystical flights given expression in a rather undeveloped German vernacular. Often the ideas of the Schoolmen incited the spiritual sensitivity of Eckhart, and they were transformed by him in his own experience and passed on to those eager for salvation.[1]

Undoubtedly, many of Eckhart's conceptions were more precisely expressed in the Latin theological systems of the Schoolmen,[2] but it was not primarily Eckhart, the Scholastic, who influenced his age. Rather, it was Eckhart, the preacher and mystic. His singular influence in this sphere is described by one authority as follows:

Eckhart was widely considered an authority on the spiritual life. He undertook to instruct the laity and extraregular communities—beghards and beguines as well as the *Gottesfreunde*—no less than the religious of his order, and for this purpose it was necessary to employ the vulgar tongue.[3]

The view that Eckhart became most creative in his preaching is well stated by Karrer. His contention is that as a Scholastic Eckhart is but one among many. Medieval Scholastic theology had reached its apex in the *Summa Theologica* of St. Thomas Aquinas (d. 1274), a Dominican like Eckhart, whose thought was subsequently officially acknowledged as the normative expression of Roman Catholic doctrine. In matters theological Eckhart is best understood against the backdrop of the larger Scholastic tradition and more specifically in terms of the theology of his Dominican order and of St. Thomas, the "angelic doctor." This leads Karrer to contend that as a Scholastic theologian, Eckhart taught nothing original.[4] Concerning Eckhart's unique contribution, this Roman Catholic interpreter comments as follows: "The best which he had to give was not derived by him from literary sources but far more from the god-given bent of his character, the experience of his life, and the sensitivity of his human, shepherdly understanding." [5] McDonnell likewise recognizes the importance of Eckhart's preaching. "He was best known for sermons which completed within Dominican circles that bridge between mysticism and scholasticism for regulars and extraregulars alike already presaged by Peter of Dacia a generation earlier." [6]

Hence, in this chapter I am primarily concerned with Eckhart, the mystic, as he speaks in his German sermons. May one, despite the divergent interpretations of Eckhart, point to the *leitmotif* of his thought? I believe that one may answer affirmatively. All of the thought of this mystic clusters about his understanding of the mystical union of God and the soul, the *unio mystica*. Karrer describes this emphasis in the following manner:

. . . his own personality as well as the attention he gave to the spiritual state of the audience he was addressing always led his speech—without long diversions—to return and be directed in some way to the one great theme, namely, that "God be born" in the soul.[7]

Rudolf Otto is correct in describing Eckhart's mysticism as a "mysticism of the soul." [8] It is to this union of God and the soul that Eckhart always recurs in his sermons. Another interpreter concurs with this viewpoint.

Eckhart terms this union of the soul with God the Divine Birth in the soul of the just. All his thoughts seem to circle continually around this, for him, all important truth and to seek for some new expression, some new means, of making this Divine Birth intelligible to his hearers.[9]

If the medieval prose of Eckhart's sermons be taken as normative for interpreting the manner in which he sought to make the union of the soul with God intelligible, one can see the difficulties this presented Eckhart, his hearers, the Church and subsequent interpreters of his thought. Though acknowledged by the Church and the Dominican Order as an able teacher, preacher, spiritual director, and administrator through appointment to important posts throughout his career, Eckhart—shortly before his death—was tried by the archepiscopal court of Cologne for disseminating certain heretical teachings among the laity. To this charge he replied: "If the ignorant are not taught they will never learn"; "the business of the doctor is to heal." Responding to the charge of teaching error or even heresy, Eckhart defended himself both in a public sermon and in a Latin defense on February 13, 1327, affirming: "to the extent that they (i.e. teachings) sound like or imply error, or savor of heresy, I do not and have not held any such view, nor maintained nor preached it." In addition, he declared:

If, however, anything in the aforesaid, or in other statements or writings of mine, should be false, which I do not see, I am always ready to yield to a better understanding.[10]

Eckhart appealed to the Pope for vindication but died in 1327 during the proceedings. In 1329, Pope John XXII condemned twenty-eight of his statements as heretical or dangerous. Yet Johann Tauler, an influential German Dominican mystic and disciple of Eckhart, spoke of him as "a man of prodigious learning, too profoundly versed in the subtilties of God—and nature—wisdom for many of the scholars of his day rightly to understand him." [11]

Eckhart's attempt to communicate the nature of the mystic union through his popular sermons was complicated by the relatively undeveloped state of the German vernacular of his day—a vernacular which he is regarded as having helped shape. Beyond this, Eckhart was confronted with the problem of whether the nature of the mystic union is capable of being expressed linguistically at all. Josef Quint has probed this issue in an article entitled, "Mystik and Sprache." He accepts the mystic's assertion of an experience of the ineffable. "But despite this fact, every mystic feels an inner compulsion to express his mystical experience, his vision, his mystical knowledge." [12] Eckhart reveals this attitude in a famous sentence: "If no one had been here, I would still have had to preach to this stick." [13]

Even a hurried reading of the German sermons reveals Eckhart's philosophical prowess. He is a speculative mystic without peer. That is not to imply that Eckhart was primarily interested in speculation, a point already intimated. Steinbüchel speaks to this matter as follows: "The metaphysical depth of Eckhart's entire speculation confirms us in the view that this mystic was not primarily interested in theoretical metaphysics, but in the religious and personal relation to Being." [14] To paraphrase Otto, speculation does not descend from above downwards, but ascends from the sphere of experience upwards. [15] Seen in this light, all of Eckhart's speculation is an attempt to give the clearest possible expression to the experience of the mystic union. Accordingly, it is impossible to regard Eckhart's metaphysical statements apart from their soteriological import. The latter is his primary interest. First and last, he was concerned with the idea of salvation; that is with *salus* or *Heil.* "That the soul is eternally one with the Eternal is not a scientifically interesting statement, but is that fact upon which the salvation of the soul depends." [16]

As we proceed, the linguistic difficulties inherent in Eckhart's attempt to give more clear expression to the mystic union must be borne in mind. Quint writes:

The argument which the mystic has with language in his attempt to find the most valid linguistic expression for his mystical knowledge takes the form of a battle against language, a battle, which, as Weisgerber has properly shown, is centered in the "disengagement from the word" *(Losloesung vom Wort).* This battle of the mystic with language, against a word, always takes on the most precise forms and is most visible at the point where one is dealing with the speculative mystic. That is to say, where one deals with a philosophical attempt to make the mystical vision comprehensible to the thoughtful mind.[17]

In his attempt to express what may be ultimately inexpressible, Eckhart made frequent use of paradox and metaphor.[18] Like Dionysius, the Neoplatonic mystical theologian (ca. 500), Eckhart often resorted to the ineffability of God and the mystical experience. But Eckhart was not content to stop there.

The speculative mystic's mode of thinking cannot rest content with the negative statement about the ineffable or incomprehensible inasmuch as for him everything—out of inner necessity—is dependent upon the knowing comprehension of the divine being with whom one comes in contact in the unitive state of the *unio mystica.*[19]

Thus perhaps Buettner is right in saying of Eckhart's language: "The boundaries of the inexpressible were pushed back by him to a degree only surpassed by Goethe." [20] This, of course, is one of the reasons why continuing philological studies of the Eckhart corpus are necessary before the scholar may ascertain precisely what Eckhart meant in the use of certain words.[21]

We have looked briefly at the linguistic problem which Eckhart faced and its bearing upon his description of the mystic union. Before proceeding to discuss how this union is achieved it is necessary to point out the more important influences which helped to mold his metaphysical and mystical thought. On the one hand, he was undoubtedly greatly influenced by the thought of the Neoplatonic school transmitted through Dionysius, the pseudo-Areopagite. It is in the latter tradition that we find the teaching concerning the emanation of all things from the One, the Absolute, and of their ultimate return to the ground from whence they came. This view made an emphasis on the immanence of God possible. Here, too, absorption into the One is the goal of the mystical quest.[22] It is therefore not surprising, as Underhill observes, that we find differences of language in Eckhart which point both to emmanental and immanental strains in his thought.[23] Here again, the interpreter's perspective on Eckhart effects the analysis. Gilson notes that Eckhart's thought is never simple. This accounts for the fact that some interpret Eckhart solely as a mystic while others view him as dialectician in the platonic and plotinian traditions—both with some justification.[24]

In one of his sermons Eckhart gives us something of an indication of the process involved in the quest for unity with God:

When I preach it is my wont to speak about detachment, of the duty of ridding ourselves of self and of things. Or again, of return to the impartible good, God to wit. And thirdly, on the duty of remembering the high and noble virtue God has put into the soul so that mortals may wonder about God. Fourthly, about the pure nature of God, the ineffable splendour of God. God is a word, an unspoken word.[25]

Prior to discussing the unitive state *per se,* one must seek to discover what Eckhart means by detachment. Admittedly, it is perilous to attempt to systematize Eckhart. Nevertheless, I am of the opinion that the discipline of detachment is important for comprehending Eckhart's view of the way which may issue in the mystic union. Otto, I think, does violence to Eckhart in relegating this process to the periphery of his thought.[26] Generally, the way of detachment corresponds to the traditional *Via Purgative,* the purgative way. But this way of *abgeschiedenheit,* or of renunciation, is not to be thought of simply in terms of seclusion or detachment from the world. Such an interpretation would neither be in keeping with Eckhart's involved life nor with his teaching on the active and contemplative lives.[27] When Eckhart speaks of detachment, the reference is primarily to an internal state rather than to separation from the world of things. Those who possess true inner poverty are the "poor in spirit" whom Jesus called blessed (Matt. 5:3).[28] In order for anyone to experience the union of the soul with God, he must begin with this process of "detachment."

In a sermon excerpt which some have attributed to Eckhart, he speaks of the four stages of detachment:

The first breaks in and makes away with all a man's perishable things. The second one deprives him of them altogether. The third not only takes them but makes them all forgotten as though they had not been, and all about them. The fourth degree is right in God and is God himself. When we get to this stage the King is desirous of our beauty.[29]

In his work entitled "About Disinterest," Eckhart accentuates the importance of this concept:

I have sought earnestly and with great diligence that good and high virtue by which man may draw closest to God and through which one may best approximate the idea God had of him before he was created, when there was no separation between man and God; and having delved into all this writing, so far as my intelligence would permit, I found that (high virtue) to be pure disinterest, that is, detachment from creatures. Our Lord said to Martha: *"Unum est necessarium,"* which is to say: to be untroubled and pure, one thing is necessary and that is disinterest.[30]

An examination of Eckhart's writings enables one to characterize this preparatory process more exactly. It becomes clear that it is both a detachment from the world of things and a process of increasing introversion. Eckhart writes: "The disinterested person, however, wants nothing, and neither has he anything of which he would be rid. Therefore he has no prayer, or he prays only to be uniform with God.[31] Or again:

The more subject to creatures a man is, the less he conforms to God, but the pure, disinterested heart, being void of creatures is constantly worshipping God and conforming to him, and is therefore sensitive to his influence.[32]

This path of renunciation may be regarded as a discipline of emptying or making the soul receptive to the activity of God. In the "Book of Benedictus" Eckhart writes: "In plain words: to take in, to be receptive, a thing must be empty."[33] Thus by virtue of this process of detachment the higher powers of the soul become increasingly receptive; the soul itself is prepared to become united with God. Yet Eckhart would warn us of the hindrances which keep the soul from completing the process of detachment. "First, her being too much divided, not simple (pure) enough. The soul is not simple in her relations with creatures. The second is attachment to temporal things. And thirdly, being fond of the body will prevent union with God." [34]

We may see the pinnacle of the process of detachment in Eckhart's conception of man's readiness to receive or experience God's presence. "Therefore if a heart is to be ready for him, it must be emptied out to nothingness, the condition of its maximum capacity. So, too, a disinterested heart, reduced to nothingness, is the optimum, the condition of maximum sensitivity." [35]

It has often been observed that this process of detachment is the movement of the soul from the sphere of multiplicity toward a state of simplicity and unity. Eckhart gives voice to this conviction: " . . . the soul that is to know God must be so firm and steady in God that nothing can penetrate it, neither hope nor fear, neither joy nor sorrow, neither love nor suffering, nor any other thing that can come in from without." [36] It is difficult for us as acquisitive consumers to grasp how radically Eckhart and other mystics conceived this process of renunciation——of *entwerden.* For Eckhart, it necessitated a radical self-denial. In order for the soul to be completely receptive it must even seek to transcend the space-time continuum.

Nothing hinders the soul's knowledge of God as much as time and space, for time and space are fragments, whereas God is one! And therefore, if the soul is to know God, it must know him above time and outside of space; for God is neither this nor that, as are these manifold things. God is One! [37]

In sum, the height of detachment—this highest virtue—is reached when man or the soul has entirely forgotten self and the sensate life. Now the self is no longer conscious of itself. All of life is lived in conformity to God as preparatory to the self's fulfillment in God. Eckhart gives voice to this repeated emphasis in his sermon, "The Kingdom of God Is at Hand":

If the soul is to see God, it must not look again on any temporal thing, for as long as the soul dwells on time or space or any image of them it may never know God. . . . Further, I say that if the soul is to know God, it must forget itself and lose (consciousness of) itself, for as long as it is self-aware and self-conscious, it will not see or be conscious of God. But when, for God's sake, it becomes unself-conscious and lets go of everything, it finds itself again in God, for knowing God, it therefore knows itself and everything else from which it has been cut asunder, in the divine perfection.

. . . If I am to know true being, I must know it where it is being itself, and that is in God and not where it is divided among creatures.[38]

In this highest state of detachment the soul is void of "alien images." It is prepared for the mystic union, the eternal birth of God in the soul.

If thou wilt find this noble birth, verily thou must quit the multitude and return to the startingpoint, into the ground out of which thou art come. The powers of the soul and their works, these are the multitude: memory, understanding and will, these all diversify thee, therefore thou must leave them all: sensible perception, imagination and everything wherein thou findest thyself and has thyself in view. Thereafter thou mayest find this birth, but believe me, not otherwise.[39]

In order to understand how this birth of God in the soul is brought about we need to be clear concerning Eckhart's understanding of the nature of the soul. What is it within the soul that enables it to be united with God in the mystic union? Wherein is the soul analogous to the divine nature? Eckhart reflects classical Roman Catholic doctrine in locating the *imago dei* in man's soul. He likens the soul to the pure temple in which God dwells:

The temple in which God wants to be master, strong to work his will, is the human soul, which he created and fashioned exactly like himself. We read that the Lord said: "Let us make man in our own image." And he did it. He made the human soul so much like himself that nothing else in heaven or on earth resembles him so much. That is why God wants the temple to be pure, so pure that nothing shall be in it except himself.[40]

Now one must seek to discover what Eckhart conceives the prime attribute of God to be. What is God in his essence? At this point Gilson is of considerable help in indicating what Eckhart taught in his lectures on the nature of God around the years 1313-1314.

In the first of these Questions he (Eckhart) asks himself whether, in God, being and knowing are identical, and he answers, in direct opposition to Thomas Aquinas, that God does not know because he is, but that he is because he knows *(est ipsum intelligere fundamentum ipsius esse)*. One could not more definitely subordinate the plane of being, and Eckhart does it in full agreement with the neoplatonism of the *De causis*, whose celebrated formula he adopts as his own: The first of created things is being.[41]

In one of his most highly speculative German sermons the intellective nature of God is strongly set forth.

When we take God in his being we take him in the forecourt of his habitation, for quiddity or mode is the way into the temple. Then where is God in his temple? Intellect is the temple of God wherein he is shining in his glory. Nowhere does God dwell more really than in the temple of his intellectual nature, where he is in stillness by himself, all undisturbed.[42]

The soul is likewise in its essence intellective. Herein lies Eckhart's version of the analogy of being *(analogia entis)*. The essential unity between God and the soul is based on their common intellective nature. Their correspondence is therefore predicated on an analogy of the intellect *(analogia intellectus)* rather than on an analogy of being *(analogia entis)*. Hence Eckhart can say: "Now turning to the soul, she has a drop of intellectual nature, a spark, a ray, and she has sundry powers which function in the body." [43] It is this intellective faculty of the soul which enables it to be "oned" with God; both the soul and God are similar in nature and therefore union between them is possible. The intellective aspect of this union is clearly manifest when Eckhart says: "My beatitude lies wholly in the fact that God is knowable and in my knowing him." [44]

The importance Eckhart attaches to the likeness between the essence of the soul and the divine essence cannot be overemphasized. Eckhart said: "I always have before my mind this little *quasi,* like: indeed, it is the burden of my entire teaching." [45] In another figure he likens the soul to the seed of God: ". . .the seed of God exists in us. Given a hard worker and a good director it thrives space and grows up into God whose seed it is and its fruit is likewise God's nature. Pear seed grows up into pear tree, nut seed grows up into nut tree: God seed into God, to God." [46]

Eckhart designates that which represents the essence of the soul by many names. Most often it is referred to as the spark of the soul, the *fünklein.* Ultimately, however, it beggars description.

I have said that there is one agent alone in the soul that is free. Sometimes I have called it the tabernacle of the Spirit. Other times I have called it the Light of the Spirit and again, a spark *(vönkelin).* Now I say that it is neither this nor that. It is something higher than this or that, as the sky is higher than the earth and I shall call it by a more aristocratic name than I have ever used before, even though it disowns my adulation and name, being far beyond both ("this little castle in the soul"). It is free of all names and unconscious of any kind of forms. It is at once pure and free, as God himself is, and like him is perfect unity and uniformity, so that there is no possible way to spy it out.[47]

Although the idea of the *fünklein* is common to mystics, it would be wrong to minimize its import for Eckhart on that account. Indeed, everything Eckhart teaches about the union of the soul with God is dependent upon the presence of this divine spark within the soul.[48] This inner essence of the soul is qualitatively different from all of the soul's other lower faculties which relate it to the transient world. Unlike these, it is detached from time and place. In its essence, the soul is related to eternity—to God. Moreover, all of the lower faculties or agents of the soul use means to effect their ends. For example, the soul loves with her will.[49] Thus, "all the soul's agents race for the prize but only the soul's essence receives it." [50] Within this inner citadel of the soul there is no activity; only a stillness and receptivity awaiting the birth of God in the soul. Eckhart writes:

. . . here alone is rest and habitation for this birth, this act, wherein God the Father speaks his Word, for it is intrinsically receptive of naught save the divine essence, without means. Here God enters the soul with his all, not merely with a part God enters the ground of the soul. None can touch the ground of the soul but God only.[51]

In a striking passage Eckhart illuminates the importance of this inner citadel of the soul in relation to the mystic union, the divine birth of God or of the Son in the soul.

—How does God the Father give birth to his Son in the soul: like creatures, in image and likeness? No, by my faith! but just as he gives him birth in eternity and no otherwise.
—Well, but how does he give him birth there? See. God the Father has perfect insight into himself, profound and thorough knowledge of himself by means of himself, not by means of any image. And thus God the Father gives birth to his Son, in the very oneness of the divine nature. Mark, thus it is and in no other way that God the Father gives birth to his Son in the ground and essence of the soul and thus he unites himself with her. Were any image present there would not be real union and in real union lies thy whole beatitude.[52]

Thus we find that for Eckhart everything in the Christian life is oriented toward—and finds its fulfillment in—the mystic union of the soul with God. "If anyone asks me, why do we pray, why do we fast, why do we work, why are we baptized, why—most important of all—did God become man? I answer, that God may be born in the soul and the soul be born into God." [53]

This mystic union is most often described in poetic fashion as the divine birth of God or the Son in the soul. The Word of the Father is continually being reborn within the soul which is properly prepared, that is to say, in the soul which is in a state of complete receptivity

(Gelassenheit). "The genuine Word of eternity is spoken only in eternity, where man is a desert and alien to himself and multiplicity." [54] Within the soul there exists an innate longing to experience this birth. The words Eckhart uses to describe this longing are reminiscent of Augustine, a master whom he often cites: "The soul is created for so high and great a good that it cannot possibly be at rest, but is always hurrying forward to arrive at the Eternal good, which is God, for which it was created." [55]

Eckhart's description of this union reveals that it was not simply a union with God, but with the pure Godhead, the soul's eternal ground.

I have spoken of an agent in the soul whose primitive function it is, not to reach God as he is good, or to apprehend him as he is the truth, but to go further, to the foundations, to seek him and apprehend him in his uniqueness and abstraction, in the desert of his solitude, the essence of his being. Still unsatisfied, it looks further to see what he is in his Godhead and so looks to the most intimate properties of his nature. Now, they say that there is no unity more perfect than that of the three persons in God. One might say further that there is no unity more perfect than that between the soul and God. When the soul is kissed by the Godhead, it is then completely perfected and blessed and embraced by the unity (of God). When God has touched the soul and rendered it uncreaturely, it is then as high in rank as God himself, after he has touched it. Contemplating the creature, God gives it being, and contemplating God, the creature receives its being. The soul has an intelligent, knowing essence and therefore, wherever God is, there is the soul, and wherever the soul is, there is God! [56]

As we have seen, this union can be effected because of the deiform nature of the soul. It is within this union that man is transformed; he becomes God's son. "I am his Son by virtue of the fact that he begets me in his nature and forms me in his image." [57]

Despite the fact that the state of union is strongly intellective in Eckhart's thought, the *visio Dei* goes beyond mere intellectual apprehension. Therefore, even when God reveals the higher *gnosis* or knowledge to man in the unitive state, man's joy is not primarily in knowing God, but in being one with God. This is a state beyond knowing.[58] "She (the soul) is fast asleep in the essence of God, conscious only of being there and God." [59]

It must be understood that this final state of union obtains because of the gracious activity of God; here man is passive.[60] It follows, therefore, that whenever the soul has been drawn up "beyond creaturehood into nothingness," it is due to God's gracious power. "The soul has dared to become nothing, and cannot pass from its own being into nothingness and then back again, losing its own identity in this process, except God safeguarded it." [61]

Joseph Quint, an acknowledged scholar of medieval mysticism and of Eckhart, illuminates our own conclusions in his assessment of the manner in which Eckhart's theology seeks to give expression to the soul's experience of God.

When the speculative mystic attempts to comprehend in thought the inner experience of the *unio mystica* as the mystical unification of the human soul with the absolute, and tries to succeed in realizing the *unio mystica* by way of knowledge—then this speculative thinking must be directed to the metaphysical ground of all being—especially (with regard) to the being of the human soul in the absolute being of the One: one has to deal with a speculation about unity. For the medieval mystic that means that he aspires to show that the innermost being of the soul is somehow identical with the inner being of God, because not only can like only be recognized by like, but also, only between like things is unification possible. For this reason it ought not to be surprising that for the mystical thinking of Meister Eckhart, speculation concerning the concept of unity and identity arises out of an inner mystical necessity—occupying a large place both in his German sermons and tractates as well as in his Latin *Opus Tripartitum.*[62]

This mystic union which Eckhart describes is not essentially different from that taught by other mystics. But is this an absorptionist mysticism? At one point Eckhart cites Dionysius approvingly: "Thus Dionysius says: 'This race is precisely the flight from creatures to union with the uncreated.' When the soul achieves this, it looses its identity, it absorbs God and is reduced to nothing, as the dawn at the rising of the sun." [63] It is evident that Eckhart envisages a circular process in which the soul moves out from God and ultimately returns to its source.[64] Thus the highest way in which the soul may move leads to its reunion with the One.

There is no gainsaying the intimacy of the union between the soul and God in Eckhart's teaching. He could say: "Our Lord Jesus Christ besought his Father to make us one with him: not only united but one and the same." [65] Or again: "And those other words, also from the gospel, in which our Lord declares, 'Where I am there shall also my servant be,' so thoroughly does the soul become the same being that God is, no less, and this is as true as God is God." [66]

These and similar statements by Eckhart relating to the mystic union or to the fact that "the Father begets his Son in me" led Eckhart's accusers to charge him with pantheism. While upholding the intimacy of the union with God which obtains when the Son is begotten in the soul in *The Defense,* Eckhart staunchly maintains that he is not guilty of the heresy of affirming the obliteration of the distinction between the creature and God, or between the believer and the Son. He writes:

For no man, however holy and good, becomes Christ himself or First Begotten, nor are others saved through him, nor is he the likeness of God, the only begotten Son of God; but he is *after* the likeness of God, a part of him who is truly and perfectly the Son, first begotten and heir, while we are joint-heirs as has just been said. . . .[67]

A related charge levelled to substantiate Eckhart's pantheism had to do with his holding that "a certain agent in the soil is uncreated (and that) if the whole soul were such, it would be uncreated and uncreatable." [68] Though there are ambiguities in Eckhart's sermons and writings regarding this charge, it appears that he intended to teach that the essence of the soul is created. Yet even his rejoinder to this charge points out something of an inherent ambiguity in Eckhart's thought on this point.

It is false (to say) that any part of the soul is uncreatable but it is true that the soul is intellectual after the image (idea) and species of God, Acts 17:29. But if it were pure intellect, such as God alone is, it would be uncreated and would not be soul. So, too, if a man were entirely soul then man would be immortal: but then he would not be a man. As it is, it is true absolutely, that man is mortal.[69]

Whatever the scholarly conclusion with respect to these charges made against Eckhart may be, there is no disputing his teaching that the goal of the soul's quest lies in being unified with the Godhead. Gilson has observed that in his later writings Eckhart subordinates everything to the purity of the divine One.[70]

This is "the one" which makes us blest, and the further we are from this one the less do we be son or sons and the more imperfectly does the Holy Ghost arise in us and issue from us. And the more we approximate to the one the more really are we God's Son, his sons, and there proceeds from us God the Holy Spirit.[71]

This quotation indicates, as was previously maintained, that Eckhart's interest was first and foremost a religious one. Everything which Eckhart said concerning the birth of the Son in the soul was rooted in his religious experience. Perhaps, as Otto has suggested, Eckhart attempted to revivify traditional Christian teachings which had become arid because of Scholastic subtleties by showing their relationship to the communion of believers with God.[72] Something similar occurred in German Protestants some five hundred years later when Pietists criticized both the arridity of Protestant orthodox theology and the moribund state of the prevailing spirituality which they countered with a stress upon the necessity of a vital, personal experience of the Christian with God. Viewed from this perspective, Eckhart's doctrinal and sermonic statements represent his reflections upon the centrality of the soul's communion with God.

The recognition of the validity of relating all of Christian teaching and preaching to Christian experience whether in a Roman Catholic mystic like Eckhart or a Protestant Pietist theologian like Schleiermacher entails neither surrendering critical scrutiny of theological positions they espouse nor accepting at face value everything they taught about the Christian's experience with God. We have seen that Eckhart's detractors raised the question whether his strong emphasis upon the birth of the Son in the soul detracted from the uniqueness and efficacy of the person of Jesus Christ and his unique incarnation. He could proclaim:

This same power (i.e., the power of God in the "castle of the soul") I am speaking of, herein God blooms and thrives in all his Godhood and the spirit in God; in this very power the Father bears his only Son no less than in himself, for verily he liveth in this power, the spirit with the Father giving birth therein to his very Son, itself this selfsame Son. . . ." [73]

Or again: "Between the only Son and the soul there is no difference." [74] Thus it appears at times that man is enabled to be united by God by virtue of the power of God resident in his soul apart from any reference to the necessary mediation provided by the historical incarnation, life, ministry, death and resurrection of Jesus Christ.[75] Yet when taken as a whole, I find Eckhart's view of the mystic union more Christian than platonic in its intention and thrust.

In conclusion, it should be said that Eckhart probed the depths of the human soul as have few mystics or advocates of experiential religion either before or since his day. His teaching concerning the mystic union incited a desire in countless others to experience God in a similar manner.[76] In one sense, Eckhart's teaching concerning the mystic union is perfectly natural. The soul was created to enjoy fellowship with God. This truth was the experience and teaching of St. Augustine, perhaps the greatest mentor in the Western Catholic tradition concerning the life of the soul, who wrote in his *Confessions:*

"Our hearts are restless until they rest in thee." This was Eckhart's conviction, too. But the union of the soul with God is supernatural because it can be effected ultimately only through the grace of God. Now as then, whoever would seek to understand Eckhart must bend both heart and mind; he must know both how to act in response to God and how to wait upon him. Eckhart concludes a sermon remembering St. Benedict with these words highlighting the divine grace.

God, despite himself, is ever hanging over us some bait to lure us into him. I never give God thanks for loving me, because he cannot help it; whether he would or no it is his nature to. What I do thank him for is for not being able of his goodness to leave off loving me. To know ourselves to be installed in God, this is not hard, seeing that God himself must be working in us; for it is godly work, man acquiescing and making no resistance: he is passive while allowing God to act in him. Let us, waiting upon God, enable him to take us into him, so that becoming one with him he may be able to love us with himself. So help us God. Amen.[77]

NOTES

[1] Otto Karrer, *Meister Eckehart, Das System Seiner Religiösen Lehre Und Lebensweisheit* (München: 1926), pp. 18-19. All translations from German titles are by David L. Mueller.

[2] Ernest W. McDonnell, *The Beguines and Beghards in Medieval Culture* (New Brunswick: Rutgers University Press, 1954), p. 356.

[3] *Ibid.*, p. 356.

[4] Karrer, *op. cit.*, p. 21.

[5] *Ibid.*, p. 22.

[6] McDonnell, *op. cit.*, p. 359.

[7] Karrer, *op. cit.*, p. 20. Pfeiffer notes some of the differing estimates of Eckhart thus: "Eckhart . . . has been called the father of the German mystics, the philosophical creative genius of the German mystics and the father of German speculation." Franz Pfeiffer, *Meister Eckhart*, trans. by C. de B. Evans (London: J. M. Watkins, 1924), I, p. xi. Vol. II was published in 1931. Cited hereafter as Eckhart (Pf. Ev.).

[8] Rudolf Otto, *Mysticism East and West* (New York: Macmillan, 1932), p. 78.

[9] Odilia Funke, *Meister Eckehart* (Washington: National Capital Press, 1916), p. 93.

[10] Raymond B. Blakney, *Meister Eckhart: A Modern Translation* (New York: Harper, 1941, from *The Defense*, IV, p. 266 and I, p. 259. Cited hereafter as Eckhart-Blakney.

[11] Cited in Eckhart (Pf. Ev.), I. p. xi.

[12] Joseph Quint, "Mystik und Sprache," *Deutsche Vierteljahrsschrift für Literaturwissenschaft und Geistesgeschichte*, XXVII (1953), p. 54.

[13] Franz Pfeiffer, *Meister Eckhart* (Goettingen: Vandenhoeck & Ruprecht, 1924), p. 181. Cited hereafter as Pfeiffer.

[14] Theodor Steinbüchel, *Mensch und Gott in Frömmigkeit und Ethos der deutschen Mystik*, (Düsseldorf: Patmos, 1951), p. 172.

[15] Otto, *op. cit.*, p. 78.

[16] *Ibid.*, p. 17.

[17] Quint, *op. cit.*, p. 54.

[18] James M. Clark, *The Great German Mystics* (Oxford: Blackwell, 1949), p. 17.

[19] Quint, *op. cit.*, p. 63.

20 Herman Buettner, *Meister Eckeharts Schriften und Predigten* (Jena: Eugen Diedrichs, 1917), I, iv.

21 Quint, *op. cit.,* p. 59. This Eckhart scholar states that no complete critical text of Eckhart was available as of 1953.

22 McDonnell, *op. cit.,* pp. 359-360. Cf. Buettner, *op. cit.,* I, xxxviii-xxxix.

23 Evelyn Underhill, *Mysticism: A Study in the Nature and Development of Man's Spiritual Consciousness* (New York: E. P. Dutton, 1930), p. 101.

24 Etienne Gilson, *History of Christian Philosophy in the Middle Ages* (London: Sheed and Ward, 1955), p. 443. Cf. note 7, above.

25 Eckhart (Pf. Ev.), "The Lord Put Forth His Hand," I, p. 69.

26 Otto, *op. cit.,* pp. 29-30.

27 Ray C. Petry, "Social Responsibility and the Late Medieval Mystics," *Church History,* XXI (March, 1952), pp. 7-8.

28 Eckhart (Pf. Ev.) "The Poor in Spirit," I, p. 217.

29 Eckhart (Pf. Ev.), "Detachment Has Four Steps," I, p. 217.

30 Eckhart-Blakney, "About Disinterest," p. 82.

31 *Ibid.,* p. 89.

32 *Ibid.* Quint shows that the idea of *abgeschiedenheit* led Eckhart to create a new group of words all of which seek to give expression to this process of "disbecoming" (*entwerden*). Thus Eckhart coined words utilizing the prefixes *abe* and *ent*. Throughout his writings one finds the following words: *abeziehen, abelegen, abeloesen, entbilden, entgeisten, entwerden, op. cit.,* p. 71.

33 Eckhart (Pf. Ev.), II, p. 56.

34 *Ibid.,* p. 189.

35 Eckhart-Blakney, "About Disinterest," p. 88.

36 *Ibid.,* "The Kingdom of God Is at Hand," p. 130.

37 *Ibid.,* p. 131.

38 *Ibid.*

39 *Ibid.,* "The Eternal Birth," pp. 20–21. For this emphasis, see also Eckhart's sermon on "The Poor in Spirit" and the Tractate on "The Soul's Perfection," in Eckhart (Pf. Ev.), I, pp. 217–221; 306–308.

40 *Ibid.,* "Truth Is not Merchandise," p. 156.

41 Gilson, *op. cit.,* p. 438. Quint's study of both Eckhart's Latin and German works leads him to concur with this viewpoint. Cf. Quint, *op. cit.,* p. 65.

42 Eckhart (Pf. Ev.), "Like the Morning Star," I, p. 212.

43 *Ibid.*

44 *Ibid.,* p. 213, Cf. p. 338.

45 *Ibid.,* p. 213.

46 Eckhart (Pf. Ev.), II. p. 80.

47 Eckhart-Blakney, "God Enters a Free Soul," pp. 210–211.

48 Gilson, *op. cit.,* p. 441.

49 Eckhart (Pf. Ev.), "This Is Meister Eckhart from Whom God Hid Nothing," I, p. 4.

50 Eckhart-Blakney, "About Disinterest," p. 89.

51 Eckhart (Pf. Ev.). "This Is Meister Eckhart from Whom God Hid Nothing," I, p. 4.

52 *Ibid.,* pp. 5–6. Quint *op. cit.* includes the following passage of Eckhart cited from Phillip Strauch, "Pardisus anime intelligentis, 1919, p. 14. ". . . also wirdet daz ewige wort gesprochin innewendic in deme herz in der sele, in deme innirsten, in deme lutirsten, in deme heubite der sele, daz ist in vornuftikeit: da geschihit di gebort inne."

53 Eckhart (Pf. Ev.), II, p. 151.

54 *Ibid.,* I, p. 22.

55 Pfeiffer, *op. cit.,* p. 178.

56 Eckhart-Blakney, "Get Beyond Time," p. 214. Pfeiffer includes the following Eckhart citation making the same emphasis: *op. cit.,* p. 77: "Ze dem vierten mâle sulle wir verstân daz êwige wort, dax dâ wirt gesprochen in die blôzen sele von der blozen gotheit, dax ist unwortlich, wan diu sele enkan sin niht geworten."

57 Eckhart (Pf. Ev.), II, p. 47.

58 *Ibid.,* p. 84.

[59] *Ibid.*

[60] Pfeiffer, *op. cit.*, p. 60. In speaking of the birth of God in the soul in the sermon, "The Eternal Birth," Eckhart says: "If this work is to be done, God alone must do it, and thou must undergo it." (Eckhart, [Pf. Ev.], I, p. 21.

[61] Eckhart-Blakney, "Truth Is not Merchandise," p. 159.

[62] Quint, *op. cit.*, p. 61.

[63] Eckhart-Blakney, "About Disinterest," p. 89.

[64] See for e.g., such sermons as "Truth Is not Merchandise" and "Youth Remains in .he Soul" in Eckhart-Blakney.

[65] Eckhart (Pf. Ev.), II, p. 94.

[66] *Ibid.*, pp. 89–90.

[67] Eckhart-Blakney, "The Defense," Part IV, p. 268.

[68] *Ibid.*, Part IX, Article 8, p. 285.

[69] *Ibid.*, Regarding Eckhart's ambiguity on this point, see Blakney's comments in *ibid.*, note 15, p. 331.

[70] Gilson, *op. cit.*, p. 439; cf. Steinbüchel, *op. cit.*, pp. 212–213.

[71] Eckhart (Pf. Ev.), II, p. 64.

[72] Otto, *op. cit.*, pp. 132–133. Cf. Steinbüchel, *op. cit.*, pp. 209–223.

[73] Eckhart (Pf. Ev.), "The Castle of the Soul," I, p. 38.

[74] *Ibid.*, "St. Germanus' Day," p. 209.

[75] Funke, *op. cit.*, p. 106.

[76] McDonnell, *op. cit.*, p. 360.

[77] Eckhart (Pf. Ev.), "Sermon on St. Benedicts Day," I, p. 179.

6.

Can Theology Be
Both Cultural and Christian?
Ernst Troeltsch and the Possibility of a
Mediating Theology [1]

John Powell Clayton

Determining the proper structure of relations between Christianity and culture has been throughout the history of theology a persistent problem, to which there has been no one solution which could be prudently acclaimed *"the* Christian solution." Variety in approach to this issue is no less a feature of primitive Christianity than of theology in the modern period. Rather than a single, normative model, we find within Christian thought from the outset a family of loosely related attempts to resolve, from within the perspective of faith, the problem of the church's existence within the world.

Some facets of this highly complex cluster of problems feature in Eric Rust's writings, especially those on the philosophy of history and culture, and those on the philosophy of science. In his widely influential book *Towards a Theological Understanding of History,*[2] Professor Rust wisely rejected any facile—and, in this case, futile—attempt to sever the Gordian knot which for centuries has bound together Christianity and Western culture.[3] Indeed, in his inaugural lecture delivered upon assuming the chair of Christian philosophy at Southern Seminary, he recommended strongly that the theological task in the modern situation requires a reappraisal of the traditions, both secular and religious, in terms of which Western society has been formed and by which it continues to be influenced.[4] This programmatic essay later became an important component in his highly regarded study *Science and Faith: Towards a Theological Understanding of Nature.*[5] There he argued forcefully that "our modern Western culture has its roots in Athens and Jerusalem, and to emphasize either at the expense of the other is to minimize one important aspect of our heritage."[6]

The tendency in the European Enlightenment and afterwards to affirm the secular, but not the religious, roots of our culture has led in modern times to a refocusing of the theological problem of religion and culture. This has been occasioned largely by the call during the Enlightenment for an emancipation of the several spheres of social and cultural life from religious tutelage. In his 1784 essay in answer to the question "Was ist Aufklärung?", Kant went so far as to define *enlightenment* as man's release from his self-imposed status as a minor, unable to make decisions without direction from those guardians who, in Kant's ironic turn of phrase, "have so kindly assumed superintendence over him." [7] To be enlightened, man must be free rationally to generate rules of belief and action; but in order for this to be possible, he must be free from the fetters of heteronomously imposed authority.[8] Whether in morality or in religion, the basis for belief and action must be found within man himself, and not be imposed from the outside in the form of external authority. True religion, as well as true morality, must find its basis "within the limits of reason alone," that is, within human autonomy.

The modern refocusing of the problem of Christianity and culture occurs against the backdrop of this new sense of self-confidence, this "recovery of nerve," [9] of which Kant is one example. The history of Christian theology since the eighteenth century can be written from one point of view as a history of responses to this new situation. For the question is not simply whether that recovery of nerve occurred. No one denies this—not even the dialectical theologians! The question is, rather, its significance for the way theology is to be done.[10] And theologians since then divide according to their relative acceptance or relative rejection of this new situation.

Ernst Troeltsch, with whom we shall be principally concerned in this essay, is to be counted among those who by and large affirmed that situation and who conducted themselves theologically within its terms.[11] Troeltsch was aware as few theologians before him that the end of what he called "church culture" [12] must have profound effects upon the way Christian theology is to be done. For theology is always done within a specific context and that context is both religious and cultural. In this the theologian has no option; but he can reflect upon the significance of this two-fold context for the way theology is to be done. And that is precisely what Troeltsch sought to do in most of his writings. In doing so, he was taking his stand within that tradition of "mediating theologians" or *Vermittlungs theologen*[13] who called Schleiermacher their "church father."

I

Writing against the background of the Enlightenment, Schleiermacher saw that the new movement had revitalized every aspect of human culture except religion, which remained aloof or openly antagonistic toward the new prominence given to autonomous reason. He envisaged this stance as having a double consequence: on the one hand, religion was being starved intellectually, and, on the other, the "cultured" were being deprived of the religious resources which are necessary for human existence.[14] His worry was expressed to his friend Lücke in the rhetorical question, "Shall the knot of history unravel in such a way that Christianity is identified with barbarism and modern knowledge with unbelief?" [15] Schleiermacher is sometimes credited with having set the methodological problem for a "theology of mediation" when, a little later in the same letter, he spoke of the need to establish between Christian faith and modern knowledge an "alliance" or a "pact" [16] in which the autonomy of neither party to the treaty is threatened, an alliance in which "faith does not hinder learning, nor learning exclude faith." [17] He found intolerable the sort of partition between intellect and faith implied in Jacobi's quip that he was a pagan with his intellect and a Christian with his heart.[18] Even so, Schleiermacher did not envisage a point at which the two would intersect or overlap with one another; there is for Schleiermacher no final synthesis between intellect and feeling, philosophy and theology, culture and religion.[19] His letter to Jacobi ends with the following words: "Intellect and feeling remain also for me distinct from one another *(nebeneinander)*, but they form together a galvanic couple. The innermost life of the spirit occurs for me only in this galvanic operation, in which feeling affects intellect and intellect feeling, but in such a way that both poles remain always distinct from one another." [20] Here, as in the letter to Lücke, the two components—in the one case, learning and faith; in the other, intellect and feeling—are allowed to affect one another and yet are said to remain distinct and ever *nebeneinander*. Their relationship is said by Schleiermacher in the one place to be similar to that between partners in an alliance, and in the other to be like that between the two poles in a galvanic reaction. In both cases, however, the relationship between the two must in Schleiermacher's view satisfy two conditions: there must be a mutual dependence and interaction in which neither component is reduced to the other, indeed, in which each remains in some sense independent from the other.

The dilemma for a "theology of mediation" along Schleiermachrian lines lies precisely in this two-fold requirement: is it possible to conceive, let alone to establish, a relationship between Christianity and culture in which there is a genuine and thoroughgoing reciprocity that denies the autonomy neither of religion nor of culture? There is widespread agreement that Schleiermacher's "experiment in cultural theology," as it has been called, ultimately failed. Yet, there is no such agreement as to the reasons why it did not finally succeed. Even so, there were theologians who persisted throughout the nineteenth and into the twentieth century in the attempt to establish an appropriate mediation or *wahre Vermittlung*[21] between historical Christianity and modern culture along lines similar to those which had been suggested by Schleiermacher. Foremost among these must be included Ernst Troeltsch.[22]

Troeltsch's posthumously published *Glaubenslehre,* delivered originally as lectures at Heidelberg, demonstrates clearly that he firmly supported "the reorganization of modern theology" with which he credited Schleiermacher.[23] And he did so, not only in the obvious sense that religious self-consciousness is regarded by Troeltsch as the proper starting-point for theology, but moreover in the sense that he shared Schleiermacher's concern that history not show Christianity finally allied with barbarism and unbelief with culture.[24] In those lectures, Troeltsch—as Schleiermacher had done before him— defended the view that theology can be substantially influenced by extra-Christian sources[25] and yet remain in some sense "relatively independent." [26] It would be a mistake, however, to think that Troeltsch is here merely juggling abstract ciphers which make no contact with human existence. Far from it. Theology was for Troeltsch too serious a business for that! This becomes clearer in his *Soziallehren,* where he defined a central problem of his theological work by asking how the church can cooperate with the main, nonreligious forces of society so that together they establish a unification of culture.[27] Given the shape of the new situation after the collapse of "church culture," Troeltsch perceived two imminent dangers: *either* Christianity would withdraw into itself and become increasingly irrelevant as a cultural force *or* it would become increasingly assimilated and lose its distinctiveness as a force in society. Troeltsch intended to construct a Christian theology which avoided both these dangers. "Religion becomes a power in ordinary life only by taking up civilization *(Kultur)* into itself and giving it a special direction." He immediately added the important and frequently forgotten disclaimer, "But it always remains distinct from this civilization." [28] In undertaking to construct a theology along such lines, Troeltsch had clearly accepted the challenge given by Schleiermacher to develop a theology of mediation between religion and culture.

Not only did Troeltsch accept Schleiermacher's challenge, but he also came through the years to broaden the terms in which that problem was conceived. This he did in two ways. First, he considerably broadened the concept of culture so that it came in his writings to include not only "the cultured" elite *(die Gebildeten),* nor even just the intellectual and imaginative activities and products of a society (its *Geistesleben),* but the social and economic "infrastructure" as well. This trend in Troeltsch's developing thought runs roughly parallel to the emergence in Germany of modern, descriptive conceptions of culture out of earlier, evaluative conceptions.[29] For Schleiermacher, on the other hand, culture was conceived principally as the process of cultivating *(Culturprozess)* human capacities, in analogy with the way that plants and animals are cultivated.[30] Schleiermacher cannot, therefore, within the terms of his culture concept speak of "*a* culture." Troeltsch *can.* And that has important consequences for his understanding of what it is to mediate between religion and culture. Schleiermacher speaks typically of the problem of mediating between religion and its "cultured despisers." [31] Troeltsch, too, sometimes speaks in similar terms.[32] But he also and perhaps more characteristically speaks of the problem of mediating between a religion and a culture or a cultural epoch.[33] Schleiermacher lacked the conceptual apparatus to discuss the problem of mediation in just these terms.

Not surprisingly, the broadened conception of culture contributed, secondly, to a wider conception of the nature of religion and (as just suggested) the problem of the relationship between religion and culture. Schleiermacher had arguably reduced essential religion to "piety" or *Frömmigkeit.* Though he emphasized, both in the *Reden* and in *Der christliche Glaube,* that the religious self-consciousness necessarily finds expression at some stage of its development in both doctrine and community, Schleiermacher nonetheless treated as secondary and derived dogma and doctrine, sacrament and cultus. A not entirely dissimilar line is to be found in Troeltsch's earlier writings, though it is noticeably less the case in his writings after the appearance of the *Soziallehren*. Despite his strong emphasis there upon the "mystical" and "personal" aspects of religion,[34] there is in that and subsequent works a growing appreciation for what might be termed (following here Ninian Smart[35]) the "multidimensional" character of religion, with particular emphasis upon its social and ethical, rather than—as in some of Troeltsch's earlier writings—its psychological dimension.[36]

Troeltsch reserves his greatest scorn, as had Schleiermacher before him,[37] for those who would intellectualize religion. He frequently complained that the academic theology of his day tended to view dogma and doctrine in isolation from the total religious context of which it formed only one part and in terms of which it gained its own significance.[38] A purely ideological or doctrinal approach to relations between Christianity and culture was for him a distortion of the actual state of affairs.[39] Consequently, Troeltsch came to regard as a serious mistake any attempt to produce a purely dogmatic history of Christianity: his *Soziallehren* is intended largely as a corrective to this overly ideological approach to the history of Christianity, as typified especially in the work of Harnack and Seeberg.[40] In the brief autobiographical essay entitled "Meine Bücher," Troeltsch mentioned that his *Soziallehren* is to be understood as a parallel account to Harnack's history of dogma in the sense that he, unlike Harnack, emphasized the primacy of the socio-ethical over the doctrinal or theological aspects of Christianity.[41] This new perspective is evidenced in much of Troeltsch's "middle" and "later" work besides the study of the *Soziallehren der christlichen Kirchen und Gruppen*. In a short article on religion, economics, and society which appeared originally in 1913,[42] Troeltsch argued that no theoretical advance regarding the relationship between religion and, say, economics would be possible so long as religion were interpreted in a purely ideological way as a body of dogma or doctrine or as a system of metaphysics. Protestants are accused of having been much more guilty of this distortion than have been Roman Catholics, who are said at least to have had a deeper appreciation for the cultic and the institutional, the mythic and the irrational aspects of religion. Yet, in Troeltsch's view, neither Protestants nor Catholics have appreciated fully the significance for religion of the wider socioeconomic sphere of culture. It may very well be the case that Troeltsch himself was not entirely successful in incorporating this socioeconomic infrastructure into his theory of culture,[43] but it must be conceded that the structure of relations between

religion and culture came through the years to be conceived by
Troeltsch in much broader terms than it had been by any theologian
before him, including Schleiermacher.

II

By asking how the church can cooperate with the main secular
forces of society so that together they form a unified culture, Troeltsch
specified the terms in which he would tackle the dilemma set by
Schleiermacher. In order to have a clearer sense of the extent to which
Troeltsch may have contributed to the resolution of that dilemma, I
propose to consider some aspects of three closely related concepts
which figure prominently in Troeltsch's thought. In this section, we
shall be concerned with his notions of "reciprocity" and "limited autonomy," and in the following two sections, with Troeltsch's conception(s!)
of "compromise." In all three sections, however, the question before
us is the same: within the framework allowed by Troeltsch, how far
would it be possible to satisfy the two conditions required for the
successful resolution of Schleiermacher's dilemma? To what extent
would it be possible, within Troeltschian terms, to effect between historical Christianity and contemporary culture a relationship of mutual
influence in which the independence of neither were undermined? Expressed in somewhat more characteristically Troeltschian terms: could
religion take culture up into itself and give it a special direction and
yet remain distinct from that culture? A final answer to these questions
clearly cannot be won within the limits of a single chapter, which
can at best specify some of the lines along which an answer might
be sought. Such questions can, nonetheless, profitably guide the direction of our inquiry. How, then, does Troeltsch attempt to combine
his stress on reciprocity with his emphasis upon the autonomy of
religion within human life?

Part of Troeltsch's case against the representatives of both the older
orthodoxy and also some forms of the newer "liberalism" [44] is built
on their allegedly having failed to grasp that the relationship between
the Christian religion and the rest of culture is reciprocal without
remainder. There is in Troeltsch's view no aspect of Christianity—
not its dogma,[45] nor its ethic,[46] nor its founder[47]—which stands outside the nexus of causal relations which together constitute cultural
history. The theologians of the older orthodoxy are said to have evaded
the relativizing effects of historical consciousness by means of their
"dogmatic method" with its inherent appeal to supranatural author-

ity—whether Bible or tradition or miracle—which was held not to be continuous with ordinary history, even if it happened "within" history.[48] Proponents of some sorts of idealism are said by Troeltsch to have contrived to evade the relativizing effects of the historical consciousness by asserting that Christianity is the absolute realization of a universal religious principle.[49] And advocates of some forms of Protestant liberalism are judged to have sought security vainly either in the "Jesus of history" [50] or in a persisting "essence" of Christianity which was thought to provide a point of identity in all authentic manifestations of Christianity.[51]

Troeltsch attacked each and every one of these attempts to evade the full consequences of historical relativism. He argued in effect that the historical consciousness which arose in and after the European Enlightenment[52] calls into question not merely this or that "fact" but one's view of the past and present and even future. The historical method cannot be adopted piecemeal or applied *ad hoc.* It must be applied consistently and dispassionately in every field of learning, including Christian theology.[53] Nor did Troeltsch restrict its significance for theology merely to the way ancient texts are to be studied. Rather the historical method is said to act as a leaven which permeates the whole of theology and which in the end "bursts the confines" of earlier methods.[54]

Few would claim that he quite succeeded, and many would hold that he was somewhat overimpressed by the putatively skeptical consequences of this historical relativism.[55] It must be granted nonetheless by all that more than most theologians of his own generation—not to mention those of the next! [56]—Troeltsch did make a serious and determined effort to apply historical method to theology with utter consistency in the sense of having attempted to construct a Christian theology based on a methodology orientated toward general cultural and religious history.[57] This being the case, the not unimportant problem arises as to how Troeltsch can hope to hold together his claim that religion is an independent factor within social history and his apparently contrary claim that religion stands in a radically reciprocal relationship to the rest of society. What then are we to make of this apparent tension in his methodology?

Troeltsch laid out the main lines of his methodology in a number of scattered articles, including his essay "Über historische und dogmatische Methode in der Theologie," which was his "final word" in the controversy with Julius Kaftan and his pupil Friedrich Niebergall regarding the autonomy on *Selbständigkeit* of Christianity within the history of religion and culture.[58] Of the three principles of historical explanation outlined there, only the principle of correlation or reciprocity is of direct concern here.[59] *Reciprocity* on the mutual interaction of all historical phenomena implies for Troeltsch that "there can be no change at one point without some preceding and consequent change elsewhere, so that all historical happening is knit together in a permanent relationship of correlation, inevitably forming a current in which everything is interconnected and each single event is related to all others." [60] There is no point in history exempt from this correlative involvement or reciprocal influence. Everything is relativized—"*Alles und Jedes*"—in the sense that there can be no absolute points in history: "Every historical configuration and moment can be understood only in relationship with others and ultimately with the total context." [61]

The main difficulties, both philosophical and theological, inherent in Troeltsch's methodology are easy enough to catalog. Nor has there been hitherto any shortage of those willing to add new charges to the bill of indictment. Yet upon reading and on occasion rereading Troeltsch's writings in the light of these charges, one begins to form the view that his case is not to be so lightly decided. It certainly should not be allowed to be settled *nolo contendere!* Moreover, means by which his position can be defended are sometimes available at just those points where he at first seemed most vulnerable: for instance, his notion of *relativism.*

The phrase "historical relativism" can be construed in a number of disparate ways,[62] and in Troeltsch's writings it is by no means in every case clear precisely which sense is meant.[63] Yet within at least *one* of the meanings present in Troeltsch's writings, "relativism" does not seem to entail the "anarchy of atoms" feared by Dilthey[64] nor the loss of all moral standards and grounds for epistemic certainty.[65] There are obviously very serious philosophical difficulties attached to Troeltsch's attempt to derive norms from history and theological norms from the history of religions. Yet in relating Christianity to the course of human events, it was in no sense Troeltsch's wish to destroy norms and criteria in Christian theology. The old norms and criteria had in his view already been thoroughly discredited. It was then his hope to win new and more certain guidelines by anchoring Christian faith firmly in history.[66] Rather that a cause of *un*certainty, "relativism" is in this sense the intended basis for such certain knowledge as can be won from history.[67] To say that a given event can be properly understood only in relation to a number of contiguous events is not to say that our knowledge of that event is in some sense defective, nor that one is unable to claim certain knowledge of that event; it is simply to specify the conditions under which one can rightly claim to have certain knowledge of that event. "Relativism," in this sense of the word at least, portends no victory of skepticism over historical knowledge. This being the case, Wolfhart Pannenberg is not entirely without justification in allowing that this principle in Troeltsch's methodology poses no threat to the perspective of faith.[68]

Others have come to a very different conclusion. Walter Bodenstein, for instance, charges Troeltsch with having reduced Christianity "in the final analysis to no more than a phenomenon of cultural life, perhaps its highest and noblest, but nonetheless fixed in the frame of human-historical life in the same way as any other cultural value." [69] Yet one misses here and elsewhere when Bodenstein attempts to substantiate his charge any adequate account of Troeltsch's persistent stress on the independence of religion. Indeed, the article mentioned already, "Über historische und dogmatische Methode in der Theologie," is itself part of a controversy in which Troeltsch attempted to lay out a way in which religion could be seen as an independent factor which, despite its thoroughly reciprocal relations with the rest of culture, lives nonetheless by "its own power." [70] If this were not the case, Troeltsch observes elsewhere, religion would have nothing to contribute to culture.[71]

The emphasis upon the autonomy of religion runs throughout most of Troeltsch's writings, though the grounds on which he defended that autonomy varied considerably. Possibly the most well-known and arguably the least successful of his various approaches to the matter was his attempt to ground the autonomy of religion in a religious a priori. Having come to the conclusion that religion is in no sense exempt from the relativizing effects of historical consciousness, Troeltsch sought to avoid what seemed to him at the time a virtually inevitable conclusion—namely, that religion is "merely" a product of social conditioning[72]—by recourse to the apriority of the religious self-consciousness. This move probably owes more to Schleiermacher[73] than to Kant, even though Troeltsch claimed to have developed the notion as a legitimate extension of Kant's concept of apriority.[74] By the time he came to defend his notion of a religious a priori against Paul Spiess,[75] however, Troeltsch already entertained some doubts about its validity, and as his research carried him further into sociology and history, the notion makes increasingly infrequent appearances in his work until it finally disappears altogether.[76] But I should like to emphasize that the idea of the autonomy of religion did not disappear with it. For that idea was essential in his lifelong struggle against various forms of positivism and reductionism, including in his later works Marxism.[77] In the *Soziallehren,* for instance, he is at pains to argue that Christian faith and ethics flow from essentially religious sources and are not merely a function of social and historical conditioning.[78] Even though he eventually came to soften the claim that purely religious factors are the driving force of Christianity,[79] he never to my knowledge relinquished the view that religion is in some sense a relatively autonomous factor in society and culture.

The notion of "relative independence" or of "limited autonomy," which plays a role in the prolegomena to Troeltsch's *Glaubenslehre,*[80] may appear at first sight a contradiction in terms, something of a square circle. The word *autonomy* is in fact among those terms constantly in danger of being priced out of the market place of linguistic usage. "Knowledge" and "altruism" [81] are other examples. For we are tempted to think of such terms only in an absolute sense, so that any claim to have autonomy which does not entail absolute independence from any sort of external influence is disallowed; or, so that any claim to empirical knowledge which does not entail apodictic certainty is disallowed. The effect in each of these cases would be to disallow every claim to have autonomy or to have empirical knowledge. One could, of course, make the conditions under which one would allow such claims so astringent that the terms would have no applicability. But it would hardly be desirable. For it would, at the very least, deprive us of a number of words which have enjoyed common usage and, at the same time, artificially create the need for new words to use in those contexts where we might like to have used "autonomy" or "knowledge" or "altruism."

There are obviously degrees of autonomy, so that things may be autonomous to a greater or to a lesser extent. But we do not in fact ever ordinarily use the word "autonomy" in an absolute sense. We might say that an academic discipline is autonomous if at least some of the main propositions which it generates are irreducible to propositions of another type. But this would not preclude there being areas of overlap between it and other disciplines. Or we might say that an emotionally healthy person is autonomous in the sense of being an integrated and self-directed personality, but not in the sense of being wholly immune from all influence by other persons. These two examples are perhaps sufficient to show that the notion of "limited autonomy" is not intrinsically incoherent. And the Troeltschian notion of a "relative independence" for theology among the sciences and for Christianity in its relations with the rest of culture need not be abandoned simply as a consequence of a general argument regarding the alleged incoherence of the concept of "limited autonomy." On the other hand, it is a concept which certainly wants working out more thoroughly and more rigorously than one finds in Troeltsch's *Glaubenslehre!*

Given that Troeltsch's notion of limited autonomy within reciprocity is not irredeemably nonsensical, it is appropriate to enquire further regarding the terms in which he sought to elucidate such a relationship between Christianity and the rest of culture. In the remaining sections, we shall be concerned with *the principle of mediation* operative in Troeltsch's thought.

III

Schleiermacher had employed several metaphors in order to elucidate his conception of the proper relationship between faith and culture. They included "alliance" or "pact." Troeltsch also used mainly contractual terms when discussing the relationship between Christianity and culture. In the *Soziallehren,* for instance, he found occasion to use for such purposes all the following images: "accommodation," "agreement," "alliance," "amalgam," "coalition," "merger," "negotiated settlement." The metaphor with which his thought is most typically associated is, however, *compromise.*

Troeltsch's election to favor that metaphor was not an altogether happy choice, for its primary associations have to do largely with the mutual concession of *Realpolitik.* His defenders frequently warn that this is not at all what he meant,[82] that his use of the word "compromise" has none of the derogatory overtones which usually accompany that term. It would make a sympathetic analysis of Troeltsch's principle of mediation much less complicated if that were the case. But it is not.

Troeltsch used the word *Kompromiss* in a number of different senses, only the most obvious of which were identified by H. Richard Niebuhr in his doctoral dissertation on Troeltsch's philosophy of religion.[83] Some of these uses are clearly negative.[84] And Troeltsch allows that there are some situations in which compromise would be undesirable,[85] even immoral[86] or dishonorable.[87] More often than not, however, he employed the term in a double-sided way: compromise is necessary, but in each particular compromise something is lost as well as gained. Needless to say, Troeltsch himself thought that the gains outweighed the losses.[88] In at least this stress, he stands quite near to Harnack. For, according to the latter, the so-called "hellenization of the gospel" was both necessary for the survival of the young Christian sect and a very high price to pay for its continued existence.[89] But, in any case, there was in his view no practical alternative if the new religion were not to pass away with the age that had produced it. This double-sided emphasis is sometimes missed by Harnack's critics; [90] and a similarly double-sided emphasis is also frequently overlooked by Troeltsch's more uncritical interpreters.

What then does Troeltsch mean by *Kompromiss?* Nowhere to my knowledge does he offer an adequate definition of what in his view would count as a "compromise." Nor does he anywhere give an adequate account of the logic of compromise. That being the case, one alternate avenue of approach would be to analyze how Troeltsch applies the term, with a view toward determining from its actual usage its basic features as a principle of mediation.

Discounting its occasional and clearly casual use in earlier writings, "compromise" begins to be used as a *terminus technicus* for mediation in Troeltsch's writings from about 1900. In his study of *Die wissenschaftliche Lage und ihre Anforderung an die Theologie,* the word is introduced without explanation in special reference to the intellectual rapprochement in ancient times between the Christians and the "cultured" of the Roman Empire, in which society the new sect had gradually gained a firm standing.[91] Troeltsch there rigidly restricted the application of *Kompromiss* to the various aspects of just this alliance between Christianity and antiquity,[92] an alliance in which "culture was Christianized and (Christian) morality was secularized." [93] This narrow restriction, however, was soon to be lifted. In the course of Troeltsch's intriguing analysis of *Das historische in Kants Religionsphilosophie* which appeared four years later, Kant is reckoned to have effected through his moral philosophy[94] a compromise[95] between "positive" or historical religion and "rational" religion.[96] This compromise is also held, at another level, to have unified Christian theology and the philosophy of religion.[97] The close similarity between this extended use of *Kompromiss* and Troeltsch's earlier, historically more restricted sense is clear enough, even if we are still quite in the dark as to what precisely is a "compromise." The matter soon becomes much more complex. For he came to use the word *Kompromiss* to refer to relationships of all kinds, and not merely those between Christianity and society.

Yet all is not chaos. Leaving aside some of his more obviously casual uses of the term, Troeltsch tends to apply the word *Kompromiss* in four distinct senses, some of which can be further subdivided. The first three senses will be treated in this section; the remaining sense is to be considered separately in section four.

First, and perhaps most literally, "compromise" is used in a political or legal sense. Such compromises can be between churches and states or between churches and individual institutions within states[98] or, more poetically, between the city of God and the city of man.[99] Thus, the Elizabethan settlement[100] and the Justinian code[101] can be called "compromises," as can the alliances between Luther and the German princes.[102] There are also compromises between church law and state law.[103] But compromises in the political sense can also be agreed between states[104] or within and between the various churches.[105] The ability and willingness of the Roman Catholic Church to assimilate into itself the "sect type" is termed by Troeltsch a compromise.[106] Calvin and Bullinger[107] came to a compromise, but none was possible between Erasmus and Luther.[108] And it was perhaps as much political as vocational reasons which caused Schleiermacher to strike a compromise between the academic and the ecclesiastical character of theology.[109] Political compromise, Troeltsch remarked in a lecture written for an English audience, is generally regarded by most Germans as "the most despicable and the most vulgar trick in the book." [110] Troeltsch himself saw things otherwise. The capacity to compromise was specifically singled out as one of the attractive features of the Anglo-Saxon political tradition which was lacking within the German.[111] Yet, "compromise" in this sense surely implies mutual concession and political bargaining; there are here losses, as well as gains. It would be very naïve indeed to insist that Troeltsch's commendation of compromise in this case has none of the negative overtones which are ordinarily associated with that term! Nor can one say that this particular usage simply has no importance for Troeltsch. Its frequent and explicit presence in *Historismus und seine Überwindung* makes such an interpretation entirely untenable. Consequently, the presence of *Kompromiss* in this "ordinary" sense in Troeltsch's writings raises for us an unavoidable question: How many of the negative overtones which ordinarily accompany the word "compromise" are carried over by Troeltsch when he extends the use of that term into other contexts? For the casual way in which the term was first introduced into his writings suggests that Troeltsch was *extending* its ordinary meaning, rather than giving it an entirely new meaning, when he applied *Kompromiss* as a principle of mediation. In looking at the various ways in which Troeltsch extends the usage of "compromise," we shall want to be alert to the particular nuances in each case. Have we to do on every occasion with an agreement reached by mutual concession? Are there in each case losses as well as gains? If so, what is their specific character?

Troeltsch used the word *Kompromiss,* secondly, in an intellectual sense in reference to the mediation between different beliefs, ideas, and ideologies. Mediation of this sort can occur within a single discipline or within a single intellectual tradition. Within Christian theology, for instance, Beza is said by Troeltsch to have effected a compromise between the doctrine of the divine right of secular authority and the doctrine of the Christian's duty of passive obedience.[112] In the Roman Catholicism of the Middle Ages there is said to have been a compromise between the "patriarchal" and the "organic" principles of society, whereas in Lutheranism this compromise was dissolved in favor of the "patriarchal." [113] In both cases, the compromise is made between disparate elements which had been indigenous to Christianity virtually from the outset. Nor should one underestimate the degree of tension or even contradiction which can exist within a single tradition or minimize the struggle which is sometimes required to resolve it. Yet, such *compromises within a single tradition,* even one as complex as historical Christianity, form a distinct sub-group within Troeltsch's writings which must be distinguished from *compromises between different traditions* or systems of thought. For, whatever the differences which exist within individual traditions, there is nonetheless a shared framework for agreement and disagreement which cannot be relied upon in cross-traditional arguments. The character and consequences of the so-called "gains and losses" is also different in the two cases: for one is an *internal* adjustment and the other is an *external* accommodation. To conflate the two, and it must be admitted that Troeltsch himself does not clearly distinguish between them, is a possible source of confusion in any assessment of the viability of Troeltsch's principle of mediation. As examples of *cross-traditional compromises* within Troeltsch's writings, I would mention accommodations reached between competing secular ideologies,[114] as well as those between a given secular philosophy and a given Christian philosophy.[115] Slightly different issues are created in *cross-disciplinary compromises,* as between theology and philosophy,[116] where the basis for compromise is more problematic than in the former case. But this old chestnut is hardly unique to Troeltsch's concept of compromise! There might be good grounds for holding that the compromise between reason and revelation[117] should form on its own a distinct class of usage; for it is a tension implicit in human existence, whether one be a theologian or philosopher or whatever, even if it be in each case resolved in a different sort of way. Yet, in Troeltsch's own writings this particular compromise tends to be treated as synonymous with that between natural and supernatural philosophies of religion or between rationalism and Christian theology. It is, therefore, more properly akin to the compromise effected by Kant between "rational" religion and "positive" religion.[118]

The third main sense in which Troeltsch used *Kompromiss* differs from the second largely in scope. For he sometimes used the term in an inclusive sense in reference to compromises made between "learning" or "science" *(Wissenschaft)* and theology or between culture and Christianity.[119] From the limited number of occasions on which the term is explicitly used in this sense it is difficult to determine just what Troeltsch meant. Indeed, he seems to use *Kompromiss* on such occasions in a way that suggests he expected his readers already to know what was meant. The infrequency with which the word is used explicitly in this inclusive sense is a cause of at least momentary embarrassment for one who has claimed the *Kompromiss* is Troeltsch's main principle of mediation between Christianity and culture! Fortunately, the discomfit is short lived. For it would be a mistake to infer from this infrequency of explicit usage that compromise in the inclusive sense plays only a minor role in Troeltsch's thought. General compromises are quite often implied in those contexts where Troeltsch speaks of ethical compromises. As we have already seen, he characteristically treated the problem of mediating between Christianity and culture as a task of *Ethik,* in Schleiermacher's sense of that word. Introducing the term ethics, however, anticipates the fourth and final way in which *Kompromiss* is typically employed in Troeltsch's writings.

IV

Owing to its thematic role in the argument of *Die Soziallehren der christlichen Kirchen and Gruppen,* "compromise" is most frequently used by Troeltsch in relation to moral and ethical issues. In order to make more precise the meaning of compromises in ethical contexts, however, it is necessary to make yet another distinction. Although Troeltsch himself seems to have confused the two, we are clearly faced with very different sorts of issues when we are asked to consider making a compromise between an ethical "ideal" and the "real world" than when we are asked to consider making a compromise between, say, a religious ethical system and a secular ethical system. In the first case, the compromise under consideration would involve two logically very disparate sorts of thing, whereas in the second case it would involve things of a logically similar type, however much they may differ in detail. What precisely constitutes the compromise is also in the two cases different, such that they must be treated separately even though Troeltsch himself tended not to distinguish properly between them.

Within both religion and secular philosophy there is said to be the necessity to make compromises between ethical ideals and the practical requirements of everyday life. Jesus made no such compromise. The "Christianity of the Christ" set in radical opposition the kingdom of God and the kingdom of this world, whereas the "Christianity of the church" sought in different ways to mediate between them,[120] with Paul having established the first tentative compromise between the radical demands of the gospel and the practical requirements of the concrete world.[121] Other such compromises were subsequently established throughout the history of the Christian church.[122] This compromise between the "lofty spirituality" of Christianity and the practical needs of life must be renewed by every Christian in every moment.[123] But it is not merely a problem for theological ethics; the tension between the ethical ideal and the real world plagues philosophical ethics as well. Thus, Kant is reckoned by Troeltsch to have been a "philosopher of compromise" in his having mediated between the absolute demands of the moral imperative and the radical evil which infects man.[124] This tension belongs inherently to human existence; it is, therefore, in Troeltsch's view finally inescapable. And compromise is inevitable.[125] The specifically theological expression of just this compromise is the doctrine of justification by faith alone.[126] *Kompromiss* in this sense would not seem to have the sort of negative overtones which were certainly present in Troeltsch's use of the term in political and legal contexts. For "compromise" in this case does not seem ever to touch the absoluteness of the "ideal": the moral imperative remains categorical and the satisfaction of its demands unattainable. Nor is it entirely clear, however, that *this* sense of ethical compromise plays the central role in Troeltsch's theology of mediation which one might have assumed. It is, rather, the *other* sense of ethical compromise which plays that role.

In addition and without clearly distinguishing it from the former sense, Troeltsch talks about effecting compromises between the competing claims of different ethical systems, the one secular and the other religious. No longer directly at issue is the mediation between absolute moral demands and human frailty. At issue, rather, is the need to mediate between two accounts of relations between those demands and our daily lives. Kant, for instance, is said to have made a compromise between a rational ethic and the ethic of Jesus.[127] Troeltsch speaks also of compromises having been struck between "natural ethics" and "supranatural ethics," [128] or between "natural law" and "divine law." [129] Elsewhere he speaks of the compromise effected between the ancient "secular ethic" and the "Christian ethic." [130] This is, in fact, Troeltsch's paradigm case, it being the compromise which eventually made possible the medieval Catholic synthesis.[131]

Troeltsch's detailing of the various steps which finally led to this compromise provides the surest source for determining the contours of his conception of an inclusive compromise between Christianity and culture. In the *Soziallehren* he traces with sensitivity and more than occasional brilliance the gradual modifications both within the social context and within Christian thought which eventually made possible the multi-sided medieval synthesis, the major theological expression of which was Thomism.[132] That synthesis, which was the sole product neither of a single theologian nor of a single generation of theologians, was in good measure the product of a gradual and largely unconscious[133] reinterpretation of traditions which had for centuries shaped Western thought.[134] All the main elements, save one, which went to make up that synthesis had according to Troeltsch's analysis been available for some time.[135] These resources from Christian moral traditions and secular *lex naturae* traditions were combined in such a way that the radical character of the Christian ethic was largely preserved through the introduction of the novel concept of degrees or gradations.[136] This "creative compromise" is said by Troeltsch to have seemed to the medieval church entirely natural and quite unremarkable,[137] even though its basis was in fact *non-*Christian.[138] This was due to long-standing modifications within both

secular and religious ethical traditions which made the distance between them seem not all that great. The notion of degrees simply
completed a process which had been developing over a long period.

While it lasted, this inclusive compromise on an ethical basis gave
meaning and structure to human life. It did not go unchallenged, as
the remainder of *Die Soziallehren der christlichen Kirchen und Gruppen*
amply records! Nor in Troeltsch's view could that same compromise
hope to serve its previous unifying role for our time,[139] owing in
part to the greater diversity and complexity of contemporary social
life.[140] There are other differences. Thomism, for instance, held it to
be an endemically Christian idea that there should be a "Christian
society" or unity of culture effected on a Christian foundation.[141]
This is an assumption which Troeltsch found impossible to share, so
that he rejected any suggestion either simply to repristinate the Thomistic synthesis[142] or even to attempt to renegotiate terms for a "Christian society" on some other basis.[143] This resistance on Troeltsch's
part owes less to possible doubts about the importance of the concept
of *lex naturae*[144] than to increasing skepticism about any attempt
to reestablish in the modern world a "church-culture" and to increasing
respect for the independence *(Selbständigkeit)* and integrity of the
various spheres of culture and institutions of society.[145] But, it must
be stressed, he did not abandon the ideal of an ethical compromise.
Precisely because an inclusive compromise in the Thomistic sense is
no longer possible, the need for a new ethical compromise is in
Troeltsch's view all the more pressing.[146] And that compromise, while
more limited in scope and more complicated in structure,[147] would
be arrived at in much the same way that the earlier one had been
effected: namely, through a reshaping and reinterpretation of the traditions, both secular and religious, in terms of which modern Western
society has been formed and by which it continues to be influenced.[148]
Troeltsch was no less aware than some of his critics among the "dialectical theologians" that there are dangers and risks entailed in attempting to forge such a synthesis between Christianity and culture.[149]
Nor would he preempt the Christian community's prerogative finally
to decide whether the result would be held as "Christian."[150] The
details of Troeltsch's own material contribution to such a new cultural
synthesis have been denied us by his early death in 1923,[151] so that
we must base our judgments as to his likely significance for the future
of theology almost entirely upon his methodology,[152] one aspect of
which is the notion of compromise.

As a principle of mediation, compromise has proved more variegated than one might at first have assumed. Nor were all of the ways in which Troeltsch applied it wholly free from the negative associations of the word "compromise" in its ordinary usage. One outstanding exception in this respect was that compromise struck within the Pauline-Lutheran-Kantian tradition between the absolute demands of the moral law and the radical evil which infects man. Yet this was but one of the meanings of "compromise" in ethical contexts. What of the second main sense in which Troeltsch spoke of an ethically centered compromise? Are there perhaps in this case losses as well as gains? If so, what is their character? We shall also want to determine whether they are a direct consequence of Troeltsch's concept of compromise.

The medieval synthesis was, in Troeltsch's view, neither entirely continuous with nor a radical break from the main traditions of historical Christianity. That particular compromise, based though it was principally on non-Christian resources, is judged by Troeltsch nonetheless largely to have conserved the radical Christian ethic. In order for that compromise to be enacted, however, only certain components from among the varied elements of the Christian ethical traditions could be selected, and even those often underwent considerable reinterpretation. In the process, other components were necessarily missed out, that being one ground for subsequent theological protest against the Thomistic synthesis. But those who protested the effects of that compromise were themselves no less selective in their handling of Christian ethical traditions than those who had established the earlier compromise.

Nor could it have been otherwise, according to Troeltsch.

Some years earlier, in a series of pieces on the "essence" of Christianity, Troeltsch had argued that Christianity contains within itself elements which are mutually exclusive, so that to affirm one entails that another be denied.[153] This would mean that no statement of what is essential to Christianity could embrace all its constituent parts, some of which in any case would seem at any given time to be more important than others.[154] The results of his subsequent study of the history of Christianity from the point of view of its social teachings confirmed and reinforced his earlier, "programmatic" essay.[155] The weight of the evidence accumulated in the nearly nine hundred pages of his *Soziallehren* seems additionally to have given Troeltsch courage to state even more strongly some of the ideas guardedly suggested in

Die christliche Welt. For when he came to revise "Was heisst, 'Wesen des Christentums'?" for inclusion in the second volume of his collected writings, Troeltsch tended sometimes to intensify the argument at those points where multiplicity and novelty figure.[156] For instance, he was by then more willing to trace some of the contradictory elements present in historically developed Christianity directly back to the very origins of Christianity, to what he called its "classical period." [157] Nor would he be drawn on the question as to which elements are "more" Christian: they all belong to Christianity—and essentially so. Thus, in any coherent account of what constitutes essential Christianity at any given time, some elemental features must be missed out: defining what counts as Christian is a critical, as well as a descriptive, exercise. In "The Dogmatics of the *religionsgeschichtliche Schule,*" Troeltsch argued that the "essence" of Christianity (in this sense) can be identified neither with the sum of its manifestations nor with a single element common to all of its instances:

The nature of Christianity cannot be determined in this fashion, for a genuinely historical point of view reveals to us such a variety of interpretations, formulations, and syntheses that no single idea or impulse can dominate the whole. Thus the essence of Christianity can be understood only as the productive power of the historical Christian religion to create new interpretations and new adaptations—a power which lies deeper than any historical formulation which it may have produced.[158]

Referring later in the same article to "the indefinite content of the word Christianity," Troeltsch added:

So long as Christianity is a living religion men will be constantly differing from one another concerning what it is and what it ought to be, and they will constantly seek through new formulations to meet present conditions and to adapt it to future exigencies. . . . An unchangeable Christianity would mean the end of Christianity itself. There has never been such an unchangeable Christianity and never can be so long as it belongs genuinely to history.[159]

Among other things, this would seem to suggest that "losses" are endemic to the theological task of giving an account of the Christian faith. But are these "losses" similar to the sort associated with the mutual concession of political bargaining? In order to answer this question, it is perhaps useful to distinguish between Troeltsch's historical judgments about the Thomistic synthesis and his constructive recommendation that compromise is a legitimate object of theological activity.

As regards the Thomistic synthesis, compromise is said by Troeltsch to have been merely an unintended by-product and not the principal goal of theological construction,[160] so that it would be at the very least misleading to liken *that* accommodation too closely to the process whereby political compromises are agreed. But, in the *Soziallehren,* Troeltsch also commends to his readers compromise as a proper goal of theology. Just as it has done in various ways in the past, albeit unconsciously, Christianity is now urged firmly to seek a new basis for accommodation *(Anpassung)* with the modern world.[161] This same recommendation even more urgently dominates *Der Historismus und seine Probleme* and *Der Historismus und seine Überwindung,* in both of which synthesis and compromise are most certainly held up as proper objectives, and are not merely tolerated as unintended by-products of some more serious undertaking. This would seem also to hold for the question cited above in which Troeltsch set out the terms in which he would tackle Schleiermacher's dilemma.[162] Are we not here at least very near to the sort of compromise associated with political bargaining? There is still another important difference between them which precludes their simple identification. In compromises of a political sort, the "losses" are precisely those points conceded in the negotiating process. In Troeltsch's own case, matters are quite different: "loss" necessarily occurs in any attempt to give shape to the elemental features of Christianity, apart from any attempt to correlate that "essence" with the requirements of a particular age or group. Such "losses" are a direct consequence of his conception of the character of Christianity and are only indirectly associated with his commendation of compromise as a principle of mediation. Nor does Troeltsch rule out the likelihood that some elements which are missed out from one definition of essential Christianity might provide the basis for a future statement of Christianity's essence.

But, one might protest, does not Troeltsch's persistent emphasis upon the need for accommodation place the stress elsewhere? Is it not more nearly the case that he would on every occasion define the essence of Christianity in precisely such a way that would make it harmonious with the values and beliefs of a given time? There is perhaps some force to this objection, to the extent that Troeltsch allowed that no single definition of the essence of Christianity could be good for all times. What he meant thereby, however, is other than what is implied by the objection. For quite like another mediation theologian somewhat nearer to our time, Troeltsch also held the view that each age produces its own unique existential questions, the answers to which form the content of Christian theology.[163] "Accommodation" for Troeltsch, therefore, does not mean simple conformity. Orientating oneself to the times may also imply polemic against prevailing values and beliefs.[164] Indeed, the precise terms of the relationship between Christianity and culture at any given time remains for him an open issue,[165] which can be decided only case by case.[166]

We have seen that it will not do to defend Troeltsch's concept of compromise on the grounds that it is free from the negative overtones ordinarily associated with that term. There are losses as well as gains, though their specific character and consequences vary from use to use. Nor will it do to reject Troeltsch's concept of compromise on the grounds that there are losses as well as gains in such relations between Christianity and culture. It would have to be shown that it could be otherwise. And that we must here leave an entirely open question.

NOTES

[1] This article was written during my tenure at the University of Marburg as a Research Fellow of the Alexander von Humboldt Foundation, whose financial support I gratefully acknowledge. For her critical comments on the argument advanced here, I express gratitude to my Lancaster colleague Sarah Coakley.

[2] New York: Oxford University Press, 1963.

[3] *Ibid.,* cf. esp. pp. 245–56.

[4] "The Apologetic Task in the Modern Scene," *Review and Expositor,* (1959), pp. 178-200.

[5] New York: Oxford University Press, 1967.

[6] *Ibid.,* p. 5.

[7] *Kants Gesammelte Schriften,* ed. by the Royal Prussian (now: German) Academy of Sciences (Berlin: Georg Reimer; Walter de Gruyter & Co., 1910ff) vol. VIII, pp. 35ff.

[8] The following year (1785), Kant developed this argument further as regards morality in his *Grundlegung zur Metaphysik der Sitten,* which appears in the *Gesammelte Schriften* in vol. IV, pp. 387-463. Cf. esp. the second and third chapters, pp. 406ff, 446ff. Cf also the *Opus postumum* in *Gesammelte Schriften,* vol. XXI, pp. 103, 106. It is perhaps not irrelevant that the concept "autonomy," which had been a central political category for the Greeks in ancient times, seems to have dropped out of usage entirely during the Middle Ages and to have made its reappearance only in modern times, most importantly in the seventeenth and eighteenth centuries. See R. Pohlmann, "Autonomie," *Historisches Wörterbuch der Philosophie,* ed. by Joachim Ritter and Karlfried Gründer (Darmstadt: Wissenschaftliche Buchgesellschaft, 1971), vol. I, cols. 701-19.

[9] The phrase is from Peter Gay, *The Enlightenment: An Interpretation* (2 vols; New York: Charles Scribner's Sons, 1966 and 1969), vol. II.

[10] A similar point is made as regards historicism by Friedrich Gogarten in "Historismus," *Zwischen den Zeiten,* VIII (1924), pp. 7-25.

[11] Cf., e.g., Troeltsch's article on "Glaube und Geschichte" in the first ed. of *Die Religion in Geschichte und Gegenwart,* ed. by Michael Schiele and Leopold Zscharnack (5 vols.; Tübingen: J. C. B. Mohr, 1909-13), II, col. 1450. He was not, however, uncritical. In particular, he rejected

entirely the view that autonomy is productive, that rules of belief and behavior can be produced out of autonomy. Cf. *ibid.,* cols. 1452-3. A not entirely dissimilar argument would be advanced later by Paul Tillich, who also both affirmed and criticized modern autonomy. Cf., e.g., *Gesammelte Werke,* vol. VII: *Der Protestantismus als Kritik und Gestaltung* (Stuttgart: Evangelisches Verlagswerk, 1962), pp. 70ff. Both Troeltsch and Tillich, like Schleiermacher before them, were convinced of the peculiar power of Protestant Christianity to meet the needs of this modern, autonomous man. Cf. Troeltsch's analysis of the relationship between Protestantism and modernity in *Die Bedeutung des Protestantismus für die Entstehung der modernen Welt* (Munich and Berlin: R. Oldenbourg, 1911).

[12] Cf. *ibid.,* pp. 9ff.

[13] On some of the main varieties of mediating theology, see Martin Kähler, *Geschichte der protestantischen Dogmatik im 19. Jahrhundert* (Munich: Chr. Kaiser, 1962), pp. 82-146 and Horst Stephan and Martin Schmidt, *Geschichte der deutschen evangelischen Theologie seit dem deutschen Idealismus* (3rd. ed.; Berlin: Walter de Gruyter & Co., 1973), pp. 228-45.

[14] *Schleiermacher-Auswahl,* ed. by Heinz Bolli (Munich and Hamburg: Siebenstern Taschenbuch Verlag, 1968), p. 146.

[15] "Soll der Knoten der Geschichte so auseinander gehn; das Christentum mit der Barbarei, und die Wissenschaft mit dem Unglauben?" *Ibid.* Elsewhere Schleiermacher would, however, contrast "culture" *(Bildung)* with "barbarism." Cf. *Kleine Schriften und Predigten,* ed. by Hayo Gerdes and Emanuel Hirsch (Berlin: Walter de Gruyter & Co., 1970), vol. I, p. 51. We shall see later that Troeltsch interestingly, and significantly, misquotes Schleiermacher's question cited above. See below, note 24.

[16] *Vertrag.* It is at best misleading to translate this as "covenant," as Gerhard Spiegler does in *The Eternal Covenant: Schleiermacher's Experiment in Cultural Theology* (New York: Harper & Row, 1967). Had he meant to say "covenant," Schleiermacher—a theologian of the Reformed tradition—would surely have used the word *Bund.* An "ewige Vertrag" is simply a pact unlimited by time, as opposed to a temporary alliance.

[17] *Schleiermacher-Auswahl,* p. 149. "Learning" translates *Wissenschaft.*

[18] In a letter to Karl Leonhard Reinhold cited in *Schleiermacher-Auswahl,* p. 116. For Schleiermacher's reply, dated 30 March 1818, see *ibid.,* pp. 116-9.

[19] These three pairs of terms are not, of course, strictly parallel. The extrapolation is based, however, on Schleiermacher's letter to Jacobi and his two letters to Lücke reprinted in *ibid.,* pp. 120-75.

[20] *Ibid.,* p. 119.

[21] For the background of this epithet, see Claude Welch, *Protestant Thought in the Nineteenth Century,* vol. I, 1799-1870 (New Haven and London: Yale University Press, 1972), p. 269f.

[22] For some perceptive, though highly compressed, remarks suggesting comparisons between Schleiermacher and Troeltsch, see Ferdinand Kattenbusch, *Die deutsche Theologie seit Schleiermacher* (Giessen: Alfred Töpelmann, 1926⁵), pp. 91ff, where he treats Troeltsch as a proponent of "die neue Schleiermacherianismus"! See also B. A. Gerrish, "Ernst Troeltsch and the Possibility of a Historical Theology" in *Ernst Troeltsch and the Future of Theology,* edited by J. P. Clayton (Cambridge: Cambridge University Press, 1976), pp. 100-35.

[23] Ernst Troeltsch, *Glaubenslehre,* edited by Gertrud von le Fort (Munich and Leipzig: Duncker & Humblot, 1925), p. 1.

[24] On one occasion Troeltsch curiously misquotes Schleiermacher's question cited above in note 15: ". . . von den akademischen Lehrern ist Milde und Toleranz zu fordern, damit nicht, um mit Schleiermacher zu reden, der Knoten schliesslich so auseinandergeht, dass es das Christentum mit der Barbarei, der Unglaube aber mit der Kultur hält." *Glaubenslehre,* p. 18. The use of *Kultur* here reflects developments in German usage of that term since the time of Schleiermacher.

[25] See, e.g., *Die wissenschaftliche Lage und ihre Anforderungen an die Theologie* (Tübingen: J. C. B. Mohr, 1900), pp. 52ff; "Die Bedeutung der Geschichtlichkeit Jesu für den Glauben" (1911), repr. in the Siebenstern edition of *Die Absolutheit des Christentums und die Religionsgeschichte,* edited by Trutz Rendtorff (Munich and Hamburg: Siebenstern Taschenbuch Verlag, 1969), p. 152; *Glaubenslehre,* pp. 22ff.

[26] *Glaubenslehre,* pp. 56ff. We shall return to this problem in part two.

[27] *Gesammelte Schriften* (4 vols.; Tübingen: J. C. B. Mohr, 1912-25), vol. I, p. 12. Thus, Troeltsch defines the problem in terms of *Ethik,* in Schleiermacher's sense, namely, philosophy

of history and culture. See Schleiermacher's *Grundriss der philosophischen Ethik*, edited by August Tweston (Berlin: Reimer, 1841), p. 251 para. 50. Troeltsch regarded the philosophical *Ethik* as Schleiermacher's greatest and most original achievement. See "Die Bedeutung der Geschichtlichkeit Jesu für den Glauben," Rendtorff collection, p. 140. Like Schleiermacher, Troeltsch too wanted to ground his theology in *Ethik*, understood as "Geschichts- und Geistesphilosophie." "Geschichte und Metaphysik," *Zeitschrift für Theologie und Kirche*, VIII (1898), 27f. Even so, Troeltsch judged that the actual details of Schleiermacher's *Ethik* "no longer have anything to do with the vital problems of the present." *Gesammelte Schriften*, II, 568f. On Schleiermacher's *Ethik* see P. H. Jørgensen, *Die Ethik Schleiermachers* (Munich: Chr. Kaiser, 1959), H.-J. Birkner, *Schleiermachers christliche Sittenlehre* (Berlin: Alfred Töpelmann, 1964), and the very carefully worked out article by Eilert Herms on "Die Ethik des Wissens beim späten Schleiermacher" which appeared in the *Zeitschrift für Theologie und Kirche*, LXXIII (1976), pp. 471-523. The best study of Troeltsch's ethics remains W. F. Kasch, *Die Sozialphilosophie Ernst Troeltschs* (Tübingen: J. C. B. Mohr, 1963).

[28] Cited from *Protestantism and Progress*, trans. by W. Montgomery (1912; Boston: Beacon Press, 1958), p. 176. Cf. *Die Bedeutung des Protestantismus*, p. 87f.

[29] Cf. A. L. Kroeber and C. Kluckhohn, *Culture: A Critical Review of Concepts and Definitions* (1952; New York: Vintage Books, n. d.).

[30] Cf. *Grundriss der philosophischen Ethik*, where Schleiermacher states that the end of the *Culturprozess* of a group is the national state (p. 148 para. 138).

[31] Cf. esp. the subtitle of his famous speeches *Über die Religion*: namely, *Reden an die Gebildeten unter ihren Verächtern* (Berlin: Unger, 1799).

[32] Cf. esp. *Die wissenschaftliche Lage und ihre Anforderungen an die Theologie*.

[33] This is the way that he typically uses the term throughout *Die Soziallehren der christlichen Kirchen und Gruppen* (-*Gesammelte Schriften*, I) and the two volumes on historicism: *Der Historismus und seine Probleme* (-*Gesammelte Schriften*, III) and *Der Historismus und seine Überwindung*, edited by Friedrich von Hügel (Berlin: Pan Verlag Rolf Heise, 1924).

[34] Cf. *Gesammelte Schriften*, I, 977ff, *et passim*.

[35] Cf. *The Religious Experience of Mankind* (New York: Charles Scribner's Sons, 1976²) and *The Phenomenon of Religion* (New York: Seabury Press, 1973).

[36] Cf. "Geschichte und Metaphysik," p. 28. Even so, one must express reservation about Lessing's judgment, supported also by Pannenberg, that psychology is the fundamental element in Troeltsch's system. Eckhard Lessing, *Die Geschichtsphilosophie Ernst Troeltschs* (Hamburg: Herbert Reich, 1965), pp. 51-6. Cf. Wolfhart Pannenberg, *Wissenschaftstheorie und Theologie* (Frankfurt/Main: Suhrkamp Verlag, 1973), p. 106.

[37] *Über die Religion*, pp. 23ff, 38ff.

[38] Cf., e.g., *Gesammelte Schriften*, II, 12.

[39] For his sometimes controversial remarks on the social role of the doctrine of Christ in the history of the Christian cultus, see "Die Bedeutung der Geschichtlichkeit Jesu für den Glauben," Rendtorff collection, pp. 147ff. See also B. A. Gerrish, "Jesus, Myth, and History: Troeltsch's Stand in the 'Christ-Myth' Debate," *Journal of Religion*, LV (1975), pp. 13-35.

[40] Cf. *Gesammelte Schriften*, IV, 739ff, for his criticisms of Seeberg's tendency to intellectualize the history of Christianity.

[41] *Gesammelte Schriften*, IV, 11f, 99.

[42] *Ibid.*, pp. 21-33.

[43] As Hans Bosse has argued in *Marx, Weber, Troeltsch: Religionssoziologie und marxistische Ideologiekritik* (Munich: Chr. Kaiser, 1971²).

[44] One is made cautious in the use of this term by Hans-Joachim Birkner's "Liberale Theologie" in *Kirchen und Liberalismus im 19. Jahrhundert*, edited by Martin Schmidt and Georg Schwaiger (Göttingen: Vandenhoeck & Ruprecht, 1976), pp. 33-42.

[45] "Was heisst 'Wesen des Christentums'?", repr. *Gesammelte Schriften*, II, 386ff.

[46] *Gesammelte Schriften*, I, 986, *et passim*.

[47] "*Die Bedeutung der Geschichtlichkeit Jesu für den Glauben,*" *inter alia*.

[48] *Gesammelte Schriften*, II, 739ff.

[49] *Die Absolutheit des Christentums und die Religionsgeschichte*, repr. Rendtorff collection, pp. 32ff. For an analysis of this aspect of Troeltsch's thought, see Gunnar von Schlippe, *Die Absolutheit des Christentums bei Ernst Troeltsch auf dem Hintergrund der Denkfelder des 19. Jahrhunderts* (Neustadt/Aisch: Verlag Degener & Co., 1966).

50 *Gesammelte Schriften,* II, 213-4. Troeltsch refers there approvingly to Schweitzer's *Von Reimarus bis Wrede* (-*The Quest of the Historical Jesus*).

51 *Gesammelte Schriften,* II, 386ff. For one view of the difference between the way Troeltsch handled the questions of the essence of Christianity and of the essence religion, see Michael Pye, "Ernst Troeltsch and the End of the Problem about 'Other' Religions" in *Ernst Troeltsch and the Future of Theology,* pp. 171-95.

52 Cf., *inter alia, Gesammelte Schriften,* II, 744-5; IV, 353.

53 Cf. *Gesammelte Schriften,* II, 734.

54 *Ibid.,* p. 730.

55 For one such assessment, see P. F. Carnley, "The Poverty of Historical Scepticism" in *Christ, Faith and History: Cambridge Studies in Christology,* edited by S. W. Sykes and J. P. Clayton (Cambridge: Cambridge University Press, 1972), pp. 165-89.

56 Cf. Van A. Harvey, *The Historian and the Believer* (London: SCM, 1967).

57 *Gesammelte Schriften,* I, viii; II, 738.

58 *Gesammelte Schriften,* II, 729f. The basic texts of that controversy appeared mainly in the *Zeitschrift für Theologie und Kirche:* Troeltsch, "Die Selbständigkeit der Religion," V (1895), 361-436; VI (1896), 71-110, 167-218; J. Kaftan "Die Selbständigkeit des Christentums," VI (1896), 373-94; Troeltsch, "Geschichte und Metaphysik," VIII (1898), 1-69; Kaftan, "Erwiderung," VIII (1898), 70-96. Friedrich Niebergall published "Über die Absolutheit des Christentums" in *Theologische Arbeiten aus dem Rheinischen wissenschaftlichen Predigerverein,* IV (1900), 46-86, in which Troeltsch's "final word" (!) "Über historische und dogmatische Methode in der Theologie" also appeared. Some years later, Kaftan's brother, Theodor, published a volume entitled *Ernst Troeltsch: Ein kritische Zeitstudie* (Schleswig: Julius Bergas, 1912), which Troeltsch reviewed in the *Theologische Literaturzeitung,* XXXVII (1912), Cols. 724-8.

59 Even so, it must be remarked that this principle is not entirely unrelated to the other two, namely, criticism and analogy. For an interpretation of the latter two, see Lessing, *Die Geschichtsphilosophie Ernst Troeltschs,* pp. 20-3.

60 *Gesammelte Schriften,* II, 733. Bosse has pointed out, and I think rightly, that when in this particular article Troeltsch spoke of the reciprocity between religion and the other spheres of culture, he had in mind principally the "superstructure" of societies and had not at this point become alert to their socio-economic "infrastructure." Only after his contact with Max Weber was the notion of reciprocity broadened so as to take account of the Marxian problem of relations between superstructure and infrastructure. *Marx, Weber, Troeltsch,* p. 76. But see Hans-Georg Drescher, "Troeltsch's Intellectual Development," in *Ernst Troeltsch and the Future of Theology,* pp. 25-7.

61 *Gesammelte Schriften,* II, 737; cf. 747.

62 Cf. Georg Iggers, "Historicism," *Dictionary of the History of Ideas,* edited by P. P. Wiener (New York: Charles Scribner's Sons, 1973), pp. 456-64; G. Scholtz, "Geschichte, Historie" and "Historismus, Historizismus," *Historisches Wörterbuch der Philosophie* (1974), vol. III, cols. 344-98, 1141-7.

63 Cf. C. G. Rand, "Two Meanings of Historicism in the Writings of Dilthey, Troeltsch, and Meinecke," *Journal of the History of Ideas,* XXV (1964), 503-18.

64 *Gesammelte Schriften,* III, 125.

65 Cf., e.g., *Gesammelte Schriften,* II, 737; III, 67ff, 102, 108ff. One is struck in "Die Bedeutung der Geschichtlichkeit Jesu für den Glauben" and elsewhere by Troeltsch's confidence that historical research has given certainty to the basic facts of Christ's life and teachings. Cf. Rendtorff collection, p. 154.

66 Cf., e.g., *Gesammelte Schriften,* II, 704, 729ff; III, 110, 164ff.

67 Cf. *Religion in Geschichte und Gegenwart,* II, cols. 1452-6, esp. 1454-5; Rendtorff collection, pp. 155-6, 162, *et passim.*

68 *Grundfragen systematischer Theologie* (Göttingen: Vandenhoech & Ruprecht, 1967), pp. 46ff.

69 *Neige des Historismus: Ernst Troeltschs Entwicklungsgang* (Gütersloh: Gerd Mohn, 1959), p. 67.

70 E.g. "Die Selbständigkeit der Religion," p. 361: "Die Religion(ist) ein im Zentrum selbständiges, aus eigener Kraft sich entwickelndes und gestaltendes Lebensgebiet. . . ." In *Die wissenschaftliche Lage,* Troeltsch also speaks of religion "die in ihrer eigenen Entwicklung aus eigener Kraft allein offenbaren kann, was sie sei." (p. 51).

71 *Die Bedeutung des Protestantismus,* pp. 85ff; *Gesammelte Schriften,* II, 820.

72 *Gesammelte Schriften,* II, 755, 761.

73 Cf. "Glaube und Geschichte", p. 28.

74 *Gesammelte Schriften* II, 757f. Elsewhere he speaks of it as a "corrective" of Kant's theory: *Psychologie und Erkenntnistheorie in der Religionswissenschaft* (Tübingen: J. C. B. Mohr, 1905, 1922²), pp. 43ff. It is in fact a totally illegitimate extension of the Kantian a priori and betrays the extent to which Troeltsch misunderstood this aspect of Kant's thought—a point made early by R. Köhler in his *Der Begriff a priori in der modernen Religionsphilosophie: Eine Untersuchung zur religionsphilosophischen Methode* (Leipzig: J. C. Hinrichs, 1920), pp. 3-22. For his own studies of this side of Troeltsch's thought, see the bibliography prepared by Jacob Klapwijk in *Ernst Troeltsch and the Future of Theology,* pp. 200-14.

75 Paul Spiess, "Zur Frage des religiösen Apriori," *Zeitschrift für Religion und Gesteskultur,* III (1909), 207–15; Troeltsch, "Zur Frage des religiösen Apriori," *ibid.,* pp. 263ff, repr. in *Gesammelte Schriften,* II, 754-68.

76 But for some interesting observations on the significance of this, see A. O. Dyson, *History in the Philosophy and Theology of Ernst Troeltsch* (D. Phil. diss.: Oxford University, 1968).

77 *Gesammelte Schriften,* I, 975ff; III, 314ff.

78 *Gesammelte Schriften,* I, 25, 432, 849f, 975, etc. Cf. also *Die Bedeutung des Protestantismus,* p. 87: ". . . die Religion kommt wirklich von Religion und ihre Wirkungen sind wirklich in erster Linie religiöse."

79 As in, e.g., *Der Historismus und seine Überwindung.*

80 Pp. 56-70. The phrase is used there in several different senses, each of which would require separate analysis.

81 I owe this last example to my Lancaster colleague Professor John Benson.

82 And, it must be pointed out that Troeltsch tended to disapprove of the pragmatic compromises of political liberalism. *Gesammelte Schriften,* I, 2f.

83 *Ernst Troeltsch's Philosophy of Religion* (Ph.D. diss.; Yale, 1924), p. 270.

84 Cf. *Vernunft und Offenbarung bei Johann Gerhard und Melanchthon* (Göttingen: E. A. Huth, 1891), p. 10; "Protestantisches Christentum und Kirche in der Neuzeit," *Die Kultur der Gegenwart,* edited by Paul Hinneberg, vol. I/IV (Leipzig and Berlin: B. G. Teubner, 1906), 427; "Die Selbständigkeit der Religion," p. 366; *Gesammelte Schriften,* I, 2f, 23, 79, 227, 393, 551, etc; II, 410, 412, etc; IV, 802; *Deutscher Geist und Westeuropa,* edited by Hans Baron (Tübingen: J. C. B. Mohr, 1925), p. 7.

85 *Christian Thought: Its History and Application,* edited by Friedrich von Hügel (London: University of London Press, 1923), p. 166f, which does not appear in the German edition, *Historismus und seine Überwindung.*

86 *Der Historismus und seine Überwindung,* p. 19.

87 *Das historische in Kants Religionsphilosophie* (Berlin: Reuther & Reichard, 1904), p. 41.

88 *Gesammelte Schriften,* I, 980; *Historismus und seine Überwindung,* p. 43f.

89 This double-sided argument is found, not only in the *Dogmengeschichte,* but in the popular lectures on *Das Wesen des Christentums* as well!

90 Including Paul Tillich: see, e.g., *Perspectives on 19th and 20th Century Protestant Theology,* edited by C. E. Braaten (New York: Harper & Row, 1967) and *Systematic Theology,* vol. II (Chicago: The University of Chicago Press, 1957), pp. 140-2.

91 *Die wissenschaftliche Lage,* pp. 15-6.

92 *Ibid.,* pp. 23, 26, 28, 40, 44f, 46f.

93 *Ibid.,* p. 25. This process is not, however, restricted by Troeltsch just to morality: it includes the whole of Christianity and all the dimensions of culture, especially learning (*Wissenschaft*).

94 *Das Historische in Kants Religionsphilosophie,* p. 58.

95 In his study of the historical in Kant's philosophy of religion, Troeltsch seems to use the following interchangeably with "compromise": accommodation (p. 73), coalition (pp. 40ff), coincidence (p. 57), cooperation (p. 60, n. 1.).

96 *Ibid.,* pp. 40f, 42, 45 n. 1, 47, 59.

97 *Ibid.,* p. 47.

98 Cf. *Gesammelte Schriften* I, 811.

99 *Ibid.,* p. 156.

100 "Protestantisches Christentum und Kirche in der Neuzeit," p. 362-3.

[101] *Gesammelte Schriften,* I, 131.

[102] "Protestantisches Christentum und Kirche in der Neuzeit," p. 317.

[103] *Gesammelte Schriften,* I, 90.

[104] *Historismus und seine Überwindung,* p. 19.

[105] Some of the following examples might also be classifiable under other senses of "compromise."

[106] *Gesammelte Schriften,* I, 810.

[107] "Protestantisches Christentum und Kirche in der Neuzeit," p. 334.

[108] *Ibid.,* p. 273.

[109] "Protestantisches Christentum und Kirche in der Neuzeit," p. 449.

[110] *Der Historismus und seine Überwindung,* p. 104.

[111] *Christian Thought,* pp. 166-7.

[112] *Gesammelte Schriften,* I, 688.

[113] *Ibid.,* p. 551.

[114] Cf. "Protestantisches Christentum und Kirche in der Neuzeit," pp. 373, 377.

[115] *Ibid.,* pp. 423ff.

[116] *Die wissenschaftliche Lage,* pp. 23, 40; *Das historische in Kants Religionsphilosophie,* p. 47.

[117] *Gesammelte Schriften,* IV, 802.

[118] See above, note 96.

[119] E.g., *Die wissenschaftliche Lage,* pp. 15-6, 28, 40.

[120] "Die Bedeutung der Geschichtlichkeit Jesu," Rendtorff collection, p. 133.

[121] *Gesammelte Schriften,* I, 69; cf. also p. 507.

[122] E.g., "Protestantisches Christentum und Kirche in der Neuzeit," p. 294.

[123] *Der Historismus und seine Überwindung,* p. 77.

[124] Cf. esp. *Das historische in Kants Religionsphilosophie.*

[125] *Der Historismus und seine Überwindung,* p. 77. Cf. *Gesammelte Schriften,* I, 79, 507.

[126] *Der Historismus und seine Überwindung,* p. 21.

[127] *Das historische in Kants Religionsphilosophie,* p. 58.

[128] *Gesammelte Schriften,* I, 481.

[129] *Ibid.,* p. 393; "Protestantisches Christentum," p. 372.

[130] *Die Bedeutung des Protestantismus,* p. 39.

[131] *Gesammelte Schriften,* I, 144ff, 171ff, 252ff, *et passim.*

[132] For a highly compressed survey of that process, see *Gesammelte Schriften,* I, 330ff.

[133] *Gesammelte Schriften* I, 198ff, cf. 203. *Der Historismus und seine Überwindung,* p. 37.

[134] Here, as elsewhere in Troeltsch's writings, the focus is less on matters of passing fancy and more on long-term historical developments. See, e.g., also *Glaubenslehre,* pp. 18-9.

[135] Even so, they could not in Troeltsch's view have been combined earlier in such a compromise, because the social conditions were not right. *Gesammelte Schriften,* I, 178ff.

[136] Cf. *Ibid.,* pp. 274ff.

[137] It was seen by the church as being "von selbst." *Ibid.,* p. 202f. It was for this reason all the more powerful in its hold. *Die Bedeutung des Protestantismus,* p. 9.

[138] *Gesammelte Schriften,* I, 272ff.

[139] In addition to the conclusion of the *Soziallehren,* see "Protestantisches Christentum und Kirche in der Neuzeit," p. 451, and *Der Historismus und seine Überwindung,* pp. 41-61, esp. 56f.

[140] He warns elsewhere, however, against exaggerating the difference in this respect between the Middle Ages and modern society. *Der Historismus und seine Überwindung,* pp. 50-1.

[141] Cf. *Gesammelte Schriften,* I, 290. The notion of a "Christian society" is itself judged by Troeltsch to have been the product of a long and complicated historical process, in which a number of extra-religious factors were assimilated into Christianity. For a brief summary of that process, see *ibid.,* pp. 286ff.

[142] *Ibid.,* pp. 965-6, 979ff, 983ff.

[143] *Historismus und seine Überwindung,* pp. 41-61, esp. 52ff.

[144] See, e.g., "The Ideas of Natural Law and Humanity in World Politics," in Otto Gierke, *Natural Law and the Theory of Society,* 1500-1800 (Cambridge: Cambridge University Press, 1923).

[145] This is especially evident in the *Soziallehren* (pp. 983ff) and in *Der Historismus und*

seine Überwindung. In earlier writings, however, Troeltsch had stressed the necessity for a religious foundation for culture. (See *Die Bedeutung des Protestantismus,* p. 92.) Later, religion was treated increasingly as one element among others, all of which make unique but interlocking contributions to culture.

[146] *Gesammelte Schriften,* I, 982.

[147] As suggested, e.g., in *Historismus und seine Überwindung,* pp. 52ff.

[148] This is in fact the goal of the "cultural synthesis" advocated by Troeltsch in *Der Historismus und seine Probleme,* pp. 71ff, 164ff. This synthesis, too, would have only temporary validity, but it would—if effective—give structure to meaning and values while it lasted. Cf. *Gesammelte Schriften,* IV, 297ff, as well as *Der Historismus und seine Überwindung,* p. 60.

[149] Cf. "Ein Apfel vom Baume Kierkegaards," *Die christliche Welt,* XXXV (17 March 1921), esp. cols. 186, 188. For an assessment of the justice of Troeltsch's fate at the hands of these theologians, see Robert Morgan, "Ernst Troeltsch and the Dialectical Theology" in *Ernst Troeltsch and the Future of Theology,* pp. 33-77.

[150] See "Ein Apfel vom Baume Kierkegaards," col. 189.

[151] *Der Historismus und seine Überwindung,* constituted by five guest lectures written for delivery in England, is hardly an adequate substitute for the "contemporary cultural synthesis" promised in the closing lines of *Der Historismus und seine Probleme* (p. 772). Nor is it likely that Troeltsch could have accepted Tillich's no doubt well-intentioned claim to have produced that synthesis toward which Troeltsch strove with his own *System der Wissenschaften.* See *Gesammelte Werke,* vol. I: *Frühe Hauptwerke* (Stuttgart: Evangelisches Verlagswerk, 1959²), p. 112.

[152] On this point, see A. O. Dyson, "Ernst Troeltsch and the Possibility of a Systematic Theology" in *Ernst Troeltsch and the Future of Theology,* pp. 81-99.

[153] "Was heisst 'Wesen des Christentums'?," *Die christliche Welt,* XVII (5 June 1903), cols. 532-6, esp. 534. This is the third of six installments which appeared between 7 May and 16 July. It is not a light-handed piece of work. With an editor's sensitivity to its dense character, Martin Rade remarked in the 16 July issue of *Die christliche Welt:* "I don't know to what extent our readers have been able to follow Troeltsch in the series of articles which comes to a close with this issue. Bedtime reading it's not, but for anyone used to the diet of our best secular newpapers, surely not all that difficult." (col. 693).

[154] A point developed further in the next installment: (18 June), cols. 578-84.

[155] Rade had said that the pieces on the essence of Christianity, especially its final installment (cols. 678-83), "contain propositions with programmatic value," though it is most unlikely that he meant it in the way that Barth would later complain about Troeltsch ever proposing and never executing new "programmes." There is much sense in regarding the *Soziallehren* as the execution of much of the programme proposed in "Was heisst 'Wesen des Christentums'?." In "The Dogmatics of the *religionsgeschichtliche Schule,*" which appeared in 1913 in *The American Journal of Theology* (XVII, 1-21), Troeltsch called especial attention to his *Soziallehren* as a work in which he set forth the various definitions of essential Christianity which have prevailed at different times. (p. 13, n. 2) The two volumes on *Historismus* are also not entirely unrelated to the task of stating afresh the essence of Christianity for the present.

[156] For a spirited comparison of the two versions of "Was heisst 'Wesen des Christentums'?", see S. W. Sykes, "Ernst Troeltsch and Christianity's Essence" in *Ernst Troeltsch and the Future of Theology,* pp. 139-71.

[157] Cf. *Gesammelte Schriften,* II, 416. This surely reflects his findings in the *Soziallehren* regarding the developments of disparate ethical positions out of motifs already present in apostolic Christianity.

[158] "The Dogmatics of the *religionsgeschichtliche Schule,*" p. 12.

[159] *Ibid.,* pp. 20-1. Enormous difficulties are, of course, raised here.

[160] *Gesammelte Schriften,* I, 203; cf. *Das historische in Kants religionsphilosophie,* p. 59, and *Die Absolutheit des Christentums und die Religionsgeschichte,* Rendtorff collection, p. 131.

[161] *Gesammelte Schriften,* I, 986. Cf. also "Protestantisches Christentum und Kirche in der Neuzeit," p. 372.

[162] See above, note 27.

[163] *Gesammelte Schriften,* II, 522: "Wir fragen nicht, wie kriege ich einen gnädigen Gott? Wir fragen vielmehr, wie finde ich die Seele und die Liebe wieder? Andere Zeiten werden wieder anders fragen. Aber da ist es nun die Möglichkeit einer echten freien Glaubenslehre,

die Frage der Gegenwart bewusst zu formulieren und die Antwort als den eigentlichen heutigen Inhalt der Glaubenslehre in der einfachsten und stärksten Konzentration zu geben. . . ." Cf. Paul Tillich, *Systematic Theology*, vol. I (Chicago: University of Chicago Press, 1951), p. 49: "The question arising out of this (contemporary) experience (of meaninglessness and despair) is not, as in the Reformation, the question of a merciful God and the forgiveness of sins: . . . nor is it the question of the personal religious life or of the Christianization of culture and society. It is the question of a reality in which the self-estrangement of our existence is overcome, a reality of reconciliation and reunion, of creativity, meaning, and hope. We shall call such a reality the 'New Being'. . . . If the Christian message is understood as the message of the 'New Being,' an answer is given to the question implied in our present situation and in every human situation." I am grateful to Professor Robert Scharlemann for having called my attention to this similarity.

[164] *Glaubenslehre*, p. 18.

[165] "Ein Apfel vom Baume Kierkegaards," col. 186.

[166] "Die Kirche im Leben der Gegenwart," Rendtorff collection, p. 180.

PART II
FAITH AND THE HISTORICAL PROCESS

7.

A Point of Departure for Process Theology
Christian Natural Theology

Stuart R. Sprague

> I suggest further that many of the problems with which theologians now wrestle arise out of assumptions formed for them by more or less consciously accepted ideas of a philosophical sort. . . . That means that it is only by facing the task of natural theology directly that the Christian theologian may hope to achieve his appropriate freedom.[1]

Coordinating the emphases of faith and reason has been a part of the task of theology since the efforts of the Fathers to formulate cogent rationales for early doctrines. However, as John Cobb points out above, contemporary theology has not outgrown the need to focus its energies on this concern also. He believes that the church's consensus on this matter, which undergirded its theology for centuries, has broken down. If it is to accomplish more than simply to measure institutional success in a secular culture, it must establish a new sense of direction grounded in a significant theology. Failure to deal with the problem of relating philosophy and theology, i.e., natural theology, will inevitably lead to the fall of the church as a vibrant institution.[2]

Cobb seeks to rebuild theology using philosophical theology as the foundation of his methodology. This task falls under the rubric of natural theology. Christian natural theology thereby becomes the starting point for a Christian theology.[3] Though this is the first step, it is not a simple one. It deserves treatment on its own. In this essay Cobb's language will be examined carefully and his unique view of Christian natural theology will be set in the context both of other views of natural theology and of its importance for the rest of his theological program.

Definitions

Understanding Cobb's discussion of Christian natural theology requires a precise use of language. There are four terms which are of importance to him at this foundational stage. His methodology depends

113

on clear distinctions among theology, natural theology, Christian natural theology, and Christian philosophy.

Theology

"By theology in the broadest sense I mean any coherent statement about matters of ultimate concern that recognizes that the perspective by which it is governed is received by a community of faith." [4]

Cobb's definition is worded carefully so as to be an inclusive one. In keeping with his larger agenda of creating a credible place for theology in a secular world, it does not seek to withdraw theology into an esoteric world of its own. Theological discussion is open to a plurality of approaches to transcendence. Christian theology can no longer resort to a barrage of jargon when it relates to the marketplace of ideas. There can be secular theologies as well as theologies associated with particular religions.

On the other hand, this definition recognizes the inevitable influence that a context of growth and nurture has on any approach to transcendence. Not only does it recognize this influence, but it also stamps such influence with legitimacy. Theology is set apart from phenomenology of religion and no longer has to take a back seat to the more empirical worlds of analysis which seem to dominate the modern mind.

Natural Theology

Cobb treats two definitions of natural theology. In one sense it may be seen as "all that can be known relative to matters of ultimate concern by reason alone." [5] With reason available as a universal human power, natural theology, understood in this way, is accessible to all men and women. It may even be included in the province of philosophy. For the purpose of later identification and discussion, this definition will be referred to as the most broadly philosophical one.

Through the history of Christian thought natural theology has been conceived of in a second way. Cobb understands this to be "conclusions of philosophical inquiry supportive of some Christian teaching from data that are understood to be factually and logically independent of Christian revelation." [6] This will be referred to as the traditional Christian definition of natural theology.

Aquinas' synthesis of faith and reason in his natural theology is the classic example of this second definition. Presuming that truth was one, he had to deal with contradictory propositions which arose from revelation and reflection. For him reason was the arbitrator of any disputes. Natural theology consisted of those doctrines given in revelation which could be demonstrated by philosophical means.[7] Hence, Cobb's definition of normative natural theology comes from the Thomistic stream of Christianity. Though the synthesis of faith and reason broke down in the Renaissance, this definition of natural theology has remained in effect and continues to exert influence in some circles.[8]

This kind of natural theology normally adopts a philosophical framework in which to operate. Through Christian history four important options have been chosen, according to Cobb. He does not exclude the possibility of others, but he believes that these are the most representative ones. Roman Catholic and Protestant Scholastics appropriated Aristotelian philosophy. Deists based their system on rationalism. Hegelian philosophy has been used by theologically conservative thinkers, and some modern theologians have used creative evolution as a base.[9] Such a variety of options shows how natural theology has been and continues to be a viable influence on those who shape theological models. Rather than a static set of arguments which do not prove anything in the end, it is a process of adopting, critiquing, and rejecting various philosophical insights. It represents the highest efforts to keep Christian faith alive in a variety of contexts.

Christian Natural Theology

Christian natural theology is, for Cobb, "the attempt to justify certain Christian beliefs rationally on the basis of data that, though historically conditioned by Christian revelation, are widely held by persons who are not self-consciously Christian." [10] Cobb has made a contribution by adding a new dimension to the discussion of natural theology. The result has much in common with Thomism. Christian beliefs are justified rationally on grounds which stand outside the beliefs themselves. However, Cobb indicates that these data and philosophic grounds have been conditioned by a Christian frame of reference as well.

This definition seeks to take seriously the need for data which are accessible generally and for a recognition of the universal character of human reason. At the same time it points to the fact that no philosophical system can isolate itself from historical conditioning. Western philosophy has been indelibly shaped by Christianity. A reciprocal exchange of influence between philosophy and theology is presupposed, avoiding the problems of Thomas' synthesis.

Christian Philosophy

Christian philosophy is "any attempt to build a comprehensive scheme of ideas on the basis of distinctively Christian data." [11] Cobb is concerned here, as in his definition of Christian natural theology, to speak of both the goal of rational reflection and the data used in such efforts. The end toward which Christian philosophy strives is more expansive than that of either theology or natural theology. It seeks to be comprehensive but uses only data that arises out of a Christian context.

Reflection, for Cobb, can take the form of philosophy, building a comprehensive scheme of ideas; theology, making coherent statements about matters of ultimate concern; or natural theology, justifying religious beliefs rationally from a context of religious faith. Data used in reflection can be distinctively religious, historically conditioned by religion (recognized as such or not), or neutral as to a belief system. Using this structure with interchangeable components, a wide variety of definitions can be proposed. Cobb has simplified the process of understanding these complex theological concepts by adopting terminology that is general and flexible.

Cobb's insight is the recognition of the way in which religious belief systems shape the ratiocinative processes of their cultures. Both data collection and thought patterns are influenced to some extent. By understanding the organizational framework and following it consistently throughout, his work is significantly clarified. Christian theology, Christian natural theology, and Christian philosophy are distinct, clearly defined entities. They are closely related and fully compatible. Yet, the differences have profound methodological implications.[12]

Toward a Christian Natural Theology

The definitions Cobb proposes betray some of the reasons for his choosing to deal with natural theology at the outset of his theological program, but the full implications of this decision require further examination. This can best be done by imposing a structure and a sequence on his thought which are artificial to some extent. Though he may not have been conscious of this structure, it does seem to add coherence to a look in retrospect.

Methodological Development

A concern for Christian natural theology is characteristic of the earlier works of Cobb. Though he currently stands firmly on the positions taken there, his work has moved beyond that point today. Looking back, it can be said that "the early Cobb" represents a kind of scholastic period.[13] Between the completion of his doctoral work at the University of Chicago (1952) and the publication of *A Christian Natural Theology* (1965) he tended to deal primarily with the rational dimensions of Christian faith.

At least three reasons for this trend can be gleaned from Cobb's writings: First, his own spiritual pilgrimage led to a period of radical doubt and concern for the philosophical problems of Christianity during his graduate education. His personal faith was shattered and required reconstruction.[14] Second, Cobb's reading and study of the history of Protestant theology led him to the conclusion that its failure to examine rational presuppositions was its largest unresolved problem.[15] *Living Options in Protestant Theology* shows that modern theologians have either conceived of natural theology too narrowly or rejected it without warrant. Cobb seeks to reformulate it and make it a viable response to secular questions about God.[16] A final reason for his early focus on natural theology is that it is the first major question of methodology. With the destructive dimensions of some modern thought structures for faith, the theologian cannot afford to remain strictly within the confines of his own heritage. He or she must be conversant with the foundation on which any system rests.[17]

The sequence of Cobb's work also corresponds to this analysis. His doctoral dissertation, "The Independence of Christian Faith from Speculative Beliefs," seems to be a resolution of some of his own existential questions. *Varieties of Protestantism* (1960) and *Living Options in Protestant Theology* (1962), Cobb's first two books, deal with the history of Protestant theology and seek to describe some of its problems. *A Christian Natural Theology* (1965) is a summary of his own synthesis of the problem and his constructive proposal for a new direction in theology. It marks the end of this "period" and the major substance of his scholastic work.

Faith

The questions which lies at the heart of the whole matter is that of faith itself. Cobb's most thorough discussion of faith is in his University of Chicago dissertation. Thus, many readers do not have a complete understanding of this most basic concept. For Cobb faith is derived from a revelatory origin.[18] It can neither be born in nor supported by speculative beliefs. To anchor faith in speculative beliefs is to risk its being undermined when those beliefs are challenged by new data or experience. Any claims which later emerge out of the experience of faith as to its object or source must also be capable of formulation in such a way that they cannot be undermined by new experience or knowledge.[19]

Hume forced a major revision in Protestant theological thinking by showing that the primary rationales for Christian faith were speculative.[20] The primary emphasis of modern theology has been to reassert the meaningful dimension of faith in the face of Hume's critique. Cobb isolates three major responses to this challenge. Schleiermacher reaffirmed the feelingful and noncognitive aspects of faith. Henry Nelson Wieman sought an empirical, nonspeculative basis for faith. Tillich removed faith and its object into the realm of Being. However, these proposals all fail to sustain a dynamic, living faith. Cobb's view seeks to recognize these same problems but to go beyond the limitations of Schleiermacher, Wieman, and Tillich.

The fundamental fact about faith is that it must exist in tension. There are rational and nonrational dimensions which must be accounted for. Cobb sees in Protestantism a rich heritage of the nonrational character of the ground and source of faith.[21] Yet, he also recognizes, with Wieman, that knowledge of God cannot be different from knowledge of other realities. Supernaturalism and radical empiricism both reject this balanced tension in favor of extreme positions. Therefore, neither can be the basis of a sound theology.[22]

Cobb's solution to this problem is a creative one. He proposes that the validation of faith claims be sought in experience rather than in circular arguments based on other tenets of faith. Debate should be in the context of cosmology. "No systematic account of any important area of experience can be formulated without cosmological implications." [23] Therefore, faith claims which cannot be set in the context of a consistent cosmology cannot survive.

This proposal has several advantages to recommend it. It recognizes that faith has unavoidable philosophical implications. However, theologians are not limited to a choice between adopting the latest philosophical whim (the error of liberalism) or avoiding philosophy at all (the error of conservatism). The burden is shifted to cosmology. They may choose among various options for understanding the universe as a whole.[24] Faith may retain its nonrational dimension with integrity. Its ground and source, once accounted for cosmologically, need not be subject to speculative debate or erosion of security. Cobb's system is ultimately pluralistic, allowing each position which survives the test of experience to make its own claim of cogency.

The Rejection of Traditional Natural Theology

The constructive aspect of Cobb's program centers around natural theology. His argument begins with a rejection of natural theology in both its broadly philosophical and its traditional Christian senses. Though each may have served well before, neither speaks in a viable way to the present situation. Protestant theologians have generally rejected natural theology in its broadest philosophical sense as arrogant and self-deceptive. Claims that unaided reason can arrive at conclusions about ultimate reality are pretentious at best. Here Cobb agrees. Treatments of ultimate concerns always arise out of a faith stance. Acceptance of this kind of natural theology inevitably involves the introduction of elements which are alien to the Christian faith.[25]

The traditional Christian definition of natural theology is a refinement in that it deals only with tenets of faith which can be justified by reason with data from outside Christian revelation. Cobb also rejects this form of natural theology as a "pseudo-option." By that he means it claims to fulfill a function which cannot be accomplished. There is no way by which one can move from data which are universally given to conclusions which have both theological significance and rational certainty.[26]

Cobb's rejection of these forms of natural theology is based on both philosophical and theological grounds. His analysis of the independence of faith claims from speculative beliefs and Hume's critique of causal arguments combine to negate the possibility of natural theology philosophically. From a theological point of view the problem stems from the fact that the Judeo-Christian tradition has not drawn its models for God from philosophical reflection but from dynamic relationship. Though attempts have been made to synthesize the two sources, Cobb feels that they have failed to produce a view of God consistent with a modern Christian vision of reality.[27]

These critiques are not original with Cobb, though his analysis of faith and speculative belief is an important contribution. He points out that there is a long history of resistance by Christian theologians to any sort of philosophical input.[28] In the twentieth century this sentiment seems to have been focused in what has come to be known as neoorthodoxy. Cobb believes theologians have overreacted to the negative implications of a relationship with philosophy. Philosophy, unfortunately, has been identified with particular philosophical positions. Theologians have failed to realize that reason itself does not demand any particualr view of God. Rather, the individual philosopher comes from a rational heritage which shapes his thought. Picturing philosophy as a singular, rigid conclusion rather than a tool with which to explore new vistas of reality has caused theologians to reject a resource which could be of great value.[29]

Cobb is not proposing that philosophy be dropped altogether. The essence of his critique of natural theology is that neither philosophy nor theology can pretend to function in a vacuum, pure and free from outside influences. He is proposing a flexible relationship with reason and experience both as legitimate inputs. Philosophy and theology in dialogue can accomplish more than either could on its own.

Christian Natural Theology

In spite of claims to the contrary, Cobb believes that every theologian functions within a philosophical frame of reference. Whatever scheme of principles for structuring knowledge is chosen by a theologian is, according to him, a natural theology, understood in a different, generic sense. Here Cobb refers to the inevitable relationship which faith-claims and beliefs have to general thought patterns. His desire is to expose this reality so that a conscious choice of a natural theology can be made on the basis of examined criteria rather than acceptance of one uncritically or apathetically. Natural theology chosen as a framework in which to set Christian beliefs is, for Cobb, Christian natural theology.[30]

Cobb does allow for the possibility of doing Christian theology without a Christian natural theology. When this occurs, three features accompany it. First, a supernatural event is the basis for Christian existence. Second, nothing can be affirmed about the cause of Christian existence which has anything to do with nature or history from any other perspective. Third, the Christian faith and its implications must be formulated so that they are not relevant to any perspective other than that of faith. Once this stance has been exposed and critiqued, there is very little than can be said persuasively to one who affirms it. However, Cobb does not consider this a live option for himself nor does he feel that it corresponds to the faith described in the New Testament.[31]

If there were a consensus of philosophical opinion as to the nature of reality, the choice of a Christian natural theology would be a simple one. Since there is no consensus, the theologian has two choices. One option is to create a philosophy based on Christian data and thought patterns. This could be called Christian philosophy using the definition given above. The other option is to adopt a philosophical system which can be amended to Christian understandings without doing violence to its systematic attributes. Cobb sees the former option as a viable one but thinks the latter one has more promise. Theologians have done their best work when appropriating philosophical material from others instead of trying to create their own.[32]

Cobb proposes two criteria which should be used in the selection of a philosophical system. First, the intrinsic excellence of the structure of thought should be considered. Tests which can be applied are consistency and coherence in the explanation of experience. These tests can be objected to philosophically as presuming a rational structure of the universe, which itself cannot be affirmed. Cobb understands this objection but believes that rational structure is a more encompassing category than total irrationality.[33]

A natural theology should also be congenial to Christian faith. There seems to be a variety of philosophical options, each of which attains a high degree of reliability in relating the truths of experience. Cobb observes that these options are characterized by a significant number of norms which they have in common. They can be distinguished from one another primarily by the perception each has of the data which are to be treated in philosophy.[34] The real differences between philosophies are not rules of logic or methods of relating and correlating data. Deciding which data from experience shall be used and how those data shall be understood and treated is a far more important process. This tacit apparatus which surrounds one's approach to the world is a vision of reality. Selecting a natural theology is, essentially, choosing a philosophy whose vision of reality corresponds most closely to the experience of the individual theologian.[35]

Having established a basis on which to make a choice of philosophical systems, Cobb chooses for himself the philosophy of Alfred North Whitehead. Whitehead's work was enriched by its Christian origin. Also, Whitehead's major philosophical work came from his Gifford Lectures on natural theology. His concerns had much in common with the theologians's quest for a holistic framework. However, Cobb is aware of the problems of trying to synthesize the work of a philosopher with that of a theologian. Many theological questions were peripheral for Whitehead. His organizing principles were different, leaving the theologian the task of gathering fragments from a variety of contexts for his own purposes. Nevertheless, viewing these limitations from the perspective of other attempts at natural theology, the choice of Whitehead's thought has an advantage. It has been Christianized in a way that many of the other options could not have been, e.g., Greek philosophy.[36]

Questions Raised About Christian Natural Theology

Cobb's work has been well received by the theological community. He is thought to have made an important contribution as an analyst of modern theology and to have proposed a provocative new synthesis of Whiteheadian philosophy and Christian theology.[37] However, his methodological proposal for a Christian natural theology has not been universally accepted.

Critiques

Schubert Ogden disagrees with "Cobb's conception of the nature of natural theology and of how we arrive at a decision between its different forms."[38] He posits that Cobb is trying to incorporate two antithetical demands into one system. The search for warrants which come from common human experience and the recognition of a variety of valid theological positions seem to be contradictory. Ogden believes that Cobb has unnecessarily relativized the search for a natural theology.

Like Cobb he affirms both philosophy's search for universal warrants and the inevitable shaping of an individual thinker by historical conditioning. Unlike Cobb his system allows for ultimate philosophical consensus on any issue. Therefore, natural theology can be judged solely on the basis of its philosophical excellence. Theologians make a faith judgment that a true philosophy can be found and that it will be in harmony with Christian faith.[39] If, as Ogden believes, natural theology can be appraised from a neutral philosophical point of view, Cobb has introduced a contradiction.

Fritz Guy criticizes Cobb's use of a new concept of natural theology. He accepts the idea of natural theology as "the systematic explication of the presuppositions of Christian thought."[40] However, he does not think Cobb has lived up to the examples of Augustine and Aquinas in their selection of philosophical frameworks in which to do natural theology. Guy criticizes Cobb for not fully exploring the compatibility of the Christian vision of reality with that of Whitehead. Just as theology has ontological implications, metaphysical systems have theological implications. Theology makes some judgments on the basis of tradition and authority, elements not prominent in Whitehead. Guy feels that Whitehead has shaped Cobb's theology, rather than vice versa, in the process of arriving at a Christian natural theology. Gnosticism and deism failed because their philosophical bases did not survive criticism in the light of Christian theological norms. For Guy, Whitehead should be subjected to the same rigorous testing before being included into a theological scheme.[41]

David Tracy agrees with Cobb that theology should be philosophical, but he does not agree that the result should be called Christian natural theology. If philosophy is used only to articulate Christian beliefs clearly or to examine the Christian vision of reality, the result could be so named. However, Christian theologians can also use philosophy to examine other visions of reality and compare them to their own. When this latter function is included, the enterprise is more accurately called natural theology. Tracy believes that Cobb includes this function in his work and should avoid the ambiguity of the term "Christian natural theology." Metaphysical speculation, critical philosophy, and literature all acknowledge, but seek to transcend, their own cultural setting. Theology should also be involved in this task but is less credible when it retains parochial nomenclature. Natural theology is a philosophical discipline. Theology proper is a separate undertaking involving existential and symbolic frames of reference.[42]

Another critic of Cobb's work is Langdon Gilkey. He also rejects the Christian natural theology as an accurate label for what Cobb does. Methodologically he raises two primary issues. The first is that Cobb has let Whitehead's system shape theological conclusions. Rather than appealing to traditional Christian authority, he has let Christian notions be violated and even destroyed. Second, Gilkey accuses Cobb and process theology of not taking seriously enough the problem of discourse about God at all.[43] He concludes that, for Cobb, philosophy provides the vision of reality and Christian faith provides the topics to be discussed.[44] Hume has destroyed the underlying presupposition of metaphysics, that the universe is rationally ordered, and cast doubt on a philosophy or theology founded on metaphysical principles. Gilkey accuses Whitehead, and indirectly Cobb, of being Edwardian in the face of a growing modern consciousness. He means that process thought retains a rationalistic or idealistic base which is anachronistic in the present empirical age.[45]

Richard R. Niebuhr questions what he sees as a methodological assumption of Cobb's discussion of the need for natural theology.

Methodology seems to be a separate discipline which settles basic issues before the historical data which give rise to religious experience are considered. It is as though Cobb has placed the question of the need for and the character of natural theology before theology itself is considered.[46]

Response

Though all the issues raised in critical essays have not been dealt with specifically, a pattern can be seen in Cobb's responses which applies to a wide variety of criticism. In a response to Gilkey, Cobb asserts that he has been misunderstood on what he means by natural theology. Gilkey implies that, for Cobb, natural theology is sufficient without any reference to tradition or authority. However, Cobb understands it as only part of the total task of theology. Also, Cobb defends his use of Whitehead, saying that he has refocused emphases in light of Christian understandings. Countering Gilkey's charge of Edwardianism, he notes that presuming order instead of chaos as a metaphysical presupposition is more Christian than empirical skepticism.[47]

Commenting on Tracy's critique, Cobb indicates a willingness to use the term "Christian" natural theology less rigidly. He admits that it is not as necessary as it was earlier to indicate that theology is historically conditioned. However, he does want to maintain a second distinctive which was originally intended. On the primary issue of the relativism of philosophy, Cobb stands firm. Philosophers do have insights which transcend culture, as do theologians. Even these are limited, though. Insights must be expressed through thought patterns, and forms of expression are shaped by cultural contexts. Philosophy advances by opening new vistas of thought rather than by rearranging fundamental ideas in new combinations. Change is unpredictable and dependent on what is looked for and what is seen. All of reality cannot be seen at once. Every perspective is partial. Therefore, Cobb feels justified in retaining the term "Christian" natural theology for insights, transcendent or otherwise, that arise from a Christian context.[48]

Summary and Evaluation

The simplicity and substance of Cobb's method are impressive. Once his definitions and the specific limits of his purpose are understood, the program to establish a Christian natural theology seems to be a sound one. In the effort to make theology more philosophically credible, Cobb is not alone. However, there are no exact parallels to his concept of a Christian natural theology. Critics have not faulted his attempt to use philosophy. Rather, they have disagreed on the viability of his specific solution.

By striving to incorporate Christian faith into a vision of the whole of reality, Cobb has done a real service to theology. He is not content to use philosophy for narrowly construed purposes such as language analysis. For him it is a more encompassing category than theology itself. This may seem ironic for a theologian. Modesty at this point has not often been a characteristic of the Christian community. Some critics charge that he is letting philosophy determine the outcome of theology, as we have noted above.

I believe, however, that Cobb's modesty is not weakness in the face of philosophy. He is not saying that Whitehead, or any other particular philosophy, takes precedence over revelation or other theological categories. Where Whitehead needs correction, he is not afraid to do so. His relativism extends to philosophy as well as theology. Reality is the ultimate test.

My most serious reservation about Cobb's starting point is that he tells us very little about Christian realities. For his Christian natural theology, the major contribution of his Christian point of view was "to focus attention upon certain questions." [49] Christian faith has more to offer than a set of questions. In addition to being philosophically responsible, a Christian natural theology should be responsibly Christian. In the case of this latter norm we have little guidance from Cobb. In recent years he has turned to some topics which are specifically Christian, most notably Christology. However, even these are not univocal criteria for judging theological statements to be Christian. Cobb's ethical concerns and his personal attributes exemplify a stance that can be called Christian. We can hope that in the future he will devote his energy to spelling these out systematically for his theological program.

NOTES

[1] John B. Cobb, Jr., *A Christian Natural Theology* (Philadelphia: The Westminster Press 1965), p. 11. Hereafter referred to as *CNT*.

[2] John B. Cobb, Jr., *Living Options in Protestant Theology* (Philadelphia: The Westminster Press, 1962), pp. 8, 11. Hereafter referred to as *LOPT*.

[3] Cobb, *LOPT*, p. 313.   [4] Cobb, *CNT*, p. 252.
[5] Cobb, *CNT*, p. 259.   [6] Cobb, *LOPT*, p. 50 n. 83.
[7] Cobb, *LOPT*, pp. 18-20.
[8] Cobb, *LOPT*, p. 20. See also Paul Tillich, "The Two Types of Philosophy of Religion," in *Theology of Culture* (New York: Oxford University Press, 1959), pp. 10-29.
[9] Cobb, *LOPT*, p. 31.   [10] Cobb, *LOPT*, p. 50 n. 83.
[11] Cobb, *LOPT*, p. 50 n. 83.   [12] Cobb, *LOPT*, p. 50 n. 83.
[13] John B. Cobb, Jr., Personal interview with the author, March 18, 1975.
[14] John B. Cobb, Jr., *To Pray or Not to Pray* (Nashville: The Upper Room, 1974), pp. 5-6.
[15] Cobb, *LOPT*, pp. 8-12.
[16] Cobb, *LOPT*, p. 313 and *CNT*, pp. 261-6.
[17] Cobb, *CNT*, p. 15.
[18] John B. Cobb, Jr., "The Independence of Christian Faith from Speculative Belief," (unpublished doctor's dissertation, University of Chicago, 1953), p. 136. Hereafter referrred to as "ICF."
[19] Cobb, "ICF," pp. 133-4.   [20] Cobb, "ICF," p. 134.
[21] Cobb, "ICF," p. 134.   [22] Cobb, "ICF," p. 136.
[23] Cobb, "ICF," p. 134.   [24] Cobb, *CNT*, pp. 264-6.
[25] Cobb, *CNT*, pp. 259-60.   [26] Cobb, *LOPT*, p. 313.
[27] Cobb, *CNT*, p. 260.   [28] Cobb, *LOPT*, pp. 121-42.
[29] Cobb, *CNT*, pp. 260-1.   [30] Cobb, *LOPT*, p. 50.
[31] Cobb. *LOPT*, pp. 320-1.   [32] Cobb, *CNT*, pp. 263-4.
[33] Cobb, *CNT*, p. 264.   [34] Cobb, *CNT*, p. 265.
[35] Cobb, *CNT*, p. 266.
[36] Cobb, *CNT*, p. 268. Cobb means here that Whitehead's philosophy was influenced by Christian roots in his background. He was reared in the home of an Anglican priest, and he was shaped by the milieu of Western thought which has indelible Christian attributes. See also Victor Lowe, *Understanding Whitehead* (Baltimore: John Hopkins Press, 1966), pp. 6, 232.
[37] See Lewis S. Ford, review of John B. Cobb, Jr., *A Christian Natural Theology, Journal of Bible and Religion*, XXIV (January, 1966), 60-4, and S. Paul Schilling, review of John B. Cobb, Jr., *Living Options in Protestant Theology, Journal of Bible and Religion*, XXXI (April, 1963), 150-2.
[38] Schubert M. Ogden, review of John B. Cobb, Jr., *A Christian Natural Theology, Christian Advocate*, IX (September, 23, 1965), 11-2.
[39] *Ibid.*
[40] Fritz Guy, "Comments on a Recent Whiteheadian Doctrine of God," *Andrews University Seminary Studies*, IV (1966), 125.
[41] *Ibid.*, pp. 125-8.
[42] David Tracy, "John Cobb's Theological Method: Interpretation and Reflections,"*John Cobb's Theology in Process*, eds. David R. Griffin and Thomas J. J. Altizer (Philadelphia: The Westminster Press, 1977), pp. 27-34.
[43] Langdon Gilkey, review of John B. Cobb, Jr., *A Christian Natural Theology, Theology Today*, XXXII (January, 1966), 543-4.
[44] *Ibid.*, p. 530.
[45] *Ibid.*, p. 535.
[46] Richard R. Niebuhr, review of John B. Cobb, Jr., *Living Options in Protestant Theology, Religion in Life*, XXXII (Summer, 1963), 471-2.
[47] John B. Cobb, Jr., "Can Natural Theology Be Christian?" *Theology Today*, XXXIII (April, 1966), 140-1.
[48] John B. Cobb, Jr., "Response to Tracy," *John Cobb's Theology in Process, op. cit.*, pp. 150-4.
[49] Cobb, *CNT*, p. 269.

8.

Faith and the Parousia
G. R. Beasley-Murray

1 *He spoke to them in a parable to show that they should keep on praying and never lose heart:*
2 *There was once a judge who cared nothing for God or man,*
3 *and in the same town there was a widow who constantly came before him demanding justice against her opponent.*
4 *For a long time he refused; but in the end he said to himself, "True, I care nothing for God or man;*
5 *but this widow is so great a nuisance that I will see her righted before she wears me out with her persistence."*
6 *The Lord said, 'You hear what the unjust judge says;*
7 *and will not God vindicate his chosen, who cry out to him day and night, while he listens patiently to them? I tell you, he will vindicate them soon enough.*
8 *But when the Son of Man comes, will he find faith on earth?'*[1]

The title of the essay is prompted by the final sentence of this parable of Jesus. The question of which it consists comes as a surprising conclusion to the parable narrated. For the parable appears to encourage believers to continue in prayer, since God will surely hear them, but the question is far from assuring. It seems to envisage the possibility that faith may disappear from the earth before the coming of the Son of Man, or at least it is calculated to induce a self-examination which asks, "Will the Son of Man find faith in *me?*"

The change of mood in the question, along with its change of subject (Son of Man instead of God) has suggested a query as to whether the question originally belonged to this context. It would by no means be unusual for an isolated saying to be attached to a parable through its related content (a notable example is seen in Luke 16:1-8, to which vv. 10-13 have been attached in this manner, and in turn vv. 14-18 have been added to the latter group of sayings on account of related themes and terms). Verse 8 could owe its place in the parable through the same process. It is the fate of this little parable, however, to have suffered total dismemberment at the hands of its exegetes. It is generally agreed that the opening sentence was added by Luke to form not only an introduction to the parable but also as an interpretation of it.[2] The majority of expositors consider that Luke has thereby given a partial interpretation which fails to do justice to the main thrust of the parable. From Jülicher on, however, there has been an increasing tendency to believe that the original parable consisted only of vv. 2-5, to which Luke's introduction is clearly suitable. The parallelism between 18:2-5 and Luke 11:5-8, the parable of the friend in need, seemed to Jülicher to be so close that he was persuaded that the two parables formed a pair and that they were originally conjoined, like the two parables of the man building a tower and the king going out to battle, Luke 14:28ff,31f. They have an identical lesson, admirably expressed by Luke in 18:1, and on this Jülicher commented, "If *one* idea is assured for Jesus it is that represented in this parable." [3] By contrast 18:6-8 is thought to have a different intention; its purpose is not to emphasize the necessity of the *believer's continuance in prayer* but the assurance of *God's speedy answer* to his people's prayers. Moreover, the attitude expressed in this passage is felt to be quite unlike that of Jesus, whereas it is characteristic of the primitive Jewish church. The thought and language of the passage are also considered to be very close to those of Ecclesiasticus 35:14-20; the suggestion therefore lies to hand that 18:6-8 represents an early interpretation of the parable, based on the passage from Ecclesiasticus.[4] In this opinion many scholars concur. A refinement of it is preferred by some, who see in Luke 18:6a ("But the Lord said") an addition from Luke, and the rest of vv. 6-7 as forming an early exposition of the parable found by Luke in his source; v. 8a ("I tell you he will vindicate them soon enough") is believed to be Luke's composition, but v. 8b ("But when the Son of Man comes . . .") as taken from elsewhere; his placing v. 8b in its present position helps to bind the parable to discourse on the parousia in the preceding chapter, Luke 17:22-37.[5]

Now the faith does not stand or fall according to the solution of these issues; but once the possibilities are pointed out, we naturally wish to know wherein probability lies. The phenomenon of different parabolic elements fused together to form a new whole is not unknown in the Gospels (cf. Matt. 22:1-10 with 11-14 conjoined; and possibly Luke 19:11-27 with vv. 14 and 27 inserted from another tradition). When however it is affirmed that the thought of vv. 6-8a is not congruous with the teaching of Jesus (Jülicher), or that Jesus could not have uttered v. 8b,[6] we are dealing with issues which extend to the nature of the teaching of Jesus as a whole, and that is not simple. The concept of the justice of God is fundamental to the Bible, and not least to Jesus himself, particularly in its eschatological aspects. Observe how the Sermon on the Mount begins with Beatitudes of the kingdom and ends with a parable of judgment; the emphasis on judgment, both positive and negative, in Luke 12—13; the element of vindication implied in such sayings as Luke 12:32, Mark 14:25 with Luke 22:28-30, Matthew 25:34ff, to say nothing of the parousia passages in the Gospels. The separating of vv. 6-7 from vv. 2-5 is, as we have seen, bound up with the idea that the shortened parable forms a twin with that of the friend at midnight, Luke 11:5-8, and that vv. 6-7 are not compatible with vv. 2-5. The former of these views, despite its popularity, is doubtful, as C. Delling has shown.[7] Moreover it is no commendation of the idea that Ott found himself under the necessity of similarly reducing the parable of the friend at midnight to 11:5-7, on the ground that 11:8 was added to this parable from 18:2-5.[8] The question of the compatibility of vv. 6-8a with 2-5 will depend on our interpretation of both sections. Suffice it to say at present that there is reason for believing that the concepts embodied in vv. 2-5 are continued in vv. 6ff and that the whole parable forms a unity, possibly reflecting and applying a notion also found in a single passage well known in the day of Jesus (Ecclus. 35:14ff). Similarly, while it is true that v. 8b may have been an isolated saying, brought by Luke to this point because of its fitness to the context (extending to Luke 17:20-37), it nevertheless suits the parable so well, notably vv. 6-7, that one has to confess that Luke was remarkably fortunate to come across such a saying as v. 8b for this context, and that he was possessed of unusual insight to place it here. There are grounds for believing that the saying was uttered in connection with the immediately preceding sentences.

II

Despite differences of judgment as to the composition of the parable, widespread agreement exists as to its meaning as it now stands in Luke's Gospel. The disagreement generally centers round the issue of the extent to which the second part would qualify the first. The widow, frequently conjoined with the orphan, is a traditional figure for helplessness in the world. Similarly the treatment of the widow by a judge is an equally traditional measure of the impartiality of his justice.[9] In the parable we are confronted with a judge who fails completely in the light of this standard. As one who neither feared God nor regarded man he is represented as a man who thought little of the judgment of God, which one day he must face, or of the opinion of his fellows; i.e., he took neither seriously.[10] A widow, convinced that she was being wronged by someone,[11] besought the judge time and again to "take up her case," [12] but without success. At length, however, the judge bestirred himself, for no other reason than the desire to get rid of the complaining woman. It is assumed, though not stated, that he put into effect his resolution to act on the widow's behalf and right the wrong she suffered. The lesson is drawn: if so *unrighteous* a judge could be persuaded to aid a person in need, we may be assured that the *righteous* God will certainly take up the case of his chosen ones who cry to him day and night and will right the wrongs they suffer. This he will bring about "speedily"—whether that means "soon," or "suddenly" (as in Noah's time and at Sodom's overthrow, Luke 17:26ff). And it will take place through the agency of the Son of Man at his coming. For that day the elect must hold themselves ready.

The clue to the parable thus is felt to be the "how much more," typical of Jewish comparison, which is read into the beginning of v. 7 ("*and* will not God vindicate his chosen. . . ?"). On this basis, a unity can be sought between the two parts of the parable, in that assurance of vindication is offered when God's people *continually* cry to him; the faith which the Son of Man seeks is the root of such believing prayer; and the lesson which Luke points out in v. 1 can be applied not only to prayer generally, but to the specific need of God's people to *pray constantly for the coming redemption.*[13]

A different approach to the parable has been set forth by J. D. M. Derrett, aided by his unusual acquaintance with law in Asian society. In his view the key to the understanding of the parable is the recognition that in the Middle East it was common for two jurisdictions to exist side by side in a single land. In the Palestine of Jesus' day there were two sorts of legal jurisdiction concurrently in force. There were the courts run by the Jews in accordance with their understanding of the Torah. But from the Ptolemaic-Seleucid period on another legal system was in operation, which left the customary system in charge of religious matters (and some criminal matters, too) but superimposed on it a kind of "police" or "administrative" system. Naturally this left open the possibility of Jews forsaking their own courts to resort to Hellenistic administrative judges and to force opponents to do what their own Jewish courts would not allow. The Jewish leaders forbade their people to go to non-Jewish courts, but in fact they did not make recourse to them a ground for excommunication. Derrett suggests that the widow, instead of trusting the community court, is pictured as going straight to the administrative judge. For this she would have two good reasons: first, the judge was not bound by ordinary customs but had authority to make decisions according to his own will; and secondly, the widow was too poor to secure a lawyer (cf. Mark 12:40), so she asked the judge to "take up her case," and so to act on her behalf virtually as her advocate.

The judge would have nothing of it at first. Why did he give way to the woman? The answer is stated in the judge's own words: "This widow is so great a nuisance I will see her righted, in case by her continually coming *she finally blackens my face.*" Such is Derrett's translation of the famous word *hupopiazein,* which literally means to hit one beneath the eye, and so to give one a black eye. The term was used in a variety of ways, other than literally, but the figure of blackening the face was and is known all over Asia for disgracing a person. It reflects the phenomenon of a sallow skin turning ash-gray when disgrace is realized. To an Oriental this is a matter of enormous consequence, and he will do anything to avoid being publicly disgraced. This judge may assume the posture of fearing neither God nor man, but he recognizes that not even he can afford to lose his prestige. His soliloquy assumes the possibility that if he finally turns away this woman, his name and his status will suffer—whether through her slander or others' deduction—and so he at last yields to her importunate pleas. Now despite the gulf between this picture of an unscrupulous judge and the biblical revelation of a holy God, there is one factor which bridges the gulf: that is, *God also has a reputation and a name to maintain.* This is a common theme in the Old Testament, and it finds illustration in the Law, the Psalms, and the Prophets (see e.g., Ex. 32:12; Deut. 9:28; Ps. 74:22; 79:9; 143:11; Jer. 16:20f; and especially Ezekiel, e.g., 36:21ff; 38:23; 39:7). Accordingly the key to the parable is not in a "how much more," which is not expressed at all, but in the recognition of the element which the judge and the Lord possess in common—the name which must be preserved. It is in accordance with that name that the Lord will act for the vindication of his people.[14] On this understanding of the situation the first part of the parable is not only in harmony with the second part, but the

first part has the second in view. The parable, that is, is one, and
not two, as many of its exegetes have tried to maintain.

There is a further issue which requires consideration for a right
comprehension of the parable, and which prepares for its final thrust;
that is the meaning of the enigmatic phrase in v. 7: *kai makrothumei
ep' autois,* rendered in *The New English Bible,* "while he listens patiently to them." Every commentator has wrestled with this problem,
and Ott found it needful to devote many pages in review of the varied
modes of interpreting this phrase. The idea that it continues the question in the first part of the sentence, as in the NEB, Ott rejects on
the ground that the aorist subjunctive of the verb in the main clause
should then be continued in the last clause of the sentence instead
of being replaced by a present indicative. The King James Version
makes the verb concessive in meaning: "though he bear long with
them," and many exegetes follow this clue in varied ways. C. Spicq,
for example, renders the sentence: "Will not God bring about justice
. . . *although in fact he is slow in responding,"* or, *"in spite* of his
holding back," or, *"even if* he presents a deaf ear." [15] The "holding
back" is thought to reflect God's pity on his people, for he does not
wish them to enter unprepared into the final crisis of judgment (cf.
2 Pet. 3:9). But objection is taken to this, that *kai makrothumei* is
not concessive, for nowhere is a solitary *kai* evidenced as a concessive
particle, and such a notion would ordinarily require a participle to
express it.[16] The interpretation of Sahlin, highlighted by Jeremias,
makes the clause follow on the participial phrase "who call to him;"
the clause in which we are interested, v. 7c, is then viewed as a paratac-
tic mode of expression instead of a relative construction, and it is
rendered, "Should not God establish his right for his elect, *whom he
graciously hears if they cry day and night to him?"* [17] Again Ott objects,
on the authority of Kühner-Gert, that this does violence to the Greek
text.[18] He calls attention rather to the contribution of H. Riesenfeld,
who urged that Luke 18:7 is directly dependent on Ecclesiasticus 35:18
and must be explained in its light.[19] Certainly the parallels between
the two passages are remarkable, as will be seen from the Greek version
of the first two lines of Ecclesiasticus 35:18:

> *kai ho kurios ou me bradune*
> *oude me makrothumesei ep' autois.*

That is,

> And the Lord will not be slow
> neither will he be patient with them.

Reisenfeld however held that as the two verbs in this passage occur in parallelism they should be viewed as identical in meaning; they both express the single idea, "be tardy, keep one waiting," and that, he urged, is the intent of Luke 18:7. Ott on the contrary maintains (surely rightly) that synonymous parallelism does not demand identical meaning of verbs employed in the parallel lines;[20] that while *bradunein* does imply tardiness, *makrothumein* has the idea of holding back wrath that it may not come into action (cf. 2 Pet. 3:9). Ecclesiasticus 35:18 says that the Lord will not be tardy nor show grace to the wicked; Luke 18:7 on the contrary states that what the Lord will not do in relation to the wicked he does for the elect: he does not close his ears to their cry but graciously listens to them.

Now while this is all very pertinent, there is a further element in the relation of Ecclesiasticus 35:18 and Luke 18:7f which deserves notice. The Hebrew text of Ecclesiasticus 35, lying behind the Greek text from which our translations are made, has some important marginal readings favored by scholars, and in v. 18 the variant is striking. Ott has observed it but did not exploit it, but Derrett grasped its importance and stressed it. Interestingly, the marginal reading has been adopted by Oesterley and Box in their translation of and commentary on Ecclesiasticus in Charles's edition of the Apocrypha. They render the passage thus:

> Yea the Lord will not tarry,
>   *And the Mighty One will not refrain himself,*
> Till he smite the loins of the merciless
>   And requite vengeance to the arrogant.[21]

The marginal reading however actually makes the second line a question, presuming the answer "No":

> The Mighty One will not refrain himself, will he?

Luke 18:7 appears to turn the question demanding the answer "No" into an open one; but since it follows a question which demands the answer "Yes," it probably expects the same positive answer as the first line:

> God will vindicate his chosen ones . . . won't he?
>   And he will be gracious to them, won't he?

Now what has Jesus to do with Ecclesiasticus? Commonly it has been assumed that an adaptation of a statement in Ecclesiasticus must betray the hand of a later redactor. Derrett however points out that this book was beloved of the Qumran community. It is not inconceivable that a cardinal passage from their favorite textbook, from which they found encouragement for their anticipated role of avengers of the Lord, was cited by Jesus in a manner wholly typical of him in correction of an attitude which was wholly typical of them and which appealed greatly to the populace. The men of Qumran looked for the Mighty One to lead them in battle to "smite the loins of the merciless and requite vengeance to the arrogant." Jesus implies that that was not the task of the people of God; they needed not the sword for the achievement of redemption, but the gracious hearing of prayer for a victory beyond their power to secure and mercy for their participation in it.[22]

III

The bearing of this discussion on the understanding of Luke 18:8*b* is apparent. The Mighty One may be counted on to hear the prayers of his people. Through him their vindication will come "shortly." But how will he bring it to pass? The answer of Israel's prophets was unambiguous: it will come through the divine intervention in the Day of the Lord, as God in awesome accompaniments of theophany appears for the judgment of evil men and the deliverance of his people. By the time of Jesus, however, those who looked for the redemption of Israel were increasingly looking for the deliverance to come about through the Messiah, God's representative in his sovereign action. If the Messiah is to come *with* the kingdom, it is not a difficult step to think of him as appearing when God manifests himself *for* the kingdom. John the Baptist spoke a message to a ready audience when he proclaimed the coming of the mighty Messiah, whose winnowing fan was in his hand to gather grain for the barn and chaff for the burning (Matt. 3:12). The transition from mighty God to mighty Messiah is also silently made in Luke 18:8*a* to v. 8*b*. It must be stressed this needed no later hand for its accomplishment; it assumes the tradition of viewing the Messiah as the instrument of the divine sovereignty, and in the coming kingdom "the form of the appearance of Yahweh the Lord." [23] This, be it noted, is not dependent on New Testament christological reflection, but represents fundamental Jewish eschatological thinking as it developed in Old Testament prophecy and was emphasized in certain strands of Jewish apocalyptic thinking. That the Son of Man should be the instrument of the divine vindication, in the conquest of the antigod oppressor and in the leadership of the universal kingdom of the saints, will have been the natural way for Daniel 7:11ff to be understood in the day of Jesus—and some consider that it should be so understood by us today.[24]

We cannot, however, make a simple leap from Daniel 7 to Luke 18:8, as though this were the only saying in the Gospels concerning the Son of man. In the apocalyptic passage which precedes our parable (Luke 17:22ff), Luke follows the comparison of the Son of Man in his day to the lightning flash (17:24) by the statement, "But first he must endure much suffering and be repudiated by this generation" (Luke 17:25). This is characteristic of a whole range of teaching relating to the humiliation of the Son of man on earth, who is yet destined to be revealed as the Lord of the kingdom. The Son of man has nowhere to lay his head (Luke 9:58) and is destined to suffer rejection and death (9:22); the Lord has come to precipitate judgment but also to endure it (12:49f; cf. Mark 10:38), that his followers may have part in the kingdom of God (22:17ff,28ff; cf. Mark 14:22ff). They who acknowledge Jesus in his lowly estate as the authoritative representative of the rule of God will be acknowledged by the Son of man at the doors of the kingdom (Luke 12:8f), even as Jesus in his humiliation before the high priest and his associates tells them that they will see the Son of man at God's right hand—not only as vindicated, but also as their judge (Luke 22:69). It could be objected that a mixture of citations like this ignores the distinction between Jesus and the Son of man in such sayings as Luke 12:8f, and the hesitations of critics as to the authenticity of the Son of man sayings in the Gospels. The time is overdue, however, for a total reconsideration of the Son of man sayings in the light of increasing knowledge that has come to us of contemporary Jewish thought on the sufferings of the righteous man, the complex range of ideas relating to the Messiah in Judaism, our increased knowledge of the breadth of apocalyptic relationships in the ancient world, and the implications of the consciousness of Jesus as the bearer of the divine sovereignty in the world—an aspect of Gospel christology to which modern New Testament studies have rarely given due weight. Whatever the reason for the apparent distinction between Jesus and the Son of man in such saying as Luke 12:8f; Mark 14:62 etc., it is clear that the sayings relating to the humble Son of man identify him with Jesus, and it is difficult to deny the identity of Jesus with the apocalyptic Son of man in Mark 14:62 and its parallels.

In this connection Luke 18:38*b* is of importance, for it is likely that this very contrast of the exalted and lowly Son of man is basic to it. "When the Son of man comes, will he find faith on earth?" What sort of faith will he look for? Schuyler Brown, after a lengthy consideration of the matter, concluded that it must denote *the* faith, that which Jesus has taught his disciples, as though the question meant: "Will Christianity still exist, or will the preaching of the Christian kerygma still be going on when the Son of Man comes?" [25] I cannot imagine that even Luke thought that Jesus had such a thought in mind; it is not a natural interpretation if Luke himself was responsible for placing the saying in its present context, and still less would it be so if the saying is in its original context. If this "faith" is to be related to the teaching of Jesus, it is likely to denote the faith in God which he taught his disciples to have; and the God in whom they were to place their faith is he whose sovereignty was effectively at work in the world in and through Jesus, the representative and instrument of the sovereignly acting God. The faith of which this saying speaks is the faith which acknowledges Jesus in his humility and humiliation as the Son of man, destined to be God's executor in the vindication of his name by the humbling of the exalted and the exaltation of the lowly. Faith of this order determines entry into or exclusion from the kingdom which was manifest in Jesus, and which as Son of man he will bring to full revelation (Luke 12:6f). And it is faith of this order which prompts the earnest cry to God for the final revelation of divine sovereignty; a faith which brightly burns even when the elect are called on to endure rejection, as the Son of man endured it; a faith which continues to believe, in spite of waiting, that the answer to their prayers is sure.

This link between the faith which the Son of man will seek and the sovereignty of God operative in and through him raises the question as to whom Jesus was addressing his parable. It is generally assumed that the recipients of the parable were his disciples, since they are the last audience to be named by Luke (17:22). If this be so the disciples received from the parable not only encouragement and assurance, but a reminder of the necessity for ensuring their preparedness for the day when their prayers will be fulfilled in the kingdom's unveiling. This is in harmony with a concern of Jesus which finds continual expression in the Gospels. In the last week of his life in Jerusalem Jesus warns Peter that the developing crisis will engulf him: "But for you I have prayed that your faith may not fail; and when you have come to yourself, you must lend strength to your brothers" (Luke 22:32). Jesus is concerned that Peter may survive the trials immediately

ahead, but Peter is expected not only to survive in faith but to serve
the community also. Similarly in the ultimate crisis of the parousia
there is repeated stress on the necessity for "watchfulness," or spiritual
alertness, that the disciples may be prepared for the day and may
discharge their responsibilities to the last. The eschatological discourse
in the Synoptic Gospels is now widely recognized as a "Mahnrede,"
and exhortation in view of the end, rather than an anticipatory review
of events leading to the end. The parables of Luke 12:35-46 and of
Matthew 25:1-46 are notable in their conjunction of watchfulness with
service. To be prepared like the wise maidens for the return of the
bridegroom, for example, demands the carrying out of tasks assigned
by the Lord (Matt. 25:14-30) and by going to the aid of the least of
the brothers of the Son of man (Matt. 25:31-46).[26] Luke's conclusion
of the eschatological discourse is particularly close in spirit to the
conclusion of the parable of the widow and judge:

> Keep a watch on yourselves . . .
> *Be on the alert, pray at all times for strength to*
> *pass safely through*
> *All these imminent troubles and to stand in the*
> *presence of the Son of Man.*[27]

The teaching of Jesus, like that of the prophets of both Testaments,
assumes that there will be a people of God—the "elect"—to inherit
the kingdom for which the world was made. Luke 18:8 must not be
interpreted so as to imply that Jesus had serious doubts about that,
still less Luke, the "theologian of redemptive history," who passed
it on to us. But again like the prophets, Jesus does not cease to warn
against "ease in Zion." Faith's assurance is never equated with presumption in relation to the judgment. The Son of man seeks a living
faith, rooted in the past, active in the present, strong enough to endure
afflictions and overcome natural impatience for vindication, a faith
which expresses itself in obedient service to the end. Such service
characterized the life of the Son of man himself (Mark 10:45). Only
grace can enable a believer so to follow in his steps as to stand in
the presence of the Son of man at the last. Hence the necessity for
prayer to the end, and for *that* end (Luke 21:36).

We know that some of the parables of Jesus, among them the best
known, were addressed not to his followers but to other members of
his nation, including some who were highly critical of him (e.g., the
parables of the good Samaritan, Luke 10:25ff, the prodigal son, Luke
15:11ff, the wicked husbandmen, Mark 12:1ff). These parables have

a different "bite" according as they are heard by followers of Jesus or his opponents. Think for example of the different ways in which a Pharisee, a publican, and a disciple would hear the parable of the prodigal son. Now could the parable of the widow and judge have been spoken primarily to Jews who were not followers of Jesus, or even to a mixed company of disciples and noncommitted Jews who were interested enough in the message of Jesus to listen to him? The possibility that the latter is the case has often attracted scholars,[28] and certainly it cannot be denied. The majority of Jews who came to hear Jesus had their hopes set on the deliverance of their people in the Day of the Lord. They would have listened with approval to the parable, readily seeing in the situation of the widow a reflection of their own, and finding in the concluding assurance of vv. 6-8*a* a heartening message. The final question of v. 8*b* however would have disturbed them and caused reflection. Are not the "elect," who cry night and day to God for vindication, the covenant people, as the Scriptures teach? And yet contemporary Judaism was aware that the "elect" were not coextensive with the nation. The prophets had taught them to recognize in the elect the righteous remnant within Israel; and that restriction of the meaning of the concept had become axiomatic to many of the most ardent of Jews looking for the kingdom, above all the men of Qumran and the circle that produced the "Similitudes of Enoch"—both groups being contemporary with Jesus. The word of Jesus now gives a fresh slant on the elect: they are those in whom the Son of man at the revelation of the kingdom finds "faith." There can hardly be doubt that in such case the faith sought would include a positive attitude to the word of the kingdom proclaimed by Jesus in his ministry, and to Jesus himself as the representative of the divine sovereignty (Luke 12:8f). For Jews who look longingly and pray earnestly for the vindication of God's people through the Messiah there is an urgent question to be faced: will the Son of man find the faith he seeks in the nation? And will he find it in his hearers? The stimulating of this reflection will have been foremost in the intention of Jesus as he told the parable, for the call to the decision of faith lay at the heart of his mission. How tragic for the people who prayed for the coming of the kingdom to be disqualified from it! Hence, in Delling's words, Jesus directs the gaze of the Jewish community to "the danger of not being able to stand before the coming of the Son of Man"; and the question is put: "Will the Son of Man encounter faith in the Judaism which at the present time widely rejects him, the faith which recognizes the Son of Man in the lowly and humble man in his earthly work, who is the Servant of the Lord?" [29]

The question finds a peculiarly urgent application to Jews of our Lord's day if he had in mind those among them who sympathized with the outlook of the Qumran sectaries. It is likely that such would have been numerous, for any who approved, however, mildly, the Zealotic tendencies among the people would have had a positive feeling for the Qumran eschatology. The men of Qumran were preparing to be the army of the Lord, whom God would use as instruments of his annihilation of the wicked—Romans, Gentiles, and apostate Jews alike—and to usher in, under the messiahs of Aaron and Israel, the promised kingdom. Certainly they prayed for the vindication of God's elect, for their entire existence was oriented to the events in which it would be accomplished. And they studied among their sacred writings the book which told how the Lord, the Judge, listens to the widow whose tears run down her cheeks as she accuses the man who caused them. We have seen how they read in their copy of the passage:

> Yea, the Lord will not tarry,
>   And the Mighty One will not refrain himself, will he?
> Till he smite the loins of the merciless
>   And requite vengeance to the arrogant (Ecclus. 35:18).

The differences between this citation and Luke 18:6ff warrant attention: in the above passage the people from whom God will not "hold back" are the objects of his destructive judgment, whereas in Luke 18:7 it is his own people from whom God will not hold back, in his gracious listening to their cries; secondly the "Mighty One" in the citation is Yahweh, whose instruments of judgment the Qumran members expected to be, whereas in Luke 18:6ff the Mighty One is the Son of man, who requires no soldiers; and most extraordinary of all, the question at the end of the parable implies that the Son of man asks no one to be an instrument of his judgment, but on the contrary warns every man to look for judgment on himself and to come to terms with the true Messiah. It is one of the tragedies of history that the group of Jews who in many ways stood closer to Jesus than any other group known to us promulgated a messianism which directly contributed, through the Zealot movement, to the destruction of their nation. Holding to the hope of a messianic Priest and messianic King, they were blind to the concept of a messianic Servant. Their Messiah-Priest, like their Messiah-King, was a warrior, and the community of priests studied to be an army of priestly-warriors. That undoubtedly appealed to many in Israel who never thought to join the ranks of the Qumran monks. But Jesus recalls them to a different understanding of the way of divine vindication. Vengeance does not belong to man to execute, for judgment is in the hand of God, and his only appointed instrument of justice is the Son of man. Israel must turn from thoughts of bringing in the kingdom with the sword, for the Lord will do it soon enough through his Mighty One. And every man of Israel must recognize that he, too, as well as the men of Kittim and the rest of the despised Gentiles, must stand before the Son of man at his coming, and to him give answer concerning his relation to the God revealed in *this* Christ.

Conclusion

The underlying presupposition of the parable of the widow and the judge is the eschatological faith of the Bible.[30] God has a purpose for his world: it is the supreme good of his kingdom, and this he intends certainly to bring to pass. The establishment of the kingdom includes the triumph of justice, and this entails judgment. But the carrying out of the judgment and the revelation of the kingdom of God in power are alike achieved through the Son of man. Now all that is in essential harmony with the faith of the prophets and the apocalyptists of Israel. But on the lips of Jesus, as of his followers, there is a unique factor in this expectation: the Son of man through whom the judgment and the kingdom of God are to be universally established has already proved himself the bearer of the kingdom to man. In his ministry of authoritative word and powerful deed the judgment and the redemption of the sovereign God entered into history, and this process continues to a death and resurrection wherein judgment and redemption are expressed with eternal validity. It is *this* sovereign work of God through *this* Son of man which is to come to its completion in the vindication of God's name and people. The concept may be otherwise expressed by affirming that the kingdom of God is one and the Christ of God is one. The kingdom comes with the Christ in his incarnate life and ministry, and it is revealed in power at his parousia.

H. D. Wendland grasped this and affirmed it to hold good of the teaching of Jesus:

His entire presentation of the divine sovereignty and the certainty of being the bringer of this sovereignty comes to perfect expression in the parousia concept. Messiah and kingdom are so completely bound together that the fulfilment of the kingdom comes with the full revelation of the Messiah; that is, the Messiah becomes also the bearer of the absolute fulfilment through which the sovereignty of God comes.[31]

To a degree unknown in Judaism faith and hope are focused in a person, in the person of the Christ who is Jesus, Son of man and Son of God, the Mediator between God and man. Nothing therefore is so important as to be related to him by faith—now, and in hope of final redemption. Such faith will find its expression in the service of God and the service of man. It will not be overthrown when confronted by a cross, nor will it grow dull when men ignore the elect instead of persecuting them. Whatever the nature of their pilgrimage may have been, the Lord will set his question before them at the end: "Have you faith worthy of the name?" The Day alone will declare it. The days given to them will determine the answer given in the last day.

NOTES

[1] Luke 18:1-8, *The New English Bible*, where, however, it forms a single paragraph.

[2] For an analysis of the language of v. 1, calculated to establish the Lucan style of the sentence, see W. Ott, *Gebet und Heil, Die Bedeutung der Gebetsparänese in der lukanischen Theologie*, Studien zum Alten und Neuen Testament, ed. V. Hamp and J. Schmid, XII (Munchen, 1965), p. 19. This study contains the most exhaustive treatment of the parable which may be found. It provides a wealth of information concerning critical opinions on the issues raised in the parable.

[3] *Die Gleichnisreden Jesu*, II (Tübingen 1910), p. 283.

[4] *Op. cit.* pp. 285ff. The parallelism is not to be doubted. Since we must examine the passage later we reproduce it here in the NEB translation:

> "The Lord is a judge
> who knows no partiality. . .
> He never ignores the appeal of the orphan
> or the widow when she pours out her complaint.
> How the tears run down the widow's cheeks,
> and her cries accuse the man who caused them!
> . . .
> The prayer of the humble pierces the clouds,
> but he is not consoled until it reaches its destination.
> He does not desist until the Most High intervenes,
> gives the just their rights, and sees justice done.
> The Lord will not be slow,
> neither will he be patient with the wicked,
> until he crushes the sinews of the merciless
> and sends retribution on the heathen. . .

until he gives his people their rights
and gladdens them with his mercy."

[5] The discussions on these matters are conveniently summarized in Ott's work, pp. 24-42.

[6] E. Grässer, *Das Problem der Parusieverzögerung in den synoptischen Evangelien und in der Apostelgeschiechte* (Berlin 1957), p. 38, citing H. H. Wendt's view that the statement sounds like a pessimistic doubt of Jesus on the continuance of the success of his messianic work after his death.

[7] Das Gleichnis vom gottlosen Richter, *Studien zum Neuen Testament und zum hellenistischen Judentum* (Göttingen, 1970), pp. 204f.

[8] *Op. cit.,* pp. 26-27.

[9] For the widow, cf. Ex. 22:21ff; Isa. 1:17; Jer. 7:6; 22:3; Lam. 1:1; Jas. 1:27. For the judge, cf. especially Ps. 82:2-7. God as the ideal judge who rejects bribes and secures justice for widows and orphans is frequently mentioned, as e.g., Deut. 10:18; Ps. 68:5.

[10] Delling, *op. cit.,* pp. 208f.

[11] Jeremias considers that it must be a money-matter of some kind—a debt, or pledge, or a portion of an inheritance which is being held from her—since the law stipulated that "an authorized scholar may decide money cases sitting alone" (b. Sany. 4b [Bar]), *The Parables of Jesus,* revised ed. (London, 1963), p. 153. It could have been such an issue but not on the ground stated. The appearance before a single judge may be for quite different reasons, as we shall see.

[12] The expression is that of J. D. M. Derrett. The term *ekdikesis,* literally "vengeance," is "the technical term for administrative justice throughout the Hellenistic age," and *ekdikeson me* means, "Take up my case." See Derrett's article, "Law in the New Testament: The Parable of the Unjust Judge," *New Testament Studies,* vol. 19 (1972), pp. 186f. Further G. Schrenk, *T. D. N. T.,* vol. II, pp. 442-446.

[13] E. E. Ellis, *The Gospel of Luke,* "Century Bible" (London, 1966), p. 213.

[14] See Derrett, *op. cit.,* pp. 180-191.

[15] La parabole de la veuve obstinee et du juge inerte, aux decision impromptues (Lc. XVIII:1-8), *Revue Biblique,* vol. 68 (1961), p. 81.

[16] Ott, p. 50.

[17] H. Sahlin, Zwei Lukas-Stellen, I. Luke 6:43-45, II. Luke 18:7, *Symbolae Biblicae Upsaliensis 4* (Uppsala, 1945), p. 17. The discussion of Jeremias is in his *Parables of Jesus,* pp. 154f.

[18] "The participial construction *ton boōnton ktl.* cannot represent the place of an adverbial clause, since an adverbial clause 'never stands between the article and the substantive, or with the article follows the substantive, but always follows or precedes the substantive without article,' " Ott, p. 52, citing Kuhner-Gert, *Ausführliche Grammatik der griechischen Sprache,* Zweiter Teil, 2 Bde (Darmstadt, 1963), p. 77.

[19] Zu makrothumein (Lk. 18:7), in *Neutestamentliche Aufsätze,* Festschrift fur Josef Schmid (Regensburg, 1963), pp. 257f.

[20] H. Ljungvik independently makes the same point in criticism of Riesenfeld's view, "Zur Erklärung einer Lukas-Stelle (Luke XVIII:7)," *New Testament Studies,* vol. 10 (1964), p. 290.

[21] *Apocrypha and Pseudipigrapha of the Old Testament,* ed. R. H. Charles, vol. 1 (Oxford, 1913), p. 439.

[22] The knowledge possessed by Jesus of teaching contained in popular extracanonical literature requires more careful consideration than is commonly given to it. If the echo of Ecclus. 35:18 was, in fact, due to a redactor this would affect chiefly the wording of v. 7; the relation of the original parable to the Qumran outlook would then be less sharply defined but not necessarily excluded.

[23] The expression is that of H. H. Wolff in his illuminating discussion of the issue, Herrschaft Jahwes und Messiasgestalt im Alten Testament, *Zeitschrift fur alttestamentliche Wissenschaft* XII (1936), p. 191.

[24] Such are the implications of J. A. Emerton's arguments in his article, "The Origin of the Son of Man Imagery," *Journal of Theological Studies,* new Series IX (1958), pp. 225ff.

[25] *Apostasy and Perseverance in the Theology of Luke,* Analecta Biblica 36 (Rome, 1969), p. 45 (cf. pp. 40-46).

[26] So P. Bonnard, *L'Evangile selon St. Mattieu,* 2nd. ed., (Neuchatel, 1970), pp. 358f. Bonnard's

exposition of Matt. 25 brings out well the connection between eschatological hope and conduct of ethical worth.

[27] Luke 21:34-36. This paragraph has no parallel in Matthew and Mark, but it is so clearly echoed by Paul in his Thessalonian correspondence that we must presume at least the apostle's knowledge of a tradition close to it. The idea that Luke drew his material from Paul is inherently implausible, and would appear to be ruled out by comparable phenomena which can be observed in the relations between 1-2 Thessalonians to the versions of the discourse in Matthew and Mark. The parallels between the synoptic versions of the discourse on the last things and Paul's instruction to the Thessalonians, in ideas as well as terminology, leave no doubt in my mind, after fresh investigation of the matter, that Paul was acquainted with an early form of the discourse. The discussion of the evidence by R. Pesch (*Naherwartungen, Tradition und Redaktion in Mk. 13,* (Düsseldorf, 1968), pp. 214f) is altogether inadequate. L. Hartman gives a much fuller account of the material in his *Prophecy Interpreted,* Coniectanea Biblica, New Testament Series I (Lund, 1966), pp. 178-205; on Luke 21:34-36 see pp. 214f.

[28] See e.g., L. Gaston, *No Stone on Another,* Supplements to Novum Testamentum XXIII (Leiden 1970), pp. 353f; G. Delling, *op. cit.,* pp. 232ff. W. L. Knox thinks that Luke 18:8 reflects a half-ironic expression of regret that the hope that the Pharisees would accept the kingdom of heaven had proved illusory, *Sources of the Synoptic Gospels,* II (Cambridge, 1957), p. 114.

[29] *Op. cit.,* p. 222.

[30] So C. E. B. Cranfield: "The passage expresses what I take to be the characteristic eschatology of the New Testament as a whole," "The Parable of the Unjust Judge and the Eschatology of Luke–Acts," *Scottish Journal of Theology,* XVI (1963), p. 300.

[31] *Die Eschatologie des Reiches Gottes bei Jesus* (Gütersloh, 1931), p. 247.

9.

Revelation in the Writings of
H. Wheeler Robinson and Eric Rust
A Comparative Study

Max E. Polley

There are some remarkable parallels between the careers of Eric
Rust and his revered teacher, H. Wheeler Robinson. Robinson was
an English Baptist minister, teacher, scholar, and principal. He was
educated at Regent's Park College in London (1890), the University
of Edinburgh (1891-1895), and Mansfield College in Oxford (1895-
1900). Upon graduation from Mansfield College, he became the minister of the Pitlochry Church in Perthshire, Scotland (1900-1903) and
then served St. Michael's Church in Coventry, England (1903-1906).
In 1906 Robinson accepted the invitation to join the faculty at Rawdon
Baptist College where he remained until 1920. Robinson found himself
during these years at Rawdon College doing research and writing in
the field of the Old Testament while his courses were in the disciplines
of church history, philosophy of theism, elementary Latin, and comparative religions. In 1920 Robinson entered the major work of his life
when he became principal of Regent's Park College, London, a position
he held until his retirement in 1942. It was during Robinson's principal-
ship of Regent's Park that the college, in 1927, moved from London
to Oxford. While at Regent's Park College, Robinson devoted his
scholarship to the field of Old Testament studies where he gained
an international reputation.[1]

Eric Rust is also an English Baptist minister, teacher, and scholar.
Rust was educated at the University of London, receiving the B. Sc.
in 1930 and the M. Sc. in 1932, majoring in the physical sciences.
But his interests turned to religion and he attended Regent's Park
College in Oxford where he studied under Robinson, receiving the
B. A. degree in 1935, the M. A. degree in 1938, and the B. D. degree
in 1946. These were exciting years in Oxford as he saw the first building
of the college erected in the year 1938. Rust also began his career
as a minister in English Baptist churches, serving the Hay Hill Baptist
Church in Bath (1935-1939), the Oxford Road Baptist Church in Bir-

mingham (1940-1942), and the New Road Baptist Church in Huddersfield (1942-1946). In 1946, one year after the death of Robinson, Rust became professor of philosophy and theology at Rawdon Baptist College, a position he held until 1952. Until this point in his career, the paths of Rust and Robinson had crossed frequently. Then in 1953 Rust came to the United States, first as professor of biblical theology at Crozer Theological Seminary in Chester, Pennsylvania (1952-1953), and then as professor of Christian philosophy at Southern Baptist Theological Seminary in Louisville, Kentucky, a position he held from 1953 to his retirement.

Neither Robinson nor Rust were narrowly trained. Robinson's major field was the Old Testament, but his writings reveal solid training in the New Testament, philosophy, theology, and church history. Rust's major field is theology and philosophy, but his writings indicate a breadth of knowledge in the areas of natural science, Old and New Testaments, and church history. Both men chose to use their scholarly talents to serve the church they loved.

Throughout the writings of both Robinson and Rust runs the theme of revelation.[2] The concept of revelation so caught the imagination of Robinson that it became the very basis for his understanding of the entire Old Testament; he found it possessed a dynamic quality that provided both a summing-up of the uniqueness of Israel's religion and a means by which this sacred literature could be viewed from within. While Rust is deeply influenced by Robinson's approach to revelation, Rust's own unique training in the natural sciences and in Christian philosophy led him to explore the implications of the concept of revelation beyond the biblical materials. The purpose of this chapter is to examine how Rust has developed and expanded Robinson's understanding of the category of revelation.

In 1938 two essays by Robinson appeared in the volume *Record and Revelation,* a book which he also edited. Their general subject was "The Theology of the Old Testament," and it is significant that the first essay dealt with the philosophy of revelation.[3] Here Robinson briefly set forth the biblical belief in a historical revelation. The modern conception of revelation postulates static propositions that are eternally true, much like axioms in mathematics. But knowledge of God, for the Hebrew people with their belief in realism is conveyed "through the concrete experience of living, rather than by any intellectual construction." [4] Therefore, by revelation Robinson meant "that direct and purposive activity of God which discloses Him to man for man's good." [5] In this definition Robinson has emphasized that double aspect of revelation which figures so prominently in all his writings, its God-ward and manward nature. Sometimes he referred to the "objective" and "subjective" nature of revelation,[6] and at other times he referred to the relationship between "revelation" and "discovery," [7] but in both instances he was emphasizing the double aspect of God's acts on man's behalf and man's response to this divine activity. For Robinson, to stress the Godward aspect of revelation alone would result in a series of propositions about God far removed from the dynamic and living quality of Israel's faith.[8] This, he believed, had been done by the confessional church to its detriment. On the other hand, to emphasize the manward aspect of revelation only would involve one in an egocentric predicament in which God's will is fashioned after man's image. It is imperative, therefore, that both extremes be avoided by a balanced approach which emphasizes alike God's self-disclosure and man's faithful response. Because revelation is to, through, and for men, the subjective response to the objective act is always necessary. There would be no revelation without God's acts; there would be no revelation without man's response; it is the blending of the human and divine factors that makes revelation possible.[9] This balance Robinson maintained through the relationship between mediation and interpretation.

The idea of revelation as a blending between mediation and interpretation Robinson developed fully in The Speaker's Lectures delivered at Oxford from 1942-1945 and published posthumously under the title *Inspiration and Revelation in the Old Testament*.[10] The main thesis of this volume is that the form which revelation takes in Israel's religion is determined by two factors, the media through which God acts and the interpretative response of those who receive the revelation. The book consists of seven parts. The first three parts deal with the media through which revelation takes place—nature, man, and history.[11] For Robinson the principle of mediation was the natural point of departure in an examination of revelation in the Old Testament. He wrote:

Since it is always through some form of mediation that God draws near to man in the actuality of history and experience, the principle of mediation supplies a convenient way of entrance to our subject. It has the great advantage of bringing us to the actual point of contact (in our experience) between God and man, instead of confronting us with *a priori* speculation.[12]

But because God's acts are never revelatory until they are so interpreted, the next four parts of *Inspiration and Revelation in the Old Testament* present the response of prophet, priest, sage, and psalmist to God's activity.

There is, of course, no perfect revelation of God through the media. Although God is known, if he is known at all, through these media, still the revelation is often distorted by either the media or the interpreter or both. Nature may be a medium through which God reveals himself, but an identification of nature and God might lead to a religiously degrading nature-worship. Such a nature-worship is one of the major crises of faith which Israel encountered when she entered Canaan. One of the unique features of Israel's faith is that the human moral consciousness triumphed over nature as a superior medium of revelation, thus enabling morality to be closely related to religion.[13] In our own day, there is a tendency to interpret the physical world naturalistically, thus concealing the activity of God. Robinson was deeply concerned that for the modern man nature with its orderliness could conceal God as well as reveal him depending upon one's interpretation of it.[14]

Despite these limitations of the media of revelation,[15] God does reveal himself to us through these media. "In the light of the principle of kenosis, therefore, we shall neither look for a revelation of Spirit divorced from any medium, and consequently inexpressible, nor reject such revelation because it is conditioned by the medium it necessarily employs." [16] Robinson, although aware that no revelation is perfect, was not driven to skepticism concerning the knowledge of God. "The unknown God becomes known in the sphere of that which man *can* know." [17] He firmly believed that there is a kinship between God and man which provides sufficient basis for revelation to occur. Indeed, he regarded the limitations of the media as a blessing in disguise, for the search for truth is more important than the possession of it; pure truth belongs only to God.[18]

Rust's basic approach to revelation is the same as Robinson's. Rust touches upon the subject in a number of articles,[19] but develops the concept fully in five books: *The Christian Understanding of History* (1946), *Nature and Man in Biblical Thought* (1953), *Salvation History: A Biblical Interpretation* (1962), *Towards a Theological Understanding of History* (1963), and *Science and Faith: Towards a Theological Understanding of Nature* (1967). Even the titles of these works reveal the emphasis placed on nature, man, and history as media of revelation.

As with Robinson, Rust also develops the Godward and manward nature of revelation through an emphasis on mediation and interpretation. Rust identified two distinct traditions in our Western culture, the Greek and the Judeo-Christian ways of viewing ultimate reality and God. The Greek took the way of reason and discovery; the Hebrew-Christian, the way of faith and revelation.

The Greek approach to ultimate reality was the beginning of Western philosophy. It emphasized reason and objectivity. Reality was regarded as an object of thought, and ideas of the human reason was regarded as the basis for an understanding of reality. The real was the rational, the knowledge of the reality that underlay all appearances was to be attained by the processes of discursive reasoning.[20]

Knowledge of ultimate reality was discovered by man through the dispassionate use of reason. Such knowledge was universal, available to all who were willing to pay the price of disciplining the mind to think objectively and rationally. The emphasis is on immanence not transcendence. Reason demands that form and matter be united in such a way that ultimate reality can be discovered by logical analysis.

But there is another approach to reality, the Judeo-Christian tradition. Here the emphasis falls on revelation, not discovery; on faith, not reason; on subjectivity, not objectivity; on transcendence rather than immanence.[21]

Now the initiative in such knowledge of God lies in God himself and not in the knowing subject. Knowledge comes through revelation, not as the end result of a process of discursive reason. God is not static being but dynamic will, not an idea consequent upon a ratiocinative process but a personal mystery who discloses himself to the subject.[22]

This disclosure of God takes place through the media of nature, man, and history. It is always a hidden revelation which occurs because the media veil God as well as disclose him. "God approaches men through the medium of his creatures in the biblical understanding of revelation. The creatures may thus veil God and the mystery of God's nature and purpose remain hidden, unless our blind eyes are open to the glory of his presence."[23] Despite the mediated nature of the revelation, revelation is immediate encounter; revelation is always a mediated immediacy.[24] Man is grasped by the divine disclosure and, through faith, encounters that which is ultimate.

Thus far, Rust's position parallels Robinson's, although Rust does explore the Greek tradition of reason and discovery far more fully than did Robinson. But Rust now proceeds to place an emphasis upon the testimony and witness of prophets and apostles in the process of revelation which Robinson never developed. For Robinson, the emphasis was always upon revelation and not inspiration; the inspiration of prophet, priest, sage, and psalmist was really their response to God's revelation mediated through nature, man, and history. But for Rust the authority of revelation rests not only upon God's activity through the media but also upon man's inspired witness to the events; both the event (revelation) and the interpretation (inspiration) are God-directed. There is a greater emphasis upon the divine factor in revelation than there was in Robinson's thought.

Such witnessing is at one and the same time a proclamation and a confession. It proclaims what God has said in the concrete confrontation of history, and it confesses the faith of the witness in the living God, his own recognition of and commitment to the God who has spoken. Such witnessing is inspired, for only God can open men's eyes to his presence, lift the veil in the historical mediating event, and only God can direct aright their testimony to what they have seen and heard. The human response to revelation is faith.[25]

The interrelatedness between media and interpretation is nowhere better expressed than in Rust's term "historical images." Rust wishes to avoid the use of "myth" in presenting biblical revelation because of its nonhistorical connotations. Rather, he employs the term "historical image" in order to describe both the transcendent and the historical nature of biblical revelation. It is an intriguing use of language. The term "historical" refers to the media through which revelation becomes actualized, and the term "images" refers to man's creative and inspired response to God's activity. God's initiative is seen not only in his revelatory acts but also in the "historical images" which witness to these acts.

Now these images are not arbitrary, or bound to the time and place in which they emerge, as Bultmann contends. This brings into view the association of divine inspiration with the imagination of the prophets and witnesses . . . in the case of the prophets and apostles, the imagination is so creatively controlled by the divine Spirit that the images and symbols have divine authority. The events and images are concomitant elements in the revelation, and without either there would be no revelation.[26]

For Rust, the authority of biblical revelation rests not only upon the mighty acts of God in history but also upon the inspired language which conveys that activity. Robinson wrote simply of man's faith-response to God's activity.

For Robinson, the three main types of media through which God reveals himself are nature, man, and history. An understanding of revelation in the Old Testament is possible only after an examination of these media as they are presented in the Old Testament. Fortunately, Robinson's position on this subject is clearly stated both from a theological viewpoint in *Redemption and Revelation: In the Actuality of History* and from a biblical viewpoint in *Inspiration and Revelation in the Old Testament.* These two works supplement each other; there is no basic disagreement between them.

To understand God's revelation of himself in nature, it is necessary for twentieth-century man to understand the Hebrew conception of nature.[27] Unlike the other Semitic religions of the fertile crescent, Hebrew religion did not identify God with nature. Nature is dependent upon God as its creator and upholder, but the forces of nature are never deified. In the fertility cult of Canaan, the seasons of the year are portrayed in the myth of the dying and rising god, but in Israel there is a rejection of this cult of magic for the belief in a transcendent God who yet asserts his divine control over nature. Because nature exists owing to God's will, it can be viewed as a medium of revelation.

Nature is also understood as having a psychical life of its own through which revelation may be conveyed. Just as each physical organ of the body has its own semi-independent psychical life,[28] so the objects of nature are considered internally alive. "It is not so much a 'soul' that is ascribed to natural objects as a potential *mana,* a diffused consciousness with its own psychical (including ethical) possibilities, and its own capacity to be indwelt or made instrumental by yet higher powers, and finally by the activity of Yahweh Himself." [29] On occasion, when God wills it, these objects can come under his direct control in order to reveal his will. When Jacob wishes a revelation from God, he takes the sacred stone of Bethel and places it beneath his head so that his dreams may be inspired (Gen. 28:10-22). Robinson believed that this approach to nature is helpful in interpreting passages which were formerly understood as mere imagery. Thus Joseph's dreams in which the sheaves and the sun, moon, and stars reveal his supremacy take on new meaning if they are regarded as possessing an inner life (Gen. 37:5-11).

The divine activity in nature is exercised in three realms.[30] First, there is creation itself. Robinson believed that creation was from a preexistent chaos, but nevertheless it reveals a sovereign God who brought into being an orderly universe. God is portrayed in the creation stories and throughout the Old Testament as a divine Person who is above nature but who has condescended to manifest his grace in the creation of a world which is good. Second, this activity of God did not cease with creation but is continuous (Neh. 9:6; Jer. 10:13; Pss. 65:9-10; 147:16ff.). Indeed, nature would cease to exist if God withdrew his active conservation of it, as the speech of Elihu in the book of Job proclaims:

> If he should take back his spirit to himself,
>   and gather to himself his breath,
> all flesh would perish together,
>   all man would return to dust. (Job 34:14-15) [31]

Third, the Hebrew people look forward to the day when nature will be transformed and made to fulfill perfectly God's purpose. The eschatology of the postexilic period, while historically oriented, finds in the transformation of nature a natural means of expressing God's acts on Israel's behalf. Robinson maintained that the pictures of a transformed world are to be taken realistically, not poetically, allegorically, or symbolically; for a literal view is in harmony with the Hebraic conception of God's control of nature. Nature is, therefore, at all times, whether past, present, or future, under the direct control of God. It is this direct control that makes it a primary sphere within which God is revealed. But, again, it must be emphasized that nature is seen as the sphere of God's creation, conservative, and transformation only when it has been so interpreted by the man of faith.

The nature-miracles of the Old Testament are only an extension and intensification of the normal activity of God in nature.[32] Robinson believed that the difficulty the twentieth-century man has in accepting miracle is due to his "imposing on the Hebrew mind a modern view of Nature." [33] The modern distinction between "natural" and "supernatural" is un-Hebraic; therefore, there is a need to set it aside and approach sympathetically the Hebrew conception of nature and its wonders.[34] This Robinson accomplished by a study of three Hebrew terms used for miracles. The term 'oth for "sign" designates any physical object or event to which special meaning has been given. Twenty-five times the plagues of Egypt are called "signs." But it may also refer to a material sign, such as the red cord which Rahab hung from her window to mark her home (Joshua 2:12), or it may be an event in the life of a person, such as the death of Eli's two sons as a sign of divine judgment (1 Sam. 2:34). Therefore, there is nothing

essentially supernatural about these signs; they designate ordinary occurrences which have been interpreted in a particular way. What makes
certain signs miraculous is not the strangeness of the event but rather
the interpretation of the event as under divine control. The term
mopheth or "portent" designates any extraordinary occurrence which
is interpreted as revealing what will come to pass. The plagues of
Egypt are called "portents" nineteen times. Yet, the term "portent"
may also denote a future evil, such as the foretelling by an unknown
prophet of the destruction of the altar at Bethel (1 Kings 13:2-3), or
a future good, such as Zechariah's reference to the priests as men
who are a prophecy of the forthcoming messianic age (Zech. 3:8).
These "portents," like the "signs," attain a miraculous connotation
because of the interpretation placed upon them. They are not "supernatural" in the modern sense of the word. Robinson maintained that
the chief difference between a "sign" and a "portent" is that the former
often designates an ordinary occurrence while the latter often refers
to an extraordinary event. The term *niphla'oth* or "wonder" is close
to miracle in the modern sense, for it designates outstanding events
in nature. However, certain events designated as wonders are hardly
what would be called supernatural today; e.g., rain (Job 5:9-10), clouds
(Job 37:16), and a sea-storm (Ps. 107:23-25) are considered wonders.
These are unusual because they "are to be regarded as extensions of
the divine power which is being constantly exercised in more normal
occurrences" rather than because they interrupt the natural order.[35]
Again, it is the interpretation given these wonders as under God's
special control that makes them miraculous.

If nature-theophanies do not necessarily break the "laws of nature,"
to use a modern phrase, then when are they considered theophanic?
The answer lies solely within the prophetic interpretation of nature.
All nature is due to God's activity and those aspects which are considered uniquely revelatory have been so interpreted by the men of faith
in Israel.

Interpretation is inseparable from miracles of the Old Testament pattern.
. . . All Nature, as we have seen, is potentially miraculous, and continually
manifests the wonders of God. At particular points of time and space this
wonder may be intensified, or given a new meaning by its incorporation in
a new context.[36]

In his book *Nature and Man in Biblical Thought*, published in 1953,
Rust developed more fully Robinson's view of nature as a media of
revelation. In Chapters II-IV Rust explores the Old Testament concept
of creation, the psychic life that earth possesses, and nature-miracles

as a disclosure of God's activity. In this material he parallels Robinson's approach. But Rust continues to develop the argument through the intertestamental period (Chapter VI) and into the New Testament (Chapters VII-VIII). The healing and nature miracles of Jesus reveal that while nature is not divine, yet it is wholly dependent upon God.

He who can order the storm to cease and bring back the dead to life; who declares that the Father clothes the lilies of the field and cares for the sparrow; who in His Person reveals the power over nature which the Old Testament ascribes to God alone; He confirms our faith that though nature is not to be identified with God, it is wholly sustained by Him and may become the medium of his revelation.[37]

But Rust's approach to the scientific view of nature is different from Robinson's. Robinson held that there was a sharp contrast between the closed system of cause and effect of modern science and the Hebrew view of God's free activity in and through nature. Rust, trained in modern natural science at the University of London, sees that the terms probability and contingency and flexibility are more suitable in describing the world than is the idea of fixed laws of nature. Hence there is room for God's continuous activity to influence nature without breaking into a fixed order.

Quite evidently the realm of scientific investigation is more open to Christian interpretation than for many decades. Nature has become a field of dynamic activity in which the new is emerging and in which it is inexplicable in terms of antecedents. We are presented with a flux of patterned events in which scientific law is no longer the supreme arbiter, but just a useful descriptive category. Regular and recurrent behavior fits into such description, but a new and creative inbreak can no longer be ruled out, as in the days of mechanistic causation.[38]

Rust also adds a new dimension to his argument when he relates the Trinity to creation. Drawing upon the Church Fathers, Rust relates all three Persons of the triune God to creation. The association of the Father with creation calls for little discussion. The Son, eternally generated by the Father, is, through the logos Christology of the Apologists, associated with the divine wisdom (pattern) used by God in creating the world. Finally, the Spirit (wind) is the activity of God that hovered over the primordial waters at the beginning of creation and which sustains all life in man and enables all creatures to exist. He writes:

If the Word is the thought of God, the divine intention and purpose, the Spirit is the outgoing of that thought in activity, the expression of that purpose in action. Hence, in the Scriptures of the Old Testament, it originally meant "breath" or "wind," as we have seen. Because the Creator intends the created order in and through His Word, the actualization of the thought in creation is the work of the Holy Spirit, which hovers over the chaos, bringing order out of the confusion and light out of darkness.[39]

Some years later, in 1967, Rust returned to the subject of God's revelation through nature in his book *Science and Faith: Towards a Theological Understanding of Nature.* The relationship between science and religion is a growing concern among theologians,[40] and Rust is to be commended for his contribution to the field. While such topics as Heisenberg's indetermancy, the second law of thermodynamics, the nature and origin of life, the new world of physics, and evolutionary theories appear in the book, Rust's major purpose, as his subtitle indicates is to present a modern, scientific view of nature which is not incompatible with the Christian understanding of the universe. But if there is a conflict between the language of science and the language of theology, Rust favors the use of theological language.

Theological language can embrace scientific language and interpret it. But the reverse is not the case, since science deals only with empirical "observables." Theological language describes a total view of reality, whereas scientific language describes only a partial view. In theology the universe is understood in personal terms, but science abstracts from the person and concerns itself with the impersonal.[41]

Rust believes that it is in "the Incarnation and a sacramental universe" that the language of science and the language of theology meet.

Is not the whole universe sacramental of him who came in the Incarnation? Everywhere men are encountering Christ. What they glean in meaning in fragmentary ways is made coherent in him. . . . The universe points toward the incarnate Christ, in whom the principle of order and meaning has tabernacled in our midst.[42]

It is beyond the training of the present writer to evaluate how successfully Rust has related science and religion in his book.[43] But what is clear is that he has used his scientific and theological skills to explore in ways only hinted at in Robinson's writings the revelation of God through the media of nature.

A second area in which God reveals himself is the human consciousness.[44] The inner consciousness has a double significance for understanding God's revelation to man, for not only does it provide the primary medium by which God is known, but it also supplies the interpretative principles by which nature and history are understood as revelatory. Robinson believed that both God and man are known only by their interrelatedness.[45] "The Old Testament habitually shows man in his relation to God, not in himself as a detached unity. It also show God in His relation to man, not in the philosophical interests of 'ethical monotheism.' "[46] Neither God nor man can be known apart from their mutual relationship. Though God and man are in the same image, still their essential substance (*ruah* and *basar*) is different, which means that the nature of each can better be understood by contrasting it with its opposite. These contrasts Robinson referred to as "polar elements," aspects of divine and human nature which are understood as they enter into a relationship of attraction and repulsion. God's revelation of himself as Spirit is made known to man only when contrasted with man's flesh. In the same manner, God's revelation of himself as holy is made known to man only when contrasted with man's sin.

These contrasts, though valuable, are generalizations and therefore non-Hebraic. Consequently, Robinson chose to turn to the concrete situation of the individual man in his relation to God as more in harmony with Hebrew realism.[47] He approached this study through Hebrew psychology.[48] Man is an animated body dependent upon God for his existence. Each man, through corporate personality, is identified both with his fellowman and with God. Furthermore, this body consists of many separate organs that possess a psychical and ethical quality of their own, what Robinson referred to as "diffused consciousness." When the conception of man is combined with the belief that the Spirit of God gives life (animation) to these bodily organs, it can easily be seen how man's consciousness is a unique sphere in which revelation occurs. The parts of the body possess a quasi-independence, and the invasive Spirit of God could take possession of the organ using it as a means of revelation. God could take possession of the prophet's lips, placing the divine words into them, and thereby enabling the prophetic oracle to become the media of revelation.[49]

The moral life of man also becomes an area in which revelation is manifested.[50] If God discloses himself to man, "then we may expect the highest revelation through the highest and noblest form of mediation, i.e., through the consciousness and especially the moral consciousness of man, made in His image."[51] Morality has its origin, of course, in the social life of the group. Justice and mercy arose in nomadic times and reflect the early beliefs of the people. What is significant in Israel's religion is the transference of justice, mercy, and righteousness to God.[52] This is justified on the basis of a definite kinship between man and God. These attributes are, however, lifted to a higher level when they are transferred to God. The modern man would say that this argument from human to divine is a discovery of God through the human mind. The Hebrew mind, however, would understand the moral consciousness as equally a revelation from God. Revelation and discovery are so united that what is revealed is both God's and man's. "The moral passion for social righteousness cherished by the Hebrew prophet was a genuine 'revelation' of higher values, yet it was not less a personal 'discovery,' and these were blended into the unity of an experience which underlies the prophet's 'Thus saith the Lord.' " [53] This revelation through the moral consciousness of man Robinson referred to as "the higher anthropomorphism." There is no more direct revelation from God than this. The holy of holies in which God truly dwells is none other than the moral consciousness of man.

Rust's position on the revelation through the human consciousness is substantially the same as Robinson's. Chapter V, "Man is the Natural Order," of *Nature and Man in Biblical Thought,* presents an analysis of Hebrew psychology which parallels Robinson's approach. Through an examination of the image of God in man, Rust concludes: "What is present under the imagery and concrete realism of the story, even in its imagery, is the thought that man has endowments which fit him for kinship with God and thereby with a capacity to respond to His Word." [54]

Where Rust goes beyond Robinson's analysis of human consciousness is in his book *Science and Faith.* Using the scientific knowledge he possesses, Rust compares the Hebrew view of man with the modern scientific analysis of human nature. The Hebrew faith did not distinguish sharply between the soul and the body of man as did the Greek view of human nature. Rather, the Hebrew viewed man as a unity, a psycho-physical whole, in which personality was related to the physical body and did not exist apart from it. While it is true that in the New Testament the Greek dichotomy between soul and body begins to exert itself, still the Christian understanding of man lies within the Hebrew tradition. Man is a unity of spirit and flesh, soul and body, a psychosomatic totality. Rust finds this Judeo-Christian view of man supported by modern scientific analyses of the close relationship between man's physical and psychological nature.

The psychosomatic nature of the human person has been borne out increasingly as science has progressed. Evidently our personality, our selfhood, has its roots deep down in the physical and physiological aspects of our bodily structure. More and more we are made aware of the interrelationship of a body chemistry and our personal characteristics, of the intimate bond between the brain and our mental activity, of the implications of our genetic structure for our personal development.[55]

Rust proceeds to develop this thesis through an analysis of the relationship of mental processes and the cerebral cortex, a critique of purely naturalistic views of the nature of mind, and of a discussion of the issues raised by depth psychology. He concludes that the Judeo-Christian religious interpretation of man best accounts for human nature as we know it. As for what man ought to be, Rust finds the ideal perfectly expressed in the incarnation.

The Incarnation points to man as he should be, living in an openness to God and openness to his fellows. It is in this personal disclosure of God that man finds the integrating center of his own life and must make his existential choice. The core of self-conscious mind or spirit is the capacity to love, and without such utter commitment to others, life and thought can be empty.[56]

The third sphere in which revelation occurs is history.[57] Robinson acknowledged that from the Christian point of view history is revelatory because God is uniquely revealed in the life, death, and resurrection of Jesus Christ. Yet such an interpretation of Jesus' life is possible only because of the Hebraic faith upon which Christianity built, which saw God's purposes being accomplished in history. Israel's history is best defined as the mighty acts of God through which God reveals his will for his people. This sacred history began with the exodus event and thereafter the God of Israel was best defined as the out-of-Egypt-bringing-God. It was this God who gave his people the promised land, established the monarchy, raised up Nebuchadrezzar to take Israel into exile, and through Cyrus restored his people to the land. When Israel rebelled against her God, he, in his mercy and justice, punished her; when Israel was obedient to her God, he blessed her. According to Robinson, such an interpretation of history is based upon five "axioms."

These "axioms" are (1) the creative activity of history, (2) its actuality, (3) its values, (4) its subjective factor, and the transformation of meaning which can result from this, and (5) the inclusion of its temporal events within an external order.[58]

For Robinson, an analysis of these five characteristics of history provided an understanding of revelation through history.

The first characteristic of history from the biblical point of view is its creative actuality. Because the Hebraic faith viewed man as a moral agent who makes responsible choices, history, in which decisions are made, must be conceived as dynamic. God does assert his control over history, but this in no way prejudices the freedom of man. If history is viewed from a deterministic standpoint, then man's freedom is undermined and God is rendered unknowable. For the Hebrew, history must be conceived "as the record of a creative work of God, highly complicated through the intervention of human agents, exercising their moral liberty." [59]

The second characteristic of history from the biblical point of view is its actuality, a term which occurs often in Robinson's writings. By actuality Robinson meant "its quality of adding something new, or of expressing in a new way that which before existed only in idea." [60] History possesses a "once-for-allness" which cannot be undone; events "happen" and life is never quite the same as it was before they occurred. The event may clarify the situation or it may introduce a new category into the situation. Applying this characteristic of history to the understanding of revelation, he wrote:

Christian theology, too much influenced by Greek thought, has never done full justice to the Hebraic emphasis in Biblical revelation, the realism of the concrete event. This emphasis makes life itself, rather than the analysis of it, the true revelation of God. The actuality of history, up to and including the Incarnation, is God's supreme medium of utterance to man.[61]

Thirdly, Robinson believed that history is creative of values. Values are not abstract ideas in the mind of men but rather qualities of life-experiences which have emerged through much struggle and anguish. All moral values emerge within an historical situation, but this is not to deny that they have a divine source. Indeed, for Robinson this is the significance of history, that God chooses to reveal such values as goodness, love, mercy, and justice to man through concrete life-experiences.

History also possesses a subjective factor which consists of the power to transform the meaning of an event. Because history is never history in the abstract but always history as understood by someone, events must be given some meaning by an interpreter before they become intelligible. The Babylonian exile is regarded by the Israelites as a national disaster, but later generations see in it the womb from which Judaism is born. Because history has no meaning apart from subjective interpretation, it is useless to speak of it as consisting of "bare-events." When the phrase "the actuality of history" is used, it does not mean the event as it occurred apart from an interpreter, but rather it includes the transforming quality of interpretation. It is this subjective factor which enables history to be a medium of revelation.

The final characteristic of history from the biblical point of view is the inclusion of the temporal events within an eternal order.[62] This involved Robinson in an analysis of the biblical concepts of time and eternity. Today one thinks of time in the abstract, dividing it into units of seconds, minutes, days, weeks, and years. But in the ancient world time was always measured by the changes which occurred in a succession of concrete events. A day was not twenty-four hours but a succession of night and day; seasons were not measured in terms of months but as periods of planting and harvesting. Robinson believed that etymologically the Hebrew word for time, *'eth,* means "occurrence," denoting what one meets in life. His examination of the usage of the term led to three generalizations: (1) the word does not denote the abstract idea "time" but rather a concrete, filled time; (2) God is related to the time-order and uses it to fulfill his purposes; (3) God's acts in history never suspend the time-order. All three points have obvious implications for viewing history as the arena in which God reveals himself to man. Robinson's examination of the main Hebrew term for eternity, *'olam,* reinforced this emphasis upon concrete events. He derived its meaning from the Akkadian *ullanu* which means "remote" in time or space, designating that which was in the ancient past or will be in the distant future, usually also conveying the idea of permanence. To say that God is "eternal" does not mean that he is removed from time, but that his existence is from one end of time to the other. God does not, strictly speaking, transcend time, yet neither is he limited by time as are men. The Hebrew neither speculates about time before which there was a time nor a period after time ceases nor endless time. Eternity is simply the accumulation of many limited time-periods.

Now Robinson noted that when human time is placed into relationship with divine eternity, it is lifted above its usual limitation because God is believed to be above them. This does not mean that this relationship between time and eternity led immediately to a belief in a future life, but it does mean that the religious experience of God transcends qualitatively the normal limitations of time. Man's experience of the divine lifts him above time as a quantitative experience and becomes a new quality in his life. He continues to use a temporal term such as *'olam* to express a supratemporal experience simply because he lacks a more suitable means of expression. The Greek idea of eternity as timelessness was foreign to Hebrew thought.

Robinson's view that history is a medium of revelation made a lasting impression upon Rust. Such topics as the actuality of history, a religious interpretation of history, time and eternity are explored by Rust in articles [63] and in books.[64] Rust does not disagree with anything that has been said concerning Robinson's position. What Rust does is to develop Robinson's position in two directions: (1) he views Christ's life, death, resurrection, and second coming as the fullest expression of God's revelation through history, and (2) he places *heilsgeschichte* within the context of secular history.

Concerning the view of God's self-disclosure in Christ, Rust finds Bultmann's position too divorced from historical actuality. Rust avoids the "existential" approach to the gospel as being too subjective and rather emphasizes the historical nature of revelation. While he does not take literally the New Testament record of Jesus' life and ministry, still he rejects Bultmann's demythologizing as too radical. Jesus' miracles are interpreted in the light of the Old Testament view of miracle, not as signs to create wonder but rather as a means to reveal the nature of God if properly interpreted. Rust carries the historical nature of revelation beyond what most scholars would accept. That which most scholars would call myth, such as the virgin birth, the resurrection, and the empty tomb, Rust regards as historical.

Salvation history is grounded in historical actuality. Miracles are historically attested occurrences. The Virgin Birth is not myth, however difficult it may appear to modern man. The resurrection cannot be dismissed as the creation of faith. Rather it is the historical actuality that vindicates the cross and creates faith. Historical actuality as such must not be confused with pure symbolism even though the interpretation of it may involve us in historical imagery.[65]

Rust's view that matter is energy allows him to accept as historical actuality the biblical references to Christ's resurrection. Christ's body, at one time, can be touched and, at another time, passes through doors. Rust believes it is a higher form of body, transcending but related to physical, earthly existence.[66]

Salvation history continues with the ascension of Christ, and the belief in his coming again at the end-of-the-ages accompanied by a general resurrection. While Rust refers to this as eschatological imagery, still it is understood as a part of salvation history in linear-temporal terms. If what is to come to pass is a new mode of existence, the language by which it is conveyed is related to space and time as we know it. Rust appears to accept an apocalyptic periodization of those events related to the last times. He does not believe that Christ's coming shattered this strictly linear-temporal portrayal of the eschatological hope. Salvation history embraces the consummation. The images employed to convey the last times still possess an historical basis.[67]

Rust also places salvation history within the context of secular history. In his book *Towards a Theological Understanding of History,* Rust examines varied interpretations of history by Spengler, Vico, Toynbee, Comte, and Marx. All non-Christian approaches he views as strictly rational interpretations of history. Because God is in control of all history, Rust believes that general revelation is conveyed in secular history. This he at times equates with natural theology. But this approach to history he contrasts with the Christian understanding of history where God's activity is clearly seen. "Hence God reveals himself in a special stream of historical events which thereby bears the central meaning of all history and becomes the focal point for the actualization of that meaning." [68] For Rust, God's special revelation which began in creation and ends in the consummation contains the key to understanding all history. Salvation history is embraced by secular history and gives it meaning; general revelation occurs whenever salvation history (special revelation) interpenetrates secular history. Salvation history has a universal vision for through the scandal of particularity all secular history is redeemed.

Always we return to the incarnate, resurrected, and ascended Lord. From him our eschatology derives. We wait for the Savior who comes from heaven, our Lord Jesus Christ, whose power enables him to make all things subject unto himself. In the End, his Spirit that dwells in us now will finally lay hold on our mortal bodies, on our involvement in cultural life and the order of nature, and the whole creation will emerge no longer subject to decay. Then we shall know as we are known.[69]

Nature, man, history, these form the three major realms through which revelation is mediated. But in each case, revelation is not possible until there is a response on the part of man. "The divine revelation in Nature, Man, and History is through *acts,* which need to be interpreted through human agency to make them *words* in our ordinary sense." [70] In his book *Inspiration and Revelation in the Old Testament,* Robinson was writing a prolegomena to Old Testament theology. Therefore, in his attempt to embrace as much of the Old Testament as possible, as befits an Old Testament theology, he examined the prophet, priest, sage, and psalmist as interpreters of God's activity.

But clearly for Robinson and for Rust, the major interpreter of God's activity, the person par excellence through whom revelation comes to Israel, is the prophet. There is no substantial distinction between Robinson and Rust at this point; but Rust's interest in the fulfilment of Old Testament promise in the New Testament does lead him to examine the parallel role of the apostles in revelation more than does Robinson. It is therefore altogether fitting that this chapter close with an examination of the place of prophet and apostle in the revelatory process.[71]

The main function of prophecy is to interpret nature, man, and history as areas in which God is active.[72] Nature is interpreted not by laws of cause and effect, but as the physical universe created, sustained, and transformed by God. Through the response of faith, nature reveals the mystery, majesty, and wisdom of God; through the prophetic interpreter, nature acquires a voice to proclaim the glory of God. The prophet also interprets man as under the divine control. Here Robinson viewed the prophetic consciousness as revelatory in a two-fold sense, as both the interpreter of man and as the direct medium of revelation. Hosea looks to his own human experience with Gomer and interprets it as God's relation to Israel.[73] The solitary confessions of Jeremiah grant him access to the very mind of God.[74] But above all, it is history that receives the prophetic interpretation by which it becomes a revelation of the nature and will of God. "The changing events of political and social circumstance, always admitting a secular interpretation, were transformed by the prophets into firmly controlled activities of God." [75] All three realms are lifted to a new level of meaning by the faith of the prophet. And yet the prophet would never say that it is his interpretation that makes them revelatory. He believes that what he declares is God's word to Israel clearly seen in nature, man, and history. Where does he acquire such insight? The prophet answers that he has stood in the council of Yahweh and there received his commission to speak for God. By articulating this revelation, however, the prophet adds a new dimension to the revelation, for his words "thus saith Yahweh" liberate the word of God which thereby becomes an objective fact which accomplishes God's will. This revelation as seen in nature, man, and history is transformed through the prophetic consciousness into revelation as the spoken word which reached its culmination for Israel in the written word.

The Christian maintains that this prophetic role in revelation is continued by the New Testament apostles. It is the apostles who responded to God's activity in Jesus Christ and bore witness to it as the full revelation of God. The Christian may affirm that Jesus Christ is the Word of God incarnate, the fulfilment of the promises to Israel of old, but in so doing he must also acknowledge that this revelation comes to him through the faith of the apostles. Without the response of prophet and apostle, no revelation is possible. God has acted on behalf of man, but the act alone apart from faith is never revelatory.

[Revelation] is a particular series of historical events which itself carried the meaning and redemption of all history. In the center of it stand the interpretative figures of the witnesses, the prophets and the apostles, and those who gathered around them. To them the revelation came. Indeed they belong to the revelation itself, for without the God-given insight which was granted to them, the Word of God which came to them within their historical situation, our own faith would be impossible.[76]

These words were written by Rust. They could have been written by Robinson. Both men alike used their scholarly abilities to analyze the concept of revelation in order that it might not only be understood more fully but also be experienced more deeply. Both the communities of faith and of learning are indebted to them.

NOTES

[1] See the biography of Robinson by Ernest A. Payne, *Henry Wheeler Robinson: Scholar, Teacher, Principal, A Memoir* (London: Nisbet and Co., Ltd., 1946).

[2] There is increasing scholarly interest in the subject of revelation. See H. D. McDonald, *Ideas of Revelation: An Historical Study, A.D. 1700 to A.D. 1860* (London: Macmillan & Co., Ltd., 1959); Gerald F. Downing, *Has Christianity a Revelation?* (London: SCM Press, Ltd., 1964); Rene Latourelle, *Theology of Revelation* (Staten Island: Alba House, 1966); Avery Dulles, *Revelation and the Quest for Unity* (Washington-Cleveland: Corpus Books, 1968); Avery Dulles, *Revelation Theology: A History* (New York: Seabury Press, 1969); Wolfhart Pannenberg, ed. in association with Rolf Rendtorff, Trutz Rendtorff, and Ulrich Wilkins, *Revelation as History* (New York: Macmillan Co., 1968); E. Schillebeeckx, *Revelation and Theology*, vol. I (New York: Sheed and Ward, 1967) and vol. II (New York: Sheed and Ward, 1968).

[3] H. Wheeler Robinson, "The Theology of the Old Testament (The Philosophy of Revelation and the Characteristic Doctrines)," in H. Wheeler Robinson, ed., *Record and Revelation: Essays on the Old Testament by Members of the Society for Old Testament Study* (Oxford: At the Clarendon Press, 1951; first published, 1938), pp. 303-320.

[4] *Ibid.*, p. 303.

[5] H. Wheeler Robinson, "History and Revelation," *The Baptist Quarterly*, New Series, VII (1934-1935), 3.

[6] H. Wheeler Robinson, *Redemption and Revelation: In the Actuality of History* (London: Nisbet and Co., Ltd., 1942), pp. xxxviii-xli.

7 *Ibid.,* p. xlv; H. Wheeler Robinson, *The Christian Experience of the Holy Spirit* (London: Nisbet & Co., Ltd., 1928), pp. 75, 96; *The Religious Ideas of the Old Testament* (London: Gerald Duckworth & Co., Ltd., 1952; first published, 1913), p. 217.

8 H. Wheeler Robinson, *The Christian Experience of the Holy Spirit,* p. 26.

9 See H. Wheeler Robinson, *The Religious Ideas of the Old Testament,* pp. 24-25, 216-222.

10 The two final chapters were not delivered in the lectures but were added to form a conclusion to the work.

11 In other works Robinson listed six different types of media for revelation in the Old Testament: nature; prophetic consciousness; history; priests, kings, patriarchs, and sages; cultus; written Torah. See H. Wheeler Robinson, *Redemption and Revelation,* pp. 98-100; "The Bible as the Word of God," in H. Wheeler Robinson, ed., *The Bible in Its Ancient and English Versions* (Oxford: At the Clarendon Press, 1940), pp. 278-283; "The Theology of the Old Testament," in *Record and Revelation,* pp. 312-320.

12 H. Wheeler Robinson, *Redemption and Revelation,* p. 96.

13 *Ibid.,* pp. 126-130.

14 H. Wheeler Robinson, *The Christian Experience of the Holy Spirit,* p. 93.

15 In *The Veil of God* (London: Nisbet & Co., Ltd., 1936), Robinson examined nature, history, redemption, Scripture, the inner life, and death as areas of life which both reveal the nature of God and also hide him from us.

16 H. Wheeler Robinson, *The Christian Experience of the Holy Spirit,* p. 90.

17 H. Wheeler Robinson, *Inspiration and Revelation in the Old Testament* (Oxford: At the Clarendon Press, 1953; first published 1946), p. 277.

18 H. Wheeler Robinson, *Redemption and Revelation,* p. 21.

19 See Eric Rust, "The Possible Lines of Development of Demythologizing," *The Journal of Bible and Religion,* XXVII (January, 1959), 32-40; "Interpreting the Resurrection," *The Journal of Bible and Religion,* XXIX (January, 1961), 25-34; "The Holy Spirit, Nature, and Man," *Review and Expositor,* 63 (Spring, 1966), 157-176; "The Authority of the Scripture— The Word of God and the Bible," *Review and Expositor,* 57 (January, 1960), 26-57; "The Atoning Act of God in Christ," *Review and Expositor,* 59 (January, 1962), 57-70; "Time and Eternity in Biblical Thought," *Theology Today,* X (October, 1953), 327-356; "Nature and Man in Theological Perspective," *Review and Expositor,* 69 (Winter, 1972), 11-22.

20 Eric Rust, *Towards a Theological Understanding of History* (New York: Oxford University Press, 1963), p. 49.

21 *Ibid.,* p. 51.

22 *Ibid.,* p. 52.

23 Eric Rust, *Salvation History: A Biblical Interpretation* (Richmond: John Knox Press, 1962), p. 23. See also *Towards a Theological Understanding of History,* p. 10.

24 Eric Rust, *Towards a Theological Understanding of History,* p. 53.

25 Eric Rust, *Salvation History,* p. 27. See also "The Authority of the Scripture—The Word of God and The Bible," *Review and Expositor,* 57 (January, 1960), 38-42.

26 Eric Rust, *Salvation History,* pp. 42-43.

27 H. Wheeler Robinson, *Inspiration and Revelation in the Old Testament,* p. 4 and *Redemption and Revelation,* pp. 118-126.

28 H. Wheeler Robinson, "Hebrew Psychology in Relation to Pauline Anthropology," in *Mansfield College Essays* (London: Hodder and Stoughton, 1909), pp. 265-286 and "Hebrew Psychology," in Arthur S. Peake, Ed., *The People and the Book: Essays on the Old Testament* (Oxford: At the Clarendon Press, 1925), pp. 353-382.

29 H. Wheeler Robinson, *Inspiration and Revelation in the Old Testament,* p. 15.

30 *Ibid.,* pp. 17-33. See also *The Religious Ideas of the Old Testament,* pp. 70-76, 190-193.

31 Revised Standard Version of the Bible, copyrighted 1946, 1952, © 1971, 1973.

32 H. Wheeler Robinson, "The Nature-Miracles of the Old Testament," *The Journal of Theological Studies,* XLV (January-April, 1944), 1-12 which was reprinted as the third chapter in *Inspiration and Revelation in the Old Testament.* See also *Redemption and Revelation,* pp. 118-126 and *The Religious Ideas of the Old Testament,* pp. 107-108.

33 "The Nature-Miracles of the Old Testament," *The Journal of Theological Studies,* XLV (January-April, 1944), 1.

34 H. Wheeler Robinson, *The Religious Ideas of the Old Testament,* pp. 102-103, 107-108;

"The Cross of Jeremiah," in *The Cross in the Old Testament* (London: SCM Press, Ltd., 1955; first published, 1916), p. 181; *The Old Testament: Its Making and Meaning* (London: University of London Press, Ltd., 1953; first published, 1937), p. 138.

[35] H. Wheeler Robinson, "The Nature-Miracles of the Old Testament," *The Journal of Theological Studies,* XLV (January-April, 1944), 4-5.

[36] *Ibid.,* pp. 9-10.

[37] Eric Rust, *Nature and Man in Biblical Thought* (London: Lutterworth Press, 1953), p. 263.

[38] *Ibid.,* p. 272.

[39] *Ibid.,* p. 300.

[40] See Karl Heim, *The Transformation of the Scientific World View* (New York: Harper & Brothers, 1953); Ian G. Barbour, *Christianity and the Scientist* (New York: Association Press, 1960); Harold K. Schilling, *Science and Religion: An Interpretation of Two Communities* (New York: Charles Scribner's Son, 1962); Ian G. Barbour, ed., *Science and Religion; New Perspectives on the Dialogue* (New York: Harper & Row, 1968); M. A. Jeeves, *The Scientific Enterprise and Christian Faith* (London: Tyndale Press, 1969); Langdon Gilkey, *Religion and the Scientific Future: Reflections on Myth, Science, and Theology* (New York: Harper & Row, 1970); Harold K. Schilling, *The New Consciousness in Science and Religion* (Philadelphia: United Church Press, 1973); Ian G. Barbour, *Myths, Models, and Paradigms; A Comparative Study in Science and Religion* (New York: Harper & Row, 1974).

[41] Eric Rust, *Science and Faith: Towards a Theological Understanding of Nature* (New York: Oxford University Press, 1967), p. 129.

[42] *Ibid.,* p. 316.

[43] For critical reviews of Rust's book *Science and Faith,* see D. M. Mackay's review in *Scottish Journal of Theology,* 21 (1968), 479-481 and Harmon L. Smith's review in *Interpretation: A Journal of Bible and Theology,* XXII (July, 1968), 366-367.

[44] H. Wheeler Robinson, *Inspiration and Revelation in the Old Testament,* Part II, chs. IV-VII, pp. 49-105; *Redemption and Revelation,* pp. 131-157 which includes a reprint of "The Psychology and Metaphysic of 'Thus Saith Yahweh,'" *Zeitschrift für die alttestamentliche Wissenschaft,* Band XLI (1923), 1-15.

[45] H. Wheeler Robinson, *Inspiration and Revelation in the Old Testament,* pp. 49-62.

[46] *Ibid.,* pp. 49-50.

[47] *Ibid.,* pp. 63-77.

[48] H. Wheeler Robinson, "Hebrew Psychology in Relation to Pauline Anthropology," in *Mansfield College Essays,* pp. 265-286 and "Hebrew Psychology," in Arthur S. Peake, ed., *The People and the Book: Essays on the Old Testament,* pp. 353-382.

[49] H. Wheeler Robinson, *The Religious Ideas of the Old Testament,* pp. 83-87; "The Theology of the Old Testament," in G. Henton Davies and Alan Richardson, eds., *The Teachers' Commentary* (London: SCM Press, Ltd., 1955), p. 94.

[50] H. Wheeler Robinson, *Inspiration and Revelation in the Old Testament,* pp. 78-91; *The Religious Ideas of the Old Testament,* pp. 38-46.

[51] H. Wheeler Robinson, "The Theology of the Old Testament," in *Record and Revelation,* p. 315.

[52] H. Wheeler Robinson, *The Religious Ideas of the Old Testament,* pp. 65-70.

[53] H. Wheeler Robinson, *The Christian Experience of the Holy Spirit,* p. 96.

[54] Eric Rust, *Nature and Man in Biblical Thought,* p. 121.

[55] Eric Rust, *Science and Faith,* p. 207.

[56] *Ibid.,* pp. 269-270.

[57] H. Wheeler Robinson, *Inspiration and Revelation in the Old Testament,* pp. 106-159; *Redemption and Revelation,* pp. xxv-xlviii, 87-92; "History and Revelation," *The Baptist Quarterly,* New Series, VII (1934-1935), 1-13; *The Religious Ideas of the Old Testament,* pp. 216-222; "The Christian Gospel of Redemption," in W. R. Matthews, ed., *The Christian Faith: Essays in Explanation and Defence* (London: Eyre and Spottswood, 1936), pp. 216-223.

[58] H. Wheeler Robinson, *Redemption and Revelation,* p. xxvi.

[59] *Ibid.,* p. xxix.

[60] H. Wheeler Robinson, "History and Revelation," *The Baptist Quarterly,* New Series, VII (1934-1935), 8.

61 H. Wheeler Robinson, *Redemption and Revelation*, p. xxxv.

62 H. Wheeler Robinson, *Inspiration and Revelation in the Old Testament*, pp. 106-122; "The Christian Doctrine of Eternal Life," being a lecture by Robinson in Ernest A. Payne, *Henry Wheeler Robinson, op. cit.*, pp. 182-183.

63 Eric Rust, "Time and Eternity in Biblical Thought," *Theology Today*, X (October, 1953), 347-356; "The Possible Lines of Development of Demythologizing," *The Journal of Bible and Religion*, XXVII (January, 1959), 32-40; "The Authority of the Scripture—The Word of God and the Bible," *Review and Expositor*, 57 (January, 1960), 26-57; "Interpreting the Resurrection," *The Journal of Bible and Religion*, XXIX (January, 1961), 25-34; "The Atoning Act of God in Christ," *Review and Expositor*, 59 (January, 1962), 57-70.

64 Eric Rust, *The Christian Understanding of History; Salvation History; Towards a Theological Understanding of History*.

65 Eric Rust, *Salvation History*, p. 41; see also "Interpreting the Resurrection," *The Journal of Bible and Religion*, XXIX (January, 1961), 25-34.

66 Eric Rust, *Salvation History*, pp. 219-228.

67 Eric Rust, *Towards a Theological Understanding of History*, pp. 257-265.

68 *Ibid.*, pp. 14-15.

69 *Ibid.*, p. 265.

70 H. Wheeler Robinson, *Inspiration and Revelation in the Old Testament*, p. 159.

71 It is beyond the scope of this chapter to present Robinson's and Rust's analyses of the prophetic consciousness. Because nature, man, and history are not media of revelation apart from the prophetic-apostolic interpretation of them as such, the following section concentrates on a point which has been discussed throughout the chapter. Repetition in the argument is to emphasize the major importance of the role of interpretation in the process of revelation.

72 H. Wheeler Robinson, *Inspiration and Revelation in the Old Testament*, pp. 160-172; *The Religious Ideas of the Old Testament*, pp. 119-123; 219-222.

73 H. Wheeler Robinson, "The Cross of Hosea," in Ernest A. Payne, ed., *Two Hebrew Prophets: Studies in Hosea and Ezekiel* (London: Lutterworth Press, 1948), pp. 21-22.

74 H. Wheeler Robinson, "The Cross of Jeremiah," in *The Cross in the Old Testament*, pp. 154-173.

75 H. Wheeler Robinson, *Inspiration and Revelation in the Old Testament*, p. 163.

76 Eric Rust, "The Authority of the Scripture—The Word of God and The Bible," *Review and Expositor*, 57 (January, 1960), 38.

10.
The Apologetic Challenge of the Radical Theological Movement
Osadolor Imasogie

The radical theological or death-of-God movement of the early sixties did not come out of the blue as it were. It was the culmination of a long process of secularization which began even prior to the Renaissance and the birth of modern science. Great men like Rene Descartes (1596-1650), William Paley (1743-1805), David Hume (1711-1776), Immanuel Kant (1747-1804), George F. Hegel (1770-1831), Soren Kierkegaard (1813-1855), Karl Barth (1886-1968), Dietrich Bonhoeffer (1906-1945), etc., each in his own way, made desperate but virtually unsuccessful attempts to put out the fire of secularism. The conflagration which was constantly fuelled by people like Auguste Comte (1798-1857), Ludwig Feuerbach (1804-1872), Friedrich Nietzsche (1844-1900), Karl Marx (1818-1883), to mention only a few, and aided by the phenomenonal breakthrough in science, continued its devastation of spirituality.

While the earlier theologians who made attempts to make Christianity relevant in the face of secularism did so within the historical Christian tradition, the radical theologians attempted to achieve the same purpose at the expense of the core of Christian orthodoxy. The contention of this writer is that no authentic Christian apologetics can be done without existential acceptance of the biblical revelation as mediated through the Scriptures, historical Christian tradition, and the Holy Spirit. Thus, the burden of this chapter is threefold. Firstly, it will attempt to present, as objectively as possible, the apologetic effort which the radical theologians make to come to grips with the spiritual problems of the secular man. Secondly, it will be shown that this attempt falls short of its aim. Thirdly, it will be demonstrated that on the basis of Casserley's insight, the orthodox Christian apologist can succeed where the radical theologians fail.

167

Radical Theological Movement

The limitation imposed by the nature of such a chapter as this makes it impossible to treat all of the men in the bandwagon of the radical theological movement. Consequently only three of them who appear to be most representative of the group will be considered here. These are Thomas Altizer, William Hamilton, and Paul Matthew Van Buren.

Thomas Altizer (1923-)

Thomas Altizer is the most radical of the three radical theologians to be considered here. He, like others, is convinced that the latter half of the twentieth century is an age in which the cultural consciousness of God and the concept of transcendence are completely absent. However, he is equally convinced that the gospel message, especially its doctrine of incarnation, is still relevant for the people of the age. But in order to make its relevance available to the people, the theologian must go the route of atheism. Altizer puts this strongly when he declares:

> If there is one clear portal to the twentieth century, it is a passage through the death of God, the collapse of any meaning or reality lying beyond the newly discovered radical immanence of modern man, an immanence dissolving even the memory or shadow of transcendence.[1]

In an age where this is the case, the Christian, according to Altizer, is faced with *only* two alternatives. The Christian theologian may decide to cling to the antiquated traditional theological jargons that have become meaningless to this age. He may, on the other hand, dare to jettison the historical expression of Christianity, including the church and all it stands for, and strike out on a new path of atheism.

Altizer opts for the latter alternative, and to make it real and radical, he would reject the Bible and the claim that the canon is closed. For him historical research has revealed that "the New Testament can no longer be accorded a literal or final authority." [2] Altizer is also convinced that modern scholarship has detected a discrepancy between the biblical record and the historical Jesus. The consensus now, according to him, is that it is only

> when a particular event or saying in the Gospels can be known as being most estranged from the life and faith of the early church that it can most

clearly be judged to be a true reflection of the acts and proclamation of the historical Jesus.[3]

In view of all these conclusions, Altizer would turn to other sources, namely, Oriental mysticism and the insight of men who "are profoundly sensitive to the profanity of our civilization and yet who know a kind of faith, a means of life affirmation in the midst of that civilization." [4] Included in the list of such men are Sigmund Freud, William Blake, George Hegel, and Friedrich Nietzsche. Altizer emphasizes the fact that the last three on this list saw the Christian God as "the transcendent enemy of the fullness and the passion of Man's life in the world, and only through God's death can humanity be liberated from that repression which is the real ruler of history." [5] The radical Christian must follow the footsteps of these men and renounce the God of the church. He cannot return to "either the word or the person of the original Jesus of Nazareth." [6] Hence, he must disavow, "both the literal and the historical interpretation of the Bible, demanding instead, a pneumatic . . . understanding of the Word." [7] The goal of the radical Christian theologian is what Altizer calls a "total union with the Word." [8] What does he mean by a total union with the Word, and how does he intend to effect this if he discards Christian tradition, the Bible, and the church?

To answer these questions Altizer turns his attention to non-Christian religions, especially the Oriental religions. His aim is to prove the uniqueness of Christianity and its complete independence of the Bible and the Christian traditional expression of it. According to Altizer, Oriental mysticism is religion par excellence, when religion is defined as man's attempt to retreat from the world. Oriental mysticism "is a way of world negation" [9] by means of which the religionist attempts to dissolve the mundane forms of experience. The ultimate goal of this negation, however, is to effect "an interior recovery of a sacred Totality, a primordial Totality embodying in a unified form all those antinomies that have created and alienated and estranged existence." [10] Altizer interprets this as a detour by means of which the mystic strives to attain a total redemption. This total redemption is possible only by the dissolution of the consciousness of the fallen world. This act of dissolution is expected to usher in "the original identity of an unfallen cosmos." [11] Thus the "oriental mysticism is a backward movement to the primordial Totality." [12] On the basis of this, Altizer concludes that all religions have dialectical elements as they all strive to negate the "given" in order to reach the primordial. He substantiates this by calling attention to the Hegelian speculative philosophy which identifies religion with philosophy. As he declared, "Hegel believed that religion is identical with dialectical or true philosophical understanding in so far as both negate the Given." [13]

In the opinion of Altizer, no matter what Christianity in its traditional form may say to the contrary, it, like Oriental mysticism, is world-denying. The truth of this charge is revealed in its

nostalgia for a lost paradise, a quest for an original innocence, a cultic representation . . . of a sacred history of the past, (a longing for) a distant epiphany of Christ, a belief in a primordial God. . . .[14]

All this belies the Christian claim to the uniqueness of Christ. In order to preserve the uniqueness of Christ, the radical theologian must of necessity evolve a religionless Christianity stripped of every vestige of the traditional garb. He must, therefore, Altizer declares,

renounce every temptation to return to an original or primordial sacred or to follow a backward path leading to an earlier and presumably purer form of the Word or to seek a total silence in which both word and world will have disappeared.[15]

The uniqueness of Christ for Altizer lies in the fact that in the incarnation the sacred became the profane. But this will forever elude the Christian unless the kenosis of the spirit is understood radically. This must be done without any attempt to return by the back door to the primordial form by such devices as the idea of ascension and the transcendent God. Radical Christianity must reverse the

orthodox confession, affirming that "God is Jesus," . . . rather than "Jesus is God," . . . God becomes incarnate in the Word, and becomes fully incarnate, thereby ceasing to exist or to be present in his primordial form . . . he had . . . negated his transcendent form.[16]

In other words, when "God" died on the cross he took an irrevocable step and, ever since this historical event, has remained "a process embodying a progressive movement of spirit into flesh." [17] Hence the present " 'cultural fact' of God's absence from modern civilization is now viewed as a historical actualization in the consciousness of all men of an event which took place initially in the person of Jesus." [18] But to continue to deny this as does the Christian tradition is to misunderstand the full impact of the event. A transcendent God is a contradiction and at best a lifeless God. Only through the "realization of the death of God in human experience can faith be liberated from the authority and power of the primordial God." [19] Thus only radical Christians can celebrate the age of atheism as a historical authentication of the incarnate Word.

Unless the Christian is liberated from the backward-looking mentality of the traditional Christian church, he cannot discern the new form in which the incarnate Word manifests itself in the world today. This new form of manifestation can only be detected by embracing the profane world with all its pains and joys believing that "the center of life is everywhere and eternity is now." [20] For, as Altizer puts it, "If a contemporary epiphany of Christ has abolished all images of transcendence and emptied the transcendent realm, then we can meet that epiphany only by totally embracing the world." [21]

Altizer's apologetic program may be summarized thus: The modern world no longer experiences the divine as transcendence. Hence it is useless for the church to continue to appeal to it in theological jargons that have become meaningless. The best way to make the gospel message relevant to this godless world is to affirm that the present godless situation is the inevitable historical actualization of the Christian doctrine of incarnation. God was Jesus who died on the cross, and by dying on the cross God ceased to be and has thus been metamorphosed into the historical process. Henceforth he may be met only as one embraces the secular world in an act of life-affirmation. The contemporary immobility and silence of the church is due to its failure to come to grips with this newly discovered fact. Without this discovery the church cannot move into the discernment of the new form of the epiphany of the incarnate Word. Indeed, as he describes it, it is the church's

refusal to abandon the God of its tradition, and to free itself from those forms of faith rooted in the eternal existence and the ever continuing activity of God which has turned it away from a full movement into our world. [22]

Altizer sees no hope of success for any attempt to revitalize the traditional church as a means for meeting the need of the secular man. The break between the old and the new world views is a radical one. What is needed is "a death of God theology . . . a theology that chooses to speak at a time in which God is dead." [23] Of course, this, as has been argued, consists simply in fully embracing the secular world in an act of life-affirmation. In the process the new form of the *diffused* incarnate Word may be apprehended.

William Hamilton (1924-   )

In William Hamilton's writings one encounters a biographical account of the progression of his spiritual odyssey. First, Hamilton was concerned with the difficulty in affirming God's reality in the face of sufferings and in a secular age. At this stage he feels that God is absent and passionately lives in hope and prayer that He might "emerge on the other side." [24] His later writings reveal his final resignation that God is probably gone forever and that the Christian will have to learn to live without him. This is reflected in his answer to a point-blank question as to what he means by the death of God:

> Death of God does not refer to a disappearance of a psychological capacity . . . [it] does not mean that some ways of thinking or talking about God in traditional Christianity are done for. . . . The God whose death is believed in is the Christian God. [25]

As indicated already, Hamilton comes to his atheistic position for at least two reasons. In the first place, he is convinced that the twentieth century is a postreligious era from which the consciousness of God has been banished. Under such a circumstance it is only fair, he argues, that a new Protestant reformation should be set in motion. To substantiate this need, Hamilton goes on to describe his understanding of the earlier Protestant reformations. The first reformation, he maintains, was interpreted as a "victory for the autonomous religious personality freed from the tyranny of hierarchy and institution while man's relation to God was described as unmediated and available to all." [26] Later the neo-orthodox theologians came to view their brand of reformation not as a victory for the religious personality but as "the theological discovery of the righteous God," [27] before whom the helpless man stands in mortal dread. The emphasis then fell on justification by faith, since no man can stand justified in the presence of the righteous God.

Unlike the neo-orthodox era, the modern period is an age of optimism in man's ability to change his world. This era has no consciousness of tragedy because it has no consciousness of God. As he puts it,

> there can't be tragedies . . . because the presence of tragedy requires the presence of God or gods and the presence of the gods is just what we do not have. The death of tragedy is due to the death of God.[28]

Hamilton is under no illusion as to the despair which modern man faces, but he contends that despair is no tragedy. Man faces his despair without reference to God but convinced that "the human conditions that created it can be overcome, whether those conditions be poverty, discrimination or mental illness." [29] This new understanding demands a new form of Protestant reformation, a reformation which has nothing to do with God, guilt and forgiveness but which still takes a form of faith. Here faith cannot be understood as "a means of apprehending God at all . . . this faith is more like a place, a being with or standing beside the neighbor." [30] Understood this way, faith becomes love, he continues. "Faith," he says, "has almost collapsed into love, and the Protestant is no longer defined as the forgiven sinner . . . but as the one beside the neighbor, beside the enemy at the disposal of the man in need." [31]

Apart from the lack of a God-consciousness of the twentieth-century man, the second event that led Hamilton down the path of atheism is the problem of suffering, both as represented by the Second World War and as reflected in the writings of Dostoevsky and Camus. For him the problem of suffering

put an end . . . to the classical doctrines of Providence, and thus to the very center of the Biblical doctrine of God. A God to whom could be ascribed the death of the six million Jews in our time would be a monster.[32]

On the basis of these reasons, what is needed is a new interpretation of Christianity that denies the authenticity of any reference to the divine. With the denial of divine reference, Hamilton contends, must also go the idea of the church as the "body of Christ." The new theologian is no longer concerned with "ecclesiastical questions about what the church must do to revitalize itself . . . the theologian does not and can not go to church, . . . he is alienated . . . , he must live outside." [33] He must now move from God, the church, from the Bible, from Christendom into the world. The radical theologian can no longer take preaching, prayer, worship, ordination, and the sacraments seriously.[34] That the break with traditional Christianity is final for Hamilton is further understood in the following statement:

In the past the theologian would distinguish between God, Christendom, Christianity and the church, so a different balance of "yes" and "no" could be uttered to each. Now he finds himself equally alienated from each of the realities represented by the four terms and he says "no" to each.[35]

At this juncture one may wonder why Hamilton's radical theologian still claims to be a Christian if he renounces God, the Bible, the church, and its doctrines. Strangely enough, Hamilton has no difficulty in explaining this. The death-of-God theologian retains the name Christian

because it is the Christian God that is referred to in the phrase. . . . The Christian is also a man in relation to Jesus and the radical theologian affirming the "death of God" claims to be a Christian in this second sense as well.[36]

Jesus minus the Christ then becomes the example for the radical theologian, and his aim is to find the Jesus in his new manifestation that lies concealed in the world. If the Bible is rejected, where does the radical theologian find his knowledge of this Jesus that is hidden in the world? Hamilton simply says that the New Testament's picture is enough grounds for following his example. Hamilton asserts:

Jesus can be known, I am claiming; enough in the record can be trusted, so that the kind of things he did, the way he stood before men, the way he taught, suffered, and died, can be discerned and believed.[37]

Armed with this biblical portrayal of Jesus, the radical theologian can discern new ways in which Jesus may be found in the world. In other words, taking his life as presented in the New Testament as a criterion, the new "Jesus" can be found "concealed in the struggle for truth, justice, beauty, or by becoming Jesus to the neighbor in the world." [38]

Since the New Testament record presents Jesus as utterly dependent upon God who was very real to him, one would have thought that Hamilton would find it difficult to become attached to Jesus without his God. Hamilton considered this and came to the conclusion that Jesus' dependence upon God as portrayed in the New Testament should be interpreted as a reflection of the world view of the time in which he lived and labored. Now that that world view has been superseded by one in which the reality of God is no longer reckoned with, Jesus' consciousness of God should constitute no problem to accepting him for what he did without tying this to a God that is no more. For instance, Hamilton argues,

If Jesus' demonology and cosmology and eschatology were taken as first century views, appropriate then, not so now, needing re-interpretation and understanding but not literal assent, what is inherently different about Jesus' *theology?* [39]

Does Hamilton have a specific apologetic strategy for getting the non-Christian world to discover the Jesus concealed in this world? Hamilton denies any desire to appeal to the scientific man per se. Says he,

It is not that we want to appeal to something—secularism, say—that is out there; but because something has happened to us which we are bound to accept and accepting it we want to see what this entails for the Christian profession.[40]

He concedes that his is a Christian humanism, "if humanism means a belief that there are no viable objects of loyalty beyond man, his values, his communities, his life." [41] It would seem then that Hamilton's approach has indirect apologetic implications. First, he affirms with the scientific age that there is no transcendent reality beyond this world. Hence, man must face his problems alone, for within him lies the ability to solve them. Secondly, the Christian must affirm that for him there is something about Jesus which not only draws one to him but also demands one's allegiance. Thus Hamilton's creed reads: Jesus is the one

before whom I stand, the one whose way with others is also to be my way because there is something there, in his words, his life, his way with others, his death, that I do not find elsewhere. I am drawn, and I have given my allegiance.[42]

Thirdly, it is to be hoped that as the Christian becomes involved in selfless and sacrificial activities as a neighbor to the needy and thereby "becoming Jesus" to the needy, the world will be moved to join him. In the act of joining him and thus becoming involved with others, the non-Christian world will come to discover Jesus as the man for others. For "the Christian life is finding Jesus in your neighbor." [43]

Paul Matthew Van Buren (1924-   )

Like other radical theologians, Van Buren takes the secular age too seriously. He feels compelled to translate the gospel message into a language he considers compatible with the secular age. His purpose, as he expresses it, is to explore a suitable answer to the question: "How may a Christian who is himself a secular man understand the Gospel in a secular way?" [44] The answer to this question, according to Van Buren, "will be reached by analyzing what a man means when he uses the language of faith, when he repeats the earliest Christian confession: 'Jesus is Lord.' " [45]

Before plunging into this problem Van Buren decides to describe the secular age and how it has become impossible for the secular man to understand the language of the gospel. The secular age is "characterized by empirical attitudes, deep interest in questions of human life, this 'side of the beyond,' and a corresponding lack of interest in what were once felt to be great metaphysical questions." [46] Consequently, the secular man bases all his understanding on models drawn from human experience. He distrusts any claims to knowledge in all other ways outside an empirical frame of reference. This new human understanding transforms the latter half of the twentieth century into an age in which the concept of the Absolute has been dissolved. It becomes the period which witnesses, in the words of Van Buren, "the passing of a world-view and habit of thought or its quiet replacement by another and different habit of thought." [47] Van Buren laments the fact that this "socio-psychologial fact of our time" [48] is so widespread that no one seems to be aware of its implications until one begins to analyze the language of faith. For, as he sees it, to use the language of faith in this situation is like "attempting to operate in a world without an Absolute while using ideas and languages drawn from a world in which the idea of the Absolute had an important place." [49] This inevitably leads to confusion for a man who lives in an age where the term "God" does not constitute a point of reference.

In spite of the secular atmosphere which now prevails, Van Buren is convinced that religion is such an integral part of man's life that any true study of him cannot ignore his religious life. Hence, theology is still essential to an adequate understanding of man if and only when it is "seen in the context of human experience." [50] Understood this way theology must become

responsible to human society, not to the church. Its orientation is humanistic, not divine. Its norms must lie in the role which it performs in human life. . . . The issue is not whether certain ideas or certain ways of expressing these ideas are faithful to some inherited . . . ancient text.[51]

From this perspective Van Buren does not consider the task of the radical theologian to be different in kind from that of older theologians. For him theology has always been the difficult task of translating man's religious ideas of the past so as to make them shed light on man's deepest experiences. Therefore, for the new theologian, theology still remains "the endless task of translation, of appropriating for today and in our way the insights and wisdom of the past in such a way as to throw light on our deepest experiences." [52]

This being the case, the new theology must do justice to the present historical context. It need not feel obligated to the form and content which religion "assumed in the context of the cultures into which it was born and took shape." [53] Van Buren agrees that the Judeo-Christian religion in its ancient form had helped to shape the Western culture. But the central concern now is how to interpret it in such a way that "that religious thought might in some manner serve a constructive role in the further shaping of the human life." [54]

Having now established the need of religion as an integral part of the human life (including the life of the secular man), Van Buren turns to the task of interpreting the gospel for the secular man. Here he falls back on the modified form of Wittgenstein's "language-game." Van Buren maintains that each assertion in a "language-game" has its "home." "Different kinds of language are appropriate to different situations." [55] For instance, he continues, "the language of love is not that of biology, nor is the language of politics that of physics." [56] To understand any language, therefore, its historical context and the subject matter must be taken into account. As it has been pointed out, the secular man is empirically oriented; hence any language whose assertions cannot be verified has little appeal for him. The secular man classifies language into cognitive and noncognitive categories. "God-talk" belongs to the noncognitive category, but that does not mean that it is not verifiable in some other ways. Religious statements such as the "Lord appeared to me" fall under what he calls "sense-content" assertions. Such statements cannot be verified by the traditional empirical means; nonetheless, they are verifiable. "The way to verify a statement of sense-content is to see if the words and actions of the person who makes the statement conform to it." [57]

Van Buren does not see any point in continuing to use the term "God" in the secular age. For the term represents a dimension of life which was once regarded as the realm of the Absolute, a concept which is no longer viable in the secular era. In any case what is important is to decide "whether Christianity is fundamentally about God or about man." [58] Of course, Van Buren opts for the latter. If Christianity is fundamentally about man, then its "language about God is . . . a dated way among a number of ways of saying what it is that Christianity wants to say about man and human life and history." [59] In view of this, to continue to use the word "God" in the secular age is not only to obscure the intention of Christianity, declares Van Buren, but also to mislead modern man. In the light of this, the term "God" must be translated into language about man. In doing this translation Van Buren must first go to the New Testament to substantiate his thesis that the "Gospel, whatever else it is or has to say, concerns Jesus of Nazareth." [60] The Gospels speak of Jesus of Nazareth as an unusual individual who was utterly free, free from "anxiety and the need to establish his own identity." [61] This Jesus, according to the Gospels, was not only free from himself; he was also free from "familial claims, religious rites and obligations of his people." [62] Apart from being free from people, the Gospels go further, in the miracle stories, to present him "mythologically as being free from the limitations of natural forces," [63] even to the point of daring to "act in the place of God! He did not leave it to God to forgive men of their sins." [64] His freedom was only matched by his "openness to friends and foes." [65]

These unusual characteristics of Jesus, insists Van Buren, made such a tremendous impact on his followers that following his execution by the Roman authorities, they came to see themselves in a new light. Van Buren denies that the resurrection story refers to a historical fact. Instead, he contends that "as historians and, indeed, as proper users of the English language, we would prefer not to speak of the Easter-event as a fact at all, not in the ordinary use of the word." [66] He goes on to say that modern biological understanding "concerning the changes in cell at death," [67] completely rules out its factuality. This, however, does not mean that Easter was not significant for Jesus' followers. Somehow at Easter the disciples apparently

found themselves caught up in something like the freedom of Jesus himself, having become free men who were free to face even death without fear. Whatever it was that lay in between, and which might account for this change, is not open to our historical investigation.[68]

Van Buren is sure that every scriptural reference that presents Jesus as appearing to his disciples following his death is meant to be interpreted as a psychological "fact." For instance, Peter's announcement concerning the so-called appearance of Jesus to him should be reinterpreted accordingly. It should read: "Jesus who was dead appeared to me as a living person, awesome in aspects so as to constrain me to call him Lord." [69] Jesus himself, according to Van Buren, discouraged his followers from looking for God, who was nonexistent. For example, in answer to Philip's question concerning the "Father," Jesus in effect was saying to Philip: "Stop 'looking for the "Father,' " for we shall not find him and the quest is beside the point in any case." [70] In the same way Jesus' statement in the story of Lazarus and Dives should be reinterpreted to read:

no ghosts, no supernatural warnings or beings, no souls rising from the dead
. . . can come to prove this to us, but the message of the parables, the
human words of an imaginative human dreamer . . . is all we have.[71]

Thus, in conformity with the example of Jesus himself, the New Testament consistently "gives its answer to the question about 'God' by pointing to the man Jesus. Whatever men were looking for in looking for 'God' is to be found by finding Jesus of Nazareth." [72]

On the basis of the foregoing, Van Buren concluded that Christianity is essentially about man though couched in a language of a culture whose world view has been superseded by the current secular world view. The only way to make it relevant to the modern man, therefore, is to lead him to "understand the Gospel in a secular way by seeing it as an expression of a historical perspective." [73] Van Buren concedes that some may say that there is "more" to Christianity than its being merely "a historical perspective." However, he argues, it is "our inability to find any empirical, linguistic anchorage for that 'more' that has led to our interpretation." [74] As a historical perspective all the Gospel is saying is that on Easter day the disciples, acting against

the background of their memory of Jesus suddenly saw Jesus in a new and unexpected way. The light dawned. The history of Jesus which seemed to have been a failure, took on a new importance as the key to the meaning of history.[75]

In other words, Van Buren continues, "Jesus' freedom from himself and freedom to be for others became contagious in Easter." [76] Thus the message of Christianity, divested of its mythological wrapping and put in a language of the secular man, may be expressed as follows:

Our human life cannot be put in parentheses as preliminary, tentative, only a dress rehearsal for a later supposedly really real performance which is supposed to transcend it. To be ready for the kingdom means to start living now, in the present.[77]

To be a Christian then is to make the life of the "imaginative prophet of Nazareth a norm in one's understanding of man and human life . . . of what human life ought to be." [78] Hence Christianity is a historical perspective. For "to speak of meaning in history," insists Van Buren, "is to speak of the insight and commitment which has arisen out of or is re-inforced by one's reflection upon history." [79] In this particular case, that history happens to be the history of Jesus of Nazareth. The genuineness of one's commitment to this perspective

can be verified in one's life and action. This is all there is to Christianity.
It can be expressed more clearly and distinctly without reference to
God inasmuch as Christianity is fundamentally about man. Expressed
in this empirical language, the gospel will once again become meaningful to the secular man. In other words, Jesus' freedom from himself
and his culture, and his freedom for and openness to others may
again become "contagious" to others as the key to the understanding
of human life.

Summary

All three death-of-God theologians examined above are agreed that
this second half of the twentieth century is witnessing the cumulative
effect of the process of secularization which began over four hundred
years ago. Today, they claim, the biblical world view has been completely replaced with the scientific world view. In the scientific world
view, the universe is a closed system which is not amenable to any
interference from without that really does not exist in actuality. The
secular man is radically immanentistic and empirically oriented; hence,
anything that is not empirically verifiable in this world is not only
meaningless but also does not appeal to him. Language, therefore, is
seen as an instrument devised by man to express his empirical experience; and any attempt to stretch it to areas beyond empirical verification is not only futile but is stupid as it results in nonsensical jabbering.

In retrospect, it becomes clear that the present situation is the fulfillment of all the anticipations of the men in the past centuries whose
writings, as has been pointed out, foreshadowed secularism. For instance, the secular man's lack of significant God-consciousness is traceable to the impact of industrialization and technology which tend to
make man see only a reflection of his own image. He has transformed
nature even to the extent that the air he breathes is no longer natural
but a mixture of soot and air. The night sky is no longer resplendent
only with the natural stars and planets but also with man-made satel-
lites so that one has difficulty distinguishing one from the other. In
such a state, where man sees only his own reflection, the incentive
to meditate on the wonders of creation as the handiwork of God
becomes thin indeed. Thus the Comtean dream of the scientific age
has come true.

Discernible also in the contemporary secularism is the actualization
of the Kantian dichotomy of the knowable and unknowable aspects
of reality. This, on the theological level, was pushed farther by Barthian

transcendentalism. If God cannot be known, no matter how much man strives, what is the use of bothering one's self with the unknowable God? Jesus, on the other hand, belongs to the knowable realm since he was a historical man. That being so, the whole of the Christian faith can be built around him. Christianity must then be reduced to "historical perspective" which sees Jesus as the ideal man whose example of selfless life makes for a better life. After all, religion is about man. This echoes Feuerbach's projection theory which considers religion to be desirable when its true purpose is understood. For Feuerbach theology is anthropology.

It must be recalled that for over three hundred years after the foundation of Western culture was eaten up, it continued to exist as the overarching ethos of the Western world. As long as the facade remained intact, secularism could only smolder underneath. But with the two world wars and the consequent revelation of the powerlessness of the church and the culture that supported it to stand up for the sanctity of man, secularism emerged in its nakedness. Here the spirit of Nietzsche comes to birth, for the secular man is the Nietzschean superman. The superman in a "world come of age" has no need for any authority other than his will to affirm life and live fully here and now without moral or religious inhibition. In other words, man and his empirical experiences must forever be the yardstick for measuring all values, including religious values. Anything that is intended for his consumption must be presented in a way that is in harmony with his will.

This is the background against which the theological attempt of the death-of-God theologians should be seen and evaluated. They accept the contemporary culture at its face value. However, these theologians are convinced that the gospel message is still relevant to the secular man. They hold that Christians have a responsibility to communicate the message to this age. In order to do this, the core of the Christian message must be isolated from the mythological language of the obsolete world view in which it is preserved. Such terms as "god," "the Christ," the "Holy Spirit," "heaven," "resurrection," etc. which have reference to transcendence should be dropped as they are no longer meaningful. After all, the gospel message has always been fundamentally about man and his existence in this world. For this reason the term "Jesus" should be retained, for that was the name of the historical man around whose life and teachings the Christian loyalty is built. Jesus' life of freedom from self, from customs, and his openness to all men, both friends and foes, describe the type of life which is ideal for all men to approximate. The Christian, then, is the one who, having reflected on the life of Jesus, has come to make that life the paradigm for his own life.

The way to commend the Christian life and theology to the secular men, therefore, is to reduce Christianity to its essential, namely, the historical life of Jesus. As the Christian commits himself to the exemplification of this life in his own personal life, the freedom of Jesus of Nazareth may once again become "contagious" to others as it was to his early disciples. But in order to make this visible to the secular man, the church in its present form and language must be replaced, as it now obscures the new form in which Jesus manifests himself in the world.

It is clear from the writings of the death-of-God theologians that they are inspired by a burning desire to make the gospel message relevant to the secular man. Their problem, then, is how to present the Gospel to an age from which, they claim, transcendence is dissolved. They are convinced that the secular man has lost the capacity for the awareness of the divine because this cannot be worked into his empirical orientation. Consequently, for the secular man, they argue, all "God-talks" have lost their meanings. But due to some strange factors, according to Van Buren, man is a religious being and as such no study of man is complete without taking cognizance of this fact. If this is the case, the fundamental issue in the death-of-God movement, as it appears to this researcher, is how to meet the spiritual needs of the secular man in the secular age. The issue then can be analyzed as:

1. A search for dynamic models for speaking about God
2. A search for a workable synthesis of transcendence and immanence.
3. A search for a virile metaphysics capable of integrating personality.

The significance of Langmead Casserley for meeting these needs will now be examined. Afterwards it will be shown that these needs which the death-of-God theologians attempt to meet can be better satisfied within the historical Christian framework by utilizing Casserley's philosophical insight.

Significance of Casserley

Apologetics, as Casserley has pointed out, stands in constant danger of reductionism, and thereby the unwary Christian apologist easily loses sight of his role. The most essential ingredient in any successful apologetics is a clear understanding of the function of apologetics and its relationship to theology. Apologetics is always an agency of the Christian church, dedicated to the task of examining, declares Casserley, "how in any reigning climate of opinion, the verdicts of theology are to be communicated to those outside the church." [80] The apologist then is not out to formulate a new theology compatible with the prevalent intellectual climate. He is to find out how the truth of Christianity as formulated in the Scriptures and the theology of the historical Christianity can best be presented to contemporary culture.

In fulfilling this mission, the Christian apologist is not obligated to accept the contemporary culture uncritically and thereby seek to append Christianity to it. His obligation is to criticize the culture and question the validity of its world view and challenge it to a critical re-examination of its current view in relation to the claims of Christianity. The death-of-God theologian-apologists fail at this point. They accept the reigning cultural and intellectual climate uncritically and seek to reduce Christianity so as to fit it into the secular mold. Consequently, it would appear, in the words of Casserley, that the new apologetic-theologian is only trying to

add Christianity to the secular man's present list of affirmations, to supplement his existing way of life with a kind of distilled essence of Christianity, which would enrich but not modify his accustomed systems of thought and affirmation.[81]

Casserley, like the death-of-God apologists, agrees that this third of the twentieth century is secular. He also accepts Van Buren's contention that religious experience is an integral part of man, and no study of man is complete if this fact is not taken into account. In other words, no apologist must ignore the present cultural situation. But at the same time he must attempt to remove the consequent intellectual and cultural barriers that tend to close the secular man's eyes to his spiritual needs. He must then demonstrate that secularism as a world view is untenable. It is an abstraction from reality which ignores other areas of human experience and thus inhibits the realization of man's full potentials. The mere removal of these intellectual obstacles to spiritual awareness does not automatically result in conversion. However, in the process of questioning, the secular man may become free to consider the Christian faith in a new light and thus become open to the pleading of the Holy Spirit, insists Casserley.

The questioning of the validity of secularism must be carried out on an intelligent basis. This writer finds the emphases in Casserley's Christian philosophy of utmost significance at this point. It is, therefore, in order here to re-examine some of them as a springboard for apologetic confrontation with the secular man.

Casserley's Theory of Knowledge

Epistemologically Casserley submits that knowledge is a product of an interaction between the knower and the known. In this connection he also argues that reality is multi-dimensional and that man is constantly bombarded with signals from reality at every waking moment of his life. Knowledge becomes actualized only when man responds to these impingements from reality. Casserley also maintains that there are various levels of reality, some of which are more easily recognized than others. The whole situation is complicated by the fact that all men do not possess the same measure of sensitivity to reality in its manifold forms of expression. Some people are more sensitive to some specific aspects of reality than others. As has been explained earlier, the disparity in measure of sensitivity is not limited to the religious realm. Michael Polanyi has indicated that what he describes as the "unaccountable elements" in science are traceable to this phenomenon. The scientist is the one who possesses intuitive sensitivity which enables him to see patterns where others do not. The same may be said of the sensitivity of the artist which helps him to capture the glory of the sunset which to another man remains a commonplace occurrence until the artist has painted it on the canvas. One more point that cries out for attention here is the truth that when one concentrates his whole attention on one aspect of reality all other aspects tend to fade into the background. In view of all these observations Casserley warns that no one should rule out the possibility of contact with any particular aspect of reality just because he is not yet in contact with it. Reality then cannot be limited to the sensible world which constitutes only one level of it.

In connection with this, Casserley sees man as capable of experiencing reality on three broad levels. These are what he calls the natural, the historico-cultural, and the existential or spiritual dimensions of human experience. But man must not be reduced to any one of these, for it takes all to describe the historical man known to human experience. The secular man appears to accept only the first two levels while he rejects or neglects the third area. The death-of-God apologists accept the third level but insist that it is reduceable to the first two. To accept this is to opt for a narrow view of reality based on a defective doctrine of man. Casserley is convinced that any doctrine that equates reality and meaningfulness of an experience of it with "observable physical consequences" must be rejected as a "defective conception of verification inspired by materialism." [82]

The secular man has no logical grounds on which to base his argument that verification of the authenticity of all human experiences must be carried out by only one specified methodology. This demand becomes ridiculous when it is made on the basis that the specific method happens to be successful on one specific level of experience. Such an argument violates the canon of scientific procedure. The nature of the subject matter must determine the method of verification. What is essential in any method is that it be critical and consistent. This must be followed by recognizable effects of the area of experience on the life of him who claims knowledge to it. This leads to Casserley's thought on man's self-consciousness.

Casserley's Metaphysics of Self-consciousness

Man, says Casserley, is a self-conscious being. In the depth of his self-consciousness man becomes aware not only of himself but of his distinction from the external world around him. He is conscious of his contingency and that of the world and other existents. In this process of creature-consciousness he is also immediately aware of the Unconditioned Other—the source of all that exists. Here man comes to the realization that he is a transcendent being, "the missing link between the creative and the created." By virtue of his transcendence of the physical, the cultural and the historical which are subject to his control over which he judges, it is only reasonable to assume that he is capable of contact with spiritual reality. Put in another way, man as a being that stands on the boundary between the temporal and the eternal is capable of receiving and symbolizing signals from the dynamic *Singular* to whom he and other existents own their being. Such a doctrine of man removes the supposedly unbridgeable chasm between the so-called secular and the divine. They become two aspects of reality. Casserley has maintained that while man is a microcosm of the macrocosm in the sense that he is made up of the same chemical composition found in nature, he finds himself conscious of his transcendence of the natural order. He can contemplate his own demise as well as criticize his own thoughts and motives in addition to exercising control over nature and history. This is possible because man finds himself involved in immediate confrontation with the source of his being to whom he is responsible and accountable.

Transcendence then is not to be understood in terms of the Greek static concept. Man is immanent in nature and yet he transcends it. In the same way, God transcends the temporal, but he is also immanent everywhere in his creation, sustaining and directing it. He is not subject to the inherent temporal limitations other than the self-imposed limitation intrinsic in the persuasion of love which refuses to overawe his creatures to submission. Casserley regards transcendence and immanence as two facets of a diamond so integrally intertwined that one is meaningless without the other. What the secular man needs, Casserley admonishes, is to retire sufficiently to the depth of his self-consciousness in order to become aware of the Unconditioned dynamic Creator who subtly impinges on his consciousness in a manner consistent with "persuasion of love." It is possible that the over-stimulation from the technological age and the corresponding over-concentration on the physical have made most secular men insensitive to the pleadings of God in his immanent form. This is not new in kind but in degree intensified by the present technological development. Man has always lived in danger of indifference and unresponsiveness to God. The duty of those who are more spiritually sensitive has always been to point men to this reality. Thus the task of the contemporary apologist, though made more difficult by the changed situation, is by no means different from that of his predecessor.

Metaphysics as an Analogical Art

One other area in which Casserley's philosophy becomes significant is in his concept of metaphysics and the use of language. Traditionally metaphysics has been presented as a finished product of speculation. If God exists, according to classical metaphysics, he must first be postulated as "a certain and distinct idea" and then proved logically after the fashion of a mathematical theorem. Since Kant, this view of metaphysics has fallen into disrepute, and both Christians and philosophers have become in the main anti-metaphysical.

But, for Casserley, metaphysics is not a product of speculation. It is an analogical art by means of which man attempts to present a systematized verbalization of his experience in analogical language. Metaphysics for the Christian is a rational explication of his ontological response to the reality that meets him in the deeps of his self-consciousness. In order to do this, he has to take his self-consciousness as a being as an analogy for describing the reality that encounters him. This is why Casserley defines analogy as "a technique by means of which we impart a certain empirical resonance to a pure concept." [83] In other words, while the being of God is not to be identified with the being of the Christian, yet it can neither be said to be completely foreign; for if God is the ground of being, he is somehow analogous to being. In any case, since his own being is the highest form of living reality known intimately to man, he can do no more than use this as analogy for talking of the reality he has come to meet as the dynamic living ground of being.

The Capacity of the Human Language

The analytical philosopher, having abdicated the role of the classical philosopher in deference to science, has now reduced philosophy to analysis of meaning. For the analytical philosopher, as has been indicated earlier, the meaningfulness of any statement is either tied up with the definition of terms involved or with the possibility of its being empirically verifiable. With this stipulation the transcendent reference of language is rejected.

Casserley rejects this position on the ground that it has no basis in fact. Apart from the fact that the analytic verification principle for meaningfulness is based on the scientific world view which Casserley has described as an abstraction from reality, it also has some other shortcomings. For instance, it ignores the truth that philosophical and metaphysical as well as religious languages arise out of man's irrepressible desire to verbalize his experiences which cannot be exhaustively described in mathematic-scientific terms. As Casserley has consistently stressed, man is a unity capable of multidimensional experiences. These include the scientific or physical, moral, religious, or existential dimensions, to mention only a few. He lives in a universe of multidimensional reality. In short, man is a living existential being who finds himself involved in responsive intercourse with the dynamic multidimensional reality.

Under this view language cannot be regarded as a mere human instrument designed to handle *only temporal and tangible* matters as claimed by the analytical philosophers. While it may not be denied that language is a human creation, yet it must be insisted that it is created in man's desperate attempt to verbalize his impressions of reality given in his self-consciousness. In the words of Casserley, "if language has been evolved and perfected through time . . . as instrument of our purpose, surely . . . transcendent purposes must have had a hand in fashioning it." [84] Casserley goes on to add that any claim that language can have no transcendental reference is not only based on a misconception of transcendence but also on ignorance of the various ways in which language is used. To restrict language to the empirically verifiable and tautological statements is to limit man's self-expression to an intolerable level. Ludwig Wittgenstein found this to be the case; hence in his later writings he moved from his earlier linguistic atomism to the idea of "language games." On the basis of Casserley's epistemology even the concept of "language game" is to be rejected as inadequate. For religious language, though analogical, is rooted in objective reality. It grows out of man's desire to give verbal expression to his vital experience of the divine, the possibility of distortion notwithstanding.

The foregoing presentation of the significance of Casserley's criticism of secularism opens the way for a fresh look at the apologetic challenge of secularism. No one can intelligently deny any longer the fact that this section of the twentieth century is a transitional period. In a sense it is a period of "cultural lag." Cultural lag may be defined as the difference between the technological development and the evolvement and consolidation of new culture able to absorb the shock of the rapid material development in order to utilize its advantages in an atmosphere of cultural wholeness. During a period of "cultural lag," people generally suffer from what sociologists call *anomie*—the shock of uprootedness arising from the demolition of ancient landmarks. This being the case, the task of the apologist is not to throw overboard the historical theology of the church but to explore new ways of presenting it to this age.

Three Basic Searches

As has been argued above, the death-of-God theologian, faced with the new situation, decided to throw in the towel rather than search for new models for presenting the eternal truth of the gospel message. After summarizing the attempts of the death-of-God apologists earlier, this researcher declares that the movement can be analyzed into three basic searches. These are: (1) A search for dynamic models for speaking about God. (2) A search for workable synthesis of transcendence and immanence. (3) A search for a virile metaphysics capable of integrating personality. The remaining portion of this chapter will be devoted to an exploration of these areas.

A Search for Dynamic Models for Speaking about God

It has often been said that the present uncertainty about theological discourse is a crisis of models for talking meaningfully about God. The transformation of the Christian culture into a secular one calls for a redefinition of the traditional models and in some cases invention of new ones for speaking about God.

No longer can the Aristolelian idea of the unmoved Mover, the impassible God, appeal to the twentieth-century man. In fact, whatever term is used to describe God must be dynamic in nature. In the opinion of Paul Schilling, Christians cannot refrain from using the term "being" as a model for speaking about God. However, the term must be purged of its static coating with which it was clothed by the traditional theology influenced by Greek philosophy. Schilling defines *being* as "the power to act—in infinitely varied ways—which sustains itself through time." [85] Schilling goes further to argue that when being is so understood God's "being then becomes the enduring, dependable but dynamically functioning ground or matrix of the activity of all created being." [86] In applying the term being to God, what Casserley says about the meaning of analogy must be kept in view. After defining analogy as a technique by means of which an empirical resonance is imparted to a pure concept, Casserley goes on to warn that under no circumstance must the being of God be identified with that of man. The only being known on a firsthand basis to man is his own, and hence, in order to conceptualize God mediated in the depth of his self-consciousness, man naturally turns to his being as a paradigm for describing him.

"Depth," "Height," and "Ground of Being" have all been recently popularized by Bishop John A. T. Robinson and Paul Tillich as models for talking about God. While these terms may be suitable in speaking about God to the secular man, they must not be absolutized. As John Macquarrie declares, "the theist is not committed to defending any and every idea of God but the God who, as he believes, has made himself known in grace and judgment." [87] This remark leads to the significance of the personal models as best suited for "God-talk," provided it is clearly understood to be a model. The Christian doctrine of God is rooted in concrete events in human history. These concrete events, in the words of Ogletree, transfigured history, "taking on a dimension of significance which both sets them apart from all other experiences and at the same time conditions the meaning of experience in its totality." [88] These series of events, the Christian asserts, came to focus in Jesus, the Christ. "The task of unfolding the meaning of God consists of critical reflection on these crucial encounters in human experience." [89] In order to verbalize the result of this reflection, one is inevitably constrained to speak of God in personal terms, or as living spirit, "for these notions are the ones which most aptly point to the dynamism embodied in the events in question." [90]

Speaking in the same vein, Macquarrie insists that the fact that God makes himself known in history and especially in the history of Jesus of Nazareth makes the doctrine of the Trinity reasonable. Trinity of the Godhead, according to Macquarrie, is a theological way of describing

the movement of being from its primordial source through its expression in creation to its unitive action in building up the kingdom of God. . . . The doctrine speaks of that ceaselessly moving inner life of the Godhead of that dynamic mystery which makes possible all life and love.[91]

This way of talking about God certainly removes him from the realm of abstract metaphysics to the concrete. This researcher has already emphasized Casserley's epistemology and metaphysics of self-consciousness which annul the supposed barrier between the secular and the divine. If man is a being on the borderline between time and eternity and if his language grows out of his attempt to express his experience, then he can talk of the God who reveals himself in Christ in personal terms. The historicity of Jesus then lends empirical muscle to the personal models which the Christian uses, even though they do not exhaust the reality thus described.

A Search for a Workable Synthesis of Transcendence and Immanence

One of the thorniest problems for the secular man is that of reconciling the transcendence of God with immanence. However, a critical examination of this issue reveals that the deity whose transcendence is rejected has no resemblance to the dynamic living God of the biblical revelation. Schilling is convinced that the God rejected by the atheist has been "a deity conceived as a being or an order existing above or beyond the realm of natural and human existence, yet ruling that realm by his arbitrary will." [92] To be sure, the Christian church, influenced by Aristotelian philosophical category, in the past had tended to lean toward this view of God. On the contrary, the biblical God is presented not as "acting from the outside . . . rather he informs and interpenetrates his creation from within, so that its existence depends moment by moment on his energizing activity." [93] In other words, man does not have to look away from the world to see God, for he is to be found in the midst of life.

Macquarrie maintains that the biblical doctrines of creation, the incarnation, the church and the sacramental presence are all designed to emphasize the interrelationship between God's transcendence and immanence. It is not by accident, insists Macquarrie, that the Church Fathers linked the incarnation with the doctrine of creation. In this sense the incarnation is seen as "recapitulation of creation." [94] Macquarrie further declares:

> The incarnation focuses in a single point, what God has . . . been doing always and everywhere. If God's presence and action are often hidden, the Christian claim is that he is signally present and manifest in Jesus Christ . . . so that Christ becomes the center for the interpretation of the whole.[95]

This immanent reality of God is further emphasized in the concept of the church as the "body of Christ." By this concept the church sees itself as the social reality of man's participation in the God immanent in the historical incarnation. It affirms that the same God continues to manifest himself in the creative activity of the Holy Spirit. Thus the church, as Casserley says of man, becomes the "link between the temporal and the eternal" who manifests himself in the temporal.

The story of the inauguration of the eucharist is also relevant here. In that story Jesus Christ is described as taking bread and saying, "This is my body." In the same way he declared the wine to be his blood, enjoining the disciples to continue to re-enact this symbolism of his presence as a "remembrance" of him. In view of this the so-called hiatus between the divine and the profane must be seen as an aberration unknown to the biblical faith.

Hamilton, it will be recalled, wrestled with the problem of evil in the world and concluded that the immanence of God cannot be squared with the presence of evil. While the present purpose is not to develop a theodicy, yet it is necessary to stress that the church's doctrine of eschatology bears on this problem. The doctrine of eschatology is the church's affirmation of the presence of directedness in the historical process. God creates a moral being with all the risks inherent in the freedom of that being. The universe itself is "unfinished" and replete with contingencies. The whole creation groans in pangs of birth into the full actualization of divine redemption. So in the historicity of Jesus, the Christ, God focuses his vital involvement with his creation in the process of the actualization of his goal of creation. By this involvement God reveals that man is an acceptable instrument in the hastening of the day of complete redemption.[96] The universe has a goal. The cross and the resurrection of Christ become a model of speaking about God's immanence in the process, redemptively transmuting evil. For the meaning of the cross is that, in spite of the evil in the world, God is involved in the world and is determined to usher in the realization of his purpose in creation. The theological cash value of the cross, according to Macquarrie, can be thus expressed: "that nothing can be so mean or profane, nothing even can be so wicked, that it cannot somehow be worked upon by God's redemptive and creative love and that it can not finally serve his purpose." [97]

These are the biblical ways of expressing the synthesis of transcendence and immanence. The meaning of transcendence, contrary to the claim of the death-of-God apologists, is not that God is above the world or outside it. The fact of the incarnation forbids such an understanding. For the incarnation implies that God becomes a reality in the "reality of man's immediate experience," affirms Dewart.[98] In this act God becomes "a transcendent presence." [99] Expressed in another way, God is "immanent within all being, all existence and most particularly in all men." [100] Yet transcendence also means that God is other than and distinct from the world, though vitally involved in the life of the world. He is the ultimate source of all things, but yet the world is not an emanation of God, for he created it out of nothing.

For the secular man who may dismiss what has been said in this connection as biblical language, the insight of Rust may become apropos here. Rust suggests that to reach the secular man with the word the apologist must "start where man is and with man himself rather than with the realm of nature." [101] In speaking of the synthesis of transcendence and immanence, Rust underlines the value in the use of the models of "personal self-transcendence and intra-personal relationship." [102] While man is a psychosomatic unity, there is a mysterious depth in him that defies any attempt at domestication. The more one tries to objectify his "I-ness," the farther it recedes to the background so that no matter what one does he never grasps his "I-ness." "In this," continues Rust, "the ego is both immanent at every level of the psychosomatic whole and yet transcends it in critical reflective and moral judgment." [103] On the intrapersonal level, when a man becomes personally related to another man, there is a sense in which it can be said that interpenetration between these two separate individuals takes place. Rust points out that the reality of "love and the subtle thing which we call influence" constitute strong evidence of "how personal being can stretch beyond its somatic frontiers to envelope the others." [104]

What Rust says here tallies with Casserley's epistemology, which sees knowledge as a result of a process of interpenetration between the knower and the known. The secular man cannot deny the reality of personal self-transcendence and the personal meeting of two "I's" beyond the frontiers of their somatic entities. If this is accepted, then personal self-transcendence becomes a workable model by means of which the secular man can understand the biblical view of God. For the Christian God's transcendence means that he is "both personally present at every level of his created order, and yet transcends it as its dynamic directing and creative center." [105] With appropriate safeguards, man's experience of his personal self-transcendence and intrapersonal transcendence can be a viable analogy for conceptualizing God's transcendence and immanence.

A Search for a Virile Metaphysics Capable of Integrating Personality

Classical metaphysics in the Cartesian tradition, tended to create a dualism of matter and mind with emphasis on the mind at the expense of the body. The resultant effect has been an unfortunate bifurcation of the physical or secular from the spirit. This attitude ignores the psychosomatic wholeness of man. The failure of the attempts of Kant and Hegel to evolve a viable synthesis between the physical and the spiritual has resulted in stiff antimetaphysical movements by both philosophers and some theologians in modern times. With the works of Dorothy Emmet, Michael Polanyi, Rust and Casserley, etc., there is a ray of hope that the question of metaphysics will be reconsidered. All these writers emphasize the indispensable elements of intuition, personal commitment, and imagination in any metaphysical thinking. They insist that the metaphysician is first a living being before becoming a metaphysician so that any attempt to separate the living being from the metaphysician is forced.

Casserley, in particular, as has already been emphasized, persistently insists that metaphysics is an analogical art and never a demonstrative science. Metaphysics arises out of a prelogical assumption based on

a significant experience around which one seeks to integrate and interpret all other experiences as a whole. As a point of view from which
one surveys the whole of life so as to make sense of its diversities,
metaphysics is a function of the total man. Hence Casserley defines
it in terms of a search for the most revealing and encompassing analogies. These analogies, Casserley submits, are invariably "drawn from
that realm of human interest and experience which the philosopher
regards as most decisive and revealing." [106] So understood, human
experience must always precede metaphysical adventure. This means
that the Christian metaphysician does not arrive at God through speculation. He does not invent God, for, as Casserley maintains, man is
not even capable of inventing anything "that it totally unreal." Whatever is imagined is a distortion of some genuine human experience.
The claims of the Christian metaphysician is that in his self-consciousness he encounters God, who somehow strikes him as the one revealed
in Jesus Christ of Nazareth. Armed with this inner experience and
confirmed by his reflection on the biblical interpretation of this historical reality, the Christian metaphysician seeks to interpret life in its
totality in the light of this experience. In order to put this in words,
he has to use the analogy of his own being as a conceptual framework
for self-expression. As analogy is never in a one-to-one-correspondence
relation with the reality about which it is analogous, so the Christian
does not claim that God's being is like his. This has already been
indicated.

In view of the existence of several metaphysical systems, such as
secularism, which cry for man's attention, Casserley stipulates three
critical tests for determining the validity of any metaphysical systems.
These are breadth and momentum, openness to a further unfolding
of mystery, and consistency. Using these as criteria, a metaphysical
system that is viable must be able to give adequate explanation of
man's natural, historical, social, moral, and spiritual dimensions of
existence. These must be explained without any attempt at reductionism, since these are stubborn dimensions of life. [107] Any critical application of these tests will reveal that only theistically-based metaphysics
has the necessary breadth and momentum against which life can be
seen "steadily and whole." Hence this is the only metaphysics capable
of integrating personality. It is the only comprehensive base in which,
according to Casserley, "the context of anything is everything and
ultimately nothing is totally irrelevant to anything else." [108]

Throughout this section of this chapter attempts have been made to argue that secularism as a world view is untenable. The nature of man is such that the possibility of interaction between the divine and the secular is a reality. This is the witness of the Christian faith throughout the ages and substantiated by human experience. It has been stressed that the present apparent obscurity of this reality is the result of the "cultural lag" brought about by the scientific and technological developments which come to climax in the twentieth century. The Christian apologist can no longer ignore the contemporary culture. However, as a man who is aware of the philosophical, historical, cultural, and theological sources of the situation, he occupies a unique position in helping the secular man to come to grips with his spiritual problems. In the discharge of his responsibility he must challenge the validity of secularism while at the same time exploring new ways in which to present the Christian message. Indeed, the sensitive Christian apologist walks a tightrope here. Care must be taken to remain faithful to the faith of the universal church as he grapples with the task of singing "the song of Zion" in a new age. This he must do, fully conscious that his language and models are broken tools but tools growing out of his encounter with the living creative God once enfleshed in Jesus of Nazareth but in every age made contemporaneous by the creative spirit. His hope is that when the intellectual and cultural blinders are removed the secular man may be open to discern and respond positively to this same *transcendent* Presence in the midst of life.

NOTES

[1] Thomas Altizer, *The Gospel of Atheism* (Philadelphia: The Westminster Press, 1966), p. 22.

[2] Altizer, *The Descent into Hell: A Study of the Radical Reversal of the Christian Consciousness* (New York: J. B. Lippincott Co., 1970), p. 112.

[3] *Ibid.*, p. 114.

[4] Thomas Ogletree, *The Death of God Controversy* (New York: Abingdon Press, 1966), p. 79.

[5] Altizer, *The Gospel of Atheism*, p. 22.

[6] *Ibid.*, p. 25.   [7] *Ibid.*

[8] *Ibid.*   [9] *Ibid.*, p. 33.

[10] *Ibid.*, p. 34.   [11] *Ibid.*

[12] *Ibid.*, p. 35.   [13] *Ibid.*, p. 34.

[14] *Ibid.*, p. 39.   [15] *Ibid.*, p. 40.

[16] *Ibid.*, p. 44.

[17] Altizer, *The Gospel of Atheism*, p. 104.

[18] Ogletree, *The Death of God Controversy*, p. 86.

[19] *Ibid.*, p. 112.   [20] *Ibid.*, p. 98.

[21] Altizer, *The Descent into Hell*, p. 155.

[22] Altizer, "The Significance of the New Theology," *The Death of God Debate*, eds. Jackson Lee Ice and John Carey (Philadelphia: The Westminster Press, 1967), p. 252.

[23] *Ibid.*, p. 255.

[24] William Hamilton, "The Death of God Theologies Today," *Radical Theology and the Death of God*, eds. Altizer and Hamilton (New York: The Bobbs-Merrill Corp., Inc., 1966), p. 47.

[25] Hamilton, "Questions and Answers on the Radical Theology," *The Death of God Debate*, *op. cit.*, p. 213.

[26] Altizer and Hamilton, *Radical Theology and the Death of God*, p. 35.

[27] *Ibid.*, p. 36.

[28] Hamilton, "The New Optimism—From Prufrock to Ringo," *Radical Theology and the Death of God*, p. 165.

[29] *Ibid.*, p. 169.   [30] *Ibid.*, p. 36.

[31] *Ibid.*, pp. 36f.

[32] Ice and Carey, *The Death of God Debate*, p. 217.

[33] Altizer and Hamilton, *Radical Theology and the Death of God*, p. 88.

[34] *Ibid.*, p. 7   [35] *Ibid.*, p. 88.

[36] Ice and Carey, *op. cit.*, p. 214.

[37] *Ibid.*, p. 221.   [38] *Ibid.*

[39] *Ibid.*, p. 223.   [40] *Ibid.*, p. 225.

[41] *Ibid.*, p. 215.

[42] Hamilton, "The Shape of a Radical Theology," *The Christian Century*, Vol. LXXXII, No. 40 (October 6, 1965), p. 1221.

[43] Altizer and Hamilton, *Radical Theology and the Death of God*, p. 49.

[44] Paul M. Van Buren, *The Secular Meaning of the Gospel* (London: SCM Press, Ltd., 1963), p. xiv.

[45] *Ibid.*, pp. 2–3.   [46] *Ibid.*, pp. xiii-iv

[47] Van Buren, *Theological Explorations* (New York: The Macmillan Co., 1968), p. 30.

[48] *Ibid.*   [49] *Ibid.*, p. 34.

[50] *Ibid.*, p. 24.   [51] *Ibid.*

[52] *Ibid.*, p. 179.   [53] *Ibid.*, p. 24.

[54] *Ibid.*

[55] Van Buren, *The Secular Meaning of the Gospel*, p. 15.

[56] *Ibid.*   [57] *Ibid.*, p. 129.

[58] Ved Mehta, "Ecce Homo," *The New Theologian* (New York: Harper and Row, Publishers, 1965), p. 66.

[59] *Ibid.*

[60] Van Buren, *The Secular Meaning of the Gospel*, p. 109.

[61] *Ibid.*, p. 123.   [62] *Ibid.*, pp. 121-22.

[63] *Ibid.*, p. 122.   [64] *Ibid.*

[65] *Ibid.*, p. 121.   [66] *Ibid.*, p. 128.

[67] *Ibid.*, p. 127.   [68] *Ibid.*, p. 128.

[69] *Ibid.*, p. 129.   [70] *Ibid.*, p. 146.

[71] Van Buren, *Theological Explorations*, p. 177.

[72] Van Buren, *The Secular Meaning of the Gospels*, p. 147.

[73] *Ibid.*, p. 193.   [74] *Ibid.*, p. 198.

[75] *Ibid.*, p. 132.   [76] *Ibid.*, p. 133.

[77] Van Buren, *Theological Explorations*, p. 177.

[78] Ved Mehta, "Ecce Homo," p. 63.

[79] Van Buren, *The Secular Meaning of the Gospel*, p. 114.

[80] Langmead Casserley, "Theology and Apologetics," *Canadian Journal of Theology*, Vol. 3 (1957), p. 226.

[81] Casserley, *Apologetics and Evangelism* (Philadelphia: The Westminster Press, 1962), p. 146.

[82] Casserley, *The Christian in Philosophy* (London: Faber and Faber, 1949), p. 196.

[83] Casserley, *Toward a Theology of History* (New York: Holt, Reinhart and Winston, 1965), p. 42.

[84] Casserley, *The Christian in Philosophy*, p. 175.

[85] Paul Schilling, *God in an Age of Theism* (New York: Abingdon Press, 1969), p. 196.

[86] *Ibid.*

[87] John Macquarrie, *God and Secularity: New Directions in Theology Today*, Vol. 3 (Philadelphia: The Westminister Press, 1967), p. 111.

[88] Ogletree, *The Death of God Controversy*, p. 43.

[89] *Ibid.*   [90] *Ibid.*, p. 44.

[91] Macquarrie, *op. cit.*, pp. 113-14.

[92] Schilling, *op. cit.*, p. 147.

[93] *Ibid.*,

[94] Macquarrie, *op. cit.*, p. 133.

[95] *Ibid.*

[96] Eric Rust, *Science and Faith* (New York: Oxford University Press, 1967), pp. 300-07.

[97] Macquarrie, *God and Secularity: New Directions in Theology Today*, p. 137.

[98] Leslie Dewart, *The Future of Belief: Theism in a World Come of Age* (New York: Herder and Herder, 1966), p. 138.

[99] *Ibid.*   [100] *Ibid.*

[101] Eric Rust, *Evolutionary Philosophies and Contemporary Theology* (Philadelphia: The Westminster Press, 1969), p. 31.

[102] *Ibid.*, p. 220.   [103] *Ibid.*

[104] *Ibid.*   [105] *Ibid.*

[106] Casserley, *The Christian in Philosophy*, p. 224.

[107] It is not possible here to go into detail as to Casserley's argument. For anyone interested pages 37-54 of the original Dissertation by this author may be consulted.

[108] Casserley, *Apologetics and Evangelism*, p. 162.

PART III
FAITH AND THE BIBLICAL REVELATION

11.
The Concept of God in the Thought of Eric Rust
Richard B. Cunningham

Having recently returned to Southern Baptist Theological Seminary to follow Eric Rust in Christian philosophy, I have known him as a student, friend, colleague, and successor. Those categories place me in a unique relationship to this British-American Christian philosopher and theologian.

I well remember sitting in his class on science and religion in 1955, listening to his still very British English as he communicated his views while his thought was maturing in early middle age. For a number of years, in classes and seminars and countless conversations, I engaged great books and ideas under his provocative and creative tutelage. My intellectual debts are owed to many teachers and thinkers. But Eric Rust has had the greatest impact and shaping influence on my own thought. I have shared instinctively many of his own deepest commitments, particularly the commitment to bring historic Christianity and modernity into creative dialogue. Perhaps my greatest learning from him is at the point of methodology. Rust has always engaged problems with a carefully defined and disciplined philosophical and theological methodology.

After completing graduate studies, I was away from Southern Seminary for a number of years, most of which I taught at Golden Gate Baptist Theological Seminary in Mill Valley, California. During that time we had occasional correspondence, and of course I read his books as they were published. One expects the thought of a fertile mind to evolve and address new questions along the way. Rust has done that in a series of books. And yet despite various new dimensions, there are a number of striking threads of continuity in the pattern of his work.

During the past eighteen months I have again been in continuing close conversation with Eric Rust as he thinks from a peak posture in approaching retirement years. As he grapples with issues within the broadened horizons of his mature thought, he repeatedly strikes notes of continuity with his early thought and the theological values he has consistently affirmed wherever his own scholarly and literary journey has taken him.

Rust's own roots lie in Baptist evangelical Christianity, a dimension he has never lost either as a Christian believer and churchman or as a scholar. His own spiritual pilgrimage undoubtedly has made the personal model an existential as well as an intellectual stackpole of his thought. His early education incorporated healthy doses of science and biblical theology. His study in Old Testament theology, particularly under the tutelage of H. W. Robinson, imprinted ineradicably a theistic understanding of God wedded to a *Heilsgeschichte* view of his activity in history in revelation and redemption. Several prominent New Testament scholars, including T. W. Manson in particular, extended that vision into the New Testament.

Along the way his understanding of the biblical God was shaped in its outer limits by conciliar orthodoxy. And while he has never been tied to the verbal or metaphysical categories of the early councils, he has unapologetically affirmed what they were at least trying to say about the nature of Jesus Christ and of the triune God. Along with the biblical-historical dimensions of his thought, scientific views of evolution and process have been dialectical partners in his theological thought process. Among the more powerful influences on his conception of the natural process have been William Temple, Teilhard de Chardin, H. H. Farmer, and John Macmurray. A. N. Whitehead and his disciples have encouraged Rust to take seriously process and becoming in nature, although he repeatedly criticizes a number of basic Whiteheadian categories. Rounding off the major influences are various existentialist and personalist thinkers.

The result is a particularly fertile field of thought in which Rust has plowed furrows of biblical theology, historic Christian orthodoxy, personalism, process thought, existentialism, salvation history, and contemporary historiography. His own thought has been charted in continuing dialogue with major thinkers in the fields of science, history, philosophy, and theology.

There are many unifying elements to Rust's thought. My judgment is that perhaps the most definitive concept in his philosophical theology is his understanding of God. Rust consciously and committedly thinks as a Christian theist. That theism, as he understands it, grows out of the biblical concept of God, the essence of the Chalcedonian insights, and personalistic values. The classic theistic view of God based upon this theological triumvirate dominates Rust's work from his earliest to his latest books.

Rust carefully stated his view of God in his early book *Nature and Man in Biblical Thought*.[1] The synoptic portrait there has provided the working structure of his thought ever since. The view of God in that book has close parallels with Emil Brunner's view in his *The Christian Doctrine of God*. In the passing years, Rust has appropriated new phraseology and opened creative new dimensions in his view of God. For example, among the important ideas in his latest works he has increasingly emphasized the becoming of God, the kenotic nature of his immanental presence, his movement at the personal level through the persuasion of love, and the delight that God takes in the unfolding of the creative process. And yet, whatever additional insights have entered into his thinking, he has never deviated substantially from that early statement. And later emphases are fully compatible with and draw out implications of the basic structure of his biblical-conciliar-personalist view of God.

Many of his critiques of a wide range of philosophical and theological positions are made from his stance within classic Christian theism. Essential theistic values include God as absolute creator and sovereign lord of the universe, his transcendence and immanence, his ontological triune unity and "communityness," the personal as the key analogue to understanding the divine being, and God's love producing a self limitation of the divine power in creating the universe. Whenever any theological or philosophical position infringes upon these and similar essential elements in the doctrine of God, then Rust's criticism of such a view is predictable, even while he is open to learning from it what he can.

Because of his enduring commitment to Christian theism, Rust has never succumbed to the radical excesses of various philosophical and theological movements of the twentieth century. The problem of God-talk, secularity, the loss of transcendence, the problem of ontological models—all these have been addressed by Rust without seducing him from his basic theological commitments or philosophical methodology. He has openly acknowledged the serious challenges of various contemporary movements without despairing over the possibility of finding acceptable responses to the new problems.

Eric Rust has contended throughout his thought and writings that the historic orthodox view of God, based broadly on biblical revelation and Chalcedonian Christology, provides the most adequate model for understanding God in the modern world and for grasping God's relationship to and activity in nature and history. His work has been an effort to relate that classic understanding to the emerging scientific and philosophical insights of the modern world. He has tried to point toward a contemporary Christian metaphysic and philosophy of history that is faithful to historic trinitarian theistic theology and to contemporary scientific understandings of the universe.

In an era when Christian theism is being eroded in concession to various contemporary problems, it is useful to grasp Rust's concept of God and to understand why he thinks it is not only essential but in fact best makes sense out of the major problematic elements in both nature and history.

I. The Concept of God

Eric Rust's major theological and philosophical work has centered upon the relationship of faith to nature and history. His concept of God dominates his interpretation of man's historical existence in a universe of creative process. Our procedure will be first to examine his view of the essential dimensions of the nature of God, and then to apply and extend those ideas in further sections dealing with God's relation to nature and to history. Certain dimensions of the divine nature can be discerned only in relation to his activity within the temporal processes of nature and history.

Rust's concept of God is a clue to his philosophical and theological methodology. He has always been careful, even adamant, in identifying his work as *Christian* philosophy. It is his way of laying bare his fundamental presupposition and highlighting his philosophical frame of reference. The categories of revelation, as well as his Christian commitment, provide the center point as well as the course markers for his thought. His concept of God derives from revelation, not from rational speculation upon nature or history.

The Centrality of Revelation for Christian Philosophizing

Rust is a thoroughgoing Augustinian in his approach to religious knowledge. In contrast to classical or contemporary natural theologies, he is skeptical about the validity of reason operating on its own about ultimate questions without taking its clues from revelation. And yet he reasons with some degree of confidence when reason utilized revelation. While many basic categories of revelation baffle the mind of natural man, they are completely reasonable when the mind is enlightened by Christ.[2] In his more recent efforts to defend the Christian position and make it intelligible to thinking men, Rust utilizies natural theological categories as a philosophical bridge to the preoccupations and attitudes of secular men. But his effort is far from old style natural theologizing. His method is "Christian philosophizing," and he insists that any adequate development of natural theology presumes revelation categories.[3]

Throughout his writings, Rust has contrasted the views of God deriving from reason and natural knowledge with that of revelation as appropriated by faith. He has frequently pointed toward the contrasting Greek and Hebrew approaches to knowledge, the one prizing objective, detached rationalistic theorizing, the other, subjective, personal encounter. His understanding of revelation has consistently centered upon *Heilsgeschichte,* salvation history. God is known not through argumentative human reasoning but in his divine personal disclosures through involvement with man in the historical process of redemption. A stream of disclosures runs through the history of Israel and the Christian church, centering upon the incarnation of God in Christ. The personal self disclosure of God in revelatory events must be received by man in faith, in existential decisions by which man acts upon what he sees.[4]

The incarnation represents the final revelation in that it cannot be surpassed. Because of the uniqueness of the divine disclosure, the biblical understanding of God sets the outer boundaries of Rust's own concept of God. He does move beyond the biblical categories and the Chalcedonian conceptions, but he always applies a test of consistency with their insights. He affirms the essential intentions of Chalcedonian christological and trinitarian affirmations, but argues that the Greek metaphysical categories need to be modified by personalistic insights. What is immediately evident in the disclosure of the incarnation is a personal depth in the universe. Therefore the best models for interpreting that depth will be those taken from the personal level of existence.[5]

At this point Rust finds most natural thought to be deficient. Natural thought normally seizes upon impersonal metaphysical terms to describe the nature of God. Rust would admit that metaphysical terms can be useful to philosophical thought, but only if they are interpreted in a personal sense in light of the divine self disclosure. One may say, for example, that God is absolute, but absolute only in the personal sense of being Creator and Lord. He sustains the world by his personal will and places a personal claim upon people.

Rust contends that all natural approaches to the knowledge of God will inevitably minimize one or another of the important aspects of the being of the biblical God. During a scientific mechanistic era, natural theologies abandoned the idea of immanence for a deistic view of God. In our own modern era, one dominated by evolutionary categories of thought, the natural theologian often paints an immanental and pantheistic view of God. Beyond the limitations of our natural capacities for knowing God, sin vitiates man's quest for God, leading him often to focus upon the medium of revelation rather than to perceive God through the medium. But also since the creation rests upon the divine will of the Creator, it does not carry its meaning within itself. The creation cannot disclose its own teleological purpose. That meaning must be given in the divine self disclosure.[6]

As an Augustinian, Rust does not despise reason. If faith wants to understand the intricacies of the natural order, it requires knowledge that only science can provide. But he insists that we recognize the limits of unaided reason. Reason cannot provide sufficient final causes or grasp the divine pattern in the creative process. However, upon the basis of faith, one can turn to an empirical investigation of the world and piece together some fragments of the divine pattern in the world. Faith can supply the final causes for the world process that are beyond the grasp of pure empirical science.[7]

Rust's approach to salvation history makes ample room for revelation outside Judeo-Christian history. His treatment of the general revelation and special revelation problem has long involved a dialogue with major proponents of the debate in modern theology, thinkers like Karl Barth, Emil Brunner, John Baillie, H. H. Farmer, Paul Tillich, and various others. There is a personal disclosure of God in nature, moral law, human reason, and conscience. The disclosure not only makes man accountable before God, but it opens the possibility for a legitimate saving response to the personal revelation. All revelation is christological. The decisive element in Christianity is not its religious trappings but Christ himself. He is the final historical revelation to whom all other revelation points.[8]

The problem is, however, that sin misdirects the human will and leads to perversion of the revelation, particularly outside special revelation. The Christian faith is essential for clarifying and helping to understand the general revelation. Christ is the personal self disclosure of the God who is both immanent and transcendent, the God of the end time who has disclosed himself in history. In that disclosure, God gives the basic interpretative categories for understanding his nature and purpose.

The Nature of God

Rust's 1953 book *Nature and Man in Biblical Thought* contains his most extensive and sustained statement of the nature of the biblical God.[9] It remains a superb brief characterization of biblical theism. The major themes reflect the general sweep of dialectical theology as well as the basic biblical images. And they center around the living God who acts in history in revelation and redemption.

In the book Rust contrasts the dynamic living God of the Bible with the static philosophical God of Pure Being. The divine nature and attributes cannot be understood as metaphysical abstractions. His self disclosure occurs in his mighty redemptive acts within human history. The knowledge of God is concrete. He is known only in what he does. Therefore he is known as redeemer before he is conceived as creator. Out of theological reflection upon God's acts, the biblical thinkers developed the picture of God's nature. The dominating images for the nature of the biblical God include sovereignty, personal being, holiness, and love.

In describing God's relation to the world and his purposes within history, Rust is always careful to preserve these biblical dimensions of the divine nature. In particular, this sovereign personal God who is holy love is free in relation to the world. He is not bound to the world through any necessary connection. He is moved wholly within himself as love, and his actions are self determined. His love is unconditionally free.

God's freedom in relation to the created order is preserved by two theological ideas. One is the trinitarian understanding of God. The doctrine of the Trinity affirms that as a triune unity of love, God is in himself all that love requires. Creation of and communion with man can add nothing to the divine perfection. There is no necessary or metaphysical ground for creation. Nor is the created order a necessary stage in the movement of the Absolute Spirit to self-fulfillment. God is not an evolving deity. God's creative movement is unconditioned and free. He allows the fellowship within himself to flow out to his creatures. In recent writings, Rust emphasizes more strongly the fulfillment that the created order provides to the being of God.

But he clearly underlines that God takes pleasure in the creation and benefits from it only because he *chooses* to do so, not because he needs the creation in order to be a God of love or to actualize his own being.

A second factor preserving the divine freedom is *creatio ex nihilo*. Creation out of nothing has remained basic to Rust's thought, despite the increasing dismissal by contemporary theology of *creatio ex nihilo* as an essential theological idea. It stresses that God is not conditioned by preexistent material or by creative patterns independent of himself from which he chooses in creating. *Creatio ex nihilo* also draws a sharp distinction between God and the world, clarifying that the world is not an emanation from the super abundance of divine being. It is the basis for dismissing both pantheism and dualism as acceptable views of God. For Rust, it also makes theism more acceptable than panentheism, a view that somewhat distinguishes him among contemporary writers who utilize process as a central category of thought. The world is not a self-sufficient and completed whole. It remains dependent upon God at every point of time and space.

The doctrine of the Trinity has remained essential in Rust's thought.[10] The triune God is a given of revelation. The formulation of the doctrine, however, is not explicit in the Bible. It is the product of reflection upon the apostolic witness. Rust has consistently affirmed the intentions and essential insights of the Chalcedonian statement of the triune God and the divine-human natures of the Son. But for him Chalcedon is read through the basic personal model for God in the biblical revelation. The apostles set the problem of the Trinity. The church later formulated the doctrine in an effort to safeguard the understanding of the triune nature.

The triune God acts in creation and redemption. The personal conception of God allows Rust to relate Father, Son, and Spirit in the mutual decision to create life external to himself and to redeem that world in its fallenness. The triune God moves outside himself in a pretemporal decision, creative act, and historical redemption. Allusions to the classic doctrine of coherence or *perichoresis* preserve God's ontological unity and diversity, so that the three Persons abide perfectly in one another, yet each has his own subsistence. Interpreting Chalcedon in line with the social view of the Cappodocian Fathers, Rust thinks of God "as a mutual involvement of three personal centers of infinite being in which each perfectly envelops the others and manifests that perfection of love which Christian disclosure declares to be the essence of God." [11]

Rust's interpretation of Chalcedon within a personal model is formulated with contemporary thought forms. But he is convinced that the personal analogue is at the center of the Christian revelation, particularly as focused in a personal incarnation. He thinks that "the use of the word 'Spirit' to describe God in the Hebrew-Christian tradition takes the personal as its essential reference." [12] Rust's own understanding of the personal has been influenced by a variety of modern thinkers. The existentialists have been influential in reawakening philosophy to man's inner life and self-transcendent personhood. But that is simply a modern version of Hebrew epistemology and anthropology. Among more prominent personalist influences on Rust's thought have been Martin Buber, John Macmurray and, in recent years, Michael Polanyi.

Rust has drawn key insight from two particular models of the personal, especially as they relate to transcendence and immanence. They are personal self-transcendence and intrapersonal relationship. Taken together, they symbolize something of God's personal nature and the character of the divine-human personal relationships. The self-transcendence of personal being suggests that God is immanent in nature and yet transcends it, much as the self is immanent in every psychosomatic process and yet transcends itself in critical reflection and judgment.[13] The model of intrapersonal relationships pictures how God is immanent in his creatures and yet transcends them, much as an I and Thou are personally related and yet are mutually transcendent. True finite personhood is fulfilled only through relationship to the infinite God of love. The trinitarian view of God further fortifies our understanding of this personal relationship.

Rust allows the personal model and various process insights to modify Chalcedonian trinitarian thought at several critical points, modifications he considers fully compatible with the biblical view of God. Rust's approach to divine perfection is illustrative of his wider methodology. As a theist, Rust has argued for the divine self-sufficiency in numerous writings. He is insistent that there is no deficiency in the divine nature, and that nature and history exist out of God's gracious self-giving love.

However, Christian theology has struggled with an adequate formulation of divine perfection whenever it has assimilated the Greek understanding of divine perfection as impassibility. As a corrective, Rust finds Charles Hartshorne's suggestion that God is dipolar, both being and becoming, useful in moving theology beyond the impasse of a static view of God. The dipolar understanding allows one to stress the transcendence of a God immanent within the process, one sovereign over the process and yet enriched by it. With this view, one can conceive the world as taken into God's experience, enriching his life and serving his ultimate purposes.

On this point, Rust makes a statement that sharply reveals his own theological criterion of revelation as the guideline for our concept of God. In accepting Hartshorne's definition of God as dipolar and his view that the universe thereby enriches the divine life, Rust comments, "The Biblical testimony to the divine disclosure in history, culminating in the Incarnation, points to this." [14] In fact, the understanding of God as dynamic activity, of his delight in the creative process, and the enrichment of his own life were in Rust's thought long before he appropriated Hartshorne's terminology. God is not static being. He is perfect in being and enriching himself in the process of becoming. Rust first assimilated that idea into his thought as an Old Testament theologian.

As his thought has developed, Rust has increasingly incorporated ideas and images out of existentialist, personalist, evolutionary, and process thought. He utilizes these personal and process images to illuminate various theological categories that emerge in the biblical revelation about a personal God of dynamic activity in nature and history. Many of the dominating images of Rust's later thought are contemporary translations of major revelatory themes. These include ideas like the transcendent presence, the kenosis of immanent Spirit, the power of loving constraint, persuasion by love, the suffering of God in a sacramental universe, and divine creativity in an unfinished universe. Most of the ideas can be found expressed by other terminology or at least implicitly in Rust's earlier writings. These emerging themes can be elaborated by an examination of Rust's thought about God's purpose and activity in nature and history.[15]

II. God and Nature

Eric Rust has concentrated much of his life and energy upon the Christian understanding of nature and its relation to the scientific view of the cosmos. That concern originated during his years in the early 30's as a science student in the Royal College of Science. His views have been expressed in a series of books beginning with his early biblical study *Nature and Man in Biblical Thought* (1953). That was followed by *Science and Faith: Towards a Theological Understanding of Nature* (1967), *Evolutionary Philosophies and Contemporary Theology* (1969), and *Nature—Garden or Desert?* (1971). The basic evolutionary process is now so well established that any serious Christian philosophical effort must correlate the Christian understanding with it. In Rust's view, an intelligent Christian doctrine of creation is highly compatible with contemporary evolutionary thought.

The concept of God must shape one's understanding of the creative process. Rust's method begins by establishing theological concepts out of revelation that are an essential framework for Christian philosophizing, concepts that center upon the nature of God. He then correlates his theological perspective with evolutionary and process thought, using evolutionary categories to cover large areas of human experience in specifically Christian type thinking.[16] Our examination of his thought will follow a similar scheme.

Essential Theological Categories

Rust's own theological development is virtually paradigmatic of his philosophical method. He developed his fundamental theological categories prior to his specific effort to relate theology to scientific and, in particular, evolutionary thought. Despite surface differences, a thread of consistency runs through all of Rust's works on nature and science. His early work *Nature and Man in Biblical Thought* bears a heavy imprint of the then current dialectical theology. His later works on nature—specifically *Evolutionary Philosophies and Contemporary Theology* and *Nature—Garden or Desert?*—speak more favorably of natural theology and are concerned to utilize natural theological categories to make contact with the thought of modern secular man.

One reading of his early and later books might argue for a radical shift from revealed theology to natural theology, particularly in certain of his comments in *Evolutionary Philosophies and Contemporary Theology.* In my view, that is a misleading reading. To the contrary, the later books presume most of the basic theological categories of Rust's early thought. There is a heavier empirical emphasis in the last two books, but an empirical emphasis compatible with revelation categories. He affirms the efforts of natural theologians and philosophers discussed in *Evolutionary Philosophies,* but those he prizes most—Teilhard de

Chardin, William Temple, and John Macmurray—all think within a clear Christian theistic framework. And the views of others he selectively utilizes are ideas that coordinate with or are complementary to Christian theism. Throughout these books, as well as in his earlier works, Christian theistic revelation is the crucial criterion by which he evaluates alternative viewpoints.

Essential theological categories out of the Christian revelation that must be preserved include the personal nature of the triune God of love, *creatio ex nihilo* and *creatio continua,* along with their major implications. For Rust it is essential that God be conceived as fully personal. Throughout his books are the rich pictures of the personal nature of God, including his personal will and purpose in creation and redemption, holiness and righteousness, love and mercy, fatherhood and grace, judgment and wrath. God wills personal relationships with his personal creatures. The incarnation is the unique and final disclosure of God and the unveiling of the true personal being of man. Jesus discloses the nature of God as personal love, a triune personal unity of love.[17]

Rust insists that *creatio ex nihilo* is vital to a proper understanding of God's relationship to the world. The model of creation, like that of the personal nature of God, emerges in the divine disclosures in salvation history which culminate in the incarnation. Creation is an analogical term that must be qualified by *ex nihilo* in order to be understood. Otherwise it pictures God as an artisan or technician who requires preexistent matter. *Ex nihilo,* much like the Hebrew term *bara,* refers to a unique divine creating that does not belong to the scientific order and is not open to scientific investigation.[18]

Creatio ex nihilo points to a personal mystery in God that cannot be contained in human or empirical categories. It expresses God's sovereignty over the physical process and its total dependence upon him. It points to the transcendence of God that must not be obscured by any view of his immanence. *Creatio ex nihilo* portrays a primordial act. But more importantly, it has ontological significance, denoting a divine act that transcends space and time. It indicates that God creates out of grace, not out of inner need or external necessity. The world is created out of nothing, not out of God's own being or out of some pre-existent matter. The world is not divine or continuous with God, but it also is not opposed to God. *Creatio ex nihilo* rules out any form of dualism or pantheism. The world is creaturely but good. The incarnation itself declares the value of the world to God.

A corollary of *creatio ex nihilo* is *creatio continua,* which points toward God's continuing act of historical creativity. His upholding of the physical creation is extended into the new creation, which grows out of the incarnation and looks forward to the future transformation. One's view of God's continuing creative activity is critical for a proper conception of God's relation to the world. God's continuation of creation is sustaining creativity, not creation out of nothing in each successive moment. Such a view allows for the quasi-independence of the universe and the freedom of man. The world depends upon God for its continuing existence, but God wills that the world operate in quasi-independence according to its inherent processes and regularities. God is present and immanently active within the creation, but there is an ontological distinction between God and the world. *Creatio continua* also eliminates both deism and pantheism.

Creatio continua preserves both the immanence and transcendence of God. God creates and continually maintains an immanent law within the natural order. The regularities, as well as the contingencies and randomness of nature, are expressions of his creation of a realm over against himself that has its own ordering independent of his own being. The miraclous reflects God's sovereignty and freedom over the creative process. The miraculous represents the point at which God wills to intervene in the process he continually sustains. At the human level, freedom is the expression of man's separate responsible existence, one in which he is free to choose his own destiny.[19]

The doctrine of providence grows out of this conception of the nature of God and his creative work. The doctrine asserts that God guides and overrules the whole process of nature and history and the lives of individuals in order to fulfill his purposes. It implies that the world, man, and history must be taken seriously. God's personal purposes involve nature and history. It is critical that the intention of divine love qualify our understanding of the providential operation. The divine providence operates within this structure of continuing creation that includes human freedom and the regularities, contingencies, and randomness of the natural order.[20] God providentially preserves and accompanies the regularities and contingencies of the quasi-independent process and the free acts of human beings.[21]

To speak of God as Creator is to speak of the creative work of the triune God. When one begins with the empirical and thus the immanence of God, it is difficult to reach the transcendence. But both transcendence and immanence are affirmed in Christian theism and are built into the mystery of the trinitarian life. The personal God of love is perfect in his innermost triune being, which excludes any view that the creative process is somehow satisfaction of a divine deficiency.[22] Far from being extraneous Greek metaphysical baggage, the triune God affords the most useful analogue for understanding the divine activity in the creative process. In a straightforward apologetic offensive, Rust writes in *Science and Faith,* "In this volume we see no need to apologize for the acceptance of the orthodox Trinitarian position. We have sought to do this in earlier books." [23]

Rust utilizes the doctrine for relating the transcendence of the eternal God to the immanence of God in the world. Already in his *Nature and Man in Biblical Thought,* Rust was emphasizing the participation of the three persons of the Trinity in the work of creation. A succinct statement of his thought about the Triune creative activity, found in *Science and Faith,* is worth quoting in full:

The Father is God as the ground of creative and redemptive power; the Son or Word is the personal activity of God coming forth in creative and redemptive love; and the Holy Spirit is the immanent aspect of that love effecting the divine purpose in nature and history, and especially in the life of redeemed man. Thus we may describe the Holy Spirit as the immanence of God within his creation, effecting the divine intention of the Father as this is expressed in creative, sustaining and redemptive activity through the Son.[24]

Rust has suggested that an emphasis upon the creative activity of the Holy Spirit is a way to respond to contemporary concern with the immanence of God, a response compatible with the broad sweep of revelatory disclosure. From his Old Testament studies, Rust was aware of the Old Testament pictures of the creative role of the Spirit. C. E. Raven's *Creator Spirit* sounded a note that has remained influential as Rust has more directly addressed evolutionary process. But his lengthy excursus on "The Creator Spirit, Evolution, and Life" in *Science and Faith,*[25] and several parallel discussions in other books, is simply an elaboration and further application of an idea basic to his early thought.

Modern Theology and Evolutionary Thought

Modern theology must relate its concept of God to contemporary scientific thought. In particular, it must take account of the emerging data of scientific investigations, the facts underlying evolutionary theories, and the models by which scientists try to explain their findings.

But any correlation of theology with the natural evolutionary process must preserve essential elements of the divine disclosure about the nature of God. That commitment virtually predetermines how Rust interacts with and critiques various modern process and evolutionary thinkers.

Rust is committed to philosophical thinking within a Christian frame of reference. Consequently, he aligns himself more closely to several theistic evolutionary thinkers than he does with many elements of the process philosophy of A. N. Whitehead and his followers. He has dealt extensively with the thought of process thinkers like Whitehead, Charles Hartshorne, Norman Pittenger, and John Cobb. Rust affirms their efforts to deal seriously with the empirical process. His own thought is compatible with many of their ideas, such as their understanding of the universe as a dynamic process, of its organic interrelatedness, of its open-endedness to novelty and future creative possibilities, and their rejection of a mind-matter dualism. He finds some contributions in their descriptions of God operating within the process through the persuasion of love, and the dynamic nature of the divine perfection which allows him to be enriched by the natural process. But at the same time Rust levels a repetitive criticism at some of their basic categories. And he judges inadequate even John Cobb's effort to correct certain limitations in Whitehead's thought for more specific Christian purposes.

Much of Rust's critique of Whiteheadian process thought grows out of his theistic view of God. He criticizes the Whiteheadians' use of an organic rather than a personal model, which creates problems for their understanding of God and of human personhood. Despite their effort to preserve transcendence, their stress on immanence and the organic nature of God does not make a sufficient distinction between God and the world. Their lack of an absolute creation, as found in *creatio ex nihilo,* makes it difficult to preserve the balanced values of classic theism. That is notably the case when Whitehead, for example, postulates creativity as a primordial reality and then defines God and the world as mutually necessary, so that God requires the process quite as much as the process requires God. In this sense, process thought offers only a finite God, not the God who is absolute over creation, a God who directs but does not create the process.

Just as process thought has difficulty maintaining the divine transcendence, it has a problem establishing self-transcendence and personal identity on the part of human creatures. It is difficult to arrive at the level of the personal when one selects as a fundamental model the organic, a lower level of reality. Whiteheadian thought regards all actual occasions as momentary within the process. Actual occasions obtain satisfaction and objectivity and then perish, persisting only in objective immortality. Although Whitehead seems to leave open the possibility of personal immortality, he more explicitly speaks of human person enduring only as memories within the ongoing becoming of God. A personal conception of God and man requires more than that.[26]

Because of such deficiencies in Whiteheadian-style process thought, Rust finds more affinity with the thought of people like William Temple, H. H. Farmer, and Teilhard de Chardin. These thinkers express evolutionary philosophies without abandoning sensitivity to theistic values. Although not fully satisfied with Teilhard's immanental view of God, Rust defends him against those who accuse him of pantheism, and finds theistic dimensions to his thought. Teilhard sees persons being bound together by Spirit around a personal point Omega, preserving both the divine person and human persons. God is a personal being who is transcendent as well as immanent, who is over against as well as a sustaining presence in the world.[27]

Toward a Christian Metaphysic

Rust's current focus of interest is an effort to develop a Christian metaphysic that incorporates the Christian view of creation and evolutionary categories into a comprehensive world view. He has sketched a tentative structure in some of the thematic patterns of his last three books on science and nature. His most direct statements are found in the final sections of *Evolutionary Philosophies and Contemporary Theology* and *Nature—Garden or Desert?* We will highlight a few of his central ideas with a few broad brush strokes.

The personal is the dominating model of his whole conceptual scheme. The key to the personal is the incarnation, which discloses the full personal nature of God and man. God is seen there "as the personal self-transcendent depth of this infinite universe." [28] The incarnation also discloses that God comes to us as "a mediated presence, in and through his creatures—nature, men, and history." [29] We meet God where he presses in upon our own personal being.

Rust finds a parallel to this personal disclosure in the emergence of self-conscious spirit out of the physical process, a phenomenon that says much about the process of nature and history. A reductionism that explains the spiritual in terms of the physical is inadequate. What is demanded is a recognition that there is a kinship between the spiritual and physical, because the spiritual emerges within the physical and can then control it. Rust rejects both a mind-matter dualism and the panpsychism of some process thinkers. And yet he agrees with the emphasis of process and evolutionary philosophical thinkers in picturing nature with psychic sensitivity and responsiveness and as having inherent within the physical the potentialities that become actualized as life and mind.[30] He contends that it is important to differentiate the personal from the organic and inanimate levels of the natural process. Man uniquely embodies self-consciousness and self-transcendence, which give rise to freedom, reflective thinking, and moral claims—characteristics essential for personal relationships. Human conscious experience, which includes intuition, sympathy, and imagination, makes man capable of recognizing claims from beyond himself.[31]

The meaning of the world to God can be envisioned in such a personal content. If God is personal and the world process is an expression of his personal will and purpose, then the process is important to his own experience. The incarnate resurrected Lord who has entered and accompanies the life of our world evidences that the history of the world is integral to the life of God himself.[32] The cross and resurrection point toward the suffering redemptive love of God for even the fallen world as he redemptively gathers it into his own life. God is perfect and at the same time enriched by the world. "Thus ever perfect, his is a growing perfection of love, enriched as that love becomes actualized in a creative and redemptive world process." [33]

Kenosis is the mode by which God achieves his personal purpose in the creation. The self-emptying (kenosis) of the incarnation is continuous with the whole divine purpose in the creative process, which throughout represents the self-emptying and self-limitation of the Creator. He endows the creative process with quasi-independence, contingency, and freedom. The kenosis of Christ in the incarnation unveils the creative intention for the whole process. Therefore Christ is the climax of the creative process, and his perfect humanity is prefigured in the whole process and is the inner meaning of all creation. He is the center not only of the new humanity but also of the whole cosmos. Christ's regenerative activity moves beyond man toward a consummation that will include a new heavens and a new earth.[34]

A personal universe bound together by organic and spiritual sensitivity and directed toward the incarnation and consummation of Christ is intelligible only if God is creatively and immanently present in the process. The Word expresses the divine intention as the depth of divine love creatively confers being on God's creatures and comes to a focus in the incarnation. Such love must operate continuously within the process and direct it. The Holy Spirit represents such divine immanence and activity.[35]

God moves and guides the world process within the limits determined by his personal purposes. In conferring quasi-independence upon the universe, God actualizes the potencies he has given his creaturely world. He respects the regularities of nature, which are the guiding rails of the process. But alongside the regularities are the contingencies and randomness of the natural process. The contingencies are a way of understanding God's struggle with evil, and also are indicators of the way that novelty and newness emerge within the process. And yet the regularities described in scientific laws indicate that nature's contingencies occur within definite limits.

The transcendent presence of the Creator Spirit guides the created order to the fulfillment of the divine purpose, respecting its quasi-independence and the freedom and creativity of man. This requires that the divine power operative within the universe be a power of loving constraint. This involves a kenosis of God's immanent Spirit at the creative level. The personal character of the immanent Spirit is increasingly central in his relationship to the organic and, especially, the personal levels where he acts largely by the persuasion of love.

In allowing for contingency in the natural order and for the freedom of creativity of man, the kenosis of the immanent Spirit incurs suffering when man does not respond to the divine persuasion. A suffering God is not a new idea for Rust. From the time of his study with H. W. Robinson, he has talked about suffering love and the eternal cross in the heart of God. Man has not yet fulfilled the divine purposes as represented in the divine image. Nature and man move toward their telos as revealed in the incarnation, the one point where the estrangement in both nature and man is overcome by God's suffering love.

Within the larger perspective of Rust's thought, this fuller understanding of the kenotic presence and becoming of God in relation to a quasi-independent universe opens possibilities for genuine creativity and a sacramental experience of the world. It allows us to see "the universe as unfinished and open toward the future within the limits, natural and moral, which are set by the Creator." [36] The creation is integral to the divine purpose. The fact that human beings meet the Creator in and through nature is an expression of the sacramental character of the universe. As Rust puts it, "The whole universe can be sacramental in the sense that it mediates the presence of and points to its creator." [37]

The Christian's cosmic hope grows out of faith in the incarnate Lord who is the presence of the future. The process of salvation, which includes nature itself, is moving toward its telos. God will ultimately bring the whole creation toward its unity in Christ. The future resurrection represents a creative renewal of the whole process, when God's "all-embracing, creative, and redeeming love will gather us all in." [38] Christian believers are co-workers with God in freeing the potentialities implanted in nature by God and helping to move it toward its final consummation.[39]

Rust has a brief summation of these major insights into the nature of God in *Nature—Garden or Desert?*[40]

We have sought to think of him as the transcendent personal depth in this process who is immanently present and active within it. We have pictured him, in his triunity, as coming forth out of his depth of love in creative and redemptive activity as Word/Son and operating immanently within his creation as Spirit. We have seen the whole process as one which both enriches his life by its actuality and yet is borne by him in suffering and redemptive love. We have stressed the Incarnation as the focal point in which the creative process reaches its climax in the full and true humanity of Jesus. Here God brings his redemptive suffering to its climax and crowns his creation in the God-man. God creates a new humanity and promises a new heaven and a new earth in the risen humanity of the Christ. The Resurrection becomes the key to the future and declares that our labor as co-workers with God shall not be cast like rubbish on the void. We live in hope as well as in faith and love.

III. God and History

The personal purposes of God in the creative process come to a focus in the dimension of history. Many of the theological ideas elaborated in connection with God's relation to nature also apply to God's activity in history. Rust has written three major books on history. Much of the thought in his early *The Christian Understanding of History* (1946) is carried over and extended in *Salvation History* (1962) and in his major work *Towards a Theological Understanding of History* (1963). He has taken account of recent eschatological thinkers in sections of *Positive Religion in a Revolutionary Time* and *Nature—Garden or Desert?* Our concern here is limited to the concept of God in relation to the historical process. We will elaborate and extend certain of the themes already examined into the specific realm of history but without any attempt at an inclusive discussion of Rust's overall work on history.

The divine purposes in history grow out of God's nature as personal love and concern, God giving himself to his creatures and being glorified in the creation. Creation and history are "an act of absolutely free love, in which God wills an order of being that shall share his eternal bliss and reflect his glory. . . . He wills to give existence to his creatures and sustain that existence." [41] History is also God taking humanity more fully into the divine life. The intended personal union "of God to his creatures and of his creatures to one another is being actualized in history." [42]

The personal God is love in his essential being. He is self-sufficient agape, not eros that needs another to be fulfilled. When God moves beyond himself, he does so because he is self-giving love, not because he is deficient in his own nature. There is no internal or external necessity for God to create the world. History is not a divine movement toward self-realization. Nor is it a struggle between God and some alien power. God's will is to create and give himself to his creatures in a relationship of love. History exists as an act of sheer grace.

The doctrine of the Trinity safeguards this divine self-sufficiency. It symbolizes a God of self-sufficient internal bliss and communion within himself. From eternity he is in his triune unity and "community-ness" a giving and receiving of love. The Trinity preserves the inner mystery of God as love and illuminates the character of nature and history as grace existence. And the doctrine relates the eternal God to his self-disclosure in his threefold activity in history as Creator and Sustainer, Redeemer and Reconciler, and Re-Creator and Sanctifier. He deals with us in history in his triune nature as love.

God's personal purpose determines the way he relates to his personal creatures in and through the historical process. The doctrine of creation asserts that both the quasi-independence of the universe and the freedom of man are essential to God's historical purpose. The doctrine of providence interprets the sustaining activity of God as he preserves, accompanies, and guides the historical process toward his appointed goal. Such preservation occurs within a natural framework where free human beings are subjected to many elements of necessity and of randomness and contingency. God also preserves our historical existence by ordaining and sustaining certain orders of creation within which society functions, including sex, family, labor, and the state.[43] Because God is absolute love, he has given his human creatures the highest kind of existence, one in which we are free to decide for ourselves. Love and personal relationships cannot be coerced.

God's creative purpose is actualized in historical existence, but that existence is in a sinful, fallen world. Because alienation of the world results from the misuse of freedom, it is best pictured in terms of voluntary rebellion and, on the cosmic scale, by demonic rebellion. One result of human sin is that God ordains orders of conservation as a form of preserving historical existence. These include an awareness of moral obligation, conscience, a sense of social justice, systems of law, and the constraining power of the state. But, of course, these orders are also perverted by human sin and fall short of their ideal.[44]

Secular history is fallen existence. But even here, "we are still in the arena of encounter and personal relationship." [45] In response to sin in his world, God still acts in ways consistent with his personal purpose. The divine providence not only accompanies secular history but also takes the form of judgment within it. Judgment introduces the recurring themes of love and wrath, grace and judgment, and the ultimate triumph of divine grace. Rust does not hesitate to use the images of judgment and wrath because in his understanding they are fully consistent with his personal model for describing God's nature and activity within history.

The judgment of God is a way of interpreting God's utilization of the tragic and destructive dimensions of history. As holy love, God does not react lightly to the sin and rebellion of his creatures. "He is self consistent, and he must be true to his purpose of love." [46] When free human beings sin, they precipitate the personal wrath of God, a wrath not inconsistent with love. Without the divine reaction, sin could conquer love. There is a retributive element to wrath, but it is ultimately redemptive. And in contrast to some modern theological views, Rust contends that wrath is personal, not impersonal. "Wrath is the personal reaction of holy love in which God gives men over to the destructive consequences of their rebellion." [47] God continues to sustain his creatures in their rebellion. Yet God's government of the sinful world is manifest in his overruling of man's sinful historical activity and directing it to unintended ends, so that even evil may serve the divine purpose. On the cosmic scale, sin will yield to the eschatological triumph of grace.[48]

To assert that the divine will and purpose are being achieved in this historical process is to affirm the absolute sovereignty of God over history. The problem of history for the Christian concerns how the divine will and purpose are to be related to the contingencies of nature and to human history with its freedom, sinful rebellion, and demonic perversion. Rust has consistently argued that God's sovereignty over history can be understood only from his personal disclosure in Christ as free self-giving love. God acts always as he has revealed himself in Jesus Christ.

The crux of the problem is how to relate the omnipotence of God to this kind of world. Providence requires that God be sufficiently powerful to achieve his historical purposes. Omnipotence cannot be analogically conceived on the basis of magnified human power. Human conceptions of power are perverted by sin and usually refer to a human will-to-power that overcomes all resistance. If we attempt such an analogical picture, then we inevitably juxtapose omnipotence and love. But the divine power is the power of omnipotent love. God's power is directed toward accomplishing his purposes in creation and redemption. Personal love is at the center of such a purpose. His power is fundamentally his power to be himself and to be self-consistent as love.

God's power is such that it creates creaturely freedom, respects and encourages it. His power is great enough that he withdraws and gives free human beings a capacity to decide their destinies. He respects even the misuse of freedom. In Rust's word's, "Because freedom was necessary for God's purpose of love, God voluntarily opened the door to sin and rebellion." [49] And God's power will sustain sinners even in their rebellion against him. He preserves and accompanies them in their sinning. Secular history is the story of sin but a story of human beings who remain responsible even though fallen.[50]

In such a fallen world, redemption becomes central to realization of the divine purposes as the God of love "moves out to his creatures, creating fellowship, evoking commitment and faith." [51] One result of the world's sinful rebellion is that the key to the historical process is found in a history within history. God's unique historical self-disclosures occur in salvation history in which God acts to redeem the world. Rust's *Salvation History* remains one of the definitive statements of *Heilsgeschichte* theology. Here he provides a classic panorama of creation, sin, judgment, and redemption, tracing the saving acts of God from the election of Israel to the incarnation of God in Christ and on into eschatological hope.

Rust has extended many of those themes in *Towards a Theological Understanding of History* in which he relates salvation history to the larger historical process. In his latest books, Rust more explicitly than earlier argues that the incarnation was not simply the result of human sin. It is the climax of the creative process itself. It represents the full disclosure of the personal character of existence and thus is the turning point in human history and the revelation of its final goal. The incarnation enthrones the personal in the universe and makes us aware of our own personal nature and of the personal presence who sustains us and places his claim over us. Man as a whole is redeemed in the incarnation. By becoming man, God potentially lifted man, in the totality of his relationships, more intimately into the divine life.

Jesus is, in this sense, the incarnate eschaton, the presence in our midst of the one who stands at the end. The eschaton becomes incarnate in the historical process. The God who is at the end of the process becomes sacramentally present in history and moves history toward its consummation.[52] Through the death, resurrection, and ascension of Jesus and the gift of the Holy Spirit, "salvation history becomes contemporaneous with all history."[53] As the power of the age to come becomes operative in history, the future goal of history becomes actualized in the present.

Salvation is on a cosmic scale, but it is actualized through the creation of a new humanity within an eschatological framework. The redeemed society takes shape within the life of the church, the body of believing and committed persons. The church's servant task is to proclaim the gospel to the world, both in evangelism and in a permeation of secular culture with the redemptive influence of the gospel.[54] Christians become co-workers with God in setting free the future possibilities in man and history and in helping to move history to its final goal.[55]

Rust has always affirmed the value of the world throughout his writings on history. But the major thrust of his thought has centered on salvation history. His images for secular history have often been those of sin, the demonic, judgment, and wrath. One can detect a slight shift in emphasis in his latest understanding of secular history in *Positive Religion in a Revolutionary Time* and *Nature—Garden or Desert?* These books reflect his increasing concentration on categories of creativity, process, the unfinished universe, and the theme of eschatological hope.

God's purposes concern this world. Redemption is in the world, not out of the world. In Christ, God has said "yes" to our world. God's decisive redemptive activity is in salvation history. But the secular historical process is also sustained by God, open to his activity, and in a more limited way subjected to his lordship. In fact, the world is in some sense both God's and the devil's, existing in a tension between its fallenness and ultimate redemption. Eschatological redemption involves a transformation of this world into a new heaven and a new earth. But with all his affirmation of the world, Rust is still careful to say, "Secular history only gains ultimate meaning as it is redeemed through the activity of God in salvation history." [56]

The purpose of God will be realized only in the eschaton when it will be actualized at all levels of his creation, when the sinful rebellion will be judged and annihilated, and the whole universe will be gathered into the life of God. Then there will be "a transfigured universe in which man as personal being will become fully personal as God relates his creatures fully to one another and to himself in love." [57]

Perhaps this extended essay has justified the thesis that the concept of God is the most definitive component of Eric Rust's philosophical theology. His lifetime of theological and philosophical work on nature and history has encompassed existence from creation to consummation. The unifying concept of his thought is the personal model of the triune God of love, who wills to share himself with his free human creatures in a quasi-independent universe fractured by the rebellion of sin. His creative and redemptive activity within that evolutionary process is consistent with his personal purposes of loving man, in his freedom, into responsible personal relationships with himself. That purpose will be consummated in a transfigured universe permeated by the reality of love in the perfected fellowship of the redeemed with the eternal triune God of love.

NOTES

[1] Eric Rust, *Nature and Man in Biblical Thought* (London: Lutterworth Press, 1953), pp. 245-303.

[2] *Nature and Man,* p. 249.

[3] Eric Rust, *Evolutionary Philosophies and Contemporary Theology* (Philadelphia: The Westminster Press, 1969), pp. 36–37.

[4] Eric Rust, *Towards a Theological Understanding of History* (New York: Oxford University Press, 1963), pp. 48-54, 61-82; Eric Rust, *Science and Faith: Towards a Theological Understanding of Nature* (New York: Oxford University Press, 1967), pp. 122-126; Eric Rust, *Salvation History:*

A Biblical Interpretation (Richmond, Va.: John Knox Press, 1962), pp. 11-48.

[5] Eric Rust, *Positive Religion in a Revolutionary Time* (Philadelphia: The Westminster Press, 1970), p. 189.

[6] *Science and Faith*, p. 122; *Nature and Man*, pp. 245-248, 274-275.

[7] *Nature and Man*, pp. 245-303.

[8] *Theological Understanding of History*, pp. 75-82; *Salvation History*, pp. 11-48.

[9] *Nature and Man*, pp. 245-303.

[10] See his discussion in *Nature and Man*, pp. 294-303, and *Science and Faith*, pp. 184-191.

[11] *Evolutionary Philosophies*, p. 221.

[12] *Theological Understanding of History*, p. 139.

[13] *Evolutionary Philosophies*, p. 220.

[14] *Ibid.*, p. 218.

[15] See excellent succinct discussions in *Evolutionary Philosophies*, pp. 202-230; *Science and Faith*, pp. 300-316; *Positive Religion*, pp. 186-210; and Eric Rust, *Nature—Garden or Desert?* (Waco, Texas: Word Books, 1971), pp. 108-137.

[16] *Evolutionary Philosophies*, p. 36.

[17] *Nature—Garden or Desert?*, p. 112.

[18] *Science and Faith*, p. 138.

[19] *Theological Understanding of History*, p. 144.

[20] *Nature—Garden or Desert?*, p. 113.

[21] *Theological Understanding of History*, p. 158.

[22] *Evolutionary Philosophies*, p. 35.

[23] *Science and Faith*, p. 184.

[24] *Ibid.*, p. 184.   [25] *Ibid.*, pp. 145-200.

[26] See his critiques of Whiteheadian-style process thought in *Evolutionary Philosophies*, pp. 94-119, and especially pp. 117-119; and *Nature—Garden or Desert?*, pp. 77-81.

[27] *Evolutionary Philosophies*, pp. 215-216.

[28] *Nature—Garden or Desert?*, p. 113.

[29] *Ibid.*, p. 115.   [30] *Ibid.*, pp. 121-122.

[31] *Evolutionary Philosophies*, pp. 207-212.

[32] *Nature—Garden or Desert?*, p. 116.

[33] *Ibid.*, p. 117.   [34] *Ibid.*, pp 118-120

[35] *Ibid.*, pp. 122-123.   [36] *Ibid.*, p. 125.

[37] *Ibid.*, p. 133.   [38] *Ibid.*, p. 136.

[39] *Ibid.*, p. 136.   [40] *Ibid.*, pp. 134-135.

[41] *Theological Understanding of History*, p. 144.

[42] *Evolutionary Philosophies*, p. 227.

[43] *Theological Understanding of History*, pp. 152-155.

[44] *Ibid.*, pp. 118-127.   [45] *Ibid.*, p. 154.

[46] *Ibid.*, p. 159.   [47] *Ibid.*, p. 160.

[48] *Ibid.*, pp. 157-173.   [49] *Ibid.*, p. 117.

[50] *Ibid.*, p. 122.   [51] Ibid., p. 140.

[52] *Positive Religion*, pp. 208-209.

[53] *Theological Understanding of History*, p. 229.

[54] *Ibid.*, p. 253.

[55] *Nature—Garden or Desert?*, p. 137.

[56] *Theological Understanding of History*, p. 220.

[57] *Evolutionary Philosophies*, p. 230.

12.
Faith and Freedom
A Case Study
Paul S. Minear

When Protestant theologians seek to trace the ways in which biblical revelation shapes Christian faith, they turn almost automatically to the Pauline epistles for normative treatments of both the terms revelation and faith. Such recourse is altogether right, for those documents do in fact furnish multiple stimuli for reflection on those themes. Furthermore, when scholars seek to tap those resources, they quickly find that the corpus as a whole provides riches that are altogether too extensive to permit adequate exploitation. A common response to this exorbitance of wealth is to limit study to a single epistle. That is what I propose to do here; but I wish to take a rather unusual course. In this predicament most scholars select the text of a major epistle (e.g., Romans) as a base of operations; I prefer to select a letter which by any ordinary measurement ranks as minor. This is a letter of whose authenticity there can be no doubt; yet of its importance there appears to be great skepticism. I have in mind the tiny note to Philemon.

This skepticism is due to many features. The letter has played no role in recent discussions of Pauline theology, a fact borne out by any competent survey of the literature. Such neglect may be due to the contents of the letter, for it seems to focus on private rather than public concerns, on practical rather than on theoretical problems. There is no explicit appeal to the *kerygma* or to divine revelation through the death and resurrection of Christ. The verb "to believe" *(pisteuein)* does not appear; the noun "faith" *(pistis)* appears twice, but only in the conventional thanksgiving formula. Attention is centered not on Paul's ideas but on actions to be taken by certain secondary characters who play only obscure roles elsewhere in the Pauline mission. If we were to measure canonicity by the degree of authority which any given document actually exerts over the modern church—its authority to define faith or to guide moral behavior—this letter

224

would not be found in any contemporary canon of Scripture. In fact no recent study of this document gives any weight to its value as Scripture. At most it is commended as providing evidence for Paul's views of the institution of slavery and for his tactful diplomacy in dealing with Christians like Philemon. Yet I believe that this brief and minor epistle actually furnishes us with a superb case study of the relations between revelation, faith, and liberation, and I hope to convince readers of this position.

I begin by observing some advantages in selecting this letter for scrutiny. For one thing, it is brief enough (25 verses) to permit microscopic analysis within the space available. For another, it does not suffer from excessive familiarity on the part of readers. It has not been submerged in the sludge deposited by dogmatic wars or by homiletical overkill. It is unfamiliar enough so that we can read it as if for the first time. (This is a good moment for my reader to do just that.) It is concrete enough for us to visualize the original situation which it addressed. Unlike many other epistles, there is in this case a remarkable consensus among scholars concerning its origin and its function. Moreover, the occasion for Paul's intervention is so clearly reflected that theoretical considerations are everywhere subordinated to a single pastoral problem. As we shall see, that problem so sharply illustrates the offensiveness of Paul's gospel that it also illustrates the power of faith, not so much on Paul's part as on the part of Onesimus. For these reasons I have chosen Onesimus as a dramatic study in the relation of faith to liberation. May he provoke us to entertain some fresh thoughts on the nature of this relation.

I have just mentioned scholarly consensus regarding this letter. It is well at the outset to review the chief items in that consensus:
—author: Paul, who associated Timothy with himself
—address: Philemon, Apphia, Archippus, and their house-church
—location: Colossae
—probable founder of church: Epaphras (Col. 4:12f.)
—location of Paul: prison
—bearers of letter: Onesimus, Tychicus
—companion epistle: Colossians (4:7-9)
—neighboring churches: Laodicea, Hierapolis
—associates of Paul and Onesimus: Epaphras, Mark, Aristarchus, Demas, Luke, Jesus Justus
—objectives of Paul: to persuade a Christian owner to receive back his runaway slave without exacting the usual penalties, to treat

him as a Christian brother, to release him from slavery, to send
him back to assist Paul.

—prior episodes in story of Onesimus: his life as a slave of Philemon;
his escape; his action of defrauding his owner; his conversion
to Christ by Paul; his helpfulness to the imprisoned apostle; his
return to Philemon with Tychicus, bearing this letter from Paul.

—the status of slaves: a slave was "a person who is the property
of another person";[1] he belonged to "the least respectable type
of the least respectable class in the social scale" and was treated
by the law as having no rights.[2] For a slave to run away was
"one of the most serious offences known to ancient law." [3] In
returning, Onesimus "would place himself entirely at the mercy
of the master whom he had wronged . . . Roman law imposed
no limits to the power of the master. . . . Slaves were constantly
crucified for lighter offences than his." [4]

—appraisal of letter: Scholars agree in assigning relatively little
value. "It does not once touch upon any question of public interest
. . . [but is] wholly occupied with an incident of domestic life." [5]
Note the contrast between this appraisal and Paul's own interest
in Onesimus and his great affection for him.

Having surveyed the constants in current appraisals, we should now
review the more significant variables. Many of these were suggested
by John Knox in a study that has been widely consulted.[6] Professor
Knox argues that Onesimus' owner, the primary recipient of Paul's
plea, was not Philemon but Archippus (Philem. 1:1; Col. 4:17). Very
few other scholars have accepted this argument. Furthermore, Knox
locates Archippus' residence not in Colossae but in Laodicea; thus
this letter becomes the 'lost' letter to the Laodiceans (Col. 4:16). Again
this view has won little support. Another variable has to do with
the city in which Paul was imprisoned and from which he was writing.
Scholars differ in their preferences: Rome, Caesarea, Ephesus, or some
other city. I prefer Ephesus, without placing much weight on this
hunch. We are also at a loss to know under what circumstances Onesimus and Paul first met. The letter itself gives no indication. E. Loh-
meyer attributes this meeting to the desire of Onesimus to seek asylum
with this religious leader, in accordance with the recognized practice
of using temples as places of refuge for escaped slaves.[7] This suggestion
has not been widely adopted. I rather picture Onesimus as having
been arrested and confined in the same prison with Paul. Following
the lead of earlier commentators, Knox believes that, after receiving

freedom from Archippus, Onesimus returned to Ephesus and in time became the bishop of the church there (Ignatius, *ad Eph.* 1:3). This is an interesting but an uncertain hypothesis.

Some of these variables are well worth support. However, in developing this chapter I have adopted none of them, but have chosen to reconstruct the situation in line with the set of constants as outlined above—though with one exception. I must disclaim any support of the last constant—the current appraisal of the major values of the letter—and wish to submit a minority report in that regard.

As already noted, it is quite common to read this letter for its "sidelights on slavery in the Roman Empire." [8] And in such a reading, the letter can be viewed as "one of the landmarks in the history of emancipation." [9] It is typical to support such an appraisal with statements like this: "When a slave in his inner nature became free, the fetters gradually fell away from him of their own accord." [10] Here I detect a tendency among Christian exegetes to treat everything in the Scriptures euphemistically; one should where possible avoid saying anything negative, especially about Paul. It is a strange thing to locate a "landmark" centuries before the change that is celebrated. When "gradualness" has to be measured in centuries rather than months, it becomes the gradual movement of a glacier rather than of a social revolution. I am forced to doubt whether this letter itself exerted any influence whatever in eroding the massive power of slavery as an institution, and I believe that such euphemisms represent rather frantic efforts to say something good about a letter when one can find nothing better to say.

There is a second type of commendation for the letter which I reject, albeit not so categorically. It measures the document by its ability to disclose "the mind and heart of Paul." [11] "Nowhere does the nobility of the apostle's character receive a more vivid illustration." [12] More specifically, the letter is praised as "an expression of simple dignity, of refined courtesy, of large sympathy, and of warm personal affection." [13] In such judgments, the apostle appears as an ideal gentleman of middle-class Anglo-Saxon culture, in which Christian faith is less decisive than charming character traits. Viewed in this light, the letter becomes "a priceless memorial of the great apostle" [14] and in literary terms "one of the most beautiful letters ever written." [15]

Such admiration may be well deserved, but it seems to me that it almost wholly ignores Paul's original intentions and concerns. Negatively, we insist that he did not write this letter in order to deal with slavery as an institution, nor was he shaping a personality profile that would attract admiration or writing a letter designed to be praised for its charm and tact.[16] Such effects were far from his hopes and fears. More positively, he was wholly intent upon influencing the immediate decisions of Philemon and thereby the future work of Onesimus. Concern for those two men almost wholly supplanted self-concern (not wholly, cf. v. 20). Their attitude toward the apostle became less crucial than their attitude toward one another. If any of the three men had allowed his conception of the institution of slavery to dictate his role in the triangle, Paul's desire would have been frustrated. Similarly, any conscious desire to enhance a heroic self-image or to call attention to literary excellence would likewise have destroyed the mutual trust that was essential to the successful outcome of a most unusual and complex project. This was a strange triangle, and the strangeness consisted in this: each of the three men was most concerned with changing the attitude of the third man to the second. The more closely we study that triangular situation, the more we will be inclined to turn away from the later history of slavery and from our impressions of the apostle and to look more intently (1) at the dilemmas which Philemon would face on receiving the letter, and (2) at the struggles which Onesimus must have endured before consenting to return to his owner. When we consider the importance to Paul of these two brothers (a runaway slave and his defrauded owner) it becomes nothing less than an insult to Paul to express our appreciation of his letter in conventional terms. Thoughtless appreciation can be more destructive than thoughtful criticism.

There is every reason to apologize to Paul for such a thoughtless insult, and then to make amends by recognizing more clearly what was really of prime concern to Paul. That concern surely centered in the fate of Onesimus. Had this slave not existed, had he not agreed to return to Philemon, Paul would never have written this letter. In his earlier conversations with Paul, we may be confident that Onesimus had weighed the different options and had made his choice. On his receipt of the letter and his slave, Philemon would be forced to weigh his options and to choose one. The letter enables us as readers to enter into those triangular relationships at a point between Onesimus' decision and Philemon's. The letter may provide inadequate evidence to permit certainty in reconstructing those decisions, but it should impel us to ponder them (as if we were in Tychicus' shoes) and to reconstruct the various options, taking care to distinguish the degrees of possibility or probability in each. This process of reconstruction can be more orderly if we separate the earlier sequences in the story of Onesimus.

Scene 1. Onesimus was a slave. This was his legal and actual status; there was nothing hypothetical or metaphorical about it. His name, in fact, was one often used to indicate servile status.[17] We know nothing about the origin of this status: whether he had been born to a slave mother or captured in war or sold to pay debts. Nor do we know anything about his assignment: to field work or house work, to a craft or an industry. We know nothing about how long he had been in bonds or about how many other slaves Philemon owned. There is only one conjecture that can rank as a highly probable one. The fact that Onesimus ran away tells us what we need to know about prior conditions. The risks taken by any fugitive slave were so great that he would not have taken those risks had there not been very great provocation. Conditions must have seemed intolerable to him and wholly without prospect of amelioration. Moreover, his success in escaping indicates the likelihood that he had planned the attempt for some time. This also tells us something about his earlier relationships to Philemon, to Apphia who as Philemon's wife (a possible assumption) may have exercised some oversight of the slaves, and to Archippus (who may have been a son in this same household). We must assume that those relationships had been neither friendly nor conducive to the satisfaction of Onesimus' grievances.

Scene 2. Onesimus had made good his escape. He had left behind whatever conditions had induced rebellion, had taken in stride the dangers of recapture, and had succeeded in reaching a haven of relative security. No reconstruction of his escape can be more than hypothetical. But the fact of escape is virtually certain and thus we are encouraged to visualize him in his flight, in which he probably carried certain valuables stolen from Philemon (v. 18). Even a minimal surrender to the imagination must allow some room for picturing his fears and feelings during the escape, his frantic search for a hiding place, and the emotions of exhilaration when first he felt safe from pursuit. In those days as now, a churning gyroscope of feelings must have attended any hazardous flight from slavery to freedom. We do not know where he found a safe haven, but he seems to have found it. "It would not be safe for Onesimus to be anywhere except with the down-and-outs, the riff-raff of the population that hang about the great seaports and collect in the less reputable part of the great cities." [18] The Asian city of Ephesus, a hundred miles from Colossae, could have provided such a haven, near enough and large enough for the fugitive to find a place in which to lose himself. We have no way of knowing how long it took him to reach such a haven or how soon thereafter the next development came.

Scene 3. Here we have the first encounter between Onesimus and Paul, a meeting that presumably took place when Paul was in prison. Other Christians were also in prison, such as Aristarchus (Col. 4:10) and Epaphras (Philem. 23), who perhaps had founded the church in Colossae. Was Onesimus in prison, too, when he met these jailmates? It is possible that he was still free, for Paul may have been rather loosely detained under house-arrest, as pictured in Acts 28:16. I think it more likely, however, that Onesimus had also been under arrest. The Greek text of v. 10, "whom I begat in prison" is more ambiguous than the RSV "whose father I have become in *my* imprisonment" (there is no *my* in the Greek). If we picture this encounter as having taken place with Onesimus in prison, we cannot avoid speculating concerning the cause of his arrest. Had he been taken in a raid on a hangout of fugitive slaves? Theo Preiss is probably right in rejecting this supposition. "A slave who was caught was punished severely and sent back to his master." [19] Had he taken refuge with Paul under the right of slaves to claim asylum in religious precincts? This itinerant tentmaker would hardly have qualified as a temple, and even if he had, the slave would either have been returned to Philemon by the civil authorities or sold to another owner. I think it more likely that Onesimus had been taken into custody for some petty theft or for vagrancy. Here was an alien, without papers or friends to vouch for him. Some minor charge would have been sufficient. Whatever the reason, we are prompted to imagine the emotional effects on him of this sharp transition from freedom to bonds. To go within a short period from intolerable slavery to delicious freedom, and then to find himself in a foreign jail, surrounded by strangers—and there to meet this strange Jewish enthusiast! What a pity that this period of Onesimus' life, and this occasion for meeting Paul, are so completely obscured. Yet the fact of a meeting is clear, along with some of its repercussions.

Scene 4. Onesimus was converted to faith in Christ. Here we are back on solid ground. In prison, the vagabond apostle, jailed on charges and under conditions that are also obscure to us (cf. 2 Cor. 11:23-

28), persuaded this fugitive slave of the truth of the gospel of a crucified Messiah. The image of birth (v. 10) indicates the sudden and drastic nature of this event, with Paul as parent and Onesimus as child. During their conversations, Paul learned of the slave's connections with Philemon, and Onesimus learned of Paul's connections with the house-church in Colossae. Onesimus met at least one fellow-prisoner from his hometown, Epaphras. He was drawn into intimate contact with six or more teammates of Paul. We know nothing specific concerning the message which was effective in converting Onesimus except what may be inferred from other epistles. And we know even less concerning the responses of the fugitive to this strange gospel. We know nothing about how long the processes of rebirth required, about what resistances were evoked and overcome, about the paths taken by the convert's thoughts and feelings. Perhaps it is just as well that so private a matter should be hidden from probing eyes that might only exploit and corrupt such knowledge. We do know that in the process the slave became the spiritual child of the apostle, and his brother as well. His uselessness was transformed to usefulness (v. 11). "In the Lord" Onesimus became the brother of all others who were "in the Lord"; this new bond submerged all former distinctions. Thereafter, the infrastructure of their relations would be determined by the realities of intercessory concern.[20] Onesimus entered the circle of those whose very life testified to the authority of Paul as father-prophet-apostle. Paul, in turn, was under constraint to exercise that authority in ways that were consistent with his responsibility both to the Lord and to his children.[21] In short, the conversion of Onesimus in prison was an event that thoroughly conditioned all his subsequent relationships "in the Lord," including, of course, to that third member of the triangle, Philemon.

Scene 5. A postconversion decision on the part of Onesimus would be whether or not to return to Philemon. We know that he finally decided to return; so we must try to visualize the process by which convert and apostle arrived at that decision. The apostle makes clear his reluctance to send the slave back "home" (v. 13). The slave had every reason to be even more reluctant. We know that in dealing with the owner, Paul was unwilling to do anything without the owner's voluntary consent (v. 14). It is altogether probable that the apostle would use the same restraint in dealing with Onesimus. His conversion must have represented a free decision on his part; this strategic and difficult postconversion decision must have been equally free. And what a test of freedom—to choose to return to slavery! "Father" and "newborn child" must have talked at length about that test, especially since it affected so many brothers. As Theo Preiss observed: "in the Body of Christ personal affairs are no longer private." [22]

The tenor of the letter implies that it would have been possible for the slave to remain with Paul. There he would be free of bonds, continuing to help Paul in association with a team of congenial Christian workers. By contrast, what would Onesimus face on his return to Colossae? We can infer from the very forcefulness of Paul's appeal that Onesimus would face all the hazards of any recaptured slave. He would be wholly at the mercy of his defrauded owner. Any penalty that Philemon chose would be legal; from among those penalties the forfeiting of life itself could not be excluded. Even if Philemon proved more tolerant and exacted no such drastic penalty, he might well return the slave to his former tasks, which had originally been so onerous as to prompt the escape in the first place. Philemon would presumably be under pressure from other owners to make such an example of this runaway as to discourage imitators. Should he be too lenient, his other slaves would be encouraged to demand equality of treatment or to defect. Many other Christian communes had slaves as members; Onesimus' decision, followed by Philemon's action, would be bound to send shock-waves through them as well. So in his internal debate over whether to return, Onesimus must have weighed the consequences not only within the personal triangle—his owner, his father in Christ, himself—but also within a much wider constituency.

We can only speculate about his discussions with Paul *en route* to a decision. To Paul he owed much; he had been trying to honor that debt by some kind of personal service. Though he had possibly been in prison when he met Paul, by the time of the letter he had been freed and could return to Colossae. Paul was engaged in urging him to return. Although Paul no doubt respected his independence, his words "I am sending him back to you" (v. 12) indicate something stronger than nondirective counseling. Just as there was steel in Paul's appeal to Philemon, so there must have been steel in his conversations with Onesimus.[23] Paul probably did not hesitate to use the authority implicit in his status as parent, brother, partner, apostle. And the comparable situations of the two men would have affected the strength of this authority.[24] Paul was in prison because of his apostolic work;

Onesimus was now free. The slave could go wherever he chose; his parent remained at the mercy of others. The fact that Onesimus listened to Paul is an interesting example of the unique character of authority within this community. Christ the crucified exerted his authority over his ambassador, in chains as a mark of his vocation; this ambassador, in turn, exerted his authority over a non-prisoner—persuading him to accept again the status of a slave.[25]

It is almost impossible to explain Paul's urging or Onesimus' response except by recognizing that both men consciously stood under the authority of Christ. So momentous and so hazardous an action would not have been chosen unless both men had agreed that this represented the will of Christ. This conviction is supported by Paul's use of prepositional phrases in his letter, phrases so potent that one could say rightly that for Paul (and presumably for Onesimus) faith was defined prepositionally.

—the faith which you have *toward* the Lord Jesus
—all the good that is ours *in* Christ
—bold enough *in* Christ
—a prisoner *for* Christ Jesus
—a beloved brother . . . both *in* the flesh and *in* the Lord
—refresh my heart *in* Christ

These phrases, so frequent a punctuation in the letter Onesimus carried, almost certainly characterized the way in which Paul in oral discussions subordinated the triangular relationships to the mutual vocation under Christ. Now, they may sound to us like pious empty rhetoric, but then they must have been quite definitive of the human situation. We must take Paul seriously when he calls Onesimus "my very heart" (v. 12). All such phrases must be taken with great seriousness because the communal reality they represent can alone explain why this slave was at last willing, in spite of internal resistances and external dangers, to return to the bonds of slavery. Before his return, what John Schutz says of Paul must have become, in one way or another, true of Onesimus as well:

The phrase "in Christ" sums up for Paul the new life which belongs to the Christian. Standing "in Christ" the Christian experiences the events of Christ's death and resurrection as his own death to an old age and entrance into a new possibility of life. This newness of life so bears the contours of Christ's death and resurrection that it is never to be understood apart from those events. When one is "in Christ," he lives in that particular confluence of past, present and future which unites the this-worldly life (brother . . . in the flesh) with an already fulfilled eschatological promise of new life (brother . . . in the Lord).[26]

In addition to his respect for this ultimate authority, there must have been other factors that nudged Onesimus in the direction of a positive decision, even though we can only guess at their relative weight with him. For example, Tychicus would accompany him and presumably use his influence with Philemon by vouching for Paul's wishes and for Onesimus' sincerity. Moreover, this duo would take along a letter which supported Paul's requests with maximum urgency. By being addressed to the local congregation as well as to Philemon, this letter would solicit their understanding and support. The mention of Epaphras and other members from the church at Colossae, along with other co-workers of Paul would have the effect of making Philemon's response a matter of wide knowledge among the churches. Then, too, Paul's announcement of a forthcoming visit would carry with it an implicit warning that Philemon would soon have to give an accounting to Paul. Finally, Paul set the whole matter within the context, not of legal obligations or financial advantage, but of intercessory prayer. Petitions for the grace of the Lord stand at the beginning and at the end of the letter which Onesimus carried, reminding both slave and master of the grace that requires forgiveness of debts among all believers.[27] Because such factors as these dominated Paul's appeal to Philemon, it is reasonable to suppose that they pervaded his earlier discussions with Onesimus.

Still another set of clues may be found in the second document which the two travelers carried in their fateful journey: the epistle to the Colossians. There are, to be sure, competent scholars who challenge the authenticity of that letter, yet I still believe it probable that Philemon and his house-church received the two letters on the same day and read them at the same session. If so, it is also probable that Onesimus would have shared earlier in the conversations leading to the writing of Colossians. This leads us to ask if there is material in that letter relevant to Onesimus' situation. I think so. This second letter has two passages dealing explicitly with slavery, and hence with the previous and the potential future relations of Onesimus to his owner. On the one hand, we note the commands for slaves to obey their masters and for masters to deal justly with their slaves (3:22 to 4:1). On the other hand, the apostle insists that the barriers between slaves and free men have been transcended in the new humanity (3:11).

Many readers find little but flat contradictions between those two passages; presumably neither Paul nor Onesimus did so. The reason surely lies in the recognition of the lordship of Christ which is central to both passages. In Colossians the term commonly used for the owner of slaves *(kyrios)* is applied to Christ at least fifteen times. Similarly, the term for slave *(doulos)* is directly applied to three Christian leaders whom both Philemon and Onesimus were bound to respect: Paul, Epaphras, Tychicus (1:7; 4:7,12). This bond between these slaves and this master constrains them to "forgive each other as the Lord has forgiven you" (3:13). It is easy for a modern reader to scan such a passage as Colossians 3:1-17 as if it contained little more than moral platitudes remote form the hurly-burly of daily tasks, but to read such a passage with eyes fixed on Onesimus' inner struggle transforms conventional generalities into explosive specifics. As one example of specific relevance, consider 2:14 which speaks in a baffling way of Christ's nailing to the cross "the bond which stood against us with its legal demands." Did that bond have anything to do with the legal demands which stood against Onesimus at that very moment? Such a possibility is not to be ruled out.

Returning to the letter to Philemon, we should not overlook one of the features that may have influenced the slave's decision, as Paul hoped it would influence his owner. This feature can be defined thus: a person sent must be received as alter ego of the one who sent him. Just as believers responded to Paul as Christ's ambassador, so Paul ordered Philemon to welcome Onesimus as he would welcome Paul (v. 17).[28] Paul had already treated this slave as emissary of his master (v.13), although he recognized that his substitution would be imperfect until the master approved (vv. 14, 21). So, too, Paul pledged to cover the debts of the slave to his master, and he used this pledge to "call in" the master's debt to Paul (v. 19). This practice of substituting one debt for another discloses the extent to which the gospel had created a complex fabric of personal relationships characterized by mutual debts and mutual cancellations, relationships that are juridical as much as mystical, temporal as much as eternal, since they transformed slaves and masters into brothers, both "in the flesh" and "in the Lord" (v. 16). Onesimus' decision to return to Colossae as a personal representative of Paul was an act of trusting the strength of these new substitutionary bonds. That act of trust would in itself be a sign of the new age. "The course of history is predictable in the degree to which all men love themselves, and spontaneous in the degree to which each man loves God and through Him his neighbor." [29]

Let us summarize our conjectures concerning the pattern of influences that finally induced this slave to return to Colossae. Nothing that has been said should induce the reader to underestimate the hazards of that return. Before reaching his decision, this slave must have felt deeply the offense of the gospel, since it required him to recognize the legal rights of Philemon, to cancel out his successful effort to win his freedom, to surrender himself, and to submit himself again to the onerous bonds of slavery. The command: "Slaves . . . obey your masters" (Col. 3:22) must have encountered stubborn resistance. The process of pondering the possibility of return must have stimulated reflections concerning his earlier experience of different kinds of captivity (e.g., as a slave and as a prisoner) and different kinds of liberation (e.g., from slavery, from prison, from fear, etc.). Consequently his willingness to return must have represented the cumulative power of his new faith and the new community in faith. Discussions with the apostle and his co-workers must have been animated and prolonged, must have covered many matters, both trivial and profound. Ultimately those discussions induced an act of obedience to his new master Christ that took the form of recognizing his obligations to his former master Philemon. That action thus must have expressed his confession of the power of the gospel and of the mysterious and miraculous freedoms conferred by faith. "Hope, by linking us to what is permanent, evokes freedom in relation to circumstances, social structures, ideological movements, and anything that might be called history." [30]

Scene 6. The decision to return was followed by the actual journey with Tychicus and the arrival in Philemon's home. The active imagination will fill in these empty spaces in the story. Was the returning slave tempted to escape again, as opportunities must have been offered along the road? And what must have been Philemon's surprise and bewilderment when he opened the door? The situation provides many parallels to the story of the prodigal son—only in this case we are dealing with a slave and not a son, and with an actual rather than a hypothetical situation. In some respects Philemon's decision may have been as difficult as Onesimus'. A negative response was entirely possible and perhaps to be expected. On this side of the scales would be many considerations: self-interest, legal rights, financial advantage, pressures from other slave holders, dangers to the churches if cultural institutions were to be challenged so openly. Exegetes are prone to suppose that Philemon granted Paul's requests, but this may be due either to their veneration for Paul or to absence of contrary evidence. In any case, the test of Philemon's freedom would not be unlike the test which Onesimus had taken. A detailed analysis of this scene, however, must await another occasion.

We have completed an exploration of six scenes. Granting that our reconstructions are conjectural, we would argue that the major inferences are more probable than improbable. After all, we know the basic points in this slave's story. Those pivotal points impel us to imagine what happened within Onesimus' mind on his escape, at his conversion, in his deciding to return, and on his return to Colossae. Our imagination would be sterile indeed if we did not move out from demonstrable facts into the realm of conjecture. To leave these spaces blank would be to reduce history to a parade of puppets, though conjectures must remain that and no more, each to be tested for its relative plausibility.

Many readers will judge our series of reconstructions simply by the test of historical probabilities. Let me suggest another test as well. We have presented Onesimus as a case study of faith and freedom. In so doing we have viewed the gospel as the gift of that unique kind of freedom which prompted Onesimus to return to the conditions of servitude. The question of the canonical authority of this epistle rests with the reality of that freedom. For those who inherit and treasure this freedom, a freedom as clearly demonstrated by Onesimus' action as by Paul's theology, this document belongs in sacred Scripture; for those to whom such freedom is an illusion, this document will continue to exert no authority. But the issue will continue to rest on Onesimus' witness as much as on the cogency of Paul's authorship.

NOTES

[1] W. G. Rollins, "Slavery" in *Interpreters Dictionary of the Bible*, Supplementary Vol., p. 830.

[2] J. B. Lightfoot, *St. Paul's Epistles to the Colossians and to Philemon* (London: Macmillan, 1892), p. 309.

[3] E. F. Scott, *The Epistles of Paul to the Colossians, to Philemon and to the Ephesians* (New York: R. R. Smith, 1930), p. 99.

[4] J. B. Lightfoot, *op. cit.,* p. 312.

[5] *Ibid.,* p. 301.

[6] *Philemon Among the Letters of Paul* (Chicago: University of Chicago Press, 1935).

[7] *Die Briefe an die Kolosser und an Philemon* (Göttingen: Vandenhoeck & Ruprecht, 1930), p. 171f.

8 George Johnston, *Ephesians, Philippians, Colossians, and Philemon* (London: Nelson, 1967), p. 74.

9 E. F. Scott, *op. cit.*, p. 99.

10 *Ibid.*

11 G. Johnston, *op. cit.*, p. 74.

12 J. B. Lightfoot, *op. cit.*, p. 301.

13 *Ibid.*, p. 317.

14 E. F. Scott, *op. cit.*, p. 99.

15 *Ibid.*, p. 97.

16 Contemporary exegetes rarely recognize the force of Kierkegaard's essay, "On the Difference between a Genius and an Apostle," in *The Present Age* (London: Oxford University Press, 1940), pp. 137ff.

17 W. G. Rollins, *op. cit.*

18 Crete Gray, *Colossians and Philemon* (London: Lutterworth, 1948), p. 81.

19 Theo Preiss, *Life in Christ* (London: SCM Press, 1934), p. 35. The procedures for advertising escaped slaves and returning them are described in C. F. D. Moule, *Colossians and Philemon* (Cambridge University Press, 1957), p. 36f.

20 Gordon P. Wiles, *Paul's Intercessory Prayers* (Cambridge Unidersity Press, 1974), pp. 218-225.

21 John H. Schutz, *Paul and the Anatomy of Apostolic Authority* (Cambridge University Press, 1975), pp. 207-222.

22 Theo Preiss, *op. cit.*, p. 34.

23 C. J. Bjerkelund, *Parakalō* (Oslo: Universitetsforlaget, 1967), pp. 118-125.

24 J. H. Schutz, *op. cit.*

25 This aspect of biblical authority is explored more extensively in my *To Heal and to Reveal* (New York: Seabury Press, 1976), Chapter 1.

26 J. H. Schutz, *op. cit.*, p. 207f. I have added the bracketed phrases from Philemon 16.

27 G. P. Wiles, *op. cit.*, pp. 218-225.

28 Theo Preiss, *op. cit.*, p. 34f.

29 W. H. Auden, *Collected Poetry* (New York: Random House, 1945), p. 452.

30 J. Ellul, *The Ethics of Freedom* (Grand Rapids: Eerdmans, 1976), p. 301.

13.
What Is Truth?[1]
Frank Stagg

The principle that words have usage rather than meaning and that no word stands in a one-to-one relationship with meaning holds true for biblical words for "truth." If meaning were inherent in words, there could be only one referent per word and one word per referent, neither of which holds. It is easy to pick a word, e.g., the English word "light," and point out its varied "meanings," more properly usages. Only contextually does the audio or visual symbol "light" communicate meaning: the opposite of darkness, the opposite of heaviness, the verbal idea of descending, or whatever. For any referent there are at least as many "words" as languages, each language having one or more words for the same referent. Semantic situations or referents are one thing; semantics is something else.

What is truth? What is intended by biblical words, Hebrew or Greek, commonly rendered "truth"? What is the "truth" (the "true" God) which we are to "know" in order to have "eternal life" (John 17:3)? In what sense is truth a proper concern of the church in Christian education or otherwise? Is there a biblical view of truth? Are there biblical views of truth? No simplistic answer is in order, yet certain understandings of "truth" are traceable and offer guidance for us today. There are ancient perspectives and usages which are identifiable in Scripture and by which Christian concern for "truth" today should be informed.

Ancient Perceptions of Truth

Truth as cognitive. One way of perceiving truth is as propositional. Statements are seen as "true" or "false." So perceived, truth opposes error whether by ignorance or willful falsification. Truth thus is something about which to be informed, something to know or believe. It may be objectified or abstracted. It may become a deposit, in religious expression known as creedal. So understood, it can be verbalized and

239

thus preserved or transmitted. When truth becomes a creed, it calls for a custodian who becomes its transmitter, protector, defender, and thus savior. Revelation becomes propositional, something conceptual and cognitive. Where this perception of truth prevails, the concepts of orthodoxy and heresy emerge. People have killed people in the name of defending truth understood as propositional, cognitive, and abstract.

The cognitive view of truth is sometimes called "Greek," contrasted with an ontological view called "Hebrew." This is an oversimplification on both sides, for there is no single, pure, and unambiguous perception of truth in either Greek or Hebrew tradition. On the other hand, there is a deeply-embedded perception of truth in Scripture, both Hebrew and Greek, which sharply contrasts with a cognitive view deeply embedded in the Greek world. Jew and Greek are more than arbitrary terms, for they did designate differing cultures in the ancient world. At the same time, Jew and Greek never lived in self-contained and exclusive worlds. Interaction, interpenetration, and assimilation occurred alongside dispositions toward contrary perspective and practice. Hebrew and Greek perceptions of truth were varied, and they both diverged and converged in many patterns. Despite this, some deep currents may with some measure of truth be considered "Hebrew" or "Greek." Although he carefully qualifies his generalization, C. H. Dodd offers this judgment as to the most significant Greek and Hebrew words for truth, "*Alētheia* is fundamentally an intellectual category, *'emeth* a moral category." [2]

The Greek word most commonly rendered "truth" in English is *alētheia*. Etymologically, the word connotes "not hidden." Words are not bound to their earliest usage, but eytmology at least reflects the point of departure or original usage. Bultmann holds that *alētheia* as "nonconcealment" thus indicated

a matter or state to the extent that it is seen, indicated or expressed, and that in such seeing, indication or expression it is disclosed, or discloses itself, as it really is, with the implication, of course, that it might be concealed, falsified, truncated, or suppressed. [3]

Truth thus understood had strong ties with seeing. A parallel linkage is reflected in the ancient, Indo-European root which survives in Greek words like *eidon* (to see) and *oida* (to know) based upon the root *'id* (originally with digamma, sounded like w or v) and in the Latin *wis/*

vis, as in "wisdom" and "vision," where seeing and knowing are expressed by the same root word.

The force of *alētheia* as "unconcealed" appears in Xenophon: "to disclose *(alētheusai)* . . . the things being as being *(onta)* and the things not being as not being" (Ana. IV, 4, 15).[4] In this usage, the opposite of *alētheia* is expressed in such antonyms as *pseudos* (deception) and *doxa* (appearance or opinion).[5] Orthodoxy's preoccupation with truth in this cognitive sense and as what really is over against the false or mere appearance is anticipated in the synonymous employment of *alētheia* and *orthos* (cf. Sophocles, *Oed. Tyr.* 1220).[6] *Alētheia* can also be synonymous with *epistēmē* (knowledge) and thus have the sense of "correct doctrine." [7]

Truth as ontological. O. A. Piper, with full awareness of "the long and intricate history of terminology" as it relates to biblical perspective on truth, concludes: "Thus, while in the Greek view of truth the cognitive element predominates, it is the ontological one in the OT." [8] Truth thus used describes the being of God, his nature as constant, unchangeable, trustworthy. As truth bears upon mankind, it likewise is to be reflected in being and life. Truth thus perceived is something to be and something to do. It is not simply something to articulate, something cognitive, or something to affirm in a creed.

The Hebrew word in the Old Testament which best connotes this understanding of "truth" is *'emeth.* The word *'emeth* occurs about 126 times in the Old Testament, denoting a reality which is firm, solid, valid, or binding.[9] The noun *'emeth* is derived from the Hebrew root *'amin,* "to be firm or sure"; and it usually is rendered in the LXX by *alētheia* (87 times) or its cognates and occasionally by *dikaiosuneē* (uprightness) and *pistis* (faithfulness, fidelity).[10] The idea in *'emeth* is closely related to that of wholeness (*shalom* and *tamin*) as well as that of grace *(hesed).*[11]

The term *'emeth* can designate factuality, as in Deuteronomy 22:20, "But if the thing *(dabhar)* is true *('emeth).*"[12] It can be used for that which may be confirmed by inquiry: "Then you shall inquire and make search and ask diligently; and if it be true *('emeth)* and certain . . ." (Deut. 13:14. Cf. 17:4). Examples appear for the employment of *'emeth* with respect to the verification of a report, simply true and not false, as in the Queen of Sheba's confession to Solomon, "The report was true *('emeth)* which I heard in my own land of your affairs and of your wisdom, but I did not believe the reports until I came and my own eyes had seen it" (1 Kings 10:6f.; 2 Chron. 9:5).

In many occurrences *'emeth* seems at first glance to imply "truth" as cognitive; but upon closer examination, it turns out to have a closer reference to character and conduct. Lifted out of context, Psalm 25:4*a* could serve as a clarion call to the pursuit of orthodoxy: "In your majesty ride forth victoriously for the cause of truth"; but what follows points in another direction: "and to defend the right." The focus is upon equity and justice, loving righteousness and hating wickedness (vv. 6f.). The call is not to orthodoxy but to the triumph of right over wrong. The call to serve God in "truth" (KJV; NASB) is a call to right attitude and conduct, not to cognition, as in Joshua 24:14: "Now therefore fear the Lord, and serve him in sincerity and in faithfulness *('emeth).*" The call is to serve JHWH instead of the gods of the heathen. This same intention of *'emeth* appears in 1 Samuel 12:24f. where "to serve in truth" is to be faithful: "Only fear the Lord, and serve him faithfully *('emeth)* with all your heart. . . . But if you still do wickedly. . . ." To "walk in truth" is to be faithful to God in one's ways (1 Kings 2:4; 2 Kings 20:3). What in 2 Chronicles 31:20 is ascribed to Hezekiah as "what was good and right and faithful before the Lord his God" is referred to in 32:1 as "these acts of faithfulness" *('emeth).* Clearly, truth in these passages refers to moral integrity in one submissive to God.

The psalmist's prayer that he be led by God's light and God's truth is not a prayer for better cognitive knowledge; it is a prayer for help toward a godly life: "O send out thy light and thy truth; let them lead me, let them bring me to thy holy hill and to thy dwelling!" (43:3). So led by God's light and truth, the psalmist will enjoy the presence of God and praise him. Here light and truth issue in refuge in God and worship. To call upon God "in truth" is not to be doctrinally informed but to turn to God in reverence and love: "The Lord is near to all who call upon him, to all who call upon him in truth" (Ps. 145:18). These are those who "fear him," "cry" out to him, and "love him"; and they are opposite to "the wicked" (vv. 19f.). "Light" and "truth" are moral, not intellectual qualities.

The moral reference in *'emeth* is unambiguous in Deuteronomy 32:4, where the greatness of God is praised: "The Rock, his work is perfect; for all his ways are justice. A God of faithfulness [*'emunah*] and without iniquity, just and right is he." The same contrast between truth and iniquity appears in Daniel 9:13: "Yet we have not entreated the favor of the Lord our God, turning from our iniquities and giving heed to thy truth." This is in a context acknowledging Israel's sins and dependence upon God's great mercy (v. 18).

Truth is related to God's "law" or instruction. An example may be found in Psalm 119:142, "Thy righteousness is righteous for ever, and thy law is true." The context acknowledges the righteousness of God and the delight of one who obeys God's commandments. Of God it is said, "All thy commandments are true" (v. 151). They are not only factually true; but, more importantly in this context, behind God's commandments are his "steadfast love" and his "justice" as contrasted with those whose actions derive from "evil purpose" (vv. 149f.). Again, the moral dimension of truth appears in verse 160: "The sum of thy word is truth; and every one of thy righteous ordinances endures for ever."

Concerning Levi, the prophet Malachi says to the wicked priests of his day, "True instruction [torath 'emeth] was in his mouth, and no wrong was found on his lips" (2:6). Out of context this may seem to represent Levi as having been orthodox in his teaching, but this is not the issue in Malachi. The remaining part of the verse puts it in perspective: "He walked with me in peace and uprightness, and he turned many from iniquity" (v. 6). The wicked priests of Malachi's time have corrupted the ways of Israel. False worship, divorce, dishonesty in vows, adultery, injustice in wages, oppression of widows and orphans, etc. are their failings. The truth sadly missing from the instruction of the priests under Malachi's indictment is ontological, not merely cognitive. It related to character and life, not simply to the articulation of theology.

In Jeremiah 2:21 'emeth carries the idea of genuineness: "Yet I planted you a choice vine, wholly of pure ['emeth] seed." The *New American Standard Bible* renders 'emeth "faithful" here. The opposite of 'emeth also appears in 21: "How then have you turned degenerate and become a wild vine?" In Zechariah 'emeth can designate truth as over against falsity, and it can stand for truth as integrity: "These are the things that you shall do: Speak the truth to one another, render in your gates judgments that are true and make for peace" (8:16). Despised by contrast are "evil in your hearts against one another" and loving a "false oath" (v. 17). In this context truth is factuality but also integrity. The test here is not creedal orthodoxy but integrity of motive and act (cf. 7:9). This is the truth God requires.

The truth which belongs to piety goes deeper than words or actions;

it is ontological. It belongs to *being* itself. The psalmist, smitten with a sense of his sin, acknowledges what God requires: "Behold, thou desirest truth [*'emeth*] in the inward being; therefore teach me wisdom in my secret heart" (51:6). The cultic sacrifices (v. 16) and other external marks of piety are insufficient; what God is in himself requires that truth be in our "inward being." Truth here is "ontological," not "cognitive." It is something to be, not merely a proposition to articulate.

Psalm 15 includes truth as belonging to that which is required of those who "sojourn" in God's "tent" and "dwell" on his "holy hill" (v. 1). Such a one "speaks truth [*'emeth*] from his heart" (v. 2). There is not a hint in the psalm about a requirement of creedal orthodoxy. The truth to be spoken from the heart is moral and ethical in quality, not such because of impeccable theological articulation. One who speaks "truth from his heart" is one who "does not slander with his tongue and does no evil to his friend, nor takes up a reproach against his neighbor" (v. 3). He is one who "swears to his own hurt and does not change" (v. 4). He is one who "does not put out his money at interest, and who does not take a bribe against the innocent" (v. 5). Truth here has to do with character; it has to do with goodness. It belongs to being. It is not an abstraction for cognition and creedal affirmation. Quell observes that in this psalm to "walk blamelessly" *(tamim)* and to "do right" *(zedek)* are expressions used synonymously with to "speak truth" *('emeth)* and that "in the last resort the rational element in the concept of *'emeth* is not the essential feature." [13]

Ezekiel 18 further illustrates the close relationship between the concept of *'emeth* and moral/ethical/personal qualities which God requires in those who stand before him, with no hint as to truth perceived as creedal. The burden of the chapter is to banish forever the fallacy in the proverb, "The fathers have eaten sour grapes, and the children's teeth are set on edge" (v. 2). Sins are not inherited; rather, "the soul that sins shall die" (v. 4). Each is accountable for himself to God. With this personal accountability to God is spelled out the criteria for judgment. What matters is ontological, what flows from what one is. The "righteous" person is one who, among other things, "executes true justice [*mishpat 'emeth*] between man and man" (v. 8); and he is one of whom God can say that he "walks in my statutes, and is careful to observe my ordinances" (v. 9). The Hebrew of the latter phrase is better preserved in the NASB "so as to deal faithfully" *('emeth).* Truth here has to do with one's speech and actions as they reflect what one is.

When Hosea declared God's controversy with Israel because there was "no truth [*'emeth*], nor mercy, nor knowledge of God in the land" (4:1, KJV), the complaint was not that Israel was doctrinally unsound. Israel's problem was deeper; it was existential or ontological, not cognitive. Both RSV and NASB properly render *'emeth* as "faithfulness" here. Examples of the lack of truth are "swearing, lying, killing, stealing, and committing adultery" (v. 2). The truth required is moral and ethical, not orthodox verbalizing of theological propositions. Israel lacks "knowledge," and it is primarily the "knowledge of God" which is lacking (v. 1). Knowing God is more than knowing facts about God. The "truth" Israel needs is truth incarnated, not verbalized.

Throughout the psalms, the hymnody of Israel, the theme of truth is prominent. The rational element is not absent from it, but its deepest concern is elsewhere. It is with the character of God, of his ways, of his words. Likewise, it is a concern for the integrity of Israel under the command and care of God. In Psalm 19:9 "the ordinances of the Lord are true" *('emeth);* and this is declared in a context in which "the Law [*Torah*] of the Lord is perfect, reviving the soul" (v. 7) and where in its various expressions it is "sure," "right," "pure," "clean," "righteous," and more desirable than gold and sweeter than honey (vv. 7-10). "Torah" to the psalmist is what Scripture is to us; and its intention is the "reviving of the soul," not to be a repository of abstract truths to be embalmed in a creed. Torah reflects what God is in himself, and it intends to affect human existence. The burden of the prayer in Psalm 25 is for deliverance not only from the psalmist's enemies but also from wrong and shameful ways. He looks to God's instruction, but this instruction is not simply to inform his mind but to correct his ways. Truth in this psalm does not exclude the cognitive, but it is more than that: "Lead me in thy truth, and teach me, for thou art the God of my salvation; for thee I wait all the day long" (v. 5). This parallels the request in verse 4, "Make me to know thy ways, O Lord; teach me thy paths." The concern of the prayer is not that he be smart but that he be good. This concern runs through the psalm.

Teaching and truth are brought together in Psalm 86:11 but in such a way as to stress character and not cognition: "Teach me thy way, O Lord, that I may walk in thy truth; unite my heart to fear thy name." As in Matthew 28:20, it is obedience that is to be taught, not factual data or doctrinal correctness. The truth with which Psalm 86:11 is concerned is truth to embody and truth to do, not simply truth to confess.

In Psalm 26 to "walk in truth" (v. 3) is not to be orthodox but to be faithful: "For thy steadfast love is before my eyes, and I walk in faithfulness ['emeth] to thee." The whole psalm emphasizes the character and conduct of one walking in integrity, not the theological competence of the orthodox. Incidentally, it could be that it was just such presumption as may lurk behind this psalm which prompted Jesus to warn in the model prayer that we not challenge God: "Prove me, O Lord, and try me; test my heart and my mind" (v. 2). The psalmist is so confident of his integrity that he invites God to test him; Jesus taught his disciples to pray for deliverance from evil, not for such testing as would vendicate them (cf. Matt. 6:13). Leaving aside the issue of presumption, the psalm clearly identifies truth with integrity, ontological and not cognitive in emphasis.

In Psalm 31:5 "faithful God" is "God of truth" (NASB). God is seen as a sure "refuge"; and in this confidence the psalmist can say, "Into thy hand I commit my spirit; thou has redeemed me, O Lord, faithful ['emeth] God." God not only speaks the truth; he is true. Throughout, the psalm is an affirmation of the goodness and trustworthiness of God. His truth is to be understood in this light. Likewise in Psalm 30:9 God's 'emeth is his "faithfulness" (the RSV's "my faithfulness" should be "thy faithfulness"). God's truth is his fidelity. The psalmist wants to live so that he may praise God's truth.

Psalm 111 praises God for his goodness: his works are great and full of honor and majesty, his righteousness endures forever, and he is gracious and merciful. In this setting the term 'emeth appears twice: "The works of his hands are faithful and just ['emeth and mishpat]; and all his precepts are trustworthy, they are established for ever and ever, to be performed with faithfulness ['emeth] and uprightness" (vv. 7f.). 'Emeth can describe the dependability of God's promise: "The Lord swore to David a sure ['emeth] oath from which he will not turn back" (Ps. 132:11). This could be rendered, "JHWH swore truth to David." It ɪs not the cognitive but the moral quality of the oath which is affirmed.

Psalm 146 warns against putting one's trust in man; for man perishes, and his "plans perish" with him (v. 4). To be congratulated is the one whose hope is in God, "who keeps faith ['*emeth*] forever" (v. 6). Such hope is well placed because God is creator of all that is and because he

executes justice for the oppressed . . . gives food to the hungry . . . sets the prisoners free . . . opens the eyes of the blind . . . lifts up those who are bowed down . . . loves the righteous . . . watches over sojourners . . . upholds the widow and the fatherless . . . the way of the wicked he brings to ruin (vv. 7-9).

Central to this understanding of God is the line, "which keepeth truth for ever" (KJV). Truth in this context has special reference to God's faithfulness, but it reflects what he is as well as what he does.

In Psalm 85 truth is a moral quality, brought about in God's people as belonging to the "salvation" which God accomplishes out of his "steadfast love" *(hesed)*. Truth is poetically personified, as are love and righteousness in these beautiful lines: "Steadfast love and faithfulness [*hesed* and '*emeth*] will meet; righteousness and peace will kiss each other. Faithfulness *('emeth)* will spring up from the ground, and righteousness will look down from the sky" (vv. 10f.). These are moral qualities in God; and in the salvation he effects, they characterize the lives of his people. '*Emeth* is best rendered "faithfulness" here (RSV); but properly understood as ontological and not merely cognitive, it may be rendered "truth" (KJV and NASB).

Isaiah too can speak of truth *('emeth)* in moral terms, allying it with justice and righteousness and contrasting it with evil: "Justice is turned back, and righteousness stands afar off; for truth has fallen in public squares, and uprightness cannot enter" (59:14f.). Truth is linked with instruction in Proverbs 23:23, but even there it has a moral reference and not creedal: "Buy truth, and do not sell it; buy wisdom, instruction, and understanding." Such action will cause rejoicing to "the father of the righteous," and "he who begets a wise son will be glad in him" (v. 24). It is truth as goodness in a son which thus pleases a father. In Exodus 34:6 the moral quality of '*emeth* as truth is found in God himself: "The Lord, the Lord, a God merciful and gracious, slow to anger, and abounding in steadfast love [*hesed*] and faithfulness ['*emeth*]." The cognitive use of truth may seem to be present in Nehemiah 9:13, "Thou didst come down upon Mount Sinai, and speak with them from heaven and give them right ordinances and true laws [*toroth 'emeth*], good statutes and commandments." Even here more than the cognitive appears in context. In 9:33 the usage is moral, for wickedness is here the antonym to '*emeth:* "Yet thou hast been just in all that has come upon us, for thou has dealt faithfully ['*emeth*] and we have acted wickedly."

Truth in the New Testament

In the New Testament as in the Old may be found both the cognitive and ontological perceptions of truth. The Greek word *alētheia* appears a hundred times in the New Testament and its cognates about seventy-five times. Each usage must be sought contextually, though exhaustive tracing is beyond the limits of this essay.

Alētheia as Cognitive? Bultmann, under the caption "The Early Christian Use of *alētheia,*" finds six groups as to usage, two of which he labels "truth of statement" and "true teaching or faith." [14] So understood, *alētheia* in these usages is basically cognitive. Under contextual examination, this is not so convincing as Bultmann seems to have it. There are traces of cognitive usage; but even in the thirty or so examples cited from the New Testament, the contextual concern is prevailingly with truth as it affects personal existence and not cognition. Almost all his examples are from the Pauline tradition.

Under the caption "truth of statement," Bultmann cites six Synoptic passages (Mark 12:14,32; 14:70; Matt. 26:73; Luke 4:25; 22:59) and one from acts 26:25. Chiefly he demonstrates here that the adverb *alēthōs* and the prepositional phrase *ep' alētheias* are used interchangeably for "truly," i.e., factually true. This seems to follow. In three of these examples, Peter is "truly" or "in fact" one of Jesus' disciples, despite his denials.

Bultmann cites numerous examples of *alētheia* in the usage "true teaching or faith"; but usage here is not unambiguous, and Bultmann is less convincing. All New Testament examples are from Paul and the general epistles (some from Patristic and other writings). Of these, the examples most clearly cognitive are from the pastoral epistles. In 2 Timothy 4:4 "the truth" is set over against "myths" and in a context concerned with "sound teaching" (v. 3). Although truth here is related directly to "teaching" and has a cognitive expression, the larger context even here is explicit that the purpose of Scripture is "for teaching, reproof, correction, and discipline in righteousness, in order that the man of God may be complete, equipped for every good work" (3:16f.). Whatever the cognitive dimension of truth, its ultimate concern in Scripture is ontological or existential. It is concerned with what we are and do.

Titus 1:14 warns against "holding Jewish myths and commandments of men," for these latter are "men who reject the truth." Truth contrasted with myths and commandments of men is, indeed, cognitive in expression; but again the concern is more basic. The concern is that the readers be "sound in the faith" (v. 13), but such soundness is far more than creedal. It is personal, moral, ethical. Opposed are "liars, evil beasts, gluttons" (v. 12) and the impure whose "very minds and consciences are corrupted" (v. 15). These people are creedally proper, "confessing to know God," but they deny him in their deeds, "being stinkers [sic!], disobedient, and unfit for any good work" (v. 16). So, where the cognitive usage is most prominent, the ontological force of "truth" remains most fundamental.

Deplored in 1 Timothy 6:5 are those "destitute of the truth." Are these doctrinally deficient, lacking in cognition or propositional truth? There is not a hint of this. These are depraved in character. Pictured are those who do not correspond in character and manner to "the sound words of our Lord Jesus Christ and the teaching which is according to godliness" (v. 3). Their "heresy" is that they are conceited, ignorant, morbid in their craving for controversy over words which produce only envy, dissension, slander, suspicions, and wrangling, and that they try to use godliness for gain (vv. 4f.). These are the ones "depraved in mind and destitute of truth" (v. 5). Again, truth is basically moral, concerned with quality of personal existence, attitude, and manner. Truth is goodness, not simply what is factually correct.

The cognitive force of truth is apparent in 2 Timothy 2:18, where to hold that "the resurrection is past already" (a gnosticizing way of "spiritualizing" the resurrection) is to have "swerved from the truth." These pseudo-spiritualists are censured for wrong teaching as to the nature of the resurrection, but the weight of the passage is beyond this. The warning is against not only "godless chatter" but against "ungodliness" (v. 16). Timothy is admonished to "handle aright the word of truth" (v. 15) not just that his hearers be informed but that they be turned from "iniquity" (v. 19). Those who "oppose the truth" are "men of corrupt mind and false faith" (3:8).

In Ephesians 1:13 "the word of truth" is explicitly equated with "the gospel of your salvation." In a close parallel, probably earlier, the same equation seems implied in Colossians 1:5, "the word of the truth of the gospel." The cognitive element may be assumed here, but the immediate concern is with the "fruit" or "the inheritance" which the Holy Spirit seals for us. Even where truth is equated with "gospel," the concern is with human existence and not creedal articulation. A cognitive element is present in 1 Timothy 4:3, "those who believe and know the truth," the context having to do with "doctrines" (v. 1) and "instructions" (v. 6). Again, the burden is not with doctrine for its own sake; it is with character and conduct. The immediate concern is to protest the asceticism which views marriage and foods as evil (v. 3). One is to be "nourished" on "good doctrine" and not on "myths" (vv. 6f.), the object being "godliness" (v. 8), not orthodoxy as an end in itself. The concern earlier in the letter, that all people be saved and "come to the knowledge of the truth" (2:4), is concern for a godly life. In 2 Timothy 3:7, those "always learning but never able to come into the knowledge of the truth" are evil people, not just dull students who do not properly articulate theology. They are corrupt people like "Jannes and Jambres" (v. 8).

In Galatians 5:7 the problem with truth is not cognitive but one of distrust: "You were running well; who cut in on you so that you trust not the truth?" Cognitive understanding of truth is involved, but the failing is more of the heart than the mind. The Galatians trust their cultic practices more than the goodness and grace of God. What is at stake is not just their theology but the quality of their existence.

Bultmann finds the truth in 2 Corinthians 13:8 to fall into the category of "true teaching or faith" and to imply "true doctrine" as opposed to a *heteron* gospel (11:4). However, the contextual concern is with morality, "that you may not do wrong" and "that you may do what is right" (13:7). In 11:4 Paul does warn against "a different gospel" *(euaggelion heteron)* which opposes his own, probably a gnosticizing movement away from the historical Jesus in favor of some "spiritualized Christ." [15] Truth as cognitive and gospel as substantive are important. What one believes does matter. These matter as they affect existence, as was true at Corinth. Paul's charges against his opponents in Corinth relate both to theological difference and underlying spirit and character: "We renounce the hidden things of shame, not walking in craftiness, perverting the word of God, but in the openness of the truth, commending ourselves to the conscience of all men in the presence of God" (4:2). Paul conceded that he may fall short in articulation, "rough in speech," but not in knowledge, having spoken with sufficient clarity (11:6). His closing appeal is that the Corinthians examine themselves to test if Christ indeed be in them (13:5–7). Ultimately, the issue is not how they articulate theology but whether or not Christ lives within them! If they fail to meet this test, all is lost. Though they may be related, the ontological question overrides the cognitive.

Hebrews 10:26 is among the passages which Bultmann selects to demonstrate that "to become a Christian" is "to come into the knowledge of the truth." However, the writer is not equating salvation with dogma. It is willful "sin" which dooms one who thus lives even after having received "the knowledge of the truth." Those warned live in danger of spurning the Son of God and outraging the Spirit of grace (10:29). The call is to an unfailing commitment of faith, not simply to creedal refinement.

Bultmann finds that "the Christian faith" can be called "obedience of the truth" (1 Pet. 1:22). Interestingly, this is in a context calling for "sincere love for the brethren," loving one another "earnestly from the heart" *(ibid.)*. The salvation to which they were called prohibits malice, guile, insincerity, envy, slander, and the like (2:1). To "obey the truth" means more than creedal confession; it is to be and to behave. In 1 Timothy 3:15 "the church of the living God" is "the pillar and foundation of the truth." Out of context, the concern is elsewhere. The explicit concern is that one "may know how one ought to behave in the household of God" (v. 14). Second Peter 1:12 commends those "established in the truth," and this appears in a chapter concerned with "escape from the corruption that is in the world" (v. 4) and with the "virtue" which belongs together with "knowledge" (v. 5).

Although he does not demonstrate it, Bultmann does recognize that even where *alētheia* appears as "true teaching or faith," "this usage is still determined by the *'emeth* concept." [16] His other four groupings of early Christian usage of *alētheia* are: that which "has certainty and force," that "on which one can rely," the "real state of affairs," and *alētheia* as meaning "genuineness," "divine reality," "revelation." [17]

Alētheia as ontological. Although the ontological lurks behind or near most occurrences of *alētheia* in the New Testament, in some of Paul and much of John it is primary. It can refer to something in God or in his action. In John, *alētheia* with yet greater force appears in terms of being and doing as well as in reference to saying.

In Romans 1:18 *alētheia* is something which may be suppressed; and such suppression of the truth is iniquity. Contextually, this is knowledge about God or knowledge of God, i.e., knowing God. The latter seems to be intended. The failing of the wicked is not that they do not know about God. Knowing about God is their advantage; refusing to know God is their guilt (1:21,28). They "exchanged the truth of God for a lie" (v. 25). They did so by giving to the creature the place in their worship which properly belongs to God alone. The truth suppressed is not just information about God. Revelation is more than God's giving information about himself; it is his self-disclosure. God offers himself in personal acquaintance, not just his "biographical data sheet." In Romans 2:2, God's judgment is "according to truth," i.e., just and fair. In 2:8 truth is seen as moral, antithetical to "iniquity." Probably in 3:7 also, God's truth is moral, contrasting with our "lie." In 15:8 the "truth of God" seems to be his fidelity, his faithfulness to his promises.

In Galatians 2:14 truth has to do with attitude and behavior. When Peter and others withdrew from table fellowship in Antioch when "some from James" caught them eating with uncircumcised persons, Paul rebuked Peter for his inconsistency. Paul saw that they in this withdrawal "were not walking toward [pros] the truth of the gospel" (Gal. 2:14). The truth of the gospel here is more than a proposition; it is a way of life.

In Ephesians 4:21 "the truth in Jesus" may be cognitive or ontological. The cognitive idea may be implied in "if, indeed, ye heard him and in him were taught"; but the ontological idea is congenial to "heard him." More is implied than teaching about Jesus; the readers are expected to have heard him. The truth is "in Jesus," not just in his teaching. Ephesians 4:15 may be translated variously: "speaking the truth in love," "holding the truth in love," or even "being true in love." The Greek participle alētheuontes has no necessary implication of "speaking" or "holding"; that is added in translation. The simplest rendering and probably the best is "being true." Truth is something which we are to be, not just speak. The ontological idea is probably intended in Romans 3:4: "Let God be true [alēthōs] and every man a liar." Truth characterizes God not just in his speaking but in his being. The ontological idea is likely in the virtues commended in Philipians 4:8f, "whatsoever things are true," etc. These are things not only taught, received, and heard, but also "seen" in Paul. They belong to being, not just teaching.

It is in the writings of John that truth is most clearly moral and ontological. The Word made flesh was "full of grace and truth" (John 1:14). The Law was given through Moses, but "grace and truth came through Jesus Christ" (1:17). Jesus speaks "the truth" (8:45f.), but he also embodies the truth: "I am the way and the truth and the life" (14:6). The Holy Spirit is "the Spirit of truth" (14:17; 15:26; 16:13); but he not only speaks the truth, "the Spirit is the truth" (1 John 5:6). Of the Father it is said, "Thy word is truth" (John 17:17).

Although the cognitive idea of truth appears in John's writings (cf. John 5:33; 8:40,45,46; 16:7; 1 John 2:21), the most significant usage is the ontological. Truth is something to be of, something to be in, or something which is in oneself. We have seen this as it related to Jesus. It also pertains to those who follow him. The devil speaks lies because the truth is not in him; when he speaks lies he speaks out of his being, and the same holds for the devil's followers (John 8:44). Jesus prays that his followers be sanctified in truth (17:17). His true followers are "out of the truth" (18:37; 1 John 3:19). The truth is "in" some people but not in others (1 John 1:8; 2:4). The truth "abides" in true disciples (2 John 2), and they are found "walking in the truth" (v. 4; 3 John 4).

Truth is not just something propositional to affirm; it is something personal to do: "The one doing the truth comes to the light, that his works may be manifest that they have been wrought in God (John 3:21). Those who walk in darkness are not "doing the truth" (1 John 1:6). To John, light and darkness are moral/ethical/personal considerations, not intellectual. To walk in darkness is not to be ignorant but to be evil. To walk in light is not to be "enlightened" in our modern usage, but to be good. The liberating truth (John 8:32) is not factual knowledge; it is the truth which one comes to know in experience when he has his abiding in Christ and his word.

Verum aut Bonum

Some years ago Robert E. Cushman in an essay entitled *Verum aut Bonum* advanced the thesis that the fate of the world lies not between truth *(verum)* and error but between good *(bonum)* and evil. Although a scholar and educator, he knew humanity and history too well to be deceived by the idea that information is sufficient for an enduring world. He contended that our hope is in goodness and that the decisive struggle is between good and evil and not between information and ignorance. The case may be documented readily. The people who have most threatened the world with enslavement and ruin were not ignorant; they were evil. Such men were Domitian, Hitler, Stalin, Cortez, and all the other bigoted tyrants who have sought by brute force to enslave human beings. The wicked are more dangerous when gifted and informed.

In today's world are the twin threats of nuclear holocaust and ecological disaster. We could destroy ourselves with a big bang or fade out with a whimper, suffocating by our own poisons. This is not because we do not know better. It is because we do not have as yet enough goodness to do right. Our problem is not that we are ignorant but that we are bad. Nuclear bombs and cosmic pollution are the achievements not of the uninformed but of the most secularly "enlightened" people who have ever walked this earth. There is Ireland, e.g., with its seemingly endless civil war, years of hatred and bloodshed by two sides labeled Protestant and Catholic. It is not that there is no knowledge in Ireland; it is that there has been a breakdown in human values where such breakdown should never have occurred. There are not only the recurring wars among the Western nations, kinfolk all, but the explosive tensions in the Middle East, the tribal clashes in Africa, and wars in the making wherever the passions of humanity exceed its residue of goodness. The fate of Ireland, Middle East, Far East, Europe, the Americas, and the whole world does indeed rest between good and evil, not between truth and ignorance or error. It is not that we are not smart enough to survive; we may not be good enough. It is well that we be smart; but it is imperative that we be good.

Professor Cushman's essay poses well the issue, yet more may be said. The intention of the essay is laudable, yet it may imply too great a gap between truth and goodness. In Christian perspective they must be one thing and not two things.

Three Levels in Education

Some years ago Paul Tillich in an essay "A Theology of Education" [19] cogently analyzed three basic concepts of education, and these three options remain before us today. They have implications for our concern with the nature of truth. As he pointed out, education may take the shape of technical training, induction, or what he called "evolution," meaning humanization. Training is the most elementary level of what is called education. A child is trained from birth in the basics of eating, drinking, bodily function, speech, etc. Training proceeds in terms of riding a tricycle, memorizing the multiplication tables, or training the fingers to the keyboard of typewriter or piano. Training has its place, but this at best is secondary and offers little that is distinctively human. Animals can be trained sometimes excelling humans in aptitude for such skills. There is a place for "how to do it" courses in the curriculum of Christian education, but surely this cannot represent what Christian education is all about.

Induction represents a second level in what is called education. Induction is the process of inducting another into one's own world of values, perspectives, principles, beliefs, or ideals. All responsible people try to impart their values to others, and within limits this is proper within the educational process. Much of this takes place apart from deliberate intention, for by contagion we catch from one another our values and perspectives, hopes and fears, bias and prejudice, mores and ideals. What is antithetical to education is coercion. It is one thing to persuade, another to compel. It is to destroy and not education another when we manipulate, intimidate, brainwash, or coerce. The only thing worse than trying to impose upon another what one believes is to impose upon that one what one does not believe. God himself does not compel faith. He offers himself yet gives us the awesome freedom for receiving him into our knowledge or rejecting him. Christian education may properly offer its values, but it becomes counterproductive to the nature and goals of Christian education to impose. Education as induction offers much in the interest of truth as ontological, for all its limits and perils.

Tillich termed the highest level of education "humanistic." By this he meant the awakening of another into authentic and growing personhood, drawing out the personhood which is there. Surely, this is what Jesus intended when he came to give us life and that in abundance. Jesus is the great Liberator. Redemption in Greek *(apolytrōsis)* means liberation. Jesus came to forgive, to accept, to cleanse, to heal, to give direction, to empower, to liberate. He liberates from guilt, fear, greed, lust, hate, envy, jealousy, prejudice, or whatever it is that enslaves, degrades, or destroys. He came to call forth the personhood God had in mind in creating us. Salvation is God's work of enabling us in Christ to become true persons, nothing less, nothing more, and nothing other. It is this end which Christian education is to serve: the humanization of society and our becoming true persons in Christ. If so, the truth with which Christians must be concerned must be more than cognitive. It must have its cognitive expression; but more importantly, it must be concerned with truth as ontological, truth as belonging to personal existence.

The Faith Delivered to the Saints

There is the constant threat that not only the nature of truth be misunderstood but that we misunderstand our proper roles in relationship with the truth. Misunderstanding of Jude is a case in point. The

epistle of Jude has been for many the banner under which they offer
themselves as the custodians of the truth (the term *alētheia* does not
appear in the letter). However sincere such action may be, nothing
could be farther from the intention of Jude. Jude's concern was with
goodness, not with the correctness with which theology is articulated.
Of course sound doctrine is on the side of goodness, for doctrine is
instruction for life. Proper articulation of theology is important; that
is precisely what this chapter is attempting. But Jude was not crusading
for orthodoxy over against heretical creeds. His heavy guns were
trained on immorality, pride, arrogance, and disobedience of God's
commands. His concern was with the quality of existence in those
claiming to be followers of Jesus Christ. But let us hear him from
his own significant letter.

Jude put his intention in sharp focus: "Beloved, while making all
diligence to write to you concerning our common salvation, I found
it necessary to write to you exhorting you to agonize for the faith
once for all delivered to the saints" (v. 3). To many "faith" has been
understood as a set of doctrinal beliefs, and the injunction has been
understood as a declaration of war upon heresy. Have we really both-
ered to read the rest of the letter? This is not remotely the concern
of the letter. The threat is moral, ethical, personal, not creedal. Those
condemned are "ungodly" *(asebeis),* and they have exchanged the grace
of God for "licentiousness" *(aselgyeian),* denying the lordship of Jesus
Christ (v. 4).

Jude gives a long list of examples of what he means by those who
betray the faith. They include the Israelites who forgot the lessons
of Egypt and failed to trust God (v. 5), angels who forsook their
proper status and arrogantly assumed another (v. 6), Sodom and Go-
morrah and the cities around them which turned to fornication and
every form of immorality and idolatry (vv. 7f.), people who live by
their instincts, like animals (v. 10), rebellious people like Cain, Balaam,
and Korah (v. 11), undisciplined people who are like wild waves of
the sea or wandering stars in the sky (v. 13), people who lack holiness
(v. 14), ungodly people doing ungodly deeds and who are harsh in
their evil (v. 15), grumblers, faultfinders, people of lust and arrogance
and who flatter for advantage (v. 16), mockers (v. 18), and worldly-
minded people who cause divisions (v. 19).

What is Jude's plea as he exhorts us to contend for the faith once
for all delivered to the saints? It is a plea for decency. It is a call to
moral integrity. It is a call to a right spirit. He begins with the prayer,

"May mercy, peace, and love be multiplied to [in] you" (v. 2). Warning against the "scoffers" who follow their "ungodly passions" (v. 18) and those worldly people, devoid of the Spirit, who cause divisions (v. 19), Jude pleads: "But you, beloved, building yourselves up in the holiness of your faith and praying in the Holy Spirit, guard yourselves in the love of God, receiving the mercy of our Lord Jesus Christ unto life eternal" (vv. 20f.). Jude is not trying to start a witch-hunt or an inquisition. First of all he is calling Christians to the basic qualities of the faith: moral, ethical, personal, spiritual. Next he enjoins them to try to convince the doubtful and rescue those threatened by the evils described. In closing, Jude commends his readers to Him who is able to keep them from falling and to present them finally without blemish to God (v. 24). The faith to which Jude calls is fidelity to God, a life of goodness lived under the lordship of Jesus Christ.

The Teaching to Which We Are Delivered

Paul has a striking way of putting our relationship to doctrine: "Thanks be to God that [although] ye were slaves of sin ye became obedient from the heart unto that type of teaching to which ye were delivered" (Rom. 6:17). Teaching is doctrine. Doctrine is instruction for life. Significantly, Paul does not speak of teaching delivered to us but of our being delivered to the teaching. We are not the custodians of the teaching, but it is our custodian.

The injunction before us appears in a context designed to combat the permissiveness known as libertinism or antinomanism (Rom. 6:1 to 7:6). Some of Paul's would-be followers distorted his doctrine of grace into license. They even proposed letting sin abound that grace could abound (6:1). They saw salvation as all gift and no demand. Paul saw salvation as both the gift of God's grace and his absolute demand for a new kind of existence. He gave three illustrations for the discontinuity between the old existence outside Christ and the new existence in Christ. To be in Christ is to have died with him to the old life and to have been raised to a new kind of life (6:3-11). It is like experiencing an exchange of masters, from slaves to sin to slaves to righteousness (6:15-23). It is like being released from one spouse through death and being joined to a new spouse (7:1-6). It is in the second of these three analogies that Paul speaks of our having been delivered to a type of teaching (6:17). We now belong to the kind of teaching or doctrine which makes righteousness and not sin our master. The doctrine to which we have been delivered does not look to us to maintain truth in cognitive expression; it offers us the truth which shapes our existence.

Conclusions

What then is truth? What is our proper concern with truth? We have no need to be uncertain. Pilate's question is not left hanging. Our basic calling is clear enough. It remains to be heeded and followed, not debated.

We are known as people of the Book. Our failing is not that we have made too much of the Bible. We have made too little of it. We probably have talked too much about it, but we have not done enough about it. The Bible does not ask us to be its custodians. It does not ask us to brag on it, protect it, or defend it, or hold it up. It asks to be read, to be heard, and to be heeded. It offers us the truth to which we are to be delivered, not a truth so small that feeble and fallible little men are able to take it into their hands and save it. Schools which offer themselves as the custodians of orthodoxy, binding themselves under their own creedal formulations, do not have the freedom necessary for Christian education to occur. One of the surest ways to mute the message of the Bible is to presume to protect it. A sure way to divert attention from its message is to turn it into an abstraction over which we fight instead of a Word which is to be incarnated in us.

In current biblical study it is a sound sense of direction when we are reminded that at the deepest level it is not we who study the Scripture but it is that the Scripture is to study us. It is not placed before us for us to strike down or hold up. We are placed before it to be judged and to be directed to a new relationship with God in Jesus Christ and thus into a new quality of existence.

Let us not forget that Jesus has already announced what the big exam will be when all the nations are gathered before his throne for the final judgment. This may be found in Matthew 25:31-46. There is not a hint of an examination in theology. There is not a hint of concern about how we articulate theology. The total emphasis is upon quality of existence. Our true relationship with Christ is reflected in how we respond to human beings about us, especially in the commonplaces of life as where there is hunger, sickness, or imprisonment. This does not mean that we are saved by our good works. It means that if there is a trusting relationship between us and Christ, something of his existence rubs off on us and we come to embody something of his way of life.

If we are to know the truth which liberates, we must get closer to Jesus Christ than the sixteenth-century Reformation. Let us not forget that Paul said far more than the Reformers heard. The Reformers heard Paul correctly on the subject of salvation as the gift of God's grace. It is not clear that they heard what Paul had to say about salvation as God's demand. They heard his reply to the Judaizers who thought to earn salvation by such Mickey Mouse credentials as circumcision or cultic rites. They may not have heard his response to the libertines who wanted salvation without cost. It is not to be forgotten that Paul wrote 1 Corinthians 6:9-11 as well as texts on salvation by grace: "Do you not know that unrighteous ones will not inherit the kingdom of God; do not deceive yourselves, neither fornicators nor idolaters nor adulterers nor effeminates nor homosexuals nor thieves nor coveteous ones, nor drunkards, nor slanderers nor robbers will inherit the kingdom of God." This is not to be isolated from other Pauline perspectives, but it is to be heard alongside what he says about salvation by grace through faith. Paul knows the saved not as sinners who have received indulgence but as those who have been washed, sanctified, and made right (v. 11).

The fate of the world and the fate of each one of us does rest between good and evil. It is bound up with the truth which is goodness as well as reality. It is bound up with the truth which was incarnated in Jesus of Nazareth and which he would bring about in us. Truth is to be done; truth is that which we are to become. This is what Christian concern for truth is about. Jesus closed the Sermon on the Mount with a contrast between the wise and the foolish. The wise person is the one who hears God's word and does it; the foolish person is the one who hears God's word but does not do it. One is like a builder building on rock, the other on sand. The test of Christian concern with truth, as of everything else we engage in, is the measure of that truth which we do and become, that truth which came in Jesus Christ.

NOTES

[1] This chapter is newly written yet incorporates in part a Christian education address delivered before the Louisiana Baptist Convention, Shreveport, Louisiana on November 26, 1976.

[2] C. H. Dodd, *The Interpretation of the Fourth Gospel* (Cambridge: University Press, 1953), p. 173.

[3] Rudolf Bultmann, *"Aletheia,"* *Theological Dictionary of the New Testament,* ed. Gerhard Kittel; trans. G. W. Bromiley (Grand Rapids: Wm. B. Eerdmans, 1964), I, 238.

4 Cited by *ibid.*, fn. 18.

5 *Ibid.*

6 *Ibid.*, p. 239.

7 *Ibid.*

8 O. A. Piper, "Truth," *The Interpreter's Dictionary of the Bible*, ed. G. A. Buttrick (New York: Abingdon Press, 1962), R-Z, 714.

9 Gottfried Quell, "The OT Term *'emeth*," TDNT, I, 232.

10 *Ibid.*, p. 233.

11 *Ibid.*

12 Unless otherwise indicated, Old Testament quotations are from the Revised Standard Version (RSV); those from the New Testament are my translations. KJV stands for King James Version, and NASB for *New American Standard Bible*.

13 *Op. cit.*, p. 235.

14 *Op. cit.*, pp. 241-47.

15 See Reginald H. Fuller, "Aspects of Pauline Christology," *Review and Expositor*, LXXI (Winter, 1974) 1, 5-17, who sees Paul as having to call gnosticizing Corinthians back to Jesus, whom they would anathematize (1 Cor. 12:3) in favor of a spiritualized Christ.

16 *Op. cit.*, p. 244.

17 *Ibid.*, pp. 242-45.

18 Robert E. Cushman, *"Verum aut Bonum,"* *Religion in Life*, XVI (Winter 1946-47), pp. 25-33.

19 Paul Tillich, "A Theology of Education," *Theology of Culture*, ed. by R. C. Kimball (Oxford University Press, 1959), pp. 146-57.

14.
Imagination and Creativity as Integral to Hermeneutics
W. L. Hendricks

Religion and imagination belong together. All rationalists since the Enlightenment, including Hegel, have disparaged the imagination and regarded it and its products as belonging to a primitive reality. The imaginative aspect of the human mind is its capacity to synthesize experience at all levels and to grasp objective realities concerning which we have clues rather than controlled evidence.[1]

The past of human history is both veiled and disclosed through the media of communication by which the inner side of historical events becomes transparent to human imagination and intuitive insight.[2]

Hermeneutics and History

Professor Rust has lacked neither imagination not historical insight. It is his gift in combining these two, so wrenched apart by the nineteenth-century rationalism, that constitutes a part of his genius and his contribution to contemporary theological scholarship. Despite Professor Rust's fine sense of the balance of history and imagination, with which I am in complete sympathy, the dead hand of Hegel and the nineteenth century is emerging once more to bifurcate these two concepts which belong together as adjuncts to fruitful scholarship.

In a very sophisticated and innovative way one could point to the emphases of Wolfhart Pannenberg as "re-Hegelinizing" theology with some expense to imagination.[3] I speak of this as a sophicated historicism because the element of imagination and intuition are taken into account in the larger category of universal history. However, it seems to me, that the intuitive and imaginative are not granted full weight. Rather, they would seem to be classed by Pannenberg as elements of a "hermeneutical ontology" attributable to Schleiermacher, Heidegger, or Dilthey. Surely there is room for some enterprising doctoral candidate to explore the elements of myth, symbolism, imagination, and creativity in the thought of Pannenberg.

In a more popular view one could suggest that the "objective historical" methodology of the widely read works of Frances Schaeffer sacrifice the intuitive and imaginative elements of hermeneutics. And this in the name of objectivity and under the anathema assigned to all things subjective.[4]

In one way, all must pay their debt to Hegel. The pendulum does swing. Professor Rust has taught and written over enough years to recognize some specters of the past which appear in new ways to raise issues some of us felt were settled. A fresh reading of Rust's books at this time is especially apropos for young theologs, lest they think too much of history, universal or objective, and too little of imagination and intuition.

Hermeneutics is indeed the "name of the game"; and I should like to suggest that imagination is an integral part of hermeneutics. It should not be suggested as with Pannenberg, that "psychological hermeneutics" is the alternative to historical knowledge. Granted liberal biblical scholars have read more of themselves into their work than they were consciously aware of doing. It is incontrovertible that "historically objective" conservative scholars gave lip service only to presuppositions. Perhaps what is being sought is a sense of balance wherein hermeneutics with an unabashed acknowledgement of imagination and intuition is the larger dialectical element in the synthesis it forms with history. If I read him properly, Professor Rust would agree with this kind of unbalanced synthesis. Certainly history, for him, is neither objective nor universal but is captured by the symbolic and the poetic. Much has been written about what history is, but nothing more trenchant has been proposed as a definition than the venerable tautology "history is what historians write." What they wrote and what they meant is the historical focus. Why they wrote as they did and what they mean is the hermeneutical focus. Both foci are essential. The latter seems to me more preformative in striving to "get at reality." And indigenous to this hermeneutical task is creative imagination controlled by the rationality of historical research and probability. For this reason, I am coming to see structuralism as a viable hermeneutical tool—the successor of "theological exegesis" and the heir of *Heilsgeschichte*.[5]

This chapter is not an exercise in structuralism. It is from a prestructuralist period when intuitive insights and historico-critical principles were jockeying for positions in my hermeneutical priorities. This chapter is (1) an attempt to identify with Dr. Rust's position of history as involving imagination, (2) an attempt to articulate some characteristics of imagination and creativity, and (3) a specific test case pertaining to historical study as to how the imaginative process may be brought to bear on a problem in New Testament studies. My appreciation for Professor Rust and my preference for imagination in hermeneutics as the larger portion of the dialectic formed with historical studies have been confessed. The more elusive process of defining imagination and creativity is the next task.

Hermeneutics, Imagination, and Creativity

Dictionaries are frustrating arbiters of words and meaning. On the one hand, they gain their concepts from the specialists in various fields, and on the other hand, they wind up being the crystallized concepts which those specialists in turn must consult in order to define their disciplines. The situation is reminiscent of an Emily Post story. That redoubtable social arbiter once asked a department store clerk about the appropriateness of a table setting only to have the clerk pull out a copy of Mrs. Post's book thereby consulting the expert. Dictionary definitions are dull, but necessary, and they are necessarily succinct and incomplete. *The Unabridged Edition of the Random House Dictionary of the English Language*[6] has eight definitions of imagination. Fortunately the first one is the more precise and agreeable to the sense intruded here. "1. the action of imaging, or of forming mental images or concepts of what is not actually present to the senses." Unfortunately, definition number five is the commonly accepted notion of imagination. "5. the product of imagining; a conception or mental creation, often a baseless or fanciful one." The same fate attends the terms *symbolic* and *mythical* as Professor Rust asserts in the quotations offered above. But as Socrates reminds us, each man has the right to define his art. And as Mortimer Adler asserts each reader is obliged to understand an author's definition of his terms. Imagination is forming mental images; it does not necessarily follow that those images are "baseless or fanciful." Through the formation of images, hypotheses, and supposition all knowledge has advanced.[7]

Harold Rugg of Columbia University, has an epochal study of imagination in which he extracts from numerous case studies four steps in the imaginative process. They are: (1) a preparatory conscious period of baffled struggle; (2) an interlude when the specific problem is pushed out of conscious thought and is fulminated over at the subconscious level; (3) a flash of insight which gives clues to the resolution of the problem; and (4) a period of verification.[8] Biblical hermeneutics is not exempt from this process. Granted at the minimal level of functioning a beginning student does not utilize this process to articulate the present or perfect tense of a Greek verb. Yet at a more advanced level the grammarian's imagination should struggle with a hypothesis as to why the author of the Fourth Gospel prefers the perfect tense to the imperfect. The process of verification of imaginative hypothesis about historical manuscripts is less cogent than in controlled scientific experiment of a biological nature. But it may be assumed that all twentieth-century historians who have read Collingwood and recognized the naivete of Von Rank will settle for convincing probability rather than empirical verification concerning their hypotheses and historical reconstructions. The subjective process of imagination in biblical exegesis sparks new interpretations. These interpretations, in turn, gain acceptance and move toward the more "objective" pole of probability as converging lines of convincing argument and rationale are offered. It would seem that this is the way that new theological heroes are born and best-sellers are written, even while standing on the shoulders of "the past." Rote and repetition are not enough. Ideas *de novo* are rare indeed. What happens even among those who espouse history as the larger side of the dialectic is an imaginative reinterpretation of the past. Historians "hermeneut" history. Archivists record and preserve the past without imagination. I have taught ministers for two decades. What is most lacking among their skills is imagination and/or the recognition of the need for it.

Creativity also is essential to hermeneutics. The abstract noun "creativity" is highly prized but rarely defined. There are the elitist British views and the egalatarian-social-development theories espoused in America. A creative entity in order to be so named should contain four elements: (1) a basic idea or conception, (2) an embodied or articulated form, (3) novelty, and (4) usefulness. Hermeneutics, as that science which seeks to interpret the past to, and in the light of, the present, must surely involve creativity. Specialists in defining and describing creativity have posited three elements in the process of creativity. (1) Fluency is the rush and flow of images and ideas. (2) There is a kind of receptivity of all phenomena and a sagacity in the solution of those phenomena which are significant and pertinent. This process is aided by insight and intuition. (3) There is a motivational force in creativity called zeal. It is this component which provides the persistence and possibly the patience to be creative.[9]

Imagination and creativity are essential in adequate hermeneutics.

And adequate hermeneutics are essentially involved with historical documents. All scholarship in the historical disciplines involves both historical method and hermeneutics. Pannenberg's dialectic is correct. I cannot, however, agree that he has chosen the better part by selecting universal history as the larger element in the dialectic over against hermeneutics. For me, the reverse is preferable because it seems more plausible to begin with the thinking selves of the community of scholars and work toward the universal contexts embodied in the tests. I am unable to determine if it was Socrates, Kant, Heidegger, Kierkegaard, or common sense that gave me this "intuition." But I cannot be persuaded that this process is more "subjective" than coming to historical texts (embodying either specifics of universal history or the exclusive propositions of a divine objective history) with a hidden agenda. This is true even when that agenda is creatively incorporated or imaginatively reconstructed in the historical texts.

A test case of this stated preference for the priority of imagination and creativity in hermeneutics in explicating a specific historical text follows. It could be strengthened by a structuralist comparison and/ or by a formal analysis of a psychological hermeneutic. Space permits neither.[10]

Hermeneutics: A Test Case on a Historical Document Involving Creativity and Imagination

The test case chosen has to do with the relation of Ignatius to Paul and the specific hypothesis that a reference in Ignatius' letters gives an imaginative clue to an intriguing riddle in New Testament studies, namely the fate of the Pauline letters to Laodicea.[11]

The relationship of Ignatius of Antioch to Paul the apostle may be approached from the literary dependence of Ignatius on Paul and from the viewpoint of secondary historical relationships. That Paul influenced Ignatius is part of what "every school boy knows" about patristics. That Ignatius may throw some light on the Pauline corpus is far from demonstrated heretofore, and doubtless herein.

Preliminary Remarks

After preliminary remarks about Ignatius' life and works, the first focus of this chapter is a general survey of some of the more important literature assessing the influence of Paul on Ignatius. In the second part of the chapter a hypothesis concerning Paul's writing will be developed from a historical reference of Ignatius.

Ignatius and His Epistles. Historically, little is known about the *curriculum vitae* of Ignatius. If the ancients had known which babies would become famous men, they would doubtless have marked the year of their birth more carefully. As it stands, the notoriety and historicity of the ancient world is reckoned from the time of death. It is, indeed, because of Ignatius' death that we know anything about him or have any literary remains from him. Internal testimony from his letters indicates that Ignatius was going to Rome to die. External evidence (Polycarp, Irenaeus, Theophilus of Antioch, Origen, Eusebius, Athanasius, Basil of Caesarea, Hieronymus, John Chrysostom, Theodoret, Socrates, John of Antioch, Gelasius, Pseudo-Dionynsius, Ephraemus, patriarch of Theopolitus, Job Monarchus, Eugarius, Gildas the Wise, Stephen Gobarus, Anastasius of Sinai, Anastasius of Antioch, Gregory the Great, Leontius of Byzantium, Antiochus Monarchus, Pascale Chronicle, Theodorus the Presbyter, Maximus, Andreas Cretensis, John of Damascus, Antionus of Melissa, Bede the Presbyter, Theodorus Studites, Michael Syngelus, Nicephorus the Patriarch, Anastasius the Librarian, Freculphus, Bishop of Lepovia, John of Malala, and Photius of Constaninople) of the thirty-nine authors from the second to the tenth century attest his martyrdom and/or cite his works.[12] The time of his martyrdom was in the second half of Trajan's reign, i.e., 107-117.[13]

Eusebius indicates that Ignatius was the third bishop of Antioch after Peter and Euodius.[14] Previously the same author cites Ignatius as second bishop of Antioch and Euodius as the first.[15]

There has been much disputation about the correspondence of Ignatius as to what may be considered genuine and what spurious. Modern scholarship has generally accepted (following Lightfoot) the seven epistles listed by Eusebius.[16] These are: Ephesians, Magnesians, Trallians, and Romans, the four epistles written at Smyrna and Philadelphians, Smyrnaeans, and the letter to Polycarp written and dispatched from Troas. Additional epistles attributed to Ignatius or addressed to him are: The Epistle of Mary Cassabola to Ignatius, the Epistle of Ignatius to Mary Cassabola, the Epistle to the Tarsians, to the Antiochians, to Hero (Ignatius' successor at Antioch), to the Philippians, two epistles to St. John, and one epistle to the Virgin Mary. For purposes of this chapter we shall use the "genuine epistles" i.e., the seven mentioned by Eusebius.

It is, however, of passing interest to note the intriguing work of Milton Perry Brown [17] in which he uses the genuine works of Ignatius and those of Pseudo-Ignatius for a study of linguistic criteria of authorship. Of particular concern to a discussion of the canon are the following statements:

> It is clear, that although Ign[atius] venerates Paul, ranks him along side Peter among the Apostles, and quotes six or seven of Paul's letters (including Ephesians), there is not yet a full blown canonical status for that Apostle's works.[18]

> The New Testament is probably still a great distance away from its ultimate definition, and even the Pauline Corpus has not in Ign[atius] attained the degree of sanctity and authority that would later be bestowed upon it.[19]

By way of contrast Brown says:

> Psuedo I[gnatius] very definitely feels the sanctity and canonical authority of the (Pauline) passages which he quotes; they are for him on a par with the Old Testament, if not superior to it. . . . In Philippians he singles out Paul as *ho apostolos* and quotes his I Corinthians 15:53 and 6:9-10 among others. . . The practice of our writer (Pseudo I) in so many respects points quite clearly to a "Closed Canon." [20]

If one were convinced by Brown's linguistic arguments, a response to the old question of when the canon was closed might well be: "Between the Epistles of Ignatius." Maybe this pragmatic question would stir long overdue activity on the dating of the Pseudo-Ignatian Epistles.

The Literary Relationship Between Paul and Ignatius

A literary relationship between Paul and Ignatius is "an assured result of scholarship," but the extent and specifics of this influence are greatly divergent according to individual scholars.

A brief resumé of various treatments of this relationship will serve as something of a bibliographical essay. Two principal ways of identifying literary dependence are: (1) linguistic affinities, involving quotes, allusions, and vocabulary studies; and (2) ideological and theological similarities pertaining to clusters of ideas and thought motifs.

Linguistic Affinities. The sources for a study of linguistic affinities are obviously the texts of Paul and of Ignatius, standard lexicons, (e.g., Arndt and Gingrich) and work lists such as Goodspeed's *Index Patristicus* and *Index Apologeticus.*

Milton Brown gives valuable word lists of Ignatius' letters and related sources which use Ignatius' terms.[21] Brown's primary purpose is to establish "greater objectivity and steadier ground for agreement in dealing with questions of authenticity." [22] By using the generally recognized genuine epistles of Ignatius vis-à-vis the spurious epistles, he seeks to illustrate and strengthen a method of linguistic comparisons used by New Testament scholars, especially on the Pauline corpus. Incidentally, but convincingly, he also illustrates the linguistic similarities of Ignatius to Paul by noting their common vocabulary and by indicating such in secondary ways throughout his work and in the word list.

Albert E. Barnett's *Paul Becomes a Literary Influence* [23] describes the rise of interest in Paul through the first half of the second century. He contends that interest in Paul's letters was sparked by the publication of Luke-Acts, that Ephesians was an encyclical epistle written by someone other than Paul as a cover letter for the collection, and that Ignatius' epistles were written during the time of popularity of Paul's letters in the first decades of the second century. Barnett knows that while there are no direct quotations from Paul's letters in Ignatius, there are thirty-nine allusions (rated on a Scale of A [practical certainty], and B [a high degree of probability]). He furthermore finds forty-one "possible literary reminiscences."

He concludes: "It is clear that Ignatius knew I Corinthians, Romans, and Ephesians and that he very probably knew Galatians, Philippians, and Colossians. He may also have known II Corinthians, I and II Thessalonians, and Philemon." [24] Barnett's list of parallels between Ignatius and Paul are given in Appendix C of this chapter. Appendices A and B are respectively the notations of Lightfoot and Kirsopp Lake. The latter are much less complete than Barnett's list, nevertheless they serve to document the more obvious allusions of Ignatius to Paul's works. Appendices D and E are, respectively, the lists of Cyril Richardson [25] and Dean Inge. [26]

The following conclusions about Ignatius' knowledge and use of Paul will summarize the linguistic affinities between the two.

(1) Ignatius refers to Paul by name twice. Ephesians 12:2: "You (the Ephesians) are the passage (parados) for these who are being slain for the sake of God, fellow initiates with Paul, who was right blessed, in whose footsteps may I be found when I shall attain to God, who in every Epistle makes mention of you in Jesus Christ." And Romans 4:3 "I do not order you as did Peter and Paul; they were Apostles, I am a convict; they were free, I am even until now a slave."

(2) There are no direct quotations from any Pauline epistles.

(3) There are allusions in the Ignatian epistles to all of the Pauline epistles and the pastorals.

(4) The five major lists of allusions consulted contained a total of 198 references (Lightfoot 7, Lake 34, Barnett 39, Richardson 47, Inge 71).

(5) Of these instances all five commentators agree unanimously on only one allusion (Ephesians 18:1 of I Corinthians 1:20).

(6) Four commentators agree on 19 of 198 allusions. (see Appendix F).

These figures point up the perils of "parallelomania" and illustrate the difficulty in assessing literary dependence. One may account for difficulty in pin-pointing direct quotations either to (1) Paul's frequent use of terms and phrases, thereby making it difficult for one to isolate a primary reference, or (2) the commonality of a general Christian vocabulary which would point to a broader use of words and phrases beyond the two authors under consideration. At best one may say that the literary influence of Paul on Ignatius was diffuse and difficult to document with any degree of specificness. An agreement of four major scholarly lists on only 19 points of 198 is certainly less than impressive.

Ideological and Theological Similarities of Paul and Ignatius. The linguistic affinities and literary allusions are the first step in assessing that Ignatius knew and used Paul's writings. The more significant questions are the substantial ones that involve what ideas Ignatius shares with Paul and what Pauline ideas are notably missing from Ignatius. The subtleties of how Ignatius appropriated Pauline ideas and the fine exposition of Ignatius independence in his Paulinism must await an enterprising doctoral dissertation.[27]

One of the influences of the *religionsgeschichtliche Schule* on Rudolph Bultmann is seen in his inclusion of the works of the Apostolic Fathers in his New Testament theology. Ignatius' works are discussed in Volume II of *The Theology of the New Testament* [28] in the section entitled "The Development Toward the Ancient Church." They are treated specifically under the topic the "Core of the Development," namely, Christology and Soteriology. Bultmann's views as to the relation of Ignatius to Paul may be summarized as follows:

Ignatius' thought, while showing an originality unique among the Apostolic Fathers, casts a light back on Paul. Early Christian eschatology has been "realized" in Ignatius in such fashion that there is but one allusion to the future coming of Christ (Poly. 3:2). Cosmic catastro-

phe and apocalyptic expectation, future oriented in Paul, have occurred, for Ignatius in Jesus' birth, death, and resurrection. Paul's
"union with Christ" figure is adopted, but it is sacramentalized by
Ignatius, however, in a total rather than a sacramentarian way.

As with Paul, Ignatius sees spirit as the sphere of the Christian,
but for Ignatius it is the other-worldly sphere rather than Paul's power
of right conduct. Ignatius does not see "flesh" as the locus of sin.
Rather it is the sphere of transitoriness and weakness. Ignatius speaks
frequently of the flesh of Christ, and "even the things done in the
flesh are spiritual, for it is in Jesus Christ that you do them all"
(Ephesians 8:2). "Being crucified with Christ" is for Paul a constant
battle with sin and renunciation of the world; for Ignatius this is
the *initatio Christi via* a martyr's death. Ignatius' concept of faith is
vital rather than forensic; he does not oppose faith to works, and he
thereby misses the sharpness of Paul's idea of justification. Freedom
is for Ignatius, in contradistinction to Paul's present posture of authentic existence, a future prospect attained after death.

Cyril Richardson in his monograph on Ignatius [29] suggests that
Ignatius knew Paul "not as a reflective thinker mediates upon a great
master, but as a fervent practical bishop admires an apostle and martyr.
He never really penetrated to the roots of Pauline thinking." [30]

Richardson cites as areas of agreement between Paul and Ignatius
the ideas of: Christ as the object of faith; the necessity of the Christian's
personal fellowship with Christ—especially seen in the use of the dying-
rising metaphor; Christ's death as central to the plan of God for man's
redemption and the defeat of the heavenly powers hostile to man;
faith is characterized by a moral life summarized by agape; full fellowship with Christ can be realized only after the resurrection; and a
stress on the unity of the church in the eucharist.

Richardson suggests that salvation as deliverance from flesh and
renewal by the indwelling Spirit, bulwarks of Pauline thought, are
lacking in Ignatius. Other insights of Paul not shared by Ignatius
are the fatherhood of God, as it pertains to men; the second coming
of Christ; faith as complete receptivity; and the idea of the lordship
of Christ as an effective power vis-à-vis a formal designation.

It is at the point of church order and the office of ministry that
Ignatius is best known. The contribution of Ignatius vis-à-vis Paul is
assessed in vastly different ways as they relate to the office of bishop.

Walter Bauer considers Ignatius' view of monoepiscopacy to be
an exception to the prevailing church order of the day. It is Bauer's

evaluation that Ignatius' view is "unparalled in the history of the ancient church." [31] Bauer considers that Ignatius is exuberant and "time and again loses all sense of proportion." [32] One must evaluate Ignatius' expressions with great care. Ignatius in his views of monoepiscopacy is not so much "depicting the actual situation" as "portraying the ideal." He is dealing with admonition rather than description. He is writing in a factious time when the reality of monoepiscopacy is desirable. The paucity of the material about the episcopacy at Antioch itself is a forceful argument against Ignatius representing the historical norm for his day. Ignatius' struggle against heresy was the motivation for his vocality about the monoepiscopacy. [33]

One need not leave the Protestant community to find a dissenting view to that of Bauer. H. E. W. Turner [34] has written *per contra* Bauer. He feels that the "Ignation quadrilateral" (one God, one Christ, one Church, one Bishop) is based on principle not expedience, on Ignatius' conviction and not his circumstance.

A Roman Catholic view that Ignatius' teachings on episcopacy are logical extension of Paul is expressed by John B. O'Conner. [35] O'Conner finds in Ignatius the legitimate extension of apostolic insights in the following Ignatian teachings: (1) the heirarchy of the church instituted by Christ; (2) the threefold character of the heirarchy; (3) the order of episcopacy superior to priesthood; and (4) the primacy of the See of Rome. [36]

Ignatius is indebted to Paul by absorption of many of Paul's insights. He is most different from Paul at the point of uniting faith and works— especially the "work" of martyrdom in a way which, as Bultmann says, misses the point of a radical view of justification by faith alone.

What is needed are further monographs on theological aspects of Paul's insights and the development and rescensions of those in the Ignatian epistles. Particularly fruitful would be both linguistic and theological comparisons of the pastoral epistles and the Ignatian corpus.

Although verbal comparisons and theological insights reflect that Ignatius was a "Paulinist," in all fairness our study has revealed that the relation of Paul and Ignatius has often been overdrawn.

A Historical Relationship: More or Less. It is not news that the Ignatian epistles were influenced by the Pauline epistles. It is intriguing to develop a hypothesis about a "lost epistle of Paul" partly from a reference of Ignatius. In Ignatius' epistle to the Ephesians (Ephesian 12:2) Onesimus is cited as the bishop of Ephesus. I agree with John

Knox that this Onesimus is the slave of the canonical Philemon.[37]
From this Ignatian reference we enter backwards into the world of
Paul. There is some degree of probability that Ignatius' Onesimus,
the same as our canonical Onesimus, was instrumental in collecting
and editing the epistles of Paul. In such a case there is a historical
relationship between Paul and Ignatius in the person of Onesimus. I
would like to deduce from this historical relationship a hypothesis
concerning the "lost" Laodicean letter of Paul.

The genuineness of Colossians and Philemon as Pauline epistles is
regarded as demonstrated.[38] The relationship of Colossians and Philemon is close in that they were written at approximately the same
time and sent to their respective destinations by Tychicus and Onesimus (Col. 4:7-9).[39] Knox has convincingly demonstrated that the Colossian *Haustafelen* about slaves (3:18 to 4:1) has reference to the
special case of Onesimus.[40] According to Colossians 4:16 there was
a letter to the Laodiceans sent at the approximate time as the letter
to Colossae. In Colossians the Colossian Christians are encouraged
to exchange their letter with the Laodiceans.

Knox and Goodspeed argue that our canonical letter to Philemon
is the Laodicean letter.[41] Failing to accept the canonical Philemon
as the Laodicean letter, one is required to provide other solutions.
It is generally acknowledged that the apocryphal Epistle to the Laodiceans is the late forgery.[43] The Marcionite notion that our canonical
Ephesians is the Laodicean letter is likewise unconvincing. The most
persistent and obvious solution to the fate of the Laodicean letter is
that it was "lost." Harrison's suggestion [44] that it was destroyed in
an earthquake in the Lycus Valley in A.D. 60 is unacceptable to me,
for I accept the later date of composition from Rome as the dating
and provenance of Colossians and therefore of "Laodiceans."

I would like to propose that the fate of the Laodicean letter is
implicit in Colossians and Philemon and is bound up with the fate
of Pauline influence in Laodicea in the late first and early second
century.

One connection of Colossians and Philemon is Archippus. It is plaus-
able to assume, with Goodspeed,[45] that Archippus was the overseer
at Laodicea. In such instance he would have been the recipient or
guardian of the epistle to Laodicea. This suggestion is fortified by
the indirect address to Archippus *via* the Colossians (4:17). The implicit
assumption of Colossians 4:17 is that Archippus is not fulfilling his
ministry and is being upbraided by Paul, who brings also the influence

of the neighboring Colossian church to bear in striving to secure the cooperation of Archippus.

The supposition may be plausible that if Colossians contained a veiled correction of Archippus, the Laodicean pastor, how much more might have the direct letter. Moule seems persuasive against Knox and Goodspeed that the letter of Philemon is not the Laodicean letter, and that the service Archippus is encouraged to do is more than that of returning Onesimus to Paul for Christian ministry.[46] Indeed, Knox's arguments for Archippus as owner of Onesimus and Philemon as pastor of Colossae seem unconvincing.

My suggestion concerning the context of Onesimus and Archippus, the lost letter to Laodicea, and the broader relations of the Pauline letters would be as follows:

Epaphras, a native of the Lycus valley became acquainted with the Christian faith as the results of Paul's labors at Ephesus. Epaphras returned to Colossae to help bring into being a small Christian community and to assume the leadership of it. From this church the congregations of Hieropolis and Laodicea came into being. Epaphras later joins Paul in Rome where both are "in bonds." [47]

Onesimus, a runaway slave is brought into contact with Paul, embraces Christianity, and is sent back to Colossae [48] with the letter of Philemon. His traveling companion is Tychicus who bears the epistle to Colossae and the official Laodicean letter.

Archippus, the overseer of the Laodicean church, is indirectly upbraided by Paul in the Colossian epistle (4:17). (Note the disjunctive address rather than the direct address lending credence that Paul exhorts the Colossians to encourage Archippus, who is not immediately one of them, to perform his ministry well.) If Archippus was minister at Laodicea, it is reasonable to assume that Paul, who never passed up an opportunity for correction and direct exhortation, upbraided Archippus more forcefully in the Laodicean epistle than in Colossians. It is entirely possible that Archippus, who may not, like other Christians of the Lycus valley, have known Paul personally, rejected and suppressed if not destroyed the letter to the Laodiceans.

It is a matter of record that John the Revelator found Laodicea deficient in warmth to apostolic witness (Rev. 3:14-22). It is Bauer's contention that the churches of the Lycus valley rejected orthodoxy in the second century and that the "Colossian heretics" prevailed.[49]

The solution to the preservation of two of three of Paul's Lycus valley letters [50] lies in the person of Onesimus who would doubtless have had access to Philemon, have rescued the Colossian epistle, but could not and did retrieve that Laodicean letter from Archippus who did not "take heed to fulfill the ministry he had received from the Lord," nor did he take kindly to Paul's injunction that he do so.[51]

Behold what a spate of speculation a simple reference of Ignatius to Onesimus has brought! There was literary, or at least vocabulary, dependence of Ignatius on Paul, *more* or less. There may be, in a reference of Ignatius, a historical clue to Paul's epistle to the Laodiceans, more or *less*.

Conclusion

In this example of hermeneutics, it is hoped that the process of imagination and creativity are demonstrated. The verification possibilities are slender, since it is an *argumentum e silencio*. I have employed a hermeneutic which takes seriously the constant of certain psychological elements of human nature, such as its unwillingness to be reproved and adds the historical arguments of Bauer about the defection of the churches in the Lycus valley. The attempt has been an illustration of the dialogical model of the relation of hermeneutics and history. The larger side of getting at the ancient setting rests on the intuitive, imaginative, and creative elements brought to a hermeneutical system. These are combined with the historical skills of exegeting the situation. The thesis has been that imagination and creativity are integral to hermeneutics. Certainly they are integral to the works of Professor Rust who viewed all theological realities as involving the imagination and who put together creative and challenging ideas in the performance of his theological scholarship.

NOTES

[1] Eric C. Rust, *Towards a Theological Understanding of History* (New York: Oxford University Press, 1963), pp. 85-86.

[2] *Ibid.*, p. 65.

[3] Cf. Pannenberg's "Hermeneutics and Universal History" in *History and Hermeneutic.* Vol. 4 of *Journal for Theology and the Church,* ed. by Robert W. Funk in association with Gerhard Ebeling (New York: Harper and Row, 1967), pp. 122-153. See Frank Tupper's "The Theology of Wolfhart Pannenberg" for a favorable analysis of Pannenberg's theology. For popular introductions to Pannenberg's thought see John Newhaus' "Wolfhart Pannenberg: Profile of a Theologian" in Pannenberg's *Theology and the Kingdom of God* (Philadelphia: Westminster Press, 1969), pp. 9-51; and Pannenberg's article "Appearance as the Arrival of the Future" in *New Theology* No. 5 edited by Martin F. Marty and Dean G. Peerman (New York: Macmillan Co., 1968).

4 Cf. for example Frances Schaeffer's *The God Who Is There* (Downers Grove, Illinois: Inter—Varsity Press, 1968). Cf. my review in *Southwestern Journal of Theology* and Francis Schaeffer, *How Should We Then Live* (Old Tappan, New Jersey: Fleming H. Revell and Company, 1976), and the review of Yandall Woodfin in *Southwestern Journal of Theology* (Spring 1977). See also the perceptive analysis of Schaeffer by Jack Rogers' "Francis Schaeffer: The Province and the Problem" in *The Reformed Journal* (May, 1977), pp. 12-15; (June, 1977), pp. 15-19.

5 See Dan O. Via, Jr. *Kerygma and Comedy in the New Testament: A Structuralist Approach to Hermeneutic.* (Philadelphia: Fortress Press, 1975). For a popular introduction to structuralism, see Daniel Patte, *What Is Structural Exegesis* (Philadelphia: Fortress Press, 1976).

6 New York: Random House, 1967.

7 This is no less true for science and mother nature than for philosophy and theology. See Thomas Kulen, *The Structure of Scientific Revolution* (Chicago: University of Chicago Press, 1962).

8 Harold Rugg, *Imagination* (New York: Harper and Row, Publishers, 1963). See especially Part One.

9 See Professor Cyril Burt's Foreword to Arthur Koestler's *The Act of Creation* (New York: The Macmillan Company, 1964), pp. 13-21.

10 For example, the genre of the epistle and personal injunctions within it could be set up to parallel and correlate with the personal injunctions of Colossians in such a way as to strengthen the following argument. Word studies of such crucial terms as *eipon* are the necessary parts of objective grammatical studies. The factor of psychological pride, a perennial part of human nature, might well be seen as an "existential" element in the following interpretation. My position is that the predictable actions of persons stung by rebuke are as cogent as tenses of Greek verbs in constructing a viable hermeneutic.

For material to provide parallels appropriate for a structuralist paradigm with Paul's letters see: William G. Doty, *Letters in Primitive Christianity* in the *New Testament Series,* edited by Dan O. Via, Jr. (Philadelphia: Fortress Press, 1973). Unfortunately this work does not deal adequately with the "informal" elements of Paul's letters. See also John Lee White's *The Body of the Greek Letter* in the SBL Dissertation Series 2, 1972. See also Dorothy Brooke, *Private Letters Pagan and Christian* (London: Ernest Benn, Limited, 1929), and Chan-Hie Kinn, *The Familiar Letter of Recommendation,* SBL Dissertation Series 4, 1972; and John Lee White, *The Form and Structure of the Official Petition,* SBL Dissertation Series 5, 1972. See also W. Hersey Davis, *Greek Papyri of the First Century* (New York: Harper and Brothers, 1933).

11 This paper was presented both to the Southwest Regional New Testament Section of the Society of Biblical Literature and to a study seminar in the Southwest called "The Seminar for the Development of Early Christianity." It has not heretofore appeared in print.

12 William Cureton, ed., *Corpus Ignatianum* (London: Francis and John Rivington, 1849).

13 Cf. Gerald G. Walsh, *The Letter of St. Ignatius of Antioch,* "The Fathers of the Church," vol. 1. (New York: CIMA Publishing Co., Inc., 1947), pp. 83-86.

14 Eusebius, *Ecclesiastical History,* 3, 36.

15 *Ibid.,* 3, 22.

16 For complete studies concerning critical editions of Ignatius' works see: J. B. Lightfoot, *The Apostolic Fathers* (London: Macmillan and Co., 1898); Cureton, *Corpus Ignatium;* Kirsopp Lake, *The Apostolic Fathers,* 2 vols. (London: William Heineman, 1919) 1:166-171; Reinoud Weijenborg, *Les Lettres d'Ignace d' Antioche,* tr. Barthelemy Heroux (Leiden: E. J. Brill, 1969).

17 *The Authentic Writings of Ignatius* (Durham, N. C.: Duke University Press, 1963).

18 Brown, p. 95.

19 *Ibid.,* p. 94.

20 *Ibid.,* p. 116.

21 Brown, Appendix A.

22 *Ibid.,* p. x.

23 Chicago: University of Chicago Press, 1941.

24 *Ibid.,* p. 170. It is difficult to comprehend why Barnett includes 2 Thessalonians and Philemon since his major 39 references contain no allusions to those books.

25 *The Christianity of Ignatius of Antioch* (New York: Columbia University Press, 1935).

26 *The New Testament in the Apostolic Fathers* (Oxford: Oxford University Press. N. I.).

27 Such might well be patterned after Christian Mowrer, *Ignatius von Antiochien und das*

Johannesevangelium, Abhandlungen fur Theologie des Alten und Neuen Testaments (Zurich: Zwingli Verlag, 1949).

[28] Translated by Kendrick Grobel (London: SCM Press, 1958), pp. 191-199.

[29] *The Christianity of Ignatius of Antioch.*

[30] *Ibid.,* p. 67.

[31] *Orthodoxy and Heresy in Earliest Christianity,* translated by a team from the Philadelphia seminar on Christian Origins (Philadelphia: Fortress Press, 1971), pp. 60ff.

[32] *Ibid.,* p. 61.

[33] *Ibid.,* pp. 60-70.

[34] *The Pattern of Christian Truth* (London: A. R. Mowbray, 1954), pp. 59-64, being the Bampton lectures of 1954.

[35] *The Catholic Encyclopedia,* 1910, vol. 7, pp. 644ff. Note the radical changes made in the treatment of Ignatius in the latest edition of the same encyclopedia.

[36] *Ibid.,* VII, 646.

[37] *Philemon Among the Letters of Paul* (London: Collins, 1960), pp. 85ff.

[38] Cf. Moule, "Colossians and Philemon," *The Cambridge Greek Testament Commentary, in loco.*

[39] Cf. John Knox, *Philemon.*

[40] *Ibid.,* pp. 31-38.

[41] *Ibid.,* p. 38. Cf. E. J. Goodspeed, *New Solutions of New Testament Problems* (Chicago: The University of Chicago Press, 1933).

[42] Moule, pp. 14ff.

[43] Cf. M. R. James, *The Apocryphal New Testament* (Oxford: Oxford University Press, 1924), pp. 479ff.

[44] Cf. P. N. Harrison, "Onesimus and Philemon," *Anglican Theological Review,* vol. XXXII (October, 1950), pp. 268-94.

[45] E. J. Goodspeed, *The Meaning of Ephesians,* p. 6.

[46] Moule, p. 14ff.

[47] Although it is impossible to know the occasion for Epaphras imprisonment, it may be assumed that Epaphras was a prisoner with Paul, even as Aristarchus was (Colossians 4:10), else Epaphras would have returned to the Lycus valley bearing Paul's letter in order to set things right in the church at Colossae.

[48] Goodspeed's note that the "one of you" as applied to Onesimus' way indeed mean one of you in the Lycus valley not just one of you at Colossae (*Meaning of Ephesians,* p. 8) is instructive at this point. See however, Moule's rebuttal.

[49] The hypothesis that Archippus suppressed the Laodicean letter gains some support from Walter Bauer's contention that Laodicea was in the hands of the heretics by the time of Ignatius. His reasoning is based on the unfavorable account of Laodicea in the Apocalypse and silence of Ignatius to the churches of the Lycus valley. Cf. Bauer, pp. 77ff.

[50] The authorship of the Ephesian letter, as to whether it is Pauline or whether it is a cover letter to replace the Laodiceans' letter is of no material substance to the point we are here asserting.

[51] It could be argued that Nympha is hostess of the house church at Colossae and that Archippus is host and overseer of the house church at Laodicea. This would mean that in addition to addressing Philemon and Apphia at Colossae, Paul is also in Philemon sending greetings to Archippus at Laodicea about whom he has grave concern. It is not unreasonable to assume with Moule that Archippus is the son of Philemon and Apphia, but it would not necessarily follow that he was in Colossae. In fact, my argument would be strengthened to suppose Archippus, was the grown son of Philemon and Apphia, and that he was the overseer at Laodicea. It would, therefore, be expeditious of Paul to address Archippus through his parents.

Appendix A

Lightfoot's list of literary dependence of Ignatius
on Paul. Total of 7.

Ephesians
10:2   Colossians 1:23
16:1-2 1 Corinthians 6:9,10; Galatians 5:21
18:1   1 Corinthians 1:20
19:3   Romans 6:4

Magnesians
none

Smyrnaeans
none

Romans
5:2 1 Corinthians 4:4

Philadelphians
3:3 1 Corinthians 6:9

Trallians
none

To Polycarp
5:1 Ephesians 5:29

Appendix B

Kirsopp Lake's list; total of 34.

To the Ephesians
8:2   cf. Romans 6:5
10:1 1 Thessalonians 5:17
10:3 Colossians 1:23; Romans 4:20;
       1 Corinthians 16:13
14:1 1 Timothy 1:5
15:3 1 Corinthians 3:16

16:1 1 Corinthians 6:9-10; Ephesians
      5:5
18:1 Galatians 5:11; 1 Corinthians 1:20
18:2 Romans 1:3; 2 Timothy 2:8
19:3 Romans 6:4
20:2 Romans 1:3

To the Magnesians
10:2 1 Corinthians 5:7

To the Romans
2:1   1 Thessalonians 2:4
*4:3 1 Corinthians 7:22
5:1   1 Corinthians 4:4
6:1   1 Corinthians 9:15
7:3   Romans 1:3; 2 Timothy 2:8
9:2   1 Corinthians 15:8-9

To the Smyrnaeans
Proleg. 1 1 Corinthians 1:7
    1:1   Romans 1:3
    1:2   Ephesians 2:16
    4:2   Philippians 4:13
   10:2 2 Timothy 1:16
   11:3 Philippians 3:15

To the Trallians
2:2   1 Corinthians 4:1
5:1   1 Corinthians 3:1-2
5:2   Colossians 1:16; 2 Corinthians
      12:1-7
9:2   1 Corinthians 15:12ff
12:3 1 Corinthians 9:27

To the Philadelphians
3:3   1 Corinthians 6:9-16
4:1   1 Corinthians 10:16-17
7:1   1 Corinthians 2:10

Ignatius to Polycarp
1:2   Ephesians 4:2
4:3   1 Timothy 6:2
*5:1 Ephesians 5:25,29
6:2   2 Timothy 2:4

Appendix C

A. E. Barnett's list; total of 39.

Ephesians

Inscription-cf.	Ephesians 1:3-12	18:1	1 Corinthians 1:18-23
1:1	Ephesians 5:1		(Gal. 5:11)
2:1	Colossians 1:7	18:2	Romans 1:3,4
8:2	Romans 8:5,8	19:3	Romans 6:4
12:2	Ephesians 1:9	20:1	Ephesians 2:15
15:3	1 Corinthians 3:16,17	20:2	Romans 1:3,4
16:1	1 Corinthians 6:9,10		

Magnesians

2:1	Colossians 1:7; 4:7
10:2	1 Corinthians 5:7

Romans

2:1	1 Thessalonians 2:4
4:3	1 Corinthians 7:22
5:1	1 Corinthians 4:4
6:1	1 Corinthians 9:15
7:3	Romans 1:3
9:2	1 Corinthians 15:8,9

Smyrnaeans

Inscription	1 Corinthians 1:1,7
1:1	Romans 1:3,4
1:2	Ephesians 2:15,16
4:2	Philippians 4:13
11:3	Philippians 3:15

Trallians

2:3	1 Corinthians 4:1
5:1	1 Corinthians 3:1-3
5:2	Colossians 1:16
10:1	1 Corinthians 15:14,15,32
12:3	1 Corinthians 9:27

Philadelphians

1:1	Galatians 1:1
3:3	1 Corinthians 6:9,10
4:1	1 Corinthians 10:16,17
6:3	2 Corinthians 1:12
7:1	1 Corinthians 2:10
7:2	1 Corinthians 3:16

Polycarp

1:2	Ephesians 4:2-4
5:1,2	Ephesians 5:25,29
6:2	Ephesians 6:13-17

Appendix D

Richardson's parallels. His listing is determined by the relation of references to the canonical materials. Richardson's view is that Ignatius reflects familiarity only with the canonical 1 Corinthians and Ephesians.

Ignatius	Paul
Ephesians 18:1	1 Corinthians 1:18-23
Ephesians 16:1	1 Corinthians 6:9,10
Romans 5:1	1 Corinthians 4:4
Magnesians 10:3	1 Corinthians 5:7
Romans 9:2	1 Corinthians 15:8-10
Ephesians 15:3	1 Corinthians 3:16
Ephesians 9:1	1 Corinthians 3:10-17

Trallians 2:3	1 Corinthians 4:1
Trallians 5:1	1 Corinthians 3:1
Trallians 12:3	1 Corinthians 9:27
Romans 4:3	1 Corinthians 7:22
Phil. 7:1	1 Corinthians 2:10
Smyr. Proleg.	1 Corinthians 1:7
Ephesians 2:3	1 Corinthians 1:10
Smyr. 1:2	1 Corinthians 12:27
Ephesians 4:2	1 Corinthians 6:15
Magnesians 5:2	1 Corinthians 2:12; 11:32
Romans 3:3; 7:1	
Phil. 4:1	1 Corinthians 10:16,17
Phil. 4:1	1 Corinthians 11:27ff
Smyr. 7:1	
Polycarp 5:1	Ephesians 5:25
Polycarp 1:2	Ephesians 4:2
Ephesians 20:1	Ephesians 2:15; 4:24
Ephesians 1:1	Ephesians 5:1
Ephesians 1:9	Ephesians 3:9
Polycarp 6:2	Ephesians 6:13-17
Ephesians 9:1	Ephesians 2:20-22
Smyr. Proleg.	Ephesians 1:6
Ephesians 19:2	Ephesians 5:18ff
Phil. 9:1	Ephesians 2:18
Ephesians 20:1	Ephesians 1:10; 3:2,9

Other tentative allusions

Ignatius	Paul
Trallians 5:2	2 Corinthians 12:1-7
Ephesians 18:1	Galatians 5:11
Ephesians 16:1	Galatians 5:21
Phil. 3:3	1 Corinthians 6:9,10
Ephesians 8:2	Romans 8:5-8
Ephesians 19:3	Romans 6:4
Smyr. 1:1	Romans 1:3,4
Romans 2:1	1 Thessalonians 2:4
Smyr. 11:3	Philippians 3:15
Smyr. 4:2	Philippians 4:13
Ephesians 10:2	Colossians 1:23
Ephesians 15:2	Colossians 3:16
Smyr. 1:1	Galatians 2:20
Magnesians 5:2	Romans 6:3ff
Smyr. 4:2	Colossians 1:24

Appendix E

Inge in Oxford Press, *The New Testament in the Apostolic Fathers*

Ephesians 16:1	1 Corinthians 6:9-10
Ephesians 18:1	1 Corinthians 1:18-20
Magnesians 10:3	1 Corinthians 5:7
Romans 5:1	1 Corinthians 4:4
Romans 9:2	1 Corinthians 15:8-10
Ephesians 15:3	1 Corinthians 3:16
Trallians 2:3	1 Corinthians 4:1
Trallians 5:1	1 Corinthians 3:1-2
Trallians 12:3	1 Corinthians 9:27
Romans 4:3	1 Corinthians 7:22
Romans 6:1	1 Corinthians 9:15
Philadelphians 4:1	1 Corinthians 10:16-17
Philadelphians 7:1	1 Corinthians 2:10
Ephesians 2:2	1 Corinthians 16:18
Ephesians 2:3	1 Corinthians 1:10
Ephesians 4:2	1 Corinthians 6:15
Ephesians 8:2	1 Corinthians 2:14
Ephesians 9:1	1 Corinthians 3:10-17
Ephesians 10:2; 20:1	1 Corinthians 15:58
Ephesians 11:1	1 Corinthians 7:29
Ephesians 17:2	1 Corinthians 1:24,30
Ephesians 20:1	1 Corinthians 15:45,47
Trallians 6:1	1 Corinthians 7:10
Trallians 11:2	1 Corinthians 12:12
Ephesians Inscription	Ephesians 1:3ff
Polycarp 5:1	Ephesians 5:25
Ephesians 20:1	Ephesians 2:15; 4:24
Smyr. 1:1	Ephesians 2:16
Polycarp. 1:2	Ephesians 4:2
Ephesians 1:1	Ephesians 5:1
Ephesians 9:1	Ephesians 2:20-22
Ephesians 19	Ephesians 3:9
Polycarp 6:2	Ephesians 6:13-17
Ephesians 8:2	Romans 8:5,8
Ephesians 19:3	Romans 6:4
Smyr. 1:1	Romans 1:3,9
Ephesians Inscription	Romans 15:29
Ephesians 15:3	2 Corinthians 6:16
Trallians 9:2	2 Corinthians 4:14
Phil. 6:3	2 Corinthians 1:12 et al
Phil. 1:1	Galatians 1:1
Ephesians 16:1	Galatians 5:21
Ephesians 18:1	Galatians 5:11

Trallians 10:1

Romans 7:2

Smyr. 4:2

Smyr. 11:3

Phil. 8:2

Ephesians 14:1; 20:1

Magnesians 8:1

Polycarp 4:3

Romans 9:2

Smyr. 4:2

Ephesians 21

Polycarp 6:2

Ephesians 17:1

Trallians 7:2

Romans 2:2

Magnesians 8:1

Polycarp 6:1

Ephesians 2:1

Ephesians 10:2

Ephesians 17:2

Ephesians 19:2

Smyr. 1:2

Smyr. 1:2

Ephesians 10:1

Romans 2:1

Romans 10:3

Ephesians 2:2

Galatians 2:21

Galatians 6:14

Philippians 4:13

Philippians 3:15

Philippians 2:3,5

1 Timothy 1:3-5

1 Timothy 6:2

1 Timothy 1:13

1 Timothy 1:12

2 Timothy 1:16

2 Timothy 2:3

2 Timothy 3:6

2 Timothy 1:2

2 Timothy 4:6

Titus 1:14

Titus 1:7

Colossians 1:7; 4:7

Colossians 1:23

Colossians 2:2

Colossians 1:25

Colossians 2:14

Colossians 1:18

1 Thessalonians 5:17

1 Thessalonians 2:4

2 Thessalonians 3:5

Philemon 20

Appendix F

Ephesians

10:1-2 cf.	Colossians 1:23	Lightfoot, Lake, Richardson, Inge
16:1 cf.	1 Corinthians 6:9-10	Lightfoot, Lake, Barnett, Inge
*18:1 cf.	1 Corinthians 1:20	Lightfoot, Lake, Barnett, Richardson, Inge

Magnesians

10:2	1 Corinthians 5:7	Lake, Barnett, Richardson, Inge

Trallians

2:2-3	1 Corinthians 4:1	Lake, Barnett, Richardson, Inge
5:1	1 Corinthians 3:1-2	Lake, Barnett, Richardson, Inge
12:3	1 Corinthians 9:27	Lake, Barnett, Richardson, Inge

Romans

2:1	1 Thessalonians 2:4	Lake, Barnett, Richardson, Inge
4:3	1 Corinthians 7:22	Lake, Barnett, Richardson, Inge
5:2	1 Corinthians 4:4	Lightfoot, Lake, Barnett, Inge
9:2	1 Corinthians 15:8-9	Lake, Barnett, Richardson, Inge

* Philadelphians

3:3	1 Corinthians 6:9-10	Lightfoot, Lake, Barnett, Richardson
4:1	1 Corinthians 10:16-17	Lake, Barnett, Richardson, Inge
7:1	1 Corinthians 2:10	Lake, Barnett, Richardson, Inge

Smyrnaeans

Inscription	1 Corinthians 1:7	Lake, Barnett, Richardson
1:1	Romans 1:3-4	Lake, Barnett, Richardson, Inge
4:2	Philippians 4:13	Lake, Barnett, Richardson, Inge
11:3	Philippians 3:15	Lake, Barnett, Richardson, Inge

Polycarp

1:2	Ephesians 4:2	Lake, Barnett, Richardson, Inge
5:1	Ephesians 5:25	Lake, Barnett, Richardson, Inge

Lightfoot	7 References
Lake	34 References
Barnett	39 References
Richardson	47 References
Inge	71 References

RESULTS:

Composite number of references	198
Number of allusions agreed on by all five compilers	1
Number of allusions agreed on by four compilers	19

15.
Prophecy and Revelation
R. E. Clements

The relationship between biblical criticism and theology has been one marked by stresses and tensions since the latter part of the eighteenth century, when biblical criticism began to adopt more trenchant and wide-ranging goals for itself. The attempts to lay bare the complicated structure and composition of the Old Testament literature have gone hand in hand with the recognition that each literary unit, or collection of units, is related to a particular period in the history of the people of God. Nowhere has this been more dramatically evident than in the Pentateuch, even though it required almost a century of painstaking labor to establish the main literary stages in the formation of this great body of literature. Equally dramatic, however, has been the change in the understanding of prophecy which, although less spectacular from the point of view of pure literary criticism, has been even more far-reaching from the perspective of theology. The great achievements of Old Testament literary criticism have gone hand in hand with the claim that it was the great Israelite prophets who were the major pioneers in introducing a new conception of God into Israel.[1] Through the prophets there came to full consciousness the rich moral monotheism which was the crowning theological achievement of Israelite faith. This was its most important intellectual legacy which it passed on to Christianity to Judaism and to Islam. Viewed from this perspective the prophets were seen as the fountainhead of revelation in the Old Testament. Opinions have differed as to whether Moses should be included as one of the prophets; so that the starting point of the revelatory process has been rather variously defined, but nonetheless this revelatory sequence of great prophetic figures has come to be viewed as central to the theological achievement of the Old Testament.

Biblical criticism, when applied to the prophets, has regarded itself as capable of exposing the very groundwork of the human experience which made possible the reception of the divine revelation in the prophet's own consciousness. Although direct knowledge of the experience itself cannot be recovered, at least in the primary levels of the literary deposits of the books which they have left, the prophets bear testimony to a knowledge of God which can still be defined and interpreted by theologians.

That the prophets stand at the fountainhead of revelation in the Old Testament has remained an influential feature of biblical criticism, yet it necessarily poses considerable problems for the theologian, especially the theologian who is committed to a recognition of the uniqueness and normative character of the biblical revelation. The prophets did not formulate their messages in the propositional categories of the modern theologian. Hence, their words and sayings do not take the form of theological propositions, and these latter can only be gleaned by a process of inference and careful probing of the underlying assumptions and ideas present in what the prophets actually said. Even here, however, as we shall have occasion to note further, the prophets were poets and their ideas and concepts were possessed of the breadth and mystery which belongs to poetic imagery. The more closely their sayings are examined, the more evident it becomes that the borderlines between metaphor, poetic image, and myth are not easy to draw with the kind of precision which the theologian, called upon to defend his ideas and concepts metaphysically, is required to seek. The sayings of the prophets therefore may be regarded as a most significant datum of religious experience and insight which the biblical critic may hope to be able to place in a known historical context, but which, nevertheless, does not provide the theologian with a readily intelligible set of basic doctrines.[2]

Two further difficulties for the theologian may be noted in connection with the way in which modern biblical criticism has understood and interpreted the prophets. The first of these arises from the fact that from the perspective of the structure and order of the Hebrew Old Testament canon the prophets have been understood to represent a secondary level of revelation to that contained in the Pentateuch—the Law—of Judaism. This structural order is not simply a question of literary convenience but has historically been reflected at a very basic level in the interpretation of the prophets and has contributed markedly to the main lines of hermeneutical approach to them. Most of all, this has been so in Judaism where the belief that the Law antedates and underlies the preaching of the prophets, and must always be accorded priority over them, is given prominence in the liturgical use made of them. Over the past half-century of biblical research the question of the historical relationship of the prophets to the Law has manifested itself again and again and has been the subject of very varied conclusions.[3] Yet in fact this issue must be treated as primarily one concerning the date of the Decalogue, or of any other nucleus of laws and regulations which are to be found in the Pentateuch. It is evident from a literary point of view that each of the collections which now comprise the Law and the Prophets contains both pre-, and post-, exilic material; each contains older and later elements and their mutual interrelationship cannot be reduced to the level of a single simple formula. Neither of the assertions; that the Law is to be accorded priority over prophecy, or that prophecy must be seen as having supplied the revelatory impulses for the development of the Law, can do adequate justice to the complex literary and historical overlapping that has taken place to produce these great collections of the Old Testament. The canonical collections of Law and Prophets, as two major literary units, more or less grew up together in Israel as twin witnesses to God's revelatory action in the life of the nation. Each contains material that might more neutrally be described as "historical," and the many contacts and interconnections which exist between the two parts precludes their assimilation into the categories of monochrome formulas. It is only at the literary level of the later stages of the shaping of the canon that the two parts came to be separated into independent and self-contained collections of material. As historical source criticism has shown, there were stages at which the source materials of the two collections overlapped, since not only are there Deuteronomic features to be found prominently in the Former Prophets, but most critics are still agreed that the earliest Pentateuchal sources (J and E) at one time carried their accounts forward to recount the story of the occupation of the land which was promised to the patriarchs, and which is now included in the Prophets. It may be argued therefore that the literary structure of the Hebrew Old Testament canon has been produced as the end product of a long process of literary and theological activity in ancient Israel. The course of this process cannot be ignored in any attempt to interpret the Old Testament as a theological whole. If the structure of the canon firmly gives priority to the Law, as the fountainhead of revelation in the Old Testament, and endeavors to place the Prophets in relation to this, then this fact must be taken fully into account in interpreting the various books of the Prophets. In this respect the many attempts to place Moses among the prophets, as is to be seen, for example, in the later writings of B. Duhm,[4] cannot be allowed to obscure the fact that the Old Testament tradition itself came to make a clear distinction between the role of Moses as the mediator and originator of the religion of Yahweh and other prophets (Num. 12:6-8). If prophecy is to be singled out as the primary medium of revelation in the Old Testament, then it certainly requires a very full and careful investigation into the reasons why the form of the Old Testament canon does not accord with this view.

A second factor also has an important bearing on the question of prophecy and revelation in relation to the rise of biblical criticism and the theological use made of the sayings of the Old Testament prophets. For the early Christians the interpretation of the events surrounding Jesus of Nazareth, the evaluation of who he was, and the meaning that was attached to his death and resurrection all found explanation from the contention that he was "the one of whom the prophets had spoken" (cf. esp. Luke 24:25,27; Acts 3:18, etc.) Broadly speaking this contention that Jesus was the "fulfillment" of Old Testament prophecy has been subsumed under the heading of the messianic hope, although the category of "Messiah" was only one of the titles and themes that had come to epitomize the prophetic message.[5] Nevertheless, the argument from prophecy provided a, and in many respects the most important, point of apologetic for the early Christians. What had happened in Jesus had happened "according to the Scriptures (1 Cor. 15:3), and the only way to appropriate the meaning of these events was to search the Old Testament Scriptures to see how they had been foretold long ago. It is widely recognized that this pattern of early Christian scriptural exegesis was not a novel method which the early church had created, but was rooted in current patterns of biblical interpretation already found in Judaism. The most easily accessible and striking examples of such pre-Christian Jewish biblical interpretation, especially of prophecy, are to be seen in the biblical commentaries from Qumran.[6] What was distinctive of the early Christian appeal to such biblical exegesis was the claim that the fulfillment had already arrived, and was no longer awaited at some undefined, though near, future time. This Christian argument from prophecy was clearly of most immediate appeal to Jews, for whom the Old Testament Scriptures were an already accepted datum of religious life and faith. However, there is no reason to suppose that such an argument was only of significance for such, since Gentiles also were capable of consulting the original prophecies and of evaluating the wisdom of the divine providence which had foretold the gift of salvation for mankind through the mouths of ancient prophets.

In the life of the Christian church the appeal to prophecy in this fashion still survives in hymnody, and even more strongly, in traditional liturgical patterns and themes which have shown a remarkable tenacity and appeal. It is also of primary importance to New Testament scholars to understand the manner of the appeal to ancient texts, understood as prophetic foretellings of the mission and person of the Messiah, in the light of contemporary Jewish interpretation. Yet in the first half of the eighteenth century the previously accepted pattern of Christian appeal to Old Testament prophecy came under criticism and attack. Clearest and most straightforward of the proponents of this attack was Anthony Collins, the English deist, whose two books *Discourse of the Grounds and Reasons of the Christian Religion* (1724) and *Scheme of Literal Prophecy Considered* (1727) [7] attacked the traditional Christian interpretation of certain prophecies drawn from the Old Testament. He showed, with the aid of a rudimentary but adequate form of historico-critical exegesis, that the texts which Christians had appealed to as foretellings of the coming of the Messiah had not originally been intended to make such a reference. The simplest and clearest example of this is to be seen in his interpretation of the Immanuel prophecy of Isaiah 7:14. This could not originally have referred to the birth of a royal savior occurring centuries after Isaiah's time, as Matthew 1:23 interprets it, since the text shows that the birth of the child was to be a sign to Isaiah's contemporary Ahaz. Collins, with remarkable perspicacity, argued that the prophecy had originally referred to the expected birth of a son to the prophet himself. Only by a pattern of secondary exegesis could the prophecy be made to refer to the birth of Jesus of Nazareth. In spite of a spirited defense of the accepted pattern of "messianic" interpretation of this and other prophecies by Thomas Sherlock [8] and others, the days of such a traditional Christian apologetic were numbered. With the rise of historicism in the latter half of the eighteenth century a new form of Christian apologetic emerged in which the whole span of history covered in the Old Testament was regarded as leading up to the concluding and climactic event in the life, death, and resurrection of Jesus of Nazareth. This was the point at which a national history came to an end and a universal history began.[9] In this way the entire history of Israel could be claimed to be "messianic" in the sense that it could be held to lead up, by a kind of divinely guided providence, to the age of universal fulfillment in the formation of the early Christian community. By this means the old argument from prophecy came to be detached from the sayings of individual prophets and to some extent even from the preaching of the prophets altogether, and attached rather to events and insights which are more broadly scattered throughout the Old Testament.

At the same time as this new historicist adaptation of the argument from prophecy appeared there emerged also through the Romantic movement, inspired most of all by the writings of J. G. Herder, a fresh approach to the prophets which radically separated them from the traditional concern with specific messianic pronouncements.[10] The prophets were poets—seers in the truest sense that they had grasped the visionary nature of reality and through their images, strictures, and insights had called men to a higher understanding of human life and destiny. The prophet-poets were man's guide to the divine, not through the logic of metaphysics, but through the images of truth, beauty, and righteousness which they presented. There is no doubt that the new Romantic view of prophecy came to exercise a dramatic influence on Old Testament studies in Germany in the nineteenth century, ultimately reaching into Great Britian, most notably through the work of W. Robertson Smith. His book, *The Prophets of Israel,*[11] first introduced the new "critical" view of prophecy to a wide British public and provided a rich recasting of the traditional formula that the prophets of the Old Testament were the divinely given preparation for the coming of the Christ. Yet this was no longer explained in terms of specific messianic prophecies, but rather was argued on the grounds that they were the pioneers of the Kingdom of God, the thinkers and seers of new divine order of righteousness and justice which broke free from the primitive world of magic, superstition, and cultic taboo. Once again the old "argument from prophecy" re-appeared in a new form, this time with a fresh and direct appeal to the preaching of the Old Testament prophets as the recognizable historical precursors of Jesus of Nazareth. Like him they had heralded the advent of the kingdom of God, although in less explicit terms and from a more distant vantage point of time. The fact that the traditional "messianic" prophecies were now almost entirely abandoned, and ceased to be regarded as authentic foretellings of the coming of a Messiah, was regarded as of lesser importance than the belief that they had, in other ways, prepared a path in the wilderness for the coming of Jesus. They laid the foundations of the moral understanding of the kingdom of God which came to full fruition with him.

Important as they are, neither of these two major nineteenth-century attempts to rehabilitate the traditional argument from prophecy can be said to provide an adequate modern alternative to it. They leave many questions unanswered. At bottom it may in fact be asked whether either of them can legitimately be called new versions of the argument from prophecy at all, for they are in many respects totally different arguments. That the Old Testament history finds its natural fulfillment in the New Testament and in the birth of the early Christian church is a significant line of Christian apologetic, but it is not a self-evident truth. It calls for further investigation as to how far the belief that certain ancient prophecies had been fulfilled provided an important feature of the sense of continuity between the first Christians and the Judaism out of which they emerged. In many respects the growing separation of Jews from Christians raised new questions about such an interpretation of the fulfillment of prophecy, since this was certainly not how the ancient prophets anticipated the era of salvation.[12] Furthermore, such a claim to fulfillment raises the issue of the need for resolving the tension which the modern critic feels to exist between the understanding of prophecy evident in the New Testament documents and that which the Old Testament scholar can discern in respect of the more original meaning which historico-critical discipline can bring to light. This certainly has contributed to the situation in which the use of the Bible by systematic theologians differs very markedly from that of Old Testament experts. More than this, however, it has given rise to a position in which there is a great difference between departments of Old and New Testament so far as the theological evaluation of the former is concerned. This immediately becomes apparent over such issues as that of the messianic hope where very diverse perspectives and patterns of interpretation begin to show themselves. Each looks at the phenomenon of prophecy, and especially at its value as revelation, from a different viewpoint. What is left unexplained, is how these different viewpoints have come into existence.

It has become customary to argue that the interpretation to be found in the New Testament of the prophetic foretelling of the person and mission of Jesus of Nazareth as the messiah is no more than one aspect of the cultural and historical connection of the New Testament with its particular Jewish-Hellenistic environment. The classic expression of this is to be found in J. S. Semler's theory of "accommodation" by which the language, ideas, and forms of the New Testament revelation are necessarily presented in the dress of its own contemporary, predominantly Jewish, environment.[13] That Jesus of Nazareth is the Messiah is itself an accommodation to the contemporary Jewish expectation, since the significance of his person for mankind must inevitably transcend this Jewish concept. On such terms the argument from prophecy becomes one among many of the conceptual means by which the revelation of God in Jesus came to be appropriated by the early church. Attractive as such a theory of accommodation is, it clearly has serious weaknesses and even dangers. It may be questioned, for example, whether the category of the "fulfillment" of Old Testament prophecy does not have a more substantial place in the New Testament than simply to serve as a convenient means of understanding what would otherwise have transcended the categories of human reason.[14] Is Jesus' birth and life as a Jew simply an accident of history, which might theoretically have been exchanged for a life as a Chinese or a Persian, or some other race, so far as his revelatory significance for mankind is concerned? Or is his being a Jew a substantial and necessary part of our understanding of who he is, and how God has chosen to reveal himself in and through him? The question is, admittedly, an entirely speculative one, but it has an important bearing on our approach to the Bible and our use of it in the modern world. It raises the serious difficulty that any attempt to separate the person of Jesus from his Jewishness, or even to understand the significance of his person without the aid of such Jewish categories as "Messiah," or "Son of man," is to reduce our understanding of him to minimal proportions. It would be to abandon the "Jesus of history," already a problem enough for theological evaluation, to the realm of impossible questions. However other matters of great importance also belong with this question. The argument from prophecy in its New Testament form is not simply a convenient way of explaining the significance of the person of Jesus, but it is, from another perspective, an argument that the revelation of God in the Old and New Testaments has been a single, purposeful, and connected series of divine acts. Neither in the Old or New Testaments do we find the claim that God's revelation has been limited to a single action, accomplished at one stroke in one life. It is an extended activity, and the argument that the revelation of God in Jesus is the fulfillment of Old Testament prophecy is primarily an argument that such revelation is both continuous with, as well as a fulfillment of, such prophecy. It is hard to see how any assertion that the New Testament interpretation of Old Testament prophecy is simply a reflection of the contemporary form of scriptural exegesis can be upheld without also implying that the entire relationship between the two Testaments is equally invalidated, and in reality no more than an accommodation to the accidental facts of history. There would then be no essential, or intrinsic, connection between the two Testaments, but merely the accidental historical fact that for most of the early Christian community the Old Testament happened to provide the ideas and concepts which enabled them to attain to a proper self-understanding and a true awareness of God.[15]

Certainly such a position is defensible and has been defended by a number of scholars, yet its effect is ultimately to reduce the range and character of the biblical revelation to an extraordinarily narrow compass. Effectively it asserts that the only true revelation of God is to be found in the New Testament, and the foretellings of this which were believed to be found in the Old Testament prophets were simply a preparation which did not partake in any essential way of the nature of the revelation itself. Certainly the critical view of prophecy, as it emerged in the nineteenth century, did not subscribe to this view, and sought to see in the Old Testament prophets a more substantial and recognizable revelation of God, even though it no longer related this in anything more than a very peripheral manner to specific "messianic" foretellings of the age of salvation that was to come. Yet this only highlights still further the problem that we are left with: that the ancient New Testament view of the character and content of revelation through Israelite prophecy differs very greatly from more modern attempts to understand what is revelatory about their message. Can we simply ignore this dichotomy, or is it not rather an important obligation for the biblical theologian who is concerned about the nature of revelation to try more earnestly to understand the two in relation to each other?

Yet another point should be noted here, even though its full implications cannot be pursued at any length. The claim that the New Testament interpretation of the fulfillment of Old Testament prophecy through the mission and message of Jesus of Nazareth can be upheld in its essential content, but set aside in its detailed citation of proof-texts, result in a heightening of the divorce between the early Christian church and its own contemporary Jewish world. Surprisingly, in view of the early Jewish-Christian dialogue whether or not prophecy had been fulfilled in Jesus, the pattern of scriptural citation and argument which is found in the New Testament binds the early church very closely to Jewish life and thought both before and during the first Christian century. The theory of accommodation and the virtual abandonment by Christian scholars of the claim that the New Testament use of prophetic texts bears any convincing relationship to their original meaning has tended to heighten the sense of separation between Christians and Jews. The early church and Judaism are regarded as having no more than an accidental relationship governed by the facts of history, rather than a more essential theological one determined by the fact that they are both founded upon the same basis of revelation in the Law and Prophets given in the Old Testament. This is in line with the belief that the early Christian formulation of the argument from prophecy is no longer historically defensible, but simply reflects the fact that the early Christians were men of their time and used the methods of scriptural interpretation current in their time. While it would be unfair and unnecessary to blame Christian interpretation of the Old Testament for the tragic reluctance of European Christendom to react more strongly against the persecution of European Jews in the twentieth century, it is very salutary to note that Christian commitment to the Old Testament has not always gone hand in hand with a measure of Christian commitment to Judaism. Is there not a sense in which any Christian attempt to defend the claim that the prophets of Israel were the forerunners of Jesus of Nazareth is committed to understand this in some way recognizably related to that in which the early Christians understood it? This means in relation to the citation and interpretation of certain proof-texts as a divinely given foretelling of the salvation which God had purposed to bring in and through his ancient people of Israel. Hence, modern attempts to understand prophecy as a revelation of God which base themselves exclusively upon critical efforts to get back to the prophet's "original" meaning have been compelled to look for the essential content of this in very different areas from those which have traditionally been accepted by Christians and Jews. What is required, however, is a stronger effort to understand the nature of divine revelation as Jews and Christians have actually understood it to have been given. This means that critical work on the meaning of the prophets' sayings must be examined and interpreted with a full awareness of the way in which these sayings were developed and re-interpreted by later ages of Jews to establish a very full and intricate understanding of them. It is this which provides the foundation for the early Christian claim that such prophecies had been "fulfilled" in Jesus, for it is only by understanding this type of reinterpretation that any historically credible content can be given to the concept of "fulfillment." What constitutes a "fulfillment" is determined by what has to be "fulfilled," and this is largely governed by the way in which the ancient scriptures of the Old Testament were understood at the time.

We may pause at this point to consider the issue as we have sought to present it so far. The early Christian church gave a very prominent place to its argument from prophecy which asserted that in the person of Jesus the salvation had arrived which had been foretold by divine revelation through the Old Testament prophets. This is supported by means of a careful citation and interpretation of certain passages from the Old Testament, primarily drawn from the collections of the Prophets, but spilling over into the Psalms quite extensively, and also into other parts of the Old Testament canon. That these prophets were the forerunners of Jesus has continued to be strongly defended by modern biblical research, almost entirely on a Christian basis, but usually with a total, or near total, abandonment of the particular texts and passages which the early Christians interpreted in this fashion. Such abandonment has been necessitated by modern historico-critical exegesis of the texts concerned. Instead other passages from the prophets have been elevated to a new position of eminence, and it should not pass unremarked that the trend has been to concentrate heavily upon the role of the prophets as heralds of judgment in reaffirming their role as the forerunners of Jesus, the Messiah. Our contention is that the effects of this recasting of the traditional argument from prophecy are more extensive than are usually admitted, and are sufficient to raise the question whether it can any longer justifiably be termed an argument from prophecy at all. Even more seriously it must raise doubts about the whole claim to divine revelation in prophecy since the understanding of what is revealed is made the subject of very far-reaching changes at different times and by different generations of interpreters. In the interests of avoiding the apparent arbitrariness and subjectivity of the methods of interpreting prophecy in the New Testament, a new basis of critical exegetical interpretation is set up which nevertheless does not avoid the arbitrariness and subjectivity of the modern scholar's estimation of what truly prepares the way for Jesus. Paradoxically, however, we find in the last two decades of New Testament research, especially where it has been most deeply concerned to explore the Jewish background of the New Testament, a renewed interest in the assumptions, methods, and aims of early Jewish and Christian Scripture exegesis. The result has been that the use of citations from the Old Testament in the New has come to acquire revived interest and respect as a foundational level of the theology-forming process present in the New Testament.[16] No longer can it be dismissed as a form of contemporary apologetic, useful for argument in the communities to which the Gospel was first addressed, but of no lasting importance once the church had moved out from its original first-century Jewish environment. The importance of biblical citation and interpretation in the New Testament, coupled with the failure of critical Old Testament scholarship to establish a more satisfactory alternative explanation of the nature and content of revelation in the Old Testament prophets, both prompt us to ask whether we ought not now to return to a more strenuous endeavor to understand and evaluate the interpretation of prophecy given in the New Testament.

Some points may be made by way of suggestion as to how and why this should be done. At the onset we must hold fast to the basic contention that there can be no abandoning of historico-critical method. However this itself requires that we should give fuller attention to the extensive history of interpretation of prophecy which exists in the Old Testament prophetic books themselves. This is of direct relevance to understanding how the New Testament interprets the Old. To abandon such methodology would leave each interpreter free to see in the prophetic texts whatever meaning he regards as appropriate, or as ultimately intended to be there by God, and this would be to abandon the gains of two centuries of painstaking labor. This is in effect what W. Vischer attempted to do in his interpretation of the prophetic literature.[17] He attempts to leap wildly across the great historical and ideological gaps which separate the original saying of the prophets from the way in which the New Testament interprets them as foretellings of a future age of salvation. Having abandoned the probably historical setting of the original prophecies as establishing a recognizable context of meaning by which they are to be understood, Vischer leaves himself free to set up a theological context of meaning which he regards as appropriate from the christological convictions of the New Testament. On this procedure the kind of objections which long ago Anthony Collins made against those of his own contemporaries who interpreted prophecy in this way would simply be set aside. But they cannot be set aside, for in themselves they are valid and correct, and the original historical setting and circumstance of the prophet must be allowed to establish criteria by which his sayings are to be understood. They need not, however, be allowed to exhaust the meaning of a prophecy, which should probably be viewed in a larger context.

Here we come up against certain basic theological and literary features which have a bearing on the way in which prophecy is to be understood. What do words like "meaning" and "fulfillment" connote in regard to prophecy? We naturally assume that these concepts should be interpreted in an acceptable historical and critical fashion as referring to the way in which the prophet himself envisaged his words taking effect and being realised through events (Hebrew uses particularly the two verbs *hēkīm (kūm)* and *hāyāh* for this; cf. Isa. 7:7). Yet the New Testament insists that it was of the nature of prophecy that the original authors did not, and could not, fully know the way in which their words would take effect and therefore be fulfilled. They themselves sought to understand the mysterious significance of the sayings that they were called upon to utter, as 1 Peter 1:10-12 asserts. Such a view is not as uncritical and theologically arbitrary as may at first appear. The prophet foretold events by means of a given range of broadly dramatic images, pronouncing the coming of wars, famine, or other misfortunes as judgments from God, or conversely heralding days of restoration, peace, and plenty as the blessings of God. Often the identity of the oppressor, or the deliverer, and even the time scale within which the events were expected to take place are left unmentioned. Naturally it is throughout to be assumed that the prophet was implying that these events would happen in what was for him a relatively near future, since they were expected to affect the lives of his hearers. When events subsequently happened which could plausibly be regarded as falling within the category which the prophet had foretold, then there represented a fulfillment. If, as we may often suppose the case to have been, the prophet were still active, then he himself would be the best judge of whether his words had been fulfilled. By such means he gained in stature and respect, and subsequent sayings of his acquired all the greater significance for his hearers. Even when events did not turn out as the original saying quite evidently expected, the prophet was free to reinterpret his prophecy by relating some other event to it. An instructive example of this is to be found in Ezekiel's reinterpretation of his prophecy about the fall of Tyre to Nebuchadnezzar when events turned out differently from the way in which they were anticipated (Ezek. 29:17-20; cf. Ezek. 26—28). This is only a very simple example, however, of what must consistently have been a very complex and continuing process. H. W. Wolff, when he comes to consider the question of the fulfillment of Amos's threats of judgment upon Israel, especially of the overthrowing of the sanctuary of Bethel (Amos 9:1), points to an extended sequence of relatively disconnected events.[18] Prophecies were in fact seldom of such a kind that their fulfillment could be exclusively identified with only one sequence of events. This in itself has been a major contributory factor in creating difficulty in understanding the sayings of the prophets. Without a guide as to the date of a prophecy a great number of possibilities present themselves. More particularly from the point of view of the redaction of the prophetic books, fresh events, far beyond those circumstances originally envisaged by the prophet, could later be regarded as falling within the category of their fulfillment. Even more strikingly we find also that prophecies were not regarded as "dead," once they had been fulfilled, but rather came sometimes to be regarded as open to yet further "fulfillments" of an almost limitless nature. This is clearly one reason why so much prophetic literature has survived in the Old Testament, for had it become "dead" once it had been fulfilled, it would have lost all further relevance or interest for people. Instead we find that a "fulfilled" prophecy seems to have elicited all the greater respect once events had appeared to confirm its divine origin so that its value for interpreting other, still future, events became all the greater. If Wolff's interpretation of the fulfillment of Amos' threats is correct then this would certainly have been the case in respect of his forewarnings of doom. We may note here how Ezekiel 7:1-9 takes up the threat of the coming of "the end" upon Israel which harks back to the earlier prophecy of Amos 8:1-2. Not only does this show a reactivation of a prophecy originally given more than one and a half centuries earlier, but it also shows how a different understanding of what constituted Israel could be involved in this. If such an extended pattern of fulfillments was accepted in interpreting the threats of doom, even more is this feature evident in regard to prophetic promises of hope and restoration. Sixth-century prophecies regarding the restoration of Israel undoubtedly expected a near fulfillment of their promises. Yet it is these prophecies which have provided the groundwork of subsequent Jewish eschatology and of its messianic hope, with its belief that a great era of restoration and salvation awaited Israel in the future. It is this expectation which has created the eschato-

logical dimension which colors the commentaries from Qumran, especially 1QHab, and which produced the background against which
the drama of the life and work of Jesus came to be seen. The reinterpretation of the "seventy years" of exile of Jeremiah 29:10 in Daniel
9:24 represents an instructive example of this from within the Old
Testament canon. However, such a phenomenon of reinterpretation
begins much earlier and is to be found in the general structuring
and literary arrangement of the prophetic corpus of the canon.

In such a context the range of possible fulfillments of prophetic
sayings becomes considerable, pointing to a wide variety of historical
events of different ages. Consequently it may be felt that the critical
scholar has no alternative but to restrict himself to considering the
find of fulfillment which the original prophet alone could have envisaged. Yet this is, in itself, not as simple as may at first appear. When
we ask, "What is the meaning of a prophecy?" we cannot ignore
the fact that such meaning could only be understood in relation to
the events by which the prophecy was thought to be fulfilled. Yet
even the original prophet himself could not have known precisely
how his prophecy would be substantiated by events, since only what
happened after he had delivered it could determine this. The "meaning"
of any prophecy, therefore, must be held to be in some measure determined, not only by the sense that the original prophet intended his
words to convey, but by the subsequent events which men believed
to have been illuminated and interpreted by them. To some extent
the "fulfillment" helped to determine the meaning. When Matthew
1:23 therefore points to the birth of Jesus of Nazareth as the fulfillment
of the prophecy of Isaiah 7:14 it is not out of keeping with the fact
that prophecies of this kind were regarded as acquiring fulfillment
over a very long period of time, far beyond the circumstances that
the prophet himself could have envisaged. Not only so, but we find
that the "Immanuel prophecy" of Isaiah 7:14 is already given two
earlier interpretations in the book of Isaiah, the first of these in Isaiah
8:8, construing it as a threat of divine judgment upon Judah. The
second, in Isaiah 8:10, quite contrastingly understands the name to
be an assurance of salvation for Judah when challenged by the threat
of the nations. The first reinterpretation of the name appears to come
from Isaiah himself, whilst the second is undoubtedly from a later
time. The precise historical situation in which this later interpretation
emerged is disputed by commentators, but in any case it reveals the
important history of exegesis of the original prophetic saying which

lies incorporated into the present book of Isaiah. Possibly yet a third interpretation of the Immanuel prophecy is to be found in Micah 5:3, although in this case it is not the name which is interpreted but the special significance of the time of the birth of the child. Just as strikingly we find a whole sequence of interpretations given in the book of Isaiah to the name of Isaiah's child Shear-Jashub—"A Remnant Will Return"—of Isaiah 7:3. Hence, in Isaiah 10:20-23 we have a series of three separate prophecies concerning the role of the remnant, now quite freshly interpreted as the remnant of Israel, which is very different from the original interpretation given in Isaiah 7:7-9. Yet a fourth interpretation of the name in a similar vein, is to be found in Isaiah 10:11, whilst an exposition of the name in its original sense, and probably deriving from the original prophet, is to be found in Isaiah 17:3. If we insist on the view that the only authentic meaning of the prophecy is that which was given by the prophet himself in Isaiah 7:7-9, then we fail to do justice to the nature of the prophetic book which we have. Certainly the Bible itself, both in the Old and New Testament, presents us with a very complex picture of how revelation is to be found in prophecy, which goes far beyond the kind of limitations which modern scholarship has tended to impose upon itself in the interests of a historico-critical exegesis. In the end this results in the production of a strangely "unhistorical" conception of revelation through prophecy because it is not that which the biblical writers themselves accepted or worked with.

The aim of this chapter is not to establish a plea for a return to the uncontrolled and fanciful interpretative patterns of "Christ in all the Scriptures," which were customary in an age of theological investigation undisciplined by the methods of historical exegesis. The plea is rather in another direction: for a more resolutely disciplined historical approach to the problem of revelation in prophecy. This must be concerned to understand prophecy as it was understood at the time it was given by those who heard it, and subsequently by the compilers of the books of the prophets, then later still by those who collected these books into a canon. Finally it must be concerned to understand the interpretation of prophecy that contributed to the expansion of the Old Testament to include the New, so that the two Testaments could be related by resort to a scheme of promise and fulfillment. Only in this way can we obtain a truly historical perspective upon the way in which revelation was considered to have been given through the mouths of the prophets of the Old Testament. Whilst there is much important and useful information in commentaries upon individual prophetic books suggesting how such revelation was believed to have taken place, there is a surprising dearth of studies of the nature of biblical prophecy dealing with these points. Instead, what we have in the place of studies of biblical prophecy as a literary phenomenon are a great many semi-biographies of the prophets, or of the prophets and their times, which concentrate almost exclusively upon the circumstances of the original sayings of the great prophetic figures of Israel and say next to nothing about the way in which later generations of Israelites and Jews understood their words to be a revelation from God. All too implicit in such an approach has been the assumption that later generations of Jews, and later the earliest Christians, largely misunderstood the prophets, and it is we who can now restore them to their proper places. Yet such an approach has only appeared to succeed by dismissing large parts of the prophetic literature of the Old Testament as "secondary," and by creating a type of interpretation in which the use of prophecy in the New Testament is made to appear totally disconnected from its purported original meaning in the Old Testament. It is to be hoped that in the future a more comprehensive approach will become a basic part of future Old Testament studies, so that research into the prophets will be able to contribute more significantly to an understanding of the New Testament documents, with their use of Old Testament citations, to the history of Christian theology, and not least, to a deeper awareness that Judaism also is heir to the prophetic revelation of the Old Testament.

NOTES

[1] A short survey of the critical study of prophecy in the nineteenth century is given by W. Baumgartner, "Die Auffassungen des 19. Jahrhunderts vom Israelitischen Prophetismus," *Archiv für Kulturgeschichte* 15 (1922), p. 21-35, reprinted in *Zum Alten Testament und seiner Umwelt* (Leiden, 1959), p. 27-41.

[2] The classic expression of the attempt to set out the theological significance of the prophets' preaching in this manner is the work by B. Duhm, *Die Theologie der Propheten,* (Bonn, 1875). However Duhm's later work in *Israels Propheten,* 2nd ed., (Tübingen, 1922), considerably modified his earlier positions.

[3] An outline survey is given by W. Zimmerlie, *The Law and the Prophets,* trans. R. E. Clements, (Oxford, 1965). A more recent attempt to deal with the question afresh from the Jewish side is to be found in R. V. Bergren, *The Prophets and the Law* (Monographs of the Hebrew Union College IV), (Cincinnati, New York, Los Angeles, Jerusalem, 1974).

[4] B. Duhm, *Israels Propheten,* p. 29-40.

[5] Cf. C. K. Barret, "The Interpretation of the Old Testament in the New," *The Cambridge History of the Bible from the Beginnings to Jerome,* ed. P. R. Ackroyd and C. F. Evans, (Cambridge, 1970), p. 405.

[6] Cf. F. F. Bruce, *Biblical Exegesis in the Qumran Texts,* (London, 1960).

[7] A valuable survey of the work and thought of A. Collins is to be found in J. O'Higgins, S. J., *Anthony Collins. The Man and His Works* (International Archives of the History of Ideas 35), (The Hague, 1970).

[8] T. Sherlock, *The Use and Intent of Prophecy in the Several Ages of the World,* (London, 1725). A brief extract on "The Limitation of Prophecy" is contained in *Religious Thought in the Eighteenth Century. Illustrated from the Writers of the Period,* ed. J. M. Creed and J. M. Boys Smith, (Cambridge, 1934), p. 61-64.

[9] Cf. H. Ewald, *The History of Israel,* trans. R. Martineau, 8 vols., 4th ed., (London, 1883), who states (p. 10) "the history comes to its close with Christ."

[10] Cf. especially in J. G. Herder, *The Spirit of Hebrew Poetry,* trans. James Marsh, (Burlington, 1833; rep. Naperville, 1971), Bk. II, p. 35ff.

[11] W. Robertson Smith, *The Prophets of Israel,* (Edinburgh, 1882; 2nd ed. London, 1895). Cf. also *The Old Testament in the Jewish Church,* (Edinburgh, 1881), p. 268-304.

[12] As is shown, for example, by the prominent place given in Christian apologetic to the necessity that the Messiah should be rejected by his own people. Cf. Luke 9:22 and Stephen's apology in Acts 7:2-53.

[13] For J. S. Semler's work and the theory of "accommodation" cf. G. Hornig, *Die Anfänge der historisch-kritischen Theologie. Johann Salomo Semler Schriftverständnis und seine Stellung zu Luther* (Forschungen zur systematischen Theologie und Religionsphilosophie 8), (Lund-Göttingen, 1961), p. 219ff.

[14] B. Lindars makes a modern attempt to restate the "accommodation" theory in "The Place of the Old Testament in the Formation of New Testament Theology. Prolegomena," New Test. Studies 23 (1977), p. 59-66. Cf. especially note 15, p. 64: "The use of the Old Testament—whether in direct quotations, in allusions, or in the employment of biblical themes—is primarily a mode of expression for early Christian thought, arising from a contemporary understanding of the meaning of scripture. There is no sign of a direct interest in the Old Testament for its own sake, as at Qumran."

[15] The question of the nature of this relationship is discussed by F. Hesse, *Das Alte Testament als Buch der Kirche,* (Gütersloh, 1966), p. 24ff.

[16] Cf. especially F. F. Bruce, *This is That,* (Exeter, 1968).

[17] W. Vischer, *Das Christuszeugnis des Alten Testaments,* Pt. II, Die Propheten, 2nd ed., (Zollikon-Zürich, 1946).

[18] H. H. Wolff, "Das Ebde des Heiligtums in Bethel," *Archäologie und Altes Testament. Festschrift K. Galling 70. Geburtstag,* (Tübingen, 1970), pp. 287-298.

PART IV
FAITH AND THE NATURAL ORDER

16.
Creation Through Alternative Histories
William G. Pollard

In the second part of his book *Science and Faith,* Eric Rust [1] reviews naturalistic neo-Darwinian theories of the evolution of life and of man under the heading "The Creator Spirit, Evolution, and Life." He contrasts these theories with the thought of Thorpe, Polanyi, Teilhard de Chardin, and others who argue that such naturalistic theories are not adequate to account for the creative achievements of evolution. In various ways they insist that an inner drive, or "nisus," propelling living matter toward the achievement of ever new emergent levels of being and consciousness is required, which natural selection operating on changing mutations in the germ pools of populations is unable to account for. Accepting the validity of these arguments, Rust proceeds to an analysis of the theology of divine creativity as carried out through evolutionary processes. He argues persuasively for identifying the immanent agent of process creation through evolution with the third person of the Trinity, rather than with the second person as in traditional views based on non-process immediate creation by edict.

A few years after the publication of Rust's book, a widely read and persuasive defense of naturalistic theories of evolution was published by the eminent molecular biologist Jacques Monod under the title *Chance and Necessity.* [2] It is the purpose of this essay to demonstrate that Monod failed to appreciate the full meaning of chance in science and the role which it plays in history. When this role is properly understood and incorporated in Monod's exposition, it changes his thesis in such a way as to fully accommodate Rust's interpretation of divine creativity in evolution. Traditional naturalistic theories have looked on evolution as a deterministic process controlled entirely by the necessities of natural law. The importance of Monod's contribution was to show that modern molecular biology requires a combination of necessity with chance. An important consequence of this, which

Monod fails to recognize, is that a scientific account of an evolutionary process involving chance must lead to an immense number of alternative histories of life. Among these many possible alternatives, science has no means for deciding which are purposive or teleological and which are not. This leaves the total history of life on earth open to the same form of theological interpretation as the history, say, of Israel. It is in this way that Rust's theological interpretation of evolution is consistent with Monod. The main body of the essay is reproduced from an earlier review article on Monod's book by the author.[3]

In order to understand Monod's thought, it is necessary to discuss three key terms which he employs in quite unconventional ways. These are "animism," "vitalism," and "objective." By "animism" he does not wish to designate the usual meaning of the word as a reference to primitive religious experience prior to polytheism and monotheism. Rather, as he uses it, it means any view of the world which involves nonphysical influences of a purposive or teleological character. Thus he classifies as "animists" Spencer, Hegel, Teilhard de Chardin, Marx, and Engels. He has no use for any of them, but his real ire is aroused by only one "animist" school—the dialectical materialism of Marx and Engels. He devotes a great deal more space to this than to any of the others, and the intensity of scorn which it evokes is considerably greater. "Vitalism," on the other hand, refers to views of the world in which the same influence is asserted only for biological systems and does not apply to inorganic nature. Among vitalists he groups Bergson, Driesch, Elsasser, and Polanyi. He has no more use for them than for the "animists."

His use of the word "objective" is even more at variance with ordinary usage. The usual meaning of this word is contrasted to "subjective" and designates knowledge which is empirically and publicly verifiable. In Monod's use of the word, however, it applies not to basic laboratory science but only to the application of science to a reconstruction of history. In this usage the contrast with "objective" is not "subjective" but rather "projective" or "teleological." For example, at the outset of the first chapter he writes:

It is another story altogether with the river or the rock which we know, or believe, to have been molded by the free play of physical forces to which we cannot attribute any design, any "project" or purpose. Not, that is, if we accept the basic premise of the scientific method, to wit, that nature is *objective* and not *projective*.[4]

And again:

The cornerstone of the scientific method is the postulate that nature is objective. In other words, the *systematic* denial that "true" knowledge can be got at by interpreting phenomena in terms of final causes—that is to say of "purpose." [5]

And the final disposition of both vitalism and animism is carried out with these words:

In the eyes of modern scientific theory all these concepts are erroneous, not only for reasons of method (since in one way or another they imply abandonment of the postulate of objectivity) but for factual reasons, which will be discussed below.[6]

There are two fundamental objections to this way of conceiving the principle of objectivity in science. First, it cannot be applied to the great bulk of scientific knowledge, which is nonhistorical and unrelated to the course of events in time. Certainly in the physical sciences such laws as the Heisenberg uncertainty principle, the basis for the periodic table of elements, or the Pauli exclusion principle are independent of the question of purpose in nature. The theoretical and experimental methodologies which led to their discovery are independent of the course of events in time and so cannot be either projective or non-projective. So, too, the experimental procedures leading to the discovery of the electron, the antiproton, or the structure of DNA are by Monod's definition of the scientific method neither objective nor scientific. Even Monod's own brilliant research on the lactose system in *Escherichia coli* described on pages 72-77 of his book would have been carried out in exactly the same way by another biochemist who believes nature to be projective or purposeful. Surely there is much more to the scientific method and the principle of objectivity in science than the systematic denial of purpose.

The other objection is directly related to the primary thesis of the scientific portion of Monod's book as indicated by its title. This has to do with the real implications of the role of chance in science. These Monod fails to see. It will be my purpose in the remainder of this chapter to show that the combination of chance and necessity which he so admirably demonstrates as established for biological evolution is precisely just the necessary and sufficient condition required for any who would wish to assert that the evolutionary process is, or can logically be maintained to be, projective or purposive. If a convincing case can be made for this proposition it means that the primary thesis, chance and necessity, of the scientific chapters of Monod's book undercuts any possibility for systematically denying on scientific grounds an interpretation of phenomena in terms of purpose. It will mean that his way of stating the principle of objectivity can no longer be held to be necessary for a scientific description of nature. Scientists who, like Monod, hold to it as a basic value can work with other scientists who reject it without in any way changing the *scientific* results and conclusions of both.

Most people have gained their basic notions about chance from games of chance such as craps or roulette. In one sense this is helpful. Treatises on the mathematical theory of probability make extensive use of such games of chance as examples which illuminate general concepts. For the student this is familiar ground on which to build. His elementary experience of chance is derived from this source. At the same time, however, this circumstance leads to the widespread conviction that chance is the very opposite of purpose. This is because games of chance in the casino are played over and over hundreds of times under identical physical conditions. The outcome of such a series could never be regarded as intended in any sense. For emphasis, Monod and others often speak of "pure" chance or "blind" chance, although in the mathematical theory there is no such distinction. In mathematics the probability of a chance event is simply a number. There is no way to tell whether it is "pure" or "blind" or has any other attributes.

This conviction about chance is further enhanced by the circumstance that science is carried out in laboratories. A scientific laboratory is a highly artificial environment. It is essential to the study of a law of nature that apparatus be designed which will exclude all other laws from operating at the same time. To be successful, it must exclude all extraneous effects and accidents, because they would mask the operation of the particular law being investigated. As we now know, the laws of nature in all fields are statistical in character, involving alternatives with probabilities. Once discovered in the laboratory the law can be demonstrated over and over and often, as a teaching experiment, *is* performed over and over year after year by hundreds of students. In this sense the laboratory is like the casino. The possibility of repetition under identical conditions reinforces the impression that chance implies the opposite of purpose.

The world at large, however, is neither a casino nor a scientific laboratory. In it no "extraneous" influences or upsetting accidents are excluded. The same laws formulated in terms of games of chance or discovered in laboratories operate in the outside world, but there are no controls and everything happens at once. Every event in the evolution of life has been made up of several independent chains of cause and effect which happened to come together accidentally at the same time. Earthquakes, storms, and floods; bursts of cosmic radiation and ultraviolet light; ice ages and tropical heat, and innumerable other environmental changes combined with randomly occurring mutations of DNA codes in many species—all become locked together in the complex web of life. The decisive events of this history have little relationship to the dependable and repeatable experiences in the laboratory or the casino. Here, as we shall see shortly, our intuitive notions about the incompatibility of chance and purpose are no longer an appropriate guide. Chance and probability still play a decisive role, as Monod has so brilliantly established, but it is a role which operates in sharp contrast to that played in repeated instances under identical conditions. But first we must deal with another common misconception about chance.

This error has to do with treating chance as a causative agent in parallel with other identifiable causes in nature. It is often said of an event or process in nature that "it was due to chance," as though chance itself could be the causative agent leading to the event or determining the process. Many scientists and philosophers prior to Monod have agreed with him (in opposition to what he calls "animist" or "vitalist" interpretations of evolution) by explaining the course of events as "due to chance." By describing steps in evolution in terms of known physical, chemical, or biological statistical processes whose probabilities could in principle be determined by experiment in the laboratory today, they imply that the attribution of nonphysical causes by their opponents has been refuted, since they have demonstrated that the "real cause" was chance. By way of driving home their point they usually resort to the more emphatic designations of "pure" chance or "blind" chance. Their opponents, on the other hand, almost always accept their basic premise and devote their major efforts to proving that the events or processes under discussion could not have been due to chance. A particularly glaring example of such efforts is that of Leconte du Nouy in his book *Human Destiny*. The arguments of both camps are equally fallacious, however, because by its very nature chance simply cannot be the cause or reason for anything's happening.

It is most important to clearly understand this point, since it lies at the root of such widespread misunderstanding. The actual situation is in fact precisely the reverse. For the introduction of probability into any scientific description constitutes the one case in which *science expressly renounces an explanation in terms of natural causes.* The very idea of probability requires valid alternatives of response by a system to the same natural cause or set of causes. Insofar as these alternatives are real, the question as to why a particular one is realized in each instance must not be raised. For if it is answerable in terms of natural causes, even in principle, the idea of a probability for that alternative becomes inapplicable. Probability applies only to indeterminate events. If in the progress of science hidden variables or previously unknown causes are discovered which remove the indeterminacy by showing the several alternatives to be really different situations generated by these new causes, the description of these phenomena in terms of chance and probability is dropped. Thereafter one speaks simply of what must happen. But so long as we speak of chance at all, we have acknowledged coming to a dead end of causal explanation. The consistency of our position demands that we raise no further questions about causes.

In quantum physics the indeterminacy leading to valid alternatives with probabilities is introduced at the outset as a fundamental law of nature. In the statistical mechanics of classical physics they arise as a result of the theory of errors by which initial conditions specified with any finite accuracy become indeterminate in a time proportional to the logarithm of the initial error. In biology, as Monod points out, chance enters through the absence of any physical or chemical forces biasing the arrangement of nucleotides in a DNA code or the sequence of amino acids in a protein. Concerning the latter, Monod expresses this point as follows: "these structures are 'random' in the precise sense that, were we to know the exact order of 199 residues (i.e. amino acids) in a protein containing 200, it would be impossible to formulate any rule, theoretical or empirical, enabling us to predict the nature of the one residue not yet identified by analysis." [7] Indeed, an essential condition for the ability to code unlimited amounts of information on DNA is just that no physical or chemical forces should in any way control which of the four coding nucleosides would occupy any particular site on the code.

By way of summary we may say, then, that rather than being able to say that any course of events in nature is due to chance, we have to assert the opposite. The appearance of chance in the scientific description of such a course of events means rather that it is one of several, generally very many, alternative courses that could have been actualized and that no explanation can be given in principle as to why the particular course was actualized and not any one of the others. This is because in introducing probabilities into the laws governing the system, the possibility of any such explanation through natural causes was already *explicitly* renounced. Probability by definition requires that any particular alternative actualized in an individual instance must have no casual relationship to the other alternatives which the system might have actualized.

Some scientists are acutely unhappy with this role of chance. This has been true of physics for the past half of the century and will be true in other fields as its full implications become apparent. The most notable example is Einstein, but a few others still share his concern. Biologists like Monod have only recently had to face up to the statistical character of their laws, but the full implications of this fact have not yet dawned on them. Traditionally it has seemed essential to science to insist that given time all natural phenomena could be explained in natural terms. The one concession they were never prepared to make was that nature herself would ever force them to explicitly renounce causal explanation in any area of their science. The basic faith was that all such areas not presently explained by science would ultimately yield to such explanation. For them to allow statistical laws with probabilities is a present surrender of this basic faith. But after fifty years of experience with the inevitable, the majority of physicists are by now reconciled to this explicit renunciation of causal explanation in their science. In time biologists will also come around to such acceptance. Monod already has, but he does not yet appreciate its implications.

A good way to bring out these implications is to consider evolution in terms of a computer model. In recent years a great deal has been done with computer models of social, economic, ecological, and other complex systems with many variables. One of the best known of these models is that developed at MIT of the Club of Rome and published under the title *The Limits to Growth*. Such models can be run rapidly under a variety of assumptions and can provide a great deal of information about the behavior of complex symptoms which could not be obtained in any other way. All of them, however, as far as I know, eliminate the element of chance by modeling the system to take the most probable alternative at each point. This means that the model is "surprise free" and always generates the same results under the same set of assumptions. Those developing such models are quite aware that in this sense actual systems will behave differently from the model. The purposes for which computer models are used, however, require this kind of dependability.

In principle a computer model could be developed which would fully reflect the statistical character of the scientific laws involved in the system being modeled. The computer could be supplied with a set of random numbers and these in turn could determine alternatives in accordance with their specified probabilities. Such a model could be developed for a limited evolutionary process such as a small island with a few species. The model would reflect mutation frequencies in the gene pools of each species and selective pressures due to environmental changes and the interactions between the species. Each run of the model could start with the same initial conditions and, with modern high speed computers, project in a run of an hour or two what would happen to the system in a million years. At each stage involving the several alternatives governed by probabilities only one would be actualized. The pattern of alternatives selected along the way in a run would change the selective pressures on the different species in a way unique to that run. As a consequence the end result of each run would be different from all the others. It would be evident to those using the model that the interweaving of chance with the necessities of biology and environment opens up evolution in a way which permits a vast variety of outcomes.

Interestingly enough a greatly simplified probabilistic computer model of this type has recently been developed by a geologist for the purpose of gaining some insight into the character of the fossil record.[8] It does not include natural selection or mutation rates and so does not attempt to model the actual process of biological evolution. What it does do is to assign to each species at the end of time periods of equal but unspecified length a probability of continuing, a probability of branching into two species or subspecies, and a probability of extinction, with their sum equal to unity. Repeated runs of the computer with these highly simplified alternatives are remarkably successful in duplicating broad features of the fossil record from the first appearance of a family of organisms (e.g., conifers, trilobites, reptiles, etc.) through increasingly diversified populations of many species to the final disappearance of the family.

Evolution in common with all history differs from the computer model in that it has had only one run. We can never go back in either and see how differently things could have turned out if some very improbable eventualities had been avoided along the way. But the computer model does assure us that, as long as science involves chance governed by probabilities, evolution and history are scientifically unpredictable. Evolution on this earth could have followed a very different course than the one it did. Whatever, if anything, "caused" it to take the course it did rather than any of the others it might equally well have taken could not be a natural cause discernible to science. This is because, as we have seen, science in introducing probability explicitly renounced causal explanation.

Up to this point I suspect Monod would agree with all that I have said about the role of chance in evolution, since I have confined myself to its mathematical and scientific aspects. Disagreement will arise only when we go beyond this stage and wish to assert, with, say, Teilhard de Chardin, that the one path actually taken by evolution on earth among the myriad other paths which, scientifically speaking, it might equally well have taken is evidence of the operation of creativity and imagination at the very heart of the process. Here, in my judgment, those he rejects as "animists" and "vitalists" show a deeper wisdom and sensitivity to the meaning of the evolutionary process than does Monod. In any event his rejection of them on *scientific* grounds is certainly not justified. Indeed, his peculiar definition of objectivity falls under the weight of these considerations. There is no conceivable operation by which it could be established within science that nature either is or is not projective or purposeful. Certainly the application of science to any segment of the history of the universe—whether it be in cosmology, the origin and development of the solar system, the geological history of the earth and other planets, the evolution of life, or the history of men and nations—proceeds in exactly the same way for a projective history as it does for a non-projective history. Since the laws governing the processes in each of these histories are all statistical, all that science can assert is that they might have been different in a myriad of ways than they were and that causes within nature or science can be asserted to account for the one particular course which events in the one actualized history took. Thus his statement of the principle of objectivity really has nothing to do with science. The methods of science are in no way dependent on it and the application of science to an understanding of the course of events in the history of nature is completely neutral with respect to it. It is a disservice to science to imply that it is essential to the integrity of the scientific method that the whole history of nature be non-projective and non-purposeful.

Both the history of life on earth which we call evolution, and the history of men and nations are filled with turning points of a miraculous character. A miracle in history is not a violation of natural laws by some outside intervention in an otherwise orderly process. Rather it is the extraordinary coming together in accidental and unforseeable ways of the most improbable instances of various natural laws. Most of the time we can count on the most probable things happening. In such periods life and history seem orderly and dependable and even dull. The great creative moments in history are the unexpected events when none of this is true. Such events have been as decisive throughout the pre-human history of living organisms on earth as they have been in human history. The word "evolution," with the connotation "anti-animist" which scientists like Monod have given it, tends to hide this central fact.

There is no way to prove that a transcendent purpose or supernatural influence, such as the "animists" and "vitalists" postulate, is involved in such events. All the scientist or historian can say is that his "explanation" has to stop when he comes to chance and accident, the boundary within which the explanation of what happens within space and time in terms of other forces and structures within space and time is forever confined. If there is anything purposeful, meaningful, or providential in history, it must cross that boundary beyond space and time to exert its influence on events. In order to do so, such a supernatural influence does not have to intervene or upset established probability patterns. It needs only single happenings, accidentally combined with single instances of other happenings, to be an event. If we want to know whether a single instance was likely or unlikely, we go to the laboratory and observe the same kind of happening repeated over and over under controlled conditions. But the event in history capitalizes on single happenings and particular accidents that will never happen just that way again. A single isolated happening is neither probable nor improbable; it is simply what happened at that particular moment. Later, in reflecting on it, we may use our knowledge of the laws of nature to say what the probability was of its happening. But the fact still remains that this was what actually happened and not something else that might just as well have happened.

Further elaboration of this point is desirable because of the peculiar and rather elusive character of the concepts of chance and probability.

Unlike all other elements which enter into a scientific description of phenomena, there is no operational way of meaningfully assigning a probability to a single concrete happening. Yet at the same time we must apply our knowledge of probability, if it is to be of any use to us at all, as though it did apply to individual events. This circumstance gives to the language of probability an ambiguous character which can be the occasion for numerous misconceptions and inadvertently erroneous usages.

I can easily calculate that the chance of a four-spot coming upon the cast of a perfect die is one-sixth. If now I cast the die and a four-spot does turn up, there is no operation whatever which I can perform with respect to that throw which will prove that the probability actually realized in that throw was one-sixth. The only proof of this sort which I can undertake would apply not to this particular throw but to a very large number of repeated throws in which I might indeed satisfy myself that the four-spot does come up one-sixth of the time. In most scientific applications of probability theory this difficulty is not crucial, either because it does not matter what comes up in a single throw or because all that is being studied anyhow is the pattern formed by a large number of repeated throws. But it becomes a very different matter when say, a man's life depends on a four turning up, and a four does turn up. It is doubtful whether, in reflecting on this event thereafter, he could ever be satisfied by the simple assertion that the chance of his living then was exactly one-sixth. Would he not always wonder why it was that, when a four-spot was just what was needed, it was a four-spot which turned up?

It is only when we are dealing with a large number of repeated instances at a given time that probabilities are actualized in events. In the field of natural phenomena this is the basis on which science rests. In the field of affairs, it is the basis for all forms of insurance underwriting, the stock exchange, and the operation of gambling establishments. History, on the other hand, involves in its most significant and determining aspects nonrepetitive events. The crucial events of history, the turning points if you wish, are singular, and the assignment of probabilities to them is either fruitless or misleading. A life insurance company could specify fairly accurately the probability of the death during the coming year of any one of the present heads of state of the nations of the world. The effect on world history of the actual death of one of them would, however, in no way be measured by the probability of its occurrence. Again, geneticists may be able to state accurately the probability of some of the mutations which have been crucial in setting the course of the evolutionary process. The knowledge of such probabilities is, however, of little assistance to the paleontologist who seeks to understand the course which was actually taken.

There is a stark and sturdy impregnability about events which constitutes their singularity. It is indeed just this impregnability which gives an elemental character to the barrier which chance and accident throw up in the path of a purely scientific understanding of history. The difficulty with the attempt to understand history in scientific terms is that generally the role of any given event in shaping history is entirely unrelated to the manner in which that same event fits into the probability pattern formed by the class of all such events when repeated a large number of times under the same conditions. The determination of the probability of throwing a four-spot with a given die is a proper subject for scientific investigation. It cannot, however, illuminate in any way the mystery for the man whose life was saved because in a single throw a four-spot actually did turn up.

It is interesting that even Monod at one point confesses to a sense of the hidden creative and therefore "animist" energies evident in evolution which Bergson and Teilhard de Chardin so persuasively express. There is in the following passage an implied acknowledgment of the force of the "vitalist" or "animist" insight with possibly some nostalgia for its demise:

When one ponders on the tremendous journey of evolution over the past three billion years or so, the prodigious wealth of structures it has engendered, and the extraordinarily effective teleonomic performances of living beings, from bacteria to man, one may well find oneself beginning to doubt again whether all this could conceivably be the product of an enormous lottery presided over by natural selection, blindly picking the rare winners from among numbers drawn at utter random.

While one's conviction may be restored by a detailed review of the accumulated modern evidence that this conception alone is compatible with the facts (notably with the molecular mechanisms of replication, mutation, and translation), it affords no synthetic, intuitive, and immediate grasp of the vast sweep of evolution. The miracle stands "explained"; it does not strike us as any less miraculous. As Francois Mauriac wrote, "What this professor says is far more incredible than what we poor Christians believe." [9]

Several observations are necessary to clarify the implications of this summary passage. By speaking of chance in evolution as an "enormous lottery" he evokes the image of the casino with all its connotations of purposelessness. So does the loaded phrase "numbers drawn at utter random." But as we have seen, chance does not operate this way in history. The great and decisive turning points in the history of life through which its creative achievements have been realized are the result of an extraordinary coming together in unforeseeable ways of the most improbable instances of natural laws. They are nothing like an "enormous lottery" or drawing numbers at utter random. It is the fact of chance in the laws of nature which makes such rare and improbable turning points a scientific possibility. The history of life on earth has indeed seen the picking of some very "rare winners," but whether they were picked "blindly" or intentionally science is powerless to decide.

It is important in this connection to recognize the immensity of time involved in the evolution of life. In the life span of individual cells or organisms, the "molecular mechanisms of replication, mutation, and translation" are indeed regular and beautifully balanced as Monod has so clearly described in his book. But the great creative turning points in evolution, the miraculous emergents through which its remarkable achievements have been actualized, are measured by the life span of species and whole populations and are separated by periods of millions of years. They involve such extreme improbabilities that ideas of the role of chance and probability derived from games of chance or controlled experiments in the laboratory are of little value in understanding them. All that science can say about them is that they were possible. But from a theological perspective they illuminate the reality of that transcendent influence operating within the natural order by which the Creator Spirit ultimately achieves his goals.

It is probable that the great majority of the readers of Monod's book see in "chance" just as much, if not more, denial of purpose as they see in the mechanistic determinism of "necessity." Even theologians carefully avoid any reference to chance because for them as well as their readers it also seems to imply the very opposite of purpose. Yet they, above all, should welcome chance because the validity of a theological interpretation of history requires the explicit renunciation of natural causation in a scientific interpretation of the same history. The only area in which science has been forced to explicitly renounce natural causation is in the introduction of probability, and therefore of chance, into scientific laws. Hopefully theologians will in time come to see this crucial role played by chance in science as providing them with the freedom they need for carrying out their task.

Biologists have only recently been forced to employ statistical modes of analysis in their science as a result of information coding in DNA and amino acid sequences in proteins. It is understandable that the full implications of the introduction of chance and probability have not yet become evident to most of them. This is not true, however, of physical scientists, who have experienced these implications in the most intimate, detailed, and universal ways for over a half a century now. Nevertheless, when they stray from their own fields, a surprising number of astronomers and physicists revert to the most naive determinism when they consider biological evolution. They express a kind of axiomatic belief that once life gets started anywhere in the universe it will inevitably evolve into intelligent beings like man. Out of this conviction, numerous astronomers have organized expensive projects designed to communicate with advanced technical civilizations on other planets. In a recent review article on cosmology, an eminent astrophysicist expresses this conviction baldly and axiomatically: "Suffice it to say that, once you have self-replication, then the entire mechanism of Darwinian selection and mutations takes over, and the evolution from the primeval slime mold to a local politician seems practically inevitable."

The evolutionist George Gaylord Simpson has discussed these expectations of physical scientists in a persuasive essay on "The Nonprevalence of Humanoids" [10] in which he says:

The assumption, so freely made by astronomers, physicists, and some biochemists, that once life gets started anywhere, humanoids will eventually and inevitably appear is plainly false. The chance of duplicating man on any other planet and its organisms have had a history identical in all essentials with that of the earth through some billions of years. Let us grant the unsubstantiated claim of millions of billions of possible planetary abodes of life; the chances of such historical duplication are still vanishingly small.

The same point has been made in a different way by Loren Eiseley who points out that the multiplanetary experiment has already been carried out for us here on earth. Some two hundred million years ago Australia, South America, and Africa were all part of a single land mass call Gondwanaland with a common flora and fauna. As a result of plate tectonics and associated sea floor spreading, they became isolated by large intervening oceans. From the beginning of such isolation until the present the evolution of life has proceeded independently on each. These three continents can, therefore, be regarded as three separate worlds or planets each maintaining life the different histories of which in a two hundred million year span are examples of the course which life might take on other planets in the universe.

It was only in Africa that the evolution of mammalian primates during the last seventy million years led to the great apes and to man. In South America the same evolution of primates over the same period led to the anatomically quite different new world monkeys. These creatures constitute a broad spectrum of species and varieties of small animals who have never left the trees or experimented with upright walking on land. The continued evolutionary development of this stock could never lead to anything like man. The evolution of mammals in Australia during the Tertiary was able to produce only marsupials. Far from producing anything like primates which might have led to some kind of humanoid, Australian evolution never succeeded in achieving even a true mammalian placenta. A contemplation of the very different histories of life on these otherwise very similar "worlds" should be adequate to dispel any illusion that there is anything inevitable about an evolutionary process elsewhere in the universe.

There is nothing in the biological laws governing evolution which makes the ultimate development of any particular species inevitable. Because of the role played by chance and probability, the evolution of life has open to it innumerable alternative paths which it might take through time. Alternative evolutionary scenarios involving no dinosaurs or primates are just as possible scientifically as the realized scenario. The fact that the one path taken by evolution here on earth ultimately led to the achievement of a creature, man, made in the image of his Creator has no scientific explanation. There is, however, an entirely adequate theological explanation in terms of the fulfillment of the purpose of God, the Creator Spirit. If humanoids have appeared anywhere else in the universe, it cannot be the result of the scientific laws of nature, but only as a result of the operation of that same Creator Spirit.

NOTES

[1] Eric Rust, Science and Faith (New York: Oxford University Press, 1967).

[2] Jacques Monod, Chance and Necessity (New York: Alfred A. Knopf, 1971).

[3] William G. Pollard, "A Critique of Jacques Monod's Chance and Necessity," Soundings, vol. 56, Winter 1973, pp. 433–445.

[4] J. Monod, Chance and Necessity, p. 3.

[5] Ibid., p. 21.   [6] Ibid., p. 41.   [7] Ibid., p. 96.

[8] David M. Raup, "Probabilistic Models in Evolutionary Paleobiology," American Scientists, 65, January-February 1977, pp. 50-57.

[9] J. Monod, Chance and Necessity, p. 138.

[10] G. G. Simpson, This View of Life: The World of an Evolutionist (New York: Harcourt Brace and World, 1964), Chapter 13.

17.
Ian T. Ramsey
The Language of Science
and the Language of Religion
Al Studdard

It was on June 30, 1860, that Bishop Wilberforce asked T. H. Huxley whether it was through his grandfather or his grandmother that he claimed simian descent. Huxley's now famous answer in part ran,

would I rather have a miserable ape for a grandfather or a man highly endowed by nature and possessing great means and influence and yet who employs those faculties and that influence for the mere purpose of introducing ridicule into a grave scientific discussion—I unhesitatingly affirm my preference for the ape.[1]

A century later the conflict between science and religion had come to be expressed as a language problem. The question is, in the light of scientific knowledge, not whether the claims of religion are true or false, but whether they make any sense at all.

Ian T. Ramsey claims that far from being mutually exclusive, the languages of science and religion are complementary. The language of science does not render the language of religion obsolete; rather the language of science requires the language of religion in order to fulfill its own goals. The purpose of this chapter is to analyze this claim of Ramsey's that the language of science requires the language of religion for its own completeness. In order to do that I must first show how it is that modern philosophy in the form of linguistic analysis shapes the issue, i.e., how linguistic analysis constitutes a challenge to religious language. After describing the challenge of the analytical movement to religious language, I will show how Ramsey combines the languages of science and religion on a single language map.

The Challenge of Linguistic Analysis

Linguistic analysis in its several forms is the answer of twentieth-century empiricism to nineteenth-century idealism. It is not possible in the space allotted to trace the several lines of analytic philosophy, yet two major strains must be mentioned, the "common-sense philosophy" of G. E. Moore and those movements informed by Ludwig Wittgenstein: logical atomism, logical positivism, and conceptual analysis. In contemporary philosophy it is not far from the mark to say that linguistic analysis and conceptual analysis are almost the same and that the Moore and Wittgenstein strains are difficult to separate. It is necessary for our interpretation of Ramsey to note briefly some of the outstanding features of the movement from logical atomism to conceptual analysis. In so doing we shall see not only how the science-religion issue evolved, but also how analytic philosophy provided some of the device which Ramsey uses to make his case for the validity of religious language.

One of the most significant features of the analytic movement is the shift of focus from truth to meaning. "What does it mean?" became a more important question than, "Is it true?" Philosophy as analysis of language is not viewed as the quest for truth but the clarification of meaning. The goal of logical atomism and the goal of Wittgenstein's early book, *Tractatus Logico-Philosophicus* are stated in Wittgenstein's own words, "The whole sense of the book might be summed up in the following words: What can be said can be said clearly, and what we cannot talk about we must consign to silence." [2]

Logical atomism, as reflected in the *Tractatus* and in *Principia Mathematica*,[3] authored by Bertrand Russell and A. N. Whitehead, took as its model for an ideally unambiguous language the language of mathematics. This ideal, combined with an atomistic metaphysics resulted in the position that meaningful language is limited to the propositions of natural science.[4] Since the world is composed of atomic facts the atomists claim, and since the purpose of language is to mirror facts directly, all meaningful language is made up of either atomic propositions or complex propositions which are truth-functional compounds of simple ones. Here is a picture-theory of language, whose sole meaning is to refer to material facts. The end result is that all meaningful propositions take the form of empirical descriptions or hypotheses.[5] This leaves no room for statements which refer to transcendent reality.

The atomistic metaphysics of logical atomism was responsible for its early decline, but one important feature of logical atomism remains to inform contemporary conceptual analysis, i.e., the notion of a "hierarchy of languages." Originally designed to indicate the relationships of simple and complex propositions, the term came to label the view that language functions at a variety of levels of logic. Mixing those levels of logic, i.e., different types of language, indiscriminately leads to linguistic confusion. In order to avoid committing this "type-trespass," [6] one must carefully observe where in the hierarchy a given statement belongs.

A more radical form of analysis appeared when Moritz Schlick and the Vienna Circle [7] made scientific method the criterion for determining the meaningfulness of any and all language. Aptly named, Logical Positivism combined the logical rigor of Cambridge with the positivism of Vienna.[8] The heart of the challenge of logical positivism to religious language lies in its use of the verification principle as the test of all synthetic statements. Schlick puts the principle this way, "The meaning of a proposition is the method of its verification." [9] A. J. Ayer spells it out in more detail: "it lays down that the meaning of a statement is determined by the way in which it can be verified, where its being verified consists in its being tested by empirical observation." [10]

Even the positivists recognized that the verification principle was too strong to be useful for natural science, since the hypotheses of natural science cannot be conclusively verified. Ayer proposed a modified version.

Some possible sense experience should be relevant to the determination of its truth or falsehood. If a putative proposition fails to satisfy this principle, and is not a tautology, then . . . it is metaphysical . . . neither true nor false, but literally senseless.[11]

This modified principle only makes conclusive verification unnecessary; it does not change the demand of positivism that all meaningful statements must be tested by empirical observation.

Now it can be said how the claims of science, from the positivist's point of view, over against the claims of religion came to be a linguistic problem. Not only is philosophy taken to be a purely analytical enterprise, but only one type of language is taken to be significant, the language of the natural sciences. Both language and philosophy were reduced to the dimensions of science. Ayer said, "Philosophy must develop into the philosophy of science." [12]

Since all statements are either tautologies, or synthetic statements to which the verification principle applies, positivism has no room for a statement which makes non-empirical claims. Any such putative claim is simply labeled as nonsense. To this category of nonsense Ayer consigned such assertions as: "There is a non-empirical world of values . . . that men have immortal souls (and) . . . that there is a transcendent God." [13]

Since all meaningful statements refer to purely spatiotemporal phenomena, the claims of religion are undercut at an even more radical point than before. It is not a question of whether they are true or false. They cannot be either true or false since they literally say nothing. Said Ayer, "We offer the theist the same comfort as we gave the moralist. His assertions cannot possibly be valid. But they cannot be invalid either." [14]

The verification principle proved too narrow a criterion for meaning, and it soon ceased to dominate the analytic movement. Ayer said in the preface to the second edition of *Language Truth and Logic* that he had not intended to deny all meaning to statements which do not pass the verification test, only "factual" and "literal" meaning.[15] This small concession reflects the changing mood of linguistic analysis as logical positivism gives way to modern conceptual analysis, in which the meaning of language is no longer taken to be the method of its verification, but its use.

The program for conceptual analysis is spelled out in Wittgenstein's *Philosophical Investigations,* where he enunciates the "use principle": "The meaning of a word is its use in the language." [16] Repudiating his earlier picture theory of language, Wittgenstein invites us to consider words as tools.

It is interesting to compare the multiplicity of tools in a language and of the way they are used, the multiplicity of kinds of word and sentence, with what the logicians have said about the structure of language (including the author of the *Tractatus Logico-Philosophicus.*) [17]

Two features of conceptual analysis are emphasized here, the heterogeneity of logic and the use principle. The heterogeneity of logic is further emphasized in Wittgenstein's talk of "language games." The whole activity of using words, both the "language and the actions into which it is woven" constitutes the game. This total phenomenon of language is what Wittgenstein calls a "form of life." [18] No rules are laid down which exclude any of these games from having significance. All are significant as they are played. While there is nothing necessarily common to all language games, there are relationships and resemblances which can be observed in varying patterns. These are called "family resemblances." [19] Thus, games can be loosely grouped into families.

The way for clearing up confusions over language for the later Wittgenstein is to put the puzzling terms back into the contexts where they are understood in ordinary language. This is known as "the appeal to the paradigm case." [20] To avoid linguistic confusion it is important to remember that one expression may in fact perform many functions and to be aware of just what game (level of language) a given expression fits.

I. T. Ramsey finds the interest of contemporary analysis in the "logical diversity of language" stimulating and constructive. Awareness of that diversity is the beginning of clearing up philosophic confusion. He believes that:

The problems of philosophy are the problems of language. . . . They arise . . . when we fail to distinguish what is logically diverse, or when we assimilate too readily phrases which in fact differ in their logical behaviour.[21]

Ramsey offers as instances in which our failure to distinguish different logical behavior such paired statements as: "lions are real," and "lions are yellow"; "I crossed the bridge," and "I crossed the equator." [22] The grammatical structure in each pair of phrases is similar. The logic is not.

Gilbert Ryle illustrates the technique that Ramsey is recommending, i.e., the separating of logical categories, to unravel a number of philosophic puzzles. His term for the mistaken assimilation of "the logical behaviour of categories whose logical behaviour differs," [23] is "category mistakes." [24] The job of philosophy is to place concepts in their proper categories, "to rectify their logical geography." [25]

In applying this method to the conflict between science and religion, Ryle says that it is a mistake to suppose that the different disciplines are giving "rival answers to the same questions." [26] We are mixing categories, making category mistakes when we suppose this. This logical mixing, says Ryle, produced poor science on the part of Bishop Ussher and poor theology on the part of T. H. Huxley.[27]

One of the most important ideas in conceptual analysis for I. T. Ramsey is the idea of a hierarchy of languages. As old (at least) as logical atomism, this device provides a way to reconcile what appear to be serious metaphysical conflicts by showing that they are merely problems arising out of mixing diverse logics. Conceptual analysis, recognizing this variety in logic, acknowledges the possibility of a wider range of significant language. It issues an invitation to the use of a language to map the logical geography of his own language.

Before proceeding to the description of Ramsey's synthesizing of the languages of science and religion, I will briefly summarize the challenge of analytic philosophy to religious language.

The materialistic metaphysics of logical atomism and the verification principle of logical positivism constitute the claim that the only significant language is, in the final analysis, the language of natural science. They constitute an even more radical challenge to religion than the older materialism, for they do not contend that religious claims are simply (on the evidence) not true, but that they do not even have any meaning. No conceivable evidence is relevant to their being true or false. It is one thing to be told that your statements are false, another to be told that your statements are not even statements.

It is not clear in the end that modern conceptual analysis is any more friendly to religious language than logical positivism; for while it does not rule out religious language as nonsense, it still does not necessarily admit that religious language has any cognitive significance. That is to say that on questions of fact, the verification principle still applies. Carl Michalson, in making this claim, parodies Ryle in saying that "the Ghost of Logical Positivism" still inhabits the machinery of linguistic analysis.[28]

There is a subtle threat in the quest for clarity in all stages of the analytic movement. It lies in the suggestion that there are no ultimate mysteries. This threat does not necessarily amount to the denial that there is something beyond the human intellect, but that if there is it would be impossible to talk about it. "This is not to deny God, but Revelation, or more accurately, it is to deny that language can be the vehicle of revealed truth."[29]

There lies a serious challenge to religious language in the assumption that philosophical thinking can only analyze. It is the denial of the possibility of constructing a synthetic world view.[30]

However, the challenge to theology of analytic philosophy is not all negative. There is a constructive one as well. The analytic movement has forced the issue of "what meaning if any attaches to the religious man's talk of God."[31] Furthermore, its contemporary insistence upon logical heterogeneity can bring a needed corrective to theological speculation, forcing the theologian to take account of the way in which theological statements differ from other types of statements, and causing him to reflect on the meaning of his own.

Ramsey uses the idea of logical heterogeneity, provided by the analytic movement to make his case for religious language. While aware of the negative aspects of linguistic analysis, he says that

The contemporary interest in language, far from being soul-destroying, can be so developed as to provide a novel inroad into the problems and controversies of theology, illuminating its claims and reforming its apologetic.[32]

A part of that job is to show how a total language map requires not only the language of science, but the language of religion as well if it is to be complete. Put another way, the language of science can never provide the schema for interpreting the whole universe.

Science and Religion: Mapping the Languages

The preceding discussion of analytic philosophy does not show that there is a necessary conflict between science and religion. What it does show is that positivism under any guise does conflict with any claim to transcendence. It makes clear, I hope, just how the centuries-old conflict between the claims of religion and the claims of science came to be expressed as a language problem. Inasmuch as the analytic movement does represent twentieth-century empiricism, one way of expressing the problem is to ask whether empiricism leaves any room for religious belief. Ramsey thinks that it does. As we approach Ramsey's attempt to reconcile the language of religion with the language of science, it will be helpful to outline some of the basic presuppositions with which he approaches the task.

First of all, Ramsey calls himself a "believing empiricist," noting that there is a crucial difference between the "believing" and the "unbelieving empiricist." [33] He believes that the successors of Locke were far too narrow in the range of experiences which they took to be significant. A "broader empiricism" is advocated by Ramsey, one which admits, not only experience reducible to the five senses, but which also allows inner experiences to count.[34] The narrow empiricism which characterized logical positivism must yield to an empiricism broad enough to include the whole range of human experience, physical and more than physical, acknowledging reality that is spatio-temporal and "more." [35]

The believing empiricist holds to the belief in transcendence. Stated in linguistic terms this claim is that not all experience is tractable in object language, that the language of science is not competent to say all that can be said of what is real. Asks Ramsey, "Are there any

facts besides 'what is observed', i.e., seen, heard, tasted, and smelt?"
He adds,

Indeed, here for the religious philosopher is the crucial question. Here is
the one ontological claim on which he cannot yield. *To have distinctly religious
language at all, there must be situations not restricted to the spatio-temporal
elements they contain.*[36]

It is this claim that is most at issue between traditional empiricism
and the religionists. The question remains whether one can maintain
such a belief in transcendence and remain, strictly speaking, an empiricist.

Along with his belief in transcendence, Ramsey holds two corollary
beliefs which are important for the discussion at hand. The first is
that transcendent reality is knowable through "disclosures," the second
that human language can be the vehicle for disclosures. Disclosures
are moments of immediate awareness which provide knowledge of a
non-experimental, non-inferential sort. From the perspective of the
receiver of such knowledge this is identical to the claim for intuition
as a way of knowing. In disclosures, that which is more than spatio-
temporal is known. Ramsey claims that not only is religious knowledge
given in disclosures, but that disclosures are a necessary part of scientific knowledge as well.[37]

Some "believing empiricists" have doubts not about transcendence
nor revelation, but about whether such knowledge can be communicated.[38] Michael Foster interprets the challenge of empiricism
in just this way, not that it denied the possibility of revelation, but
rather the possibility of communicating it in human language.[39] Ramsey believes that he can show just how language functions both to
refer to disclosures and to evoke disclosures in science and religion.

Ramsey prefaces his mapping of the languages of science and religion
by noting three attitudes which may be held toward the relationship
between science and religion: First is the view that science and religion
are mutually exclusive, and that as scientific ignorance is overcome,
religion will disappear. The second view is that while they are not
mutually exclusive, they are altogether different sorts of activity, having
no relation at all to each other. The third alternative, the one recommended by Ramsey, is

a view of science and religion which recognizes their distinctive features
. . . but also recognizes the need and possibility to comprise them in one
vision. . . . On this view, while science and religion have their characteristi-

cally different features, they can, nevertheless, as I shall argue, be harmonized in an outlook which genuinely combines both.[40]

Ramsey uses the idea of the hierarchical structure of language to harmonize the respective visions of science and religion.

The idea of a hierarchy of languages, produced by the atomists, continues to be one of the more useful devices in conceptual analysis. The theory suggests that apparently homogeneous language can be separated into a variety of logical types, each of which has a place as "a subordinate language" on a "total language map." [41] Showing the relationships of these language to each of the others is analogous to constructing an ordinary geographical map. As an ordinary map is a schematic representation of "the geographical settings of town and villages in terms of the symbols for hills and rivers, roads and railways," so

logical mapwork is somewhat similarly concerned to exhibit the propositional settings in which concepts are set, to exhibit the linguistic context in which the particular concept sentences have their place.[42]

It is by constructing such a map that Ramsey intends to show the relationship between the language of science and the language of religion.

If one begins to plot on his map the various subordinate languages, he will construct a hierarchy of languages, each having its own distinctive use or logic. However, when all of the subordinate languages are plotted, the map remains fragmented. In order to give it overall unity it will be necessary to add "index words," [43] words which belong to none of the subordinate levels but which can without type-trespass function at all levels. They must be "frame-transferable" by nature." [44]

They are words which are good clues to, and definitions of the total language scheme, as is the index of a book to the words contained in its chapters. . . . They are words which bring to a full level of concretion what is being talked about.[45]

The outstanding question is, where do these words come from?

The claim that the language of the natural sciences is the totality of factually significant language is the same as the claim that the index words are furnished by science itself, i.e., that the language of science provides the "overall scheme" [46] for understanding the world. Science writes "the total map for the whole universe." [47] Ramsey claims that the language of science is prevented from performing this integrating function by three of its regular features; "its permanent incompleteness," "its peculiar selectivity," and the "type-trespass which results when scientific language moves out of its level of logic." [48]

Ramsey characterizes scientific method primarily, though not exclusively, as a search for invariants. Its language progresses from simple observation statements at its lowest level, to the articulation of "large-scale hypotheses." [49] Its aim is to produce one "overall scheme, one total map for the whole universe." [50] It is the "peculiar selectivity" of scientific method that operates in this progression which keeps science from performing the integrating role, i.e., it progresses by selecting "uniformities and repeated patterns," [51] becoming more and more comprehensive by becoming more and more abstract. This method of attaining comprehensiveness requires that the language of science ignores numerous features of any situation which it attempts to interpret. The wider its coverage the greater its abstraction, leaving the language of science

saying less and less about that part of a concrete situation with and from which a beginning was made, in order to say more and more about the totality of facts over which scientific language is farther and farther extended. [52]

As it extends itself over a wider range of experience, science does produce new ways of speaking; however, Ramsey says, it does not integrate diverse language so much as it simply replaces older languages with newer ones. Because of this proliferation without integration within science itself, words from outside the language of science are required to unify and to provide factual reference for all of the various levels, i.e., to relate the abstractions to concrete situations.

As the language of science proceeds from observation statements to large-scale hypotheses, it requires words which are clearly not observation language. The function of the hypothesis is, not to state one more empirical observation, but to unite a number of widely divergent observation statements, e.g., apples falling and planets in motion. Newton's hypothesis to unite these and similar observations did not itself represent something observable. At the level of forming hypotheses scientific method requires language which is neither simply observational nor mathematical. Examples of such words are "mass," "power," "ether," and "entropy." [53] The questions which have to be raised here are, "What is the nature of these words? Where do they come from? What do they represent?"

Ramsey outlines two radically antithetical ways of understanding these terms, rejects them both, and proposes a third which is crucial for the relating of the language of science and religion. The first alternative sees these terms for invariants as literally descriptive labels, the second that these words talk about nothing whatsoever, i.e., that they are to be interpreted purely operationally. The first alternative provides us with too much (and often incompatible) furniture in the world, while the second leaves us with none at all.[54]

If we interpret these words operationally, we will dismiss old metaphysical terms only to replace them with new ones, fragmenting the language of science with each new development. This happens when

science develops and invariants change [and] the world becomes cluttered up with scientific furniture of the most extraordinary sort. The old hard particles have a very uneasy relationship and existence with and among electrons, protons, mesons, and the rest. And what about those wave mechanics, as well as particle mechanics? [55]

Ramsey asks of the second alternative:

Are the invariants, which are the very basis of scientific method, talking about nothing at all besides the observations they conveniently organize and link together? Can we not say that these invariants of science, in some way or another, are clues to the real world? Can we not say that in some way or another they talk distinctively about something though they do *not* talk about little teeny-weeny particles, or big whopping absolute spaces? [56]

It is clear to Ramsey that neither of these alternatives will do. One leaves us with an increasingly fragmented world, and the other leaves us in danger of having no world at all. He proposes that they are to be interpreted "informationally." [57] By this he means that these invariant terms are models which refer to facts, though in something other than a picturing relationship. How they refer and whence they arise constitute the core of Ramsey's understanding of scientific method, as well as the basis for relating the language of science and the language of religion. Its elements are: intuition and imagination on the part of the investigator as he frames his questions, and disclosure on the part of the universe. The model on which Ramsey is operating is not that of "putting nature to the test," [58] but an interpersonal "dialogue with the universe." [59] He is claiming that scientific method is best understood when the universe is considered as personal. The invariant terms in question are provided in, and refer to, the disclosure, wherein the universe discloses itself to the investigator.

The anchor of the metaphysical words of science (invariant words) in a disclosure furnishes for these words a "basis in fact, a reference which other views deny altogether or take too uncritically." [60] To view science as a dialogue with the universe highlights both the personal involvement of the scientist and the personal character of the universe.

The most complex step of scientific method, the conversion of hypotheses, further demands metaphysical terms, and this reveals another significant element in Ramsey's philosophy of science, the use of models. To illustrate how this works, Ramsey chooses the well-known wave mechanics–particle mechanics issue. Neither explanation of the nature of light is falsifiable, and each is needed under certain circumstances. Both cannot of course directly picture reality. The solution to this problem, or pseudo-problem, is to view the separate alternatives as models, imaginative pictures which give some information about the universe, but which do not copy it directly or finally. The attempt to reduce the two models by suggesting "hidden parameters," [61] reveals a misunderstanding of how models work. It fails to see that models provide only a partial picture, never a complete picture of the universe. With two irreducible models, we still have a fragmented map. A further disclosure is required, providing language which exceeds the scientific to integrate the map.

The integrator, or index, words must be words which refer to concrete experience, not abstraction. The phrase "I exist," integrates fragmented language at the personal level, Ramsey says. It is entailed by all statements about "me," yet it entails no particular statements about "me." It is one phrase which commits no type-trespass when used in any context of personal experience. It gives all statements about "me" their "concrete reference, . . . unites them all." [62] However this phrase will not serve as the ultimate index word. The integrator word for all scientific statements must be adequate to include both the personal as well as all natural phenomena in the universe. Such a word is "God." [63]

Observation statements must have index words to provide a frame or reference. Index words (religious language) need observation statements to relate them to experience. Neither religion nor science alone can provide an adequate map for the entire universe of meaningful language. They are complementary: Religion provides the integration which science needs, an affirmation of the universe, "while science gives to religion fuller and fuller relevance . . . more and more adequate discursive expression." [64]

Not only does the theist require a disclosure for the knowledge that he seeks; the scientist does, too. The methods and language of both are compatible when the limitations of each are acknowledged. This accommodation is not without cost, however. The theologian will find that he must be more cautious in his metaphysical pronouncements as well as in the observable facts which these metaphysical beliefs entail.[65] The theologian cannot be a universal expert. On the other hand, science will have to admit reality and language which cannot be verified by its techniques. (It already knows that its hypotheses are reformable.) "Theologian and scientist must meet where all meet—in the affirmation of the universe which is wonder and worship at what the universe discloses." [66]

Ramsey's attempt to reconcile the languages of science and religion interprets scientific method primarily as the search for invariants. There is another feature of scientific method which, at least superficially, appears more difficult to harmonize with religion, the "empirical verification of deductions from hypotheses." [67] This feature, says Ramsey, has no parallel in theology,[68] but instead of rendering synthesis impossible, it serves to show why both languages are needed to complete the language map.[69]

It must be recalled that in Ramsey's schema index words do not belong to any of the subordinate levels of language. Only a word from outside all subordinate levels can connect various levels without committing type-trespass.

When personal language, i.e., statements about "me," connect with observation statements, all such statements imply "I exist," while "I exist" implies no particular statements. Likewise, "God exists" is implied by all statements, while implying no particular observation statements. This is another way of saying that empirical verification applies only within the language of science. If we try to apply it to the language of religion, we cause religious language to lose its religious character, for under these conditions it becomes just one more subordinate language on the map. [70] The implications of these final descriptive paragraphs bring us to the first paragraph of the conclusion of this chapter which consists of a brief evaluation of Ramsey's position.

Conclusion

While it is not my purpose to pursue the detailed workings of religious language here (Ramsey has written more on this subject than on any other, but it is beyond the limited aim of this chapter), note must be taken of the serious difficulty involved for religious language if "God exists" implies nothing in particular. It means that any state of affairs is compatible with belief in God, i.e., the claim that God exists cannot be falsified by anything. While a disclosure gives us the certainty of God (if it does), it guarantees nothing else. No theological propositions apart from that one are certain. All are tentative. Asked what it is that we can be sure about, Ramsey replies, "God." "We can be sure about God; but we must be tentative in theology." [71]

Having already argued that all scientific statements are reformable, uncertain, Ramsey now places all theological statements save one in the same questionable status. His making the one statement, "God exists" immune to falsification renders even that one of questionable meaning, if it is supposed to state an objective fact. Here lies the second major problem, from the religious perspective, with Ramsey's reconciliation of science and religion. The question to be put to Ramsey at this point is whether or not he takes the existence of God to be a matter of objective fact at all. The alternative to this is, of course, a subjective interpretation of religious language, which means that in the final analysis talk of God refers only to our own attitudes and intentions.[72]

Ramsey vigorously defends his claim to objectivity, resisting assimilation to other philosophers of religion who reduce religious language to psychological or ethical significance. Index words, Ramsey claims, do more than simply label a commitment, an attitude toward the world; they also refer to objective facts.[73] He claims that a hierarchy of facts corresponds to the hierarchy of language, that index words have an objective reference too. The objective facts referred to by these words are, though related to spatio-temporal phenomena (and approached by them), not in themselves limited to the spatio-temporal. These words "are a part of a language system whose empirical necessity arises from the fact that experience is not exhaustively described in terms of any number of parts which are objective in any number of senses." [74]

Ramsey seems to be talking about a universe in which there are two different kinds of facts, one kind empirically measurable, the other not so measurable. His nebulous account of "metaphysical facts" leaves us uncertain as to just what they may be. The idea of a "non-objective objectivity" is as prima facie self-contradictory as G. E. Moore's well-known "non-natural properties." Ramsey's attempt to answer the criticism of Ninian Smart is most revealing on this score, for he finds himself reduced to saying that it is "a *sort* (italics mine) of fact that God exists." [75] It is not at all clear that Ramsey has defended himself against the charge of subjectivism.[76]

In order to find any meaning at all in such claims as these we have to take into account Ramsey's belief in disclosure. For it is from disclosures that religious language comes, and it is to disclosures that it refers. The final justification, says Ramsey, of such words as "God" lies "in the fact that there is a non-inferential awareness more concrete than the objective facts which characterize it abstractly and objectively." [77] Here Ramsey's case can be seen to rest on a claim to intuitive knowledge. We have to ask now what part intuition can play in empiricism.

Intuitive knowledge, by definition, can never be proven veridical by the one who claims to hold it. We are now working at the level of presuppositions, and it is here that the challenge of analytic philosophy to religious language must be met. Behind the demand for empirical verification, which is central to the analytic movement, lies an important epistemological claim, i.e., that knowledge comes only through sense experience.[78] To the extent that the analytic movement reflects this traditional understanding of empiricism, Ramsey differs from empiricists so fundamentally that there is no genuine room for conversation between them. The "believing empiricist" may in fact be right about the nature of the world and the nature of knowledge, but he has no way of proving it to anyone else. This is not to deny that others may come to agree with him, but it will be under the conditions that they too believe that they have had a similar disclosure.

Ramsey's ontology is a correlate of his epistemology. He believes in a reality which transcends the spatio-temporal, a reality which is known intuitively. Berkeley and the contemporary phenomenalists demonstrate that it is possible to be an empiricist without embracing materialism. Ramsey does not want to embrace materialism, yet he rejects both the subjective idealism of Berkeley and the skepticism of the phenomenalists. While he seems to want to live in both worlds, his comparison of "cognition" and "intuition" indicate where his commitments really lie. Intuition is superior to cognition, being more concrete and noninferential. Cognition is inferential, and can only refer to objects. Ramsey sounds strangely like a rationalist when he talks about intuition.[79]

Ramsey's use of the term "empirical" is ambiguous. Often he uses it to refer to purely sensory experience. When he characterizes disclosures he uses the term to speak of ordinary perceptual facts, the "more" which transcends them, and the situation as a whole. It is not clear just what an appeal to experience means when it is given so many meanings. Royce has said that "the mystic" is the "thorough going empiricist." [80] While the rationalist's account of experience may be correct, nevertheless it completely redefines "empiricism," producing the strange situation that rationalists become empiricists. That, in ordinary language, is a logical contradiction. It does help to identify Ramsey's philosophical position.

Having raised a question of how much empiricist Ramsey really is, we now need to ask just how "empirical" scientific method is. It is here that Ramsey shows insight into the nature of scientific method. He shows why we can no longer view the edifice of science as being built solely upon empirical observation, and as laying claim to the final truth about the world. Ramsey is in agreement with a significant part of the scientific community itself in his claim that science depends upon intuition, models, and imagination, in developing, testing, and articulating its claims.[81] The tentativeness and reformability of scientific hypotheses are well-acknowledged by scientists and philosophers of science as well as by humanists.[82]

Showing that science is less than absolute in its claims, however, does not establish the truth of Ramsey's claim to intuitive knowledge of transcendent realities. What it does show at best is that at certain levels and in certain significant ways science and religion do have much in common. We must remember though that when the scientist talks about "intuition," and "imagination," he is usually claiming something less than a guarantee of eternal truth. What intuition and imagination do for the scientist is provide hypotheses for further testing.

It must be said finally that Ramsey's plotting of the languages of science and religion on his hierarchical map is unsatisfactory. He illustrates clearly by this device what he has in mind, but good illustration is not to be taken for convincing argument. Ramsey fails at three points: (1) His rigid stratification of types of language does not reflect the complexities of language as it is used. His scheme is too simple and his divisions are too neatly separated to reflect the living organism of human language.[83] (2) Ramsey places the language of science in the subordinate position on his map. The partisans of the view that science can some day write the index words as well are by no means satisfied nor proven wrong by Ramsey's analysis. (3) The third point at which Ramsey fails is integrally connected with the first two. His placing of the respective languages of science and theology on his map, far from synthesizing them, permanently separates them in practice.

On Ramsey's own account, religious claims are not falsifiable, that is, they imply no claim about any matter of observable fact in the world; scientific claims are about observable facts. Ramsey has indeed arranged his map so that the two languages can never make conflicting claims. The fatal flaw here is that on these grounds they can never really *meet* either. Ramsey's argument is subject to one of the criticisms that David Hume made of the design argument for the existence of God: it is acceptable to neither the believer not the skeptic. It seems to me that Ramsey is tacitly endorsing the view of science and religion that he specifically rejected earlier: that while the two activities are not mutually exclusive, they are altogether different sorts of activity, having no relation at all to each other. While this arrangement does prevent conflict between the language of science and the language of religion it does not constitute synthesis.

NOTES

[1] Excerpt from a private letter, in Ashley Montagu's introduction to T. H. Huxley's *Man's Place in Nature* (Ann Arbor: University of Michigan Press, 1959) p. 2.

[2] Ludwig Wittgenstein, *Tractatus Logico-Philosophicus*, D. F. Pears and B. F. McGuinness, trans. (London: Routledge and Kegan Paul, 1961) P. 3. Hereafter this work will be referred to in text and notes as *Tractatus*. Citations taken from the main body of the book will show proposition numbers rather than page numbers.

[3] The *Principia Mathematica* was published in 1910.

[4] "The totality of true propositions is the whole of natural science." *Tractatus* 4.11.

[5] For a discussion of this idea, see Gilbert Ryle, "Ludwig Wittgenstein," *Essays on Wittgenstein's Tractatus,* Irving M. Copi and Robert W. Bread, editors (New York: The Macmillan Company, 1966) p. 4.

[6] Ramsey borrows this language from Bertrand Russell. For his discussion see, Ian T. Ramsey, *Religion and Science: Conflict and Synthesis* (London: S.P.C.K., 1964) pp. 78-79.

[7] A. J. Ayer, "The Vienna Circle," *The Revolution in Philosophy,* A. J. Ayer, *et al.* (London: The Macmillan Company, 1957) p. 70. Ayer identifies the Vienna Circle as a group of philosophers who gathered around Moritz Schlick, professor of philosophy at Vienna from 1922 to 1938. They were heavily influenced by the physical theory of Ernst Mach.

[8] *Ibid.,* p. 73.

[9] Moritz Schlick, "Meaning and Verification," *Readings in Philosophical Analysis,* Herbert Feigl and Wilfrid Sellars, editors (New York: Appleton-Century-Crofts, 1949) p. 156.

[10] Ayer, *op. cit.,* p. 75.

[11] A. J. Ayer, *Language, Truth and Logic* (New York: Dover Publications, 1946) p. 31.

[12] *Ibid.,* p. 153.

[13] *Ibid.,* p. 31.

[14] *Ibid.,* p. 116.

[15] *Ibid.,* pp. 15-16.

[16] Ludwig Wittgenstein, *Philosophical Investigations,* G. E. M. Anscombe, trans. (New York: The Macmillan Company, 1953) p. 20.

[17] *Ibid.,* p. 12 Cf. p. 6.

[18] *Ibid.*, p. 11.

[19] *Ibid.*, p. 32. "Games form a family."

[20] William Hordern, *Speaking of God: The Nature and Purpose of Religious Language* (New York: The Macmillan Company, 1964) p. 41. Cf. also Wittgenstein, *Philosophical Investigations*, p. 25.

[21] Ian T. Ramsey, "Contemporary Empiricism, Its Development and Theological Implications," *The Christian Scholar* (43:174-84, Fall, 1960) p. 179.

[22] *Ibid.*

[23] *Ibid.*, p. 180.

[24] See two books by Gilbert Ryle, *The Concept of Mind* (New York: Barnes and Noble, 1949) and *Dilemmas* (Cambridge: Cambridge University Press, 1954).

[25] John Macquarrie, *Twentieth-Century Religious Thought: The Frontiers of Philosophy and Theology* (New York: Harper and Row, 1967), p. 310.

[26] Gilbert Ryle, *Dilemmas*, p. 11.

[27] *Ibid.*, pp. 6-7.

[28] Carl Michalson, "The Ghost of Logical Positivism," *The Christian Scholar* (43:223-3-, 1960).

[29] Michael Foster, "Contemporary British Philosophy and Christian Belief," *The Christian Scholar* (43:185-98, Fall, 1960) p. 196.

[30] James Richmond, *Faith and Philosophy* (Philadelphia: J. B. Lippincott Company, 1966) p. 1977.

[31] John Macquarrie, *op. cit.*, p. 305.

[32] Ian T. Ramsey, *Religious Language: An Empirical Placing of Theological Phrases* (New York: The Macmillan Company, 1957) p. 11.

[33] Ian T. Ramsey, "Contemporary Empiricism," p. 183. Cf. also Ramsey's introduction to Locke's *The Reasonableness of Christianity* (Stanford: Stanford University Press, 1958). This also reflects William James' thought, though Ramsey does not mention James.

[35] This "More" is Ramsey's all-pervasive term.

[36] Ian T. Ramsey, "Empiricism and Religion: A Critique of Ryle's *Concept of Mind,*" *The Christian Scholar* (39:159-63, June, 1956) p. 161.

[37] Ramsey, *Religion and Science*, pp. 12-25.

[38] Thomas MacPherson, "Religion as the Inexpressible," *New Essays in Philosophical Theology*, Antony Flew and Alasdair MacIntyre, editors (London: S. C. M. Press, 1966) pp. 131-43.

[39] Michael Foster, *op. cit.*, p. 191.

[40] Ramsey, *Religion and Science*, pp. 4-5.

[41] Ian T. Ramsey, "Miracles," *The Miracles and The Resurrection*, I. T. Ramsey, *et. al.* (London: S. P. C. K., 1964) p. 2.

[42] *Ibid.*

[43] Ian T. Ramsey, "The Challenge of the Philosophy of Language," *The London Quarterly and Holborn Review* (186:52-69, October, 1961) pp. 261-262. Cf. Ramsey, *Religion's Language*, p. 67. These may be called "boundary words" or "limit words."

[44] *Ibid.*

[45] *Ibid.*

[46] Ian T. Ramsey, "Religion and Science, A Philosopher's Approach," *The Church Quarterly Review* (162:77-91, January–March, 1961) p. 87.

[47] *Ibid.*

[48] Ian T. Ramsey, "On the Possibility and Purpose of a Metaphysical Theology," *Prospect for Metaphysics*, Ian T. Ramsey, editor (New York: The Philosophical Library, Inc., 1961, pp. 153-77) p. 160.

[49] Ramsey, "Religion and Science, A Philosopher's Approach," pp. 78-79.

[50] *Ibid.*, p. 87.

[51] Ramsey, "Miracles," p. 5.

[52] *Ibid.*, p. 6.

[53] Ramsey, *Religion and Science: Conflict and Synthesis*, pp. 10, 11. "Such Words range from 'absolute space' for Newton to 'continuous creation' for Hoyle, not forgetting the all-embracing use of 'evolution' in the later nineteenth century."

[54] *Ibid.*, pp. 10-12.

[55] *Ibid.*, p. 11.   [56] *Ibid.*, p. 12.

[57] Ramsey, "Religion and Science, A Philosopher's Approach," pp. 83-84.

[58] *Ibid.*   [59] *Ibid.*, p. 85.

[60] Ramsey, *Religion and Science: Conflict and Synthesis*, p. x.

[61] *Ibid.*, p. 11. Cf. also p. 79.

[62] Ramsey, "Religion and Science, A Philosopher's Approach," p. 89.

[63] *Ibid.*   [64] *Ibid.*, p. 90.

[65] *Ibid.* Cf. Ramsey, *Religion's Language: Conflict and Synthesis*, p. 84.

[66] Ramsey, "Religion and Science, A Philosopher's Approach," p. 91.

[67] Ramsey, *Religion and Science: Conflict and Synthesis*, p. 6.

[68] *Ibid.*, p. 69.

[69] *Ibid.*, pp. 64-87, *passim.*

[70] *Ibid.*, p. 82. But as I have also emphasized in this chapter, the assertion, "God exists" has a logic similar in important respects to that of the phrase "I exist," being grounded in a disclosure, though this time of a cosmic kind. No one can therefore expect that language about God, anymore than the first-person assertions it resembles, will generate deductions capable of empirical verification. It happens, however, that this very peculiarity attaching to the logical character of "God exists" enables it, without generating the nonsense of category-confusion, to be linked with, as presupposition of, all empirical assertions.

[71] Ian T. Ramsey, *Christian Discourse: Some Logical Explorations* (London: The Oxford University Press, 1965) p. 89. Cf. Ian T. Ramsey, *On Being Sure in Religion* (London: The Athlone Press, 1963), pp. 22-23.

[72] Ninian Smart thinks that is precisely what Ramsey is doing. In his article, "The Intellectual Crisis of British Christianity," *Theology* (68, January, 1965) pp. 31-38. Smart calls Ramsey a "superstitious Atheist" and a humanist, identifying him with the humanism of R. B. Braithwaite, Ronald Hephurn, R. M. Hare, and Paul Van Buren. It is significant that Alan Richardson specifically distinguishes Ramsey from the above, citing Ramsey as an empiricist philosopher who does "not think that religious belief is only a matter of intentions and stories." *Religion in Contemporary Debate* (Philadelphia: The Westminster Press, 1966), p. 58.

[73] I. T. Ramsey, "The Challenge of the Philosophy of Language," pp. 260-61.

[74] Ian T. Ramsey, "Miracles," p. 21.

[75] Ian T. Ramsey, "Letter in response to Ninian Smart" in *Theology* (68:353, July, 1965) p. 111.

[76] Frederick Ferre says that Ramsey provides no way to distinguish between objective disclosure and illusion, that "experiencing-as-objective" is being confused with experience of the objective. Ferre says that Ramsey has only emphasized his claim, he has not defined it. Ferre, *Language, Logic and God* (New York: Harper and Row, Publisher, 1961) p. 141.

[77] Ian T. Ramsey, "Miracles," p. 21.

[78] I am not laying claim to *the* definition of "empiricism"; rather I am attempting to make some distinctions. For a discussion of the range of uses for the word "empirical," see James A. Martin, *Empirical Philosophies of Religion*, (Morningside Heights, New York: King's Crown Press, 1945) pp. 1-3. John Baillie, commenting on the verification principle says that it refers to "the region of experience as that with which natural science deals, namely, that gained through bodily senses." *The Sense of the Presence of God* (New York: Charles Scribner's Sons, 1963) p. 63.

[79] Ian T. Ramsey, "Miracles," p. 19.

[80] Cited by J. A. Martin, *loc. cit.*

[81] Good examples are: Werner Heisenberg, *Physics and Philosophy;* J. Brownoski, *Science and Human Values;* and Michael Polanyi *Personal Knowledge* and *The Study of Man.*

[82] For a readable exposition of this point of view by a contemporary philosopher of science, see Thomas Kuhn, *The Structure of Scientific Revolutions* (Chicago: University of Chicago Press, 1962).

[83] Dallas High has objected to what he considers a misuse of Wittgenstein's "language-games" analogy by those who so stratify language. See his *Language, Persons and Belief* (New York: Oxford University Press, 1967) p. 86. Stuart Hampshire says that "we cannot make a simple and absolute separation between levels of language. They have all been developed in the same context of a social life." *Thought and Action* (London: Chatto and Windus, 1959) p. 15.

18.
Scientific Knowledge as Personal Knowledge
Leroy Seat

In the preface of his distinguished book *Science and Faith,* Eric Rust states: "It will be noted how dependent this book is upon the thought of Michael Polanyi and I. T. Ramsey." [1] The purpose of this essay is to elucidate the content and explore some of the implications of the epistemological thought of Michael Polanyi, an author introduced to the writer while a graduate student by Dr. Rust, who was at that time beginning to write his book which is subtitled *Towards a Theological Understanding of Nature.*

Michael Polanyi became a master in three fields: physical science, social science, and philosophy. As a result of his intellectual pilgrimage from physical chemistry to metaphysics, Polanyi has given to the world a most valuable understanding of the nature of knowledge: a concept which he calls "personal knowledge." Since this concept has great relevance for an understanding of the nature of scientific knowledge, the writer has attempted to summarize and to explain the concept of personal knowledge in this essay. This summary will be preceded by a brief biographical statement about Polanyi and followed by an evaluation containing, among other things, some suggestions for the use of Polanyi's concept of personal knowledge in a Christian apologetic directed toward a scientific age that often seems at odds with the Christian faith.

Biographical Information

Michael Polanyi was born in Budapest, Hungary, in the year of 1891. At the age of 32 he became a member of the Kaiser Wilhelm Institute, but because of Hitler's rise to power he had to leave this position in 1933. After leaving Germany, Polanyi became professor of physical chemistry at Victoria University in Manchester, England. His status as a scientist is attested to by the fact that in 1944 he became a Fellow of the Royal Society. In 1948 Polanyi became professor of social studies at Victoria. He held this position until his retirement in 1958. Following his retirement, Polanyi lectured on his theory of knowledge at various English and American universities, including Cambridge, Edinburgh, Oxford, Yale, and Duke. He passed away in February of 1976.

Before 1946 Polanyi had published a number of scientific articles and had written briefly as a social scientist, but his first book of philosophical interest was published in that year. This book, *Science, Faith, and Society,*[2] was produced against the backdrop of a movement in England for the central planning of science, i.e., a forfeiture of the freedom of science. In opposition to this movement Polanyi called for a "dynamic free society" which enforces the tradition of science and, at the same time, assures its continuous renewal. This theme was further expanded in *The Logic of Liberty,* published in 1951.

In 1951-52 Polanyi delivered the famed Gifford Lectures in Scotland. Not only did Victoria University grant him the privilege of giving these lectures, but it also permitted him to exchange his Chair of Physical Chemistry for a professorial appointment without lecturing duties and to spend nine years almost exclusively on the preparation of this, his *magnum opus,* which was published in 1958 under the title *Personal Knowledge.*[3] Polanyi gave three lectures at the University College of North Staffordshire in 1958, and these were incorporated into *The Study of Man,* which was published the next year.[4] These lectures were intended to be an extension of *Personal Knowledge,* but they mainly recapitulated the relevant parts of the latter.

In 1960 Polanyi published a book under the title *Beyond Nihilism,* but more relevant to this study is a later work, *The Tacit Dimension,*[5] which appeared in 1967. Polanyi calls this book "an interim report on an inquiry started more than twenty years ago" (TD, p. ix). His other published writings during the last ten years of his life add little of significance to the subject of this essay and will be referred to sparingly.[6]

Summary of Polanyi's Concept of Personal Knowledge

Polanyi's most important book, *Personal Knowledge,* contains more than four hundred pages of finely written, detailed analysis of the nature of knowledge. In the space of this essay it would be impossible to give a complete summary of such a book. The writer has chosen, therefore, to state some generalizations about Polanyi's presuppositions and the philosophers to which his ideas are related and upon which, at least to some degree, they are dependent. Then a brief summary of Polanyi's purpose and central thesis will be given. This will be followed by a consideration of some of his key words, emphases, and conclusions.

Polanyi's Presuppositions

Polanyi would be the first to admit that all thinking stems from certain definite presuppositions. In fact, his work primarily deals with this matter. He stresses that "we incline to regard our own particular convictions as inescapable" (SFS, p. 25). It will be helpful, then, to take note of some of Polanyi's basic convictions.

Polanyi's philosophical orientation. Polanyi's philosophy can be described in terms of rationalism, idealism, and humanism. His rationalism is seen in his strenuous opposition to empiricism [7] and by his emphasis upon theory as of more significance than observation. He says that the main lesson to be learned from the Copernican revolution is that "we should consider as more objective that which relies to a greater measure on theory rather than on more immediate sensory experience" (PK, p. 4). Thus, he calls for abandonment of "the cruder anthropocentrism of our senses" and encourages "a more ambitious anthropocentrism of our reason" (PK, pp. 4-5).

Philosophical idealism holds that nature "is the expression of a universal Mind or Spirit that realizes itself at different levels and in different forms." [8] This seems to be the emphasis of Polanyi as seen in his view of evolution. He places strong stress upon teleology and the emergence of life from one level to another. This basic teleological force in the universe has now produced the human mind, but the process may go on towards an "unthinkable consummation." [9]

Connected with this idealism there is in Polanyi a definite relation to Renaissance humanism. One reviewer refers to him as an "aggressive humanist" with "a proclivity toward the deification of man." [10] This states the matter too strongly, but Polanyi does definitely have a high opinion of human beings and their capabilities. This is seen in his violent rejection of totalitarianism and his strict advocacy of a democratic society in which people can exercise their freedom.

Polanyi's relation to other philosophers. The main philosophers who seem to have influenced Polanyi most (or at least seem most closely related to his position) are Kant, Bergson, Dilthey, and Teilhard de Chardin. While Polanyi criticizes Kant at times and disagrees with him at some vital points, he refers to him in several places and quite clearly emphasizes with Kant that things cannot be known as they are "in themselves." [11] He also supports a kind of "moral imperative" (see PK, p. 309). There is an affinity with Bergson because of the emphasis on intuition, which Polanyi refers to as a "tacit component" of all knowledge. The relationship with Dilthey comes through the stress upon "understanding." Teilhard is obviously admired by Polanyi,[12] and the last chapter of *Personal Knowledge* bears resemblance to Teilhard's *The Phenomenon of Man.*

There is also a definite relationship between Polanyi and Augustine. Polanyi's central thesis (which will be dealt with next) is expressed in Augustinian terminology, and Augustine is quoted in various places.[13] In an article on faith and reason, it is Augustine's balance between the two that Polanyi seeks.[14]

Existential philosophy is also seen in Polanyi's work.[15] Indeed, one of the main points that Polanyi makes is that persons can never get outside themselves and their culture to make objective judgments. They have to choose between rival authorities, but this choice relies on "an ultimate commitment" (SM, p. 98).

A final matter to be mentioned at this point is Polanyi's relationship not to other philosophers but to psychologists. Polanyi's philosophy is based quite heavily upon the concepts drawn from Gestalt psychology.[16] He readily admits that he transposes "the findings of Gestalt-psychology into a theory of knowledge" (SM, p. 29). This theory is based upon the comprehension of wholes from a knowledge of parts. He emphasizes that "all kinds of rational knowing involves an existential participation of the knower in the subsidiary particulars known by him as their joint meaning or purpose" (SM, p. 32).

Polanyi's Purpose and Central Thesis

On the basis of the background just presented, it is now fitting to come to the heart of the matter. In this section, therefore, the writer has attempted to state as succinctly and as clearly as possible the central purpose and the central thesis of Polanyi's work.

Towards a postcritical philosophy. In the "Preface" of *Personal Knowledge* Polanyi says that his work is "primarily an enquiry into the nature and justification of scientific knowledge" (PK, p. xiii). But, in actuality, he deals with the whole problem of epistemology, emphasizing the impossibility of objective "proof." Later in the book he asserts: "The principal purpose of this book is to achieve a frame of mind in which I may hold firmly to what I believe to be true, even though I know that it might conceivably be false" (PK, p. 214). He also says that the aim of the book is "to re-equip men with the faculties which centuries of critical thought have taught them to distrust" (PK, p. 381). The subtitle of the book, therefore, expresses the purpose of the book: "Towards a Post-Critical Philosophy."

The heart of *Personal Knowledge* is found on pages 264-268; this is section 12 of the eighth chapter and is entitled "The Fiduciary Programme." Polanyi refers to the "critical movement" as the epoch in the philosophy of science, running from Bacon to contemporary logical empiricism, which insists that all meaning is a function of observation. But Polanyi calls for a return to the Augustinian emphasis that knowledge must be guided by antecedent belief. This is expressed in the formula *nisi credideritis, non intelligitis.* This doctrine was in the ascendancy for a thousand years, but the "faith declined and demonstrable knowledge gained superiority over it" (PK, p. 266). Beginning with the empiricism of Locke, "belief was so thoroughly discredited that . . . modern man lost his capacity to accept any explicit statement as his own belief" *(ibid.).* Belief was thought to be subjective, and thus inferior in its validity to empirical "truth." But Polanyi calls for a recognition of belief as the source of all knowledge. He says:

Tacit assent and intellectual passion, the sharing of an idiom and of cultural heritage, affiliation to a like-minded community: such are the impulses which shape our vision of the nature of things on which we rely for our mastery of things. No intelligence, however critical or original, can operate outside such a fiduciary framework.

While our acceptance of this framework is the condition for having any knowledge, this matrix can claim no self-evidence. . . . Our mind lives in action, and any attempt to specify its presuppositions produces a set of axioms which cannot tell us why we should accept them. . . .

This then is our liberation from objectivism: to realize that we can voice our ultimate convictions only from within our convictions—from within the whole system of acceptances that are logically prior to any particular assertion of our own, prior to the holding of any particular piece of knowledge (PK, pp. 266-267).

Personal Knowledge. The purpose of the book, to forward a postcritical philosophy, is based upon the central thesis of the book, *viz.* the concept of personal knowledge. Thus, the postcritical philosophy stems from a new epistemology that is neither objective nor subjective; it is personal. The currently accepted epistemology based on "complete objectivity as usually attributed to the exact sciences" is condemned as "a delusion and . . . a false ideal" (PK, p. 18). Polanyi's emphasis on "personal knowledge," therefore, is a substitute for this deficient epistemology and is presented as being "more worthy of intelligent allegiance" *(ibid.)*. This might be thought by some to eradicate science, but Polanyi believes just the opposite: "The elimination of personal knowledge from science would destroy science" (PK, p. 153).

Polanyi's thesis, in other words, is that there is a personal participation of the knower in the knowledge he believes himself to possess. He seeks to demonstrate this by showing

that into every act of knowing there enters a tacit and passionate contribution of the person knowing what is being known, and that this coefficient is no mere imperfection, but a necessary component of all knowledge. All this evidence turns into a demonstration of the utter baselessness of all alleged knowledge, unless we can wholeheartedly uphold our own convictions, even when we know that we might withhold our assent from them (PK, p. 312).

Thus, there is no proof; there is only belief, and "to believe something is a mental act" (PK, p. 313). Moreover, there is always the possibility of being wrong, for "you can only believe something that might be false." This, says Polanyi, is his argument "in a nutshell" *(ibid.)*.

Polanyi's Key Works, Emphases, and Conclusions

This section will serve to explain Polanyi's main thesis and to further expand what he means by the concept of "personal knowledge."

Objectivity. It is not hard to understand Polanyi's opinion about objectivity. He makes it quite plain in the preface of *Personal Knowledge* that according to his way of thinking "the ideal of strict objectivism is absurd" (PK, p. x). In *The Study of Man* he asserts that objectivism is "self-contradictory, meaningless, a fit subject for ridicule" (SM, p. 27). Thus, he thoroughly rejects "the ideal of scientific detachment" (PK, p. xiii). With the repudiation of objectivism comes the rejection of a strict empiricism (cf. SM, p. 21). Empiricism is "an indispensable clue to the understanding of nature," but "it does not determine its understanding" (PK, p. 150). In one of his many denunciations of "the Laplacean mind" Polanyi says that it "understands precisely nothing and that whatever it knows means precisely nothing" (PK, p. 141). Therefore, in this "enquiry into the nature and justification of scientific knowledge," there is nothing that Polanyi tries any harder to do than to show the impossibility, inadequacy, and absurdity of "scientific" objectivity.

The tacit component. The main reason why objectivity, as it is generally understood, is not possible is because there is a "tacit component" in all knowledge. In 1963 Polanyi affirmed that the concept of "the tacit knowing of reality underlies all my writings" (SFS, p. 10). What Polanyi means by this concept, which serves as the title of the second (and longest) part of *Personal Knowledge,* can be stated simply: all acts of knowing include an appraisal by the knower (PK, p. 17). Knowledge depends upon understanding, and understanding depends upon the participation of the knower in the act of knowing (cf. PK, p. 3, and SM, p. 72). In Polanyi's later book, *The Tacit Dimension,* this concept is simplified further. Here, in writing about "Tacit Knowing" (chapter one, pp. 3-25), he emphasizes the fact "we can know more than we can tell' (TD, p. 4). Thus, there is a distincition between explicit and tacit knowledge. Explicit knowledge is what is usually called knowledge, and it is capable of being clearly stated. But tacit knowledge is unformulated knowledge; it is what we know but "cannot tell" (see TD, p. 22). Explicit knowledge is based on and verified by observation, i.e., empirical tests; it is subject to critical analysis. But tacit knowledge is nonverifiable and a-critical (cf. PK, p. 264, and SM, pp. 16-17). Nevertheless, Polanyi holds that tacit knowledge is more fundamental and more important than explicit knowledge. He says that "we always know tacitly that we are holding our explicit knowledge to be true" (SM, p. 12).

This tacit component is illustrated in many ways. There is a tacit component present when one decides what constitutes evidence for a hypothesis. "Evidence" does not come so labeled in nature, but it becomes such only to the extent that it is accepted as such by observers (PK, p. 30), and where there are conflicting sets of presuppositions "the two sides do not accept the same 'facts' as facts, and still less the same 'evidence' as evidence" (PK, p. 167). Furthermore, says Polanyi, it is simply not true to say that scientists project "neutral" hypotheses and accept or reject these according to "objective" tests (SM, pp. 14-15). There are no set rules by which a hypothesis can be objectively tested (SM, p. 15). One simply accepts what he believes tacitly to be true and rejects what he believes to be false.[17] And no one, not even a scientist, "can forego selecting his evidence in the light of heuristic expectations" (PK, p. 30).[18]

Polanyi also illustrates what he means by tacit knowledge by reference to the work of the Gestalt psychologists. In *Personal Knowledge* he speaks of the subsidiary awareness that is present along with focal awareness (PK, pp. 55-58). Focal awareness centers on particulars in themselves; subsidiary awareness centers on particulars in terms of the whole. Meaning can only be gained by subsidiary awareness, but this is beyond the range of objectivity (cf. PK, p. 57). Physics and chemistry can analyze focally the parts of a machine, but the purpose and use of the machine can only be assessed in a subsidiary manner, and this involves a nonobjective judgment (SM, p. 52). The same is true for understanding persons; they cannot be known in terms of behavioral psychology (PK, pp. 332-334). In *The Tacit Dimension* Polanyi applies this concept to such simple matters of recognizing people. In such elementary acts of perception there is a tacit process of "subception" which cannot be fully explained (TD, pp. 6-7).

Polanyi also makes much of the fact that skills and connoisseurship can be acquired only through a tacit coefficient. There are no set rules by which one can "scientifically" obtain a skill or become a connoisseur. These are developed only through the personal participation of the individual in the knowledge which he gains from others. Likewise, the appraisal of probability and the assessment of order are acts of personal knowledge also (PK, p. 36).

Intellectual commitment. Polanyi makes much of what he calls "local rootedness." By this concept he means the presuppositions to which a person is committed before he begins to think. Back of all knowledge there is the pre-logical and a-critical commitment to certain implicit beliefs. No one has any clear knowledge of what his presuppositions are, and when one seeks to formulate them "they appear quite unconvincing" (PK, p. 59).[19] Moreover, there is no way to test or verify the basic set of presuppositions to which one commits himself, for "we live in the garment of our own skin" (PK, p. 64). These presuppositions are transmitted from one generation to another, and a child grows up committing himself to the presuppositions taught him. Thus, tradition is indispensable: "a society which wants to preserve a fund of personal knowledge must submit to tradition" (PK, p. 53). Knowledge, therefore, not only rests on understanding, but also on submission (commitment) to the society in which one lives (SM, p. 98). The only objectivity possible is the "objectivity" based on the premises shared by a community. This is as true for science as for any other discipline. "Science," says Polanyi, "is a system of beliefs to which we are committed: (PK, p. 171). Moreover, "the cultivation of science by society relies on public acceptance of . . . decisions as to what science is and who are scientists" (PK, p. 217). "Thus, to accord validity to science . . . is to express a faith which can be upheld only within a community" (SFS, p. 73). New theories are developed and new facts accepted only when the authority of the community is abandoned. Moreover, it can even be said that scientific "apologetics" with the purpose of "conversion" is necessary to convince others of the truth of new propositions (PK, p. 151). There is, therefore, an "ontology of commitment" behind all acts of personal knowledge (PK, p. 379). "Every act of factual knowing has the structure of commitment" (PK, p. 313).

Intellectual passion. The validity of personal knowledge rests upon the concept of intellectual passion; that is, its validity is guaranteed by the intellectual passion which impels one toward contact with reality and results in "a full measure of truth" (SM, p. 27). This is what keeps knowledge from being merely subjective: . . . "passionate participation in the act of knowing" shapes all factual knowledge and in so doing bridges "the disjunction between subjectivity and objectivity" (PK, p. 17).[20] Polanyi believes that "man can transcend his own subjectivity by striving passionately to fulfill his personal obligations to universal standards" *(ibid.).* "The effort of knowing is thus guided by a sense of obligation towards the truth" (PK, p. 63). Thus, intellectual commitment "is a responsible decision" and there is a "universal intent" in personal knowledge (PK, p. 65). A person who is free acts not as he *desires* in a purely subjective manner but as he *must* in a responsible manner (PK, p. 309).[21] There is a definite distinction between appetites and passions; appetites lead to subjective satisfaction, but intellectual passions spur one to responsible action as one seeks to apprehend truth (PK, p. 174). Thus, the theory of personal knowledge says that in making a decision, "a valid choice can be made by submitting to one's own sense of responsibility" (SM, p. 62).

Polanyi stresses that all intellectual efforts "are guided by the urge to make contact with a reality which is felt to be there already to start with, ready to be apprehended" (SFS, p. 35). When an intellectual problem arises, there is first perplexity and then effort to act in order to dispel this perplexity (PK, p. 120). This leads to what Polanyi calls "heuristic passion," the intellect striving to cross the "logical gap" created between the individual and that which he believes to exist but does not yet know (PK, p. 123). When the problem is finally solved, the discovery made, it always comes "with the conviction of its being true. It arrives accredited in advance by the heuristic craving which evoked it" (PK, p. 130). This leads to a "persuasive passion" by which one seeks to convince others of the truth of his discovery (PK, p. 150).

The heuristic passion, as manifested in science, is guided by "intellectual beauty" and a sense of rationality. Polanyi says that "the intelletual beauty of a theory is a token of its contact with reality" (PK, p. 145). Later he asserts: "Our heuristic self-giving is invariably impassioned; its guide to reality is intellectual beauty" (PK, p. 320).[22] Moreover, one makes "contact with reality in nature by recognizing what is rational in nature" (PK, p. 6). In the same way, "any critical verification of a scientific statement requires the same powers for recognizing rationality in nature as does the process of scientific discovery" (PK, p. 13). The heuristic passion, however, is not infallible, nor does the discovery always actually make contact with reality. Intellectual passions may be altogether misdirected or may be interwoven with others that are inherently erroneous (PK, p. 144). But there is only one truth (PK, pp. 315-316), and the community to which one is committed leads by general authority in this search for truth and eliminates the errors.[23]

Evaluation and Utilization of Polanyi's Concepts

In reflecting upon the monumental work of Polanyi, the writer in this critique will present both some positive and negative considerations and then conclude by proffering some suggestions for using Polanyi's central concepts in the development of an apology for the Christian faith, which is often considered to be intellectually suspect by many who have succumbed to the scientific spirit of a secular society.

Positive Considerations

On the whole, the writer believes that Polanyi's concept of personal knowledge is a valid and important concept. In an age in which science constantly threatens to become scientism and in which all intellectual disciplines—including theology and philosophy—tend to be forced into submission to positivism, it is encouraging to find a competent scientist who lays far greater stress upon faith and intellectual passion than upon strict empiricism. Of course there are those who think that Polanyi has sold his soul to irrationalism and needs, therefore, to be strongly rebuffed. Such a person is May Brodbeck of the University of Minnesota. She says that "the genus obscurantist has two species, the Lower and the Higher"—and, since Polanyi is a scientist, she classifies him as a "Higher obscurantist." The reason why he is so labeled is because Miss Brodbeck believes that he has depreciated reason in favor of faith or feeling.[24] She goes on to say that it is

"late in the day for these tender-minded assaults on the life of reason.
. . . It is time once again to stand up and be counted against the
forces of irrationalism whenever they appear, in no matter how benign
a guise." [25] However, this condemnation of Polanyi and of his concept
of personal knowledge is a *personal* judgment; it is not "scientific."
Thus, in seeking to repudiate Polanyi's thesis Miss Brodbeck has, in
effect, substantiated it. It seems to the writer that it is virtually impossible to present decisive arguments against the central concept of personal knowledge. One may analyze the paper and ink of the books
objectively, but how can there be any objective set of rules by which
the thesis is analyzed? Furthermore, one's opinion of the concept of
obscurantism depends entirely upon personal appraisal. Brodbeck's
judgment is one of condemnation, but Richard Gelwick, another reviewer, has only priase for Polanyi and his work. He specifically says
that Polanyi is not "an antiscientist, obscurantist, or incompetent
scientist." [26] And Polanyi himself speaks harshly against scientific
obscurantism! [27] This certainly gives support to the validity of his
concept of local rootedness and personal knowledge.

Negative Considerations

One can accept the central thesis of Polanyi's work and still not
agree completely with all the accompanying conclusions and correlative concepts. There does not, for example, seem to be a balanced
view of human nature in Polanyi's writing, i.e., balanced from the
Christian viewpoint. People are seen in their position as the highest
form of life in the universe, but they are not recognized as rebellious
sinners. Polanyi emphasizes that humanity is consistently seeking a
"hidden reality," which may be taken to mean "God" (see SFS, pp.
83-84). But if the biblical doctrine of sin is taken seriously, it must
be affirmed that "natural" people love darkness rather than light. In
contradistinction to the paradoxical view of persons as found in the
Bible, there appears to be more of a Greek idealism present in Polanyi
(see SM, pp. 67, 87), and this leads to what might be called an idealistic
evolutionism. Polanyi, it is true, makes mention of people's "fallen
nature" and their "propensity to do evil," but this is explained as
"the necessary condition of a morally responsible being grafted on a
bestiality through which alone it can exercise its own powers." [28]
But is there not more to sin than an evolutionary hang-over? Do all
people have a ;· ·sionate desire for truth as Polanyi suggests (see SM,
p. 62)? Polanyi states emphatically: "The freedom of the subjective

person to do as he pleases is overruled by the freedom of the responsible person to act as he must" (PK, p. 309). But is there always this compulsion and this degree of responsibility in sinful human beings?

Polanyi not only has an overly optimistic view of humanity, but he also fails to make any provision for the category of revelation. Polanyi appears to be a Christian (see especially PK, pp. 279-286), but he never has anything to say about God revealing himself. He frequently speaks about "hidden reality" but says nothing about the hidden God taking the initiative to make himself known to humankind. There is even apparent agreement with scientism's rejection of "the word made flesh" (see PK, p. 267). Certainly one can appreciate Polanyi's rejection of what has been called the "propositional" view of revelation.[29] This concept of "revealed truth" expressed in statements or propositions has been held by many theologians extending from medieval Catholicism to contemporary Protestant fundamentalism, and it is not unexpectedly rejected not only by modern scientists but also by most serious thinkers. But why must this mean a rejection of all revelation? How Polanyi could have included recognition or revelation in his writings is problematical, but that he did not is regrettable.

Here are two major areas where the writer feels that Polanyi's system is weak—but this does not affect his central thesis. And this criticism, as well as the one mentioned above, is a personal one, based on the writer's presuppositions and basic commitments. Since the central thesis remains valid, however, it is appropriate to consider in the next place some possible ways Polanyi's concepts can be used in developing a Christian apologetic for use in a scientific age.[30]

Utilizing Polanyi's Concepts in a Christian Apologetic

The Hebrews during the Babylonian exile lamented, "How can we sing a song to the Lord in a foreign land?" (Psalm 137:4, TEV). For most of this century the problem of many persons seeking to communicate the Christian faith has been, "How can we speak meaningfully about God or faith in a science-oriented world?" For several decades philosophers have been quick to point out the many "basic conceptual and methodological problems of religious language, and here the most significant influence has undoubtedly been science."[31] Largely because of the tremendous benefits reaped from science, the masses of common people came to accept science as "the supreme intellectual authority of the post-Christian age."[32] As Polanyi points out, to say, "It is unscientific," is the twentieth-century equivalent to the seventeenth-century objection which ruled supreme: "It is contrary to religion." [33]

The limitation of science. The value of scientific inquiry and of the scientific method should in no way be belittled. As Polanyi affirms:

Scientific genius has extended man's intellectual control over nature far beyond previous horizons. By secularizing man's moral passions, scientific rationalism has evoked a movement of reform which in the past hundred and fifty years has improved almost every human relationship, both public and private. A rationalist concern for welfare and for an educated and responsible citizenship has created an active mutual concern among millions of previously submerged and isolated individuals. Scientific rationalism has indeed been the main guide to intellectual, moral, and social progress since the idea of progress first gained popular acceptance about a hundred and fifty years ago.[34]

But Polanyi has also made it abundantly clear that science as well as religion depends upon personal knowledge, and neither science nor religion are free from prescientific presuppositions, commitment, or intellectual passion. While it is popularly thought that science is based upon objectivity which contrasts sharply with the subjectivity of religion, such is not the case. Following Polanyi, Leonard K. Nash in *The Nature of the Natural Sciences,* asserts:

We found in Chapters I and II that perceived "naked fact" is, if not quite mythical, at least substantially hypothetical. We find now that, in confrontation of "naked fact," scientific ideas are born of human minds suffused with extrascientific, metaphysical presuppositions.[35]

Similarly, a professor of physics at the University of Nevada states:

The ways in which scientists commit themselves to the standards of their discipline, exercise their responsibility for research of a universal and objective character, and rejoice in their discoveries are not sharply distinguishable from the religious functions of personal commitment to shared values of universal character, personal response to a calling to seek the truth and to come to know and love one another, and personal experience of revelation in response to existential difficulties. It is no longer possible to defend the old notion of value-free, impersonally objective science standing in sharp contrast with value-laden, unrealistically subjective religion.[36]

With the acceptance of Polanyi's thesis, therefore, proponents of the Christian faith are freed from responding to the present scientific age by either hostile opposition or meek submission. Even though it may often be thought that scientific method relies on nothing but systematic empiricism, hard facts, and cold logic, "this alluring conception of routinized Method is indefensible in the face of multiple objections." [37] Science, like every other intellectual discipline, is limited by the presuppositions, ideas, and theories held by the scientists. These presuppositions, ideas, and theories are like spectacles through which the natural world is observed, and "you cannot use your spectacles to scrutinize your spectacles." [38] This is the existential limitation of science, and recognition of this limitation allows religious faith to confront science on a common intellectual basis.

The necessity of faith. The scientific temper of the time has consciously and unconsciously led many to reject religious faith and "God-talk" as superstitious, unreliable, noncognitive, and spurious. But Polanyi has amply demonstrated in his writings that science as well as religious faith depends upon commitment and community support. Accordingly to Polanyi, science and religion are not separate dimensions. Since all knowledge is *personal* knowledge, there is a common ground between science and religion, and Polanyi asserts that it is on the basis of this common ground "that science should be reconciled with religion." [39] Following Polanyi, the first main conclusion in Ian G. Barbour's book *Myths, Models, and Paradigms* is this:

science is not as objective, nor religion as subjective, as the view dominant among philosophers of religion has held. Man the knower plays a crucial role throughout science. . . . Data are theory-laden; comprehensive theories are resistant to falsification; and there are no rules for paradigm choice. To be sure, each of these subjective features is more prominent in religion; . . . But in each of these features I see a difference of degree between science and religion rather than an absolute contrast.[40]

According to the concept of personal knowledge, scientific investigations as well as theological affirmations are based on the ancient aphorism *credo ut intelligam*. Thus, in Polanyi's postcritical philosophy religion is exonerated from the claims of scientism that religious knowledge is inferior to scientific knowledge because the former rests upon faith rather than reason. As a noted Belgian professor has asserted, this "enterprise of Polanyi is, in a sense, revolutionary, for it reverses a trend which has characterized the evolution of Western humanity since Descartes." [41] Thus it was in one of his earlier philosophical writings that Polanyi emphasized: "We must get rid of the obsession which forbids us to believe anything that we could conceivably doubt." [42] Then he adds: "It should have become clear by now that the method of discovering truth by eliminating everything that can be conceivably doubted is misleading." [43]

So for both science *and* religion, faith is indispensable. Since "behind the observable realm that science studies" religious faith "sees the transcendent presence, immanently active, the personal depth who sustains and redeems his creature," [44] faith in religion is more obvious than in science; nevertheless, Polanyi asserts that science "can never be more than an affirmation of certain things we believe in" and which we must hold even though we cannot prove them to be true.[45] One's scientific beliefs—as well as one's religious faith—"must be adopted responsibly, with due consideration of the evidence and with a view to universal validity. But eventually they are ultimate commitments, issued under the seal of our personal judgment." [46] Thus, the German physicist Max Planck, writing several years before Polanyi, summed up the matter well:

. . . science demands also the believing spirit. Anybody who has been seriously engaged in scientific work of any kind realizes that over the entrance to the gates of the temple of science are written the words: *Ye must have faith.* It is a quality which the scientist cannot dispense with.[47]

This recognition of the necessity of faith in scientific inquiry certainly makes religious faith far more legitimate from the scientific point of view than is ever possible for those under the sway of positivism.

The importance of community. It has been indicated above how Polanyi stressed the significance of a scientific community. Dr. Rust summarizes this point in the following words: the "personal aspect of scientific knowledge becomes very evident in the fact that science is a community effort, and that the scientific community is, at its own level, a believing and committed community." [48] In one of his essays, Polanyi refers to "the republic of science" and suggests that the community of scientists is organized in a way which resembles certain features of a body politic.[49] Since the scientific community is necessary for the continuation and development of science as it upholds and transmits presuppositions from one generation to another, so the Christian faith needs and is dependent upon the church, the community of faith. The teaching on "indoctrination" of the young within the church—both those young in faith and young in years—should not be neglected nor thought illegitimate, for the same thing is regularly done in society by the purveyors of the scientific world view. Just as the scientist, or the science-oriented person, gets support from the scientific community, so the individual Christian must have the support and sustenance of the community of faith. The Christian should accept that support and sustenance without being intimidated by those who erroneously accuse the person of faith of being influenced by group psychology or persons of authority; for the scientist is similarly influenced by the community of scientists and the authorities in his field.

Since scientific knowledge is personal knowledge just as is religious knowledge, science is not infallible, for it also relies on faith-commitment and a community of faith. Thus, the central emphasis upon personal knowledge made by Polanyi is highly significant for religious faith, for it removes much of the foundation upon which the criticism of religion by science-oriented persons is based and allows religious knowledge, faith, and community to be considered legitimate human activities.

There are other suggestions that might be made as to how Polanyi's concepts can be used in developing a Christian apologetic, but the above paragraphs indicate some of the most fruitful ways the concept of personal knowledge is helpful in affirming religious faith in this scientific age. And the writer remains grateful to his seminary professor who introduced him to the thought of Michael Polanyi—and in so many other ways helped this writer gain a deeper understanding of Christian philosophy, Christian faith, and Christian commitment.

NOTES

[1] Eric C. Rust, *Science and Faith: Towards a Theological Understanding of Nature* (New York: Oxford University Press, 1967, p. viii. References to Polanyi are made on at least twenty pages of this book, mostly in the sections on "Scientific Knowledge: Its Limitations and Implication" (pp. 38-84) and on "The Creator Spirit, Evolution, and Life" (pp. 145-200).

[2] Michael Polanyi, *Science, Faith and Society* (London: Oxford University Press, 1946). In 1964 this book was published by the University of Chicago Press both as a hardback and as a "Phoenix" paperback. This book will be referred to throughout this chapter by the abbreviation SFS, and page numbers will refer to the latter edition, which includes a twelve-page introduction written by Polanyi in 1963.

[3] Michael Polanyi, *Personal Knowledge: Towards a Post-Critical Philosophy* (New York: Harper & Row, Publishers, 1958). This book was republished by Harper and Row as a "Torchbook" in 1964. Throughout this chapter this book will be referred to by the abbreviation PK, and page numbers will refer to the latter edition.

[4] Michael Polanyi, *The Study of Man* (Chicago: University of Chicago Press, 1959). Throughout this chapter this book will be referred to by the abbreviation SM.

[5] Michael Polanyi, *The Tacit Dimension* (London: Routledge & Kegan Paul, Ltd, 1967). Throughout this chapter this book will be referred to by the abbreviation TD.

[6] Fourteen of Polanyi's essays published between 1959-1968 were edited by Marjorie Grene and published under the title *Knowing and Being: Essays by Michael Polanyi* (Chicago: University of Chicago Press, 1969). Several years later nine of Polanyi's essays written between 1945 and 1965 were compiled into a book: Fred Schwartz (ed.), *Scientific Thought and Social Reality: Essays by Michael Polanyi* (New York: International Universities Press, Inc., 1974). Polanyi's last published book was coauthored with Harry Prosch and entitled *Meaning* (Chicago: University

of Chicago Press, 1975). This book is based mainly on three series of lectures delivered by Polanyi from 1969 to 1971. Thus, the content of the book is almost completely Polanyi's, but Prosch, who during his sabbatical leave in 1968-69 worked with Polanyi at Oxford University and in the spring of 1970 collaborated with Polanyi in teaching a course on Polanyi's thought at the University of Chicago, prepared these lectures for publication in this volume. Prosch is also the author of a brief book entitled *Cooling the Modern Mind: Polanyi's Mission* (Saratoga Springs, New York: Skidmore College, 1971).

[7] See, for example, PK, pp. 150, 158, 167-170, and 266. In a 1959 essay entitled "The Two Cultures," Polanyi rejects what he calls "scientific rationalism," but this is the rationalism of science based upon strict empiricism (Grene [ed.], *Knowing and Being*, pp. 40-42). In this context Polanyi asserts: "Empirical induction, strictly applied, can yield no knowledge at all, and the mechanistic explanation of the universe is a meaningless ideal" (*ibid.*, p. 41).

[8] George F. Thomas, *Christian Ethics and Moral Philosophy* (New York: Charles Scribner's Son's, 1955), p. 148.

[9] See PK, pp. 404-405. This is the note on which the book ends.

[10] John W. Bennett, review of *The Study of Man* in *American Anthropologist*, LXII (1960), 887.

[11] See, for example, PK, pp. 269-274, and the introductory paragraphs of a 1962 essay, "The Unaccountable Element in Science," in Grene (ed.), *Knowing and Being, op. cit.*, pp. 105-106. For a brief discussion of the relationship of Polanyi's ideas to those of Kant, see R. J. Brownhill, "Michael Polanyi and the Problem of Personal Knowledge," *Journal of Religion*, XLVIII (April 1968), 115-118.

[12] Polanyi reviewed the *Phenomenon of Man* for *Saturday Review*. Here he acknowledges that he had "readily turned" to Teilhard when he rejected the current genetical theory of evolution. Michael Polanyi, "An Epic Theory of Evolution," *Saturday Review*, XLIII (January 30, 1960), 21. See also PK, p. 388.

[13] See, for example, PK, pp. 141, 181, 198, 209, 266, and 267.

[14] Michael Polanyi, "Faith and Reason," *The Journal of Religion*, XLI (October 1961), 238-239.

[15] See for example, PK, pp. 249, 318-320, 344; and SM, pp. 29, 87, and 98. Polanyi criticizes certain types of existentialism, however (see TD, pp. 58, 85). In his major writings Polanyi makes no reference to Kierkegaard, but there is an obvious connection between his idea of personal knowledge and truth and the latter's concept of truth. Compare, for example, PK, p. 286, with Søren Kierkegaard, *Concluding Scientific Postscript*, trans. David F. Swenson (Princeton: University Press, 1964), pp. 169-210. This is where Kierkegaard speaks much about truth as subjectivity.

[16] See especially PK, pp. xiii, 55-58, 97; SFS, pp. 10-11; SM, pp. 29-32; and TD, pp. 6-7, 43, 46, 95.

[17] At various places throughout *Personal Knowledge*, Polanyi shows how scientists have continued to hold onto old beliefs in spite of weighty evidence to the contrary. See especially PK, pp. 138, 292-294. The rationale for such "unscientific" procedures is given in an illuminating section called "Three Aspects of Stability" (PK, pp. 288-292). This section explains how implicit beliefs are maintained in spite of conflicting evidence. Cf. the section entitled "The Natural Selection of Scientific Theories" in Leonard K. Nash, *The Nature of the Natural Sciences* (Boston: Little, Brown and Company, 1963), pp. 272-284.

[18] For a discussion by a natural scientist of the meaning and significance of tacit knowledge see William T. Scott, "A Bridge from Science to Religion Based on Polanyi's Theory of Knowledge," *Zygon*, V (March 1970), 41-62; see especially pp. 47-50. Scott asserts that the concept of tacit knowledge is "the heart of the Polanyian system" (p. 41), and states that "the keystone of Polanyi's account of man in the world is his theory of tacit knowledge" (p. 47). Scott is also the author of "A Course in Science and Religion Following the Ideas of Michael Polanyi," *Christian Scholar*, XLVII (Spring 1964), 36-46.

[19] See also PK, pp. 60, 191, and 287.

[20] See also PK, pp. 300-303, where Polanyi discusses "the subjective, the personal and the universal."

[21] A free society is considered by Polanyi to be of the highest significance. See PK, pp. 214, 241, and the entire concluding lecture of SFS (pp. 63-84). See also chapters 12 and 13 of

Polanyi and Prosch, *Meaning, op. cit.* (pp. 182-216). In subsequent footnotes, references to this book will simply be designated *Meaning.*

[22] This is elaborated in detail in the second lecture incorporated in SFS (pp. 42-62).

[23] See also PK, pp. 135, 192, 300; and SFS, p. 71.

[24] May Brodbeck, review of *Personal Knowledge* in *American Sociological Review,* XXV (August 1960), 582-583.

[25] *Ibid.,* p. 583.

[26] Richard L. Gelwick, "Michael Polanyi—Modern Reformer," *Religion in Life,* XXXIV (Spring 1965), 225. Gelwick is one of the leading Christian scholars in the U.S. in the field of Polanyian thought. Gelwick's Th.D. dissertation completed in 1965 at the Pacific School of Religion was entitled *Michael Polanyi: "Credere Aude," His Theory of Knowledge and Its Implications for Christian Theology.* A lengthy article by Gelwick on the thought of Polanyi and its implications for Christianity was published under the title "Discovery and Theology," *Scottish Journal of Theology,* XXVIII (1975), 301-321. Finally, Gelwick has written a major book entitled *The Way of Discovery: An Introduction to the Thought of Michael Polanyi* (New York: Oxford University Press, 1977). Unfortunately, this book appeared too late to be used in preparation of this chapter.

[27] Polanyi, "An Epic Theory of Evolution," *loc. cit.*

[28] Polanyi, "Faith and Reason," *op. cit.,* p. 246.

[29] See John Hick, *Philosophy of Religion* (Englewood Cliffs, N.J.: Prentice-Hall, Inc., 1963), p. 61.

[30] Polanyi himself was the author of at least three essays that dealt with the relation of science and faith: "Science and Faith," *Question,* V (Winter 1952), 16-36, 37-45; reprinted as "Science and Conscious," *Religion in Life,* XXIII (Winter, 1953-1954), 47-58; "Faith and Reason," *Journal of Religion,* LXI (October 1961), 237-247; reprinted in Fred Schwartz (ed.), *Scientific Thought and SocialReality: Essays by Michael Polanyi* (New York: International Universities Press, Inc., 1974), pp. 116-130; and "Science and Religion: Separate Dimensions or Common Ground?", *Philosophy Today,* VII (Spring 1963), 4-14.

[31] Ian G. Barbour, *Myths, Models, and Paradigms: A Comparative Study in Science and Religion* (New York: Harper & Row, Publishers, 1974), p. 2.

[32] This statement is from a 1959 essay by Polanyi entitled "The Two Cultures" which first appeared in *Encounter,* XIII (1959), 61-64, and is included in Grene (ed.), *Knowing and Being, op. cit.,* pp. 40-46; quotation is from p. 40.

[33] *Ibid.* In the late 1970's with the problems of pollution, ecological imbalance, and the continuing stockpiling of nuclear weapons, there is more criticism of science than in the late 1950's. But even though science may no longer be the god it once was, it is still a major barrier keeping many from religious faith and commitment.

[34] This quotation is taken from the chapter entitled "Personal Knowledge" (pp. 22-45) in *Meaning,* pp. 24-25. Cf. Polanyi, "Science and Conscience," *op. cit.,* p. 58.

[35] Nash, *op. cit.,* p. 96. Nash cites Polanyi more than any other author living when this book was completed, and Polanyi acknowledged Nash's use of his views in *Meaning,* p. 57. Polanyi also said, "Thomas S. Kuhn's book *On the Structure of Scientific Revolutions* [sic] brought further confirmation of my views in detail" (*ibid.,* pp. 56-57). Kuhn, who for five years was a colleague of Nash at Harvard, makes little direct reference to Polanyi; see *The Structure of Scientific Revolutions* (second edition, enlarged; Chicago: University of Chicago Press, 1970), p. 44, for the main citation of Polanyi. But Kuhn's emphasis on the place of paradigms in science parallels Polanyi's stress on tacit knowledge. For a helpful treatment of this subject with reference to both Polanyi and Kuhn, see chapter six of Barbour, *op. cit.,* "Paradigms in Science," pp. 92-118.

[36] Scott, *op. cit.,* p. 57.

[37] Nash, *op. cit.* p. 157. At This point Nash makes reference to PK, p. 143.

[38] *Meaning,* p. 37.

[39] Polanyi, "Science and Religion," p. 14. In this essay Polanyi emphasizes that all knowledge is based on "indwelling." Then he asserts: "From the minimum of indwelling that we call observation we move without a break to the maximum of indwelling, which is a total commitment" (p. 12). Cf. Polanyi, "Faith and Reason," pp. 127-128.

[40] Barbour, *op. cit.,* p. 171.

41 Chaim Perelman, "Polanyi's Interpretation of Scientific Inquiry," in Thomas A. Langford and William H. Poteat (eds.), *Intellect and Hope: Essays in the Thought of Michael Polanyi* (Durham, N. C.: Duke University Press, 1968), p. 233. Perelman points out that in another sense Polanyi's thought is counterrevolutionary because it "goes back to an ancient tradition against which Descartes and Cartesianism fought with acknowledged success" *(ibid.)*.

42 Polanyi, "Science and Conscience," p. 58.

43 *Ibid.*

44 Rust, *op. cit.,* p. 141. The second and third sections of Part I of Dr. Rust's book deals with the nature of "Scientific Knowledge" and "Religious Knowledge," and Part II is entitled "Where the Two Forms of Knowledge and the Two Languages Meet."

45 Polanyi, "Scientific Beliefs," in Schwartz (ed.), *Scientific Thought and Social Reality,* p. 80. This essay was first published in *Ethics,* LXI (October 1950), 27-37.

46 *Ibid.*

47 Nash, *op. cit.,* p. 327, citing Max K. E. L. Planck, *Where Is Science Going?,* trans. J. Murphy (New York: Norton, 1932), p. 216. This quotation from Planck appears in an insightful section in Nash's book called "The Attitude of the Investigator" (pp. 326-333) in which, among other things, Nash asserts that "the deepest source of detachment is commitment" (p. 331).

48 Rust, *op. cit.,* p. 51. Cf. Scott, *op. cit.,* pp. 55-57.

49 Polanyi, "The Republic of Science: Its Political and Economic Theory," an essay written in 1962 and published in Grene (ed.), *Knowing and Being,* pp. 49-72; quote from p. 49. Nash, *op. cit.,* refers to the scientific community as "the invisible college" (see pp. 298-311).

19.
Leibniz and Locke
On the Relationship Between Metaphysics and Science
Robert M. Baird

R. G. Collingwood, in his *Idea of Nature,* historically traces three contrasting views of the physical world. To the Greek the natural world was a grand organism permeated by mind. In the sixteenth and seventeenth centuries the Renaissance mechanistic view prevailed: the natural world was conceived in terms of a well-ordered machine. Mechanism eventually gave way to an evolutionary conception of nature.

The middle period of Collingwood's analysis, the period of mechanism, provides the historical context for both Gottfried Leibniz and John Locke. A central philosophical problem during this period was the relationship between mind and matter. The attempts by Leibniz and Locke to cope with this issue gave rise to divergent views concerning the relationship between metaphysics and science. Their respective positions with regard to one aspect of that relationship is the focus of this chapter. Specifically, it will be argued that the metaphysical perspective of Leibniz resulted in considerable confidence in man's ability to grasp the laws governing phenomenal relationships and thus confidence in man's ability to obtain scientific knowledge. By contrast, the metaphysical perspective of Locke precluded confidence in man's ability to understand the laws governing phenomenal interaction. This resulted in a Lockean scientific agnosticism. There is an element of irony here which will be noted in the conclusion.

While acknowledging the abuses often present in metaphysical writings,[1] Leibniz defends responsible metaphysics as the source from which all the sciences ultimately derive their principles.[2] Metaphysics is the preface to all else. Nevertheless (and this is a crucial 'nevertheless') because of his native interest in science and because he recognized that "we are simple empirics in three-fourths of our actions," [3] Leibniz was concerned to distinguish clearly between the phenomenal world and its metaphysical foundations. That is, although the principles of physics can be deduced via the principle of the optimum from metaphysics, Leibniz also maintained—as noted by Leroy Loemker—that the principles of physics "can be established empirically and independently of metaphysics as well." [4] For example, in his essay "Specimen Dynamicum" Leibniz indicates how a metaphysical notion can be introduced to account for physical phenomena, but he then proceeds to demonstrate how the laws of that notion (in this case the concept of force) can be determined a posteriori or independently of metaphysics.

A careful examination of the Leibnizian analysis in "Specimen Dynamicum" clearly reveals this interest in discovering—independently of metaphysics—those laws governing phenomenal relationships. In his controversy with Descartes, Leibniz had realized the necessity of some metaphysical concept to account for physical phenomena. Descartes had argued that matter was pure extension, that the fundamental nature of matter was to occupy space. But, argued Leibniz, if a body is conceived simply as inert mass, indifferent to rest or motion, then it should be the case that when a small, light body collides with a big, heavy body the velocity of the smaller body would be completely transmitted to the larger body. One body (regardless of how small) should be able to move any other body (regardless of how large). Since such is obviously not the case, the concept of matter as pure extension, or inert mass, is unacceptable.

To provide a more adequate account of matter, Leibniz introduced the metaphysical principle of force. Force, implanted in matter by the Creator, is logically prior to extension. In fact, for Leibniz, neither extension nor motion have reality apart from force. Force is not mere potentiality as the scholastics had thought; rather, force contains within itself an actual striving or effort. This striving or effort sometimes appears to the senses, but even where it does not, it must be posited on rational grounds. Extension, according to Leibniz, is a repetition of the striving and counter-striving of force. Motion occurs in that moment when force strives for change. Leibniz interpreted his analysis as a clarification of Aristotle's notion of entelechy. But whether one calls it "entelechy," "form," or "force," such a principle, claimed Leibniz, must be introduced if one is to adequately characterize matter.

The Leibnizian distinction between the realm of metaphysics and the realm of science is depicted in the following skeletal summation of his analysis of force as it appears in "Specimen Dynamicum."

Leibniz's Division of Force[5]

I. *Active Force* (that principle whereby no matter is at perfect rest, but is always striving)
  A. *Primitive Force* (that force which belongs to the realm of metaphysics)
  B. *Derivative Force* (that force which belongs to the realm of science)
    1. *Inactive Force* (that force which is potential only, i.e., force which is a tendency toward motion)
    2. *Active Force* (that force which appears in impact)
      a. *Total Force* (that force which is comprised of both the relative and common force as described below)
      b. *Partial Force*
        (1) *Relative Force* (that force by which bodies within a closed system interact with one another)
        (2) *Common Force* (that force by which a system as a whole can produce external effects)
II. *Passive Force* (that principle whereby one body always resists the active force of another body)
  A. *Primitive Force* (that force which belongs to the realm of metaphysics)
  B. *Derivative Force* (that force which belongs to the realm of science)

The transition from the realm of metaphysics to science occurs when one reaches the level of derivative force. At this level, where bodies actually act and resist, the laws of dynamics are revealed. As a scientist, Leibniz is concerned with derivative force, for he is particularly interested in the dynamic tendency of bodies to produce modifications in one another.

As a means of demonstrating the independence of the phenomenal world from metaphysics, Leibniz proceeds to establish a posteriori "the universal rules of active forces in order to be able then to employ them for the explication of particular efficient causes." [6]

His procedure of measuring force involved two objects each weighing one pound and each suspended vertically. Now if the velocity of object A is twice the velocity of object B, empirical evidence will indicate, argued Leibniz, that object A will be raised four times as high as object B. Therefore, if the velocity of object A is two and the velocity of object B is one, A will be raised four feet whereas B will be raised one foot. The force of A is thus four times the force of B. This is clearly the case because A has done four times the work [7] of B. A has raised one pound four feet, whereas B has raised one pound only one foot. On the basis of this empirical evidence, Leibniz defined force as the product of the mass of an object times the square of its velocity.[8] Employing this concept of force, Leibniz devised other experiments in which the rules governing derivative force were used in explaining phenomenal relations.

Now the significant point of all of this is that Leibniz, the metaphysician, was convinced that one could have knowledge of the world of science independently of metaphysics, for the empirical world contains within itself the means whereby its phenomenal occurrences and relationships can be explained. Declared Leibniz: "the reason for any natural truth whatsoever is never to be sought immediately in the activity or will of God, but rather in the fact that God has enclosed *in things themselves* properties and determinations from which all their predicates can be explained." [9] So, although "the laws of nature . . . have their origin in principles superior to matter . . . nevertheless, everything takes place mechanically in matter." [10] The scientist can, in other words, provide explanations without explicit metaphysical considerations.

But what about these results of empirical investigations? To what extent can one be confident of such conclusions? To what extent can such investigations result in genuine knowledge? Does Leibniz, the rationalist, affirm that one can have scientific *knowledge* derived from the senses?

Leibniz, as is well known, distinguishes between truths of reason and truths of fact. The former are a priori and necessary; the latter are a posteriori and contingent. "Necessary truths are innate, and are proved by what is within, it not being possible to establish them through experience, as we establish truths of fact." [11] Truths of reason are verified logically, i.e., the truth is analyzed until it is reduced to an identity. Truths of fact can never be so reduced.[12] They must be verified by empirical observation.

Now here the important point is that for Leibniz, although truths of reason have a certainty superior to truths of fact or scientific truth, one is said to have knowledge of the latter.[13] In controversy with Locke, who refused to call that which is probable only knowledge, Leibniz argued, *"Opinion,* based on probability, deserves perhaps the name knowledge also." [14] It is crucial to note that Leibniz's position at this point is a direct consequence of his view of the physical world as a *well-founded* system of phenomena reflecting some "ultimate pattern of being." [15]

For Leibniz, scientific *knowledge* is knowledge of phenomenal relationships based upon sense experience, and he made explicit the criterion by means of which scientific truth can be said to be known.

I think the true *criterion* concerning the objects of the senses is the connection of the phenomena, i.e., the connection of that which takes place in different places and times, and in the experience of different men who are themselves, each to the others, very important phenomena in this respect.[16]

The conclusion is that scientific knowledge is an awareness of phenomenal relationships, the nature of which one may know even if one does not know the essences underlying the phenomena. As he unequivocally states:

. . . if indeed the definition of an actually existing substance should not be fully determined in all respects . . . we should not cease to have an infinite number of general propositions upon its subject, which would follow from reason and the other qualities which we recognize in it.[17]

Science is concerned with the outward manifestations of physical bodies, not with the inward metaphysical constitution of such bodies. Since sense perception enables one to arrive at the former, scientific knowledge is possible.

One would not be justified in concluding, however, that for Leibniz scientific knowledge is based simply upon sense experience. Leibniz agreed with Descartes that "an idea may be clear and confused at the same time." [18] Indeed, argued Leibniz, such is the nature of "ideas of sensible qualities." [19] Scientific knowledge must be arrived at, therefore, not simply by sense experience, but by sense experience rationally aided. Clear but confused ideas produced by the senses can become distinct when submitted to rational analysis. Leibniz affirmed this, though rather cumbersomely, in his claim that

the ideas of sensible qualities are confused, and the powers which should produce them furnish in consequence only ideas into which some confusion enters: thus the connections of these ideas can be known otherwise than by experience only as they are reduced to the distinct ideas which accompany them.[20]

And, for Leibniz, only when reason is allowed to judge the compatibility and connection of ideas can such ideas become distinct.[21] This methodological combining of sense experience and reason "presents a beginning in analysis which is of great use in physics." [22] For "one cannot go very certainly beyond the experiences one has had, when one is not aided by reason." [23] As Leibniz observed, we not only ask witnesses "what they have seen but also what they think." [24]

For Leibniz, then, scientific knowledge is the result both of sense experience in terms of which phenomena are discovered to be connected in a certain manner and reason in terms of which the conclusions of sense experience are further verified. Leibniz frequently illustrated this relationship between truths of fact and truths of reason by referring to the laws of optics (truths of fact) which are explained and verified by geometry (truths of reason).

With regard to the metaphysical reality underlying phenomena, three concluding observations are in order. First, such a reality is in one sense irrelevant as far as Leibniz the scientist is concerned. As a scientist he is concerned to establish—independently of metaphysics—those laws which hold between phenomena; he is not concerned with that reality which underlies phenomena. But, second, Leibniz was not simply a scientist. He was also a metaphysician. As a scientist *and* a metaphysician, he was concerned to develop a unified world view, a world view "which equally satisfies religion and science." [25] Leibniz was convinced that he had accomplished precisely this, for he had demonstrated "the possibility of inferring all physical phenomena from mechanically efficient causes," [26] while at the same time showing

. . . that mechanical laws themselves in their generality originate in higher reasons, and that, accordingly, we need a higher active cause which, however, only serves for the establishment of general and, accordingly, remote reasons. But once this is settled, then when it comes to dealing with proximate and individual causes, we have no further concern with souls or entelechies [i.e. metaphysics] . . . except for the sake of reflection on the purposes to which the divine wisdom had adhered in his ordering of things; that is, we should miss no opportunity to praise and glorify God.[27]

This relationship between metaphysics and science is summarized most succinctly by Leibniz in his claim that "these two kingdoms everywhere interpenetrate without confusing or disturbing each other's laws." [28] Finally, and most importantly for the present thesis, the very reason Leibniz was confident of man's ability to establish the laws governing phenomenal relationships independently (at least in one sense) of metaphysics was due to his confidence in the orderly nature of phenomenal relations, a confidence directly grounded in his particular metaphysical perspective.

In turning to John Locke one encounters a continually professed aversion to metaphysics. Locke's opposition to metaphysics led Maurice Cranston to conclude that "Locke brought no metaphysical preconceptions to the study of science." [29]

Granted Locke's intense interest in empirical investigations and his aversion to abstract a priori reasoning, Cranston is hardly justified in concluding that Locke was without metaphysical assumptions affecting his understanding of science. Indeed, Locke made several such assumptions which strongly influenced his epistemological views which in turn strongly influenced his perspective on science.

Locke's epistemology is founded upon the familiar Cartesian metaphysical distinction between mind and body.[30] Having concluded that what the mind knows are simply ideas, Locke defined knowledge as "nothing but *the perception of the connexion of and agreement, or disagreement and repugnancy of any of our ideas.*"[31] These ideas which constitute the objects of knowledge originate either in sensation or reflection, i.e., they originate in what is presented to the senses or in reflection upon the operations of one's own mind. Moreover, since there would be no mental operations and therefore nothing upon which to reflect if the mind were not stimulated by the ideas of sensation, sense perception itself is logically and psychologically primary.

Locke then proceeds to advance a causal theory of perception:

. . . since the extension, figure, number, and motion of bodies of an observable bigness, may be perceived at a distance by the sight, it is evident some singly imperceptible bodies, must come from them to the eyes, and thereby convey to the brain some motion; which produces there ideas which we have of them in us.[32]

This ability that bodies have to give rise to human perception Locke attributes to "the power that is in any body, by reason of its insensible primary qualities, to operate after a peculiar manner on any of our senses, and thereby produce in *us* the different ideas. . . ."[33]

These epistemological conclusions, rooted in certain metaphysical assumptions, significantly influenced Locke's analysis of scientific knowledge. He contended that the possible knowable relations between ideas may be reduced to four: identity or diversity, relation, coexistence or necessary connection, and real existence. The third of these possible relations, namely, that an idea "does or does not always coexist with some other idea in the same individual substance,"[34] is the type of relation from which is derived the subject matter of science. Moreover, whereas Locke maintained that one can have knowledge of the identity or diversity of ideas, of the agreement or disagreement of ideas in other relations, and of the actual existence of things, one *cannot* have knowledge of the coexistence of ideas or the necessary connection of ideas in individual substances. This means no less than that one cannot have scientific knowledge. His point: in science one arrives only at probability and "the highest probability amounts not to certainty, without which there can be no true knowledge." [35] Alexander Fraser has argued that Locke's favorite conclusion repeatedly drawn in his essay is that

> . . . men can have no absolute certainty, i.e., no strictly scientific knowledge, of the truth or falsehood of any *general* proposition regarding matters of fact. . . . Science, or complete knowledge of things really existing, transcends the faculties and experience of man.[36]

Locke believed that man could have intuitive knowledge of his own existence, demonstrative knowledge of God's existence, and sensory knowledge of the existence of finite beings, but scientific knowledge was beyond his capacity.

In order to appreciate Locke's conception of such human limitations, one must consider his view of substance. Again, an examination of Locke's metaphysics is necessary. Indeed, Locke's belief in the reality of substance was a metaphysical assumption. As John Yolton so clearly puts it:

> He [Locke] was not satisfied with sets of qualities furnished by experience, although he admitted that we can have no clear idea of the nature of substances except as this combination of qualities. A compulsion of reason, a rational postulate, forces him to add to the empirical qualities an unknown substratum, the abode of the real essence.[37]

In his analysis of bodies or substances, Locke introduced the notions of quality and power. Both of these concepts have been mentioned previously, but to reiterate Locke's point, "the power to produce any idea in our mind, I call [the] *quality* of the subject wherein that power is." [38] Locke distinguished three kinds of qualities in bodies: primary qualities, secondary qualities immediately perceivable, and secondary qualities mediately perceivable. By primary qualities, Locke had reference to qualities such as solidity, extension, figure, and mobility. These qualities are inseparable from the body of which they are a part. Then there are those "qualities which in truth are nothing in the objects themselves but powers to produce various sensations in us by their primary qualities." [39] Sensations thus produced are sensations of colors, sounds, tastes, and so forth. The power in a body to produce these ideas in the perceiver, Locke called secondary qualities immediately perceivable. Finally, there is "the power that is in any body, by reason of the particular constitution of its primary qualities, to make such a change in the bulk, figure, texture, and motion of *another body*, as to make it operate on our senses differently from what it did before." [40] These are the secondary qualities mediately perceivable, i.e., one is aware of them in body A only as a result of body A's effect on body B. Note that both immediately and mediately perceivable secondary qualities depend upon the constitution of the primary qualities.

This distinction between primary and secondary qualities is one of the most crucial Lockean metaphysical assumptions influencing his view of science. For the basis of Locke's argument against the possibility of scientific knowledge is his contention that "we know not the real constitution of substances." [41] Man does not know the constitution of the primary qualities of bodies upon which the secondary qualities depend. Ultimately, then, man cannot know the physical causes of secondary qualities, and without such understanding scientific knowledge is impossible. Scientific knowledge would require the perception of two kinds of necessary connections. First, one would have to be able to perceive the necessary connection between the primary qualities of a body and the ideas or sensations which it produces in the percipient, i.e., one would have to be able to perceive the necessary connection between primary qualities and secondary qualities immediately perceivable. Second, one would have to be able to perceive the necessary connection between the primary qualities of a body and the changes which it produces in the primary qualities of another body, i.e., one would have to be able to perceive the necessary connection between primary qualities and secondary qualities mediately perceivable. Scientific knowledge thus necessitates awareness of certain kinds of necessary connections which lie beyond man's ability to perceive. Scientific knowledge requires apodictic, universal affirmations or denials, but such affirmations and/or denials would be possible only if one knew the real essences of substances, only if one knew *that* upon which the behavior of bodies ultimately depends. Since such knowledge is inaccessible to man, so too is scientific knowledge.

One readily noticeable difference, then, between Leibniz and Locke is that Leibniz, contrary to Locke, believed that scientific knowledge was possible. The surface reason for this difference is that Leibniz, contrary to Locke, restricted scientific knowledge to probable knowledge of the phenomenal realm. As shall soon be noted, however, there is an underlying and quite significant reason why Leibniz was and Locke was not willing to introduce such a restriction.

Locke would agree with Leibniz that what we perceive is the phenomenal world. Moreover, Locke acknowledged that if one restricts himself to this realm, one can arrive at true and false propositions of *immediate* sense experience. As he expressed it:

. . . where the nominal essence is kept to, as the boundary of each species, and men extend the application of any general term no further than to the particular things in which the complex idea it stands for is to be found, there they are in no danger to mistake the bounds of each species, nor can be in doubt, on this account, whether any proposition be true or not.[42]

Locke even goes so far as to admit that one may be aware of "a constant and regular connexion in the ordinary course of things." [43] Despite this, Locke denies that one can have scientific knowledge. For although one may have some degree of awareness of subordinate laws, i.e., of the constant and regular connections in the ordinary course of things, nevertheless

that connexion being not discoverable in the ideas themselves, which appearing to have no necessary dependence one on another, we can attribute their connexion to nothing else but the arbitrary determination of that All-wise Agent who has made them to be, and to operate as they do, in a way wholly above our weak understandings to conceive.[44]

Since knowledge of such connections surpasses human understanding and since, for Locke, genuine scientific knowledge must go beyond phenomena to an understanding of these connections, scientific knowledge itself surpasses human understanding.

In his work *Morality and Freedom in the Philosophy of Immanuel Kant,* W. T. Jones in his analysis of Kant makes an observation in terms of which the distinction being made here between Leibniz and Locke can be clearly seen.

The observed sequence, A . . . B, say, the movement of a ball across a billiard table, may very well be the appearance to us of some underlying reality. But the question whether or not this is the case is irrelevant here and may be safely ignored, for our concern is with the character the sequence has at its own phenomenal level and with what, in particular, we mean when we judge that the sequence A . . . B is a causal sequence. It should be clear that the relations between the various items of the sequence are not affected by the fact, if it is a fact, that the sequence as a whole is the appearance of something else. . . . If all events are equally the appearance of an underlying noumena, we can determine the nature of the special relation (causality), which connects certain of these events to certain others, independently of determining what relation they all, collectively, have to this noumena.[45]

With minor alterations, Jones could very well be analyzing Leibniz's scientific perspective. Both Leibniz and Locke believed that the phenomenal world was an appearance of some underlying reality. But whereas Leibniz was convinced that phenomena itself constituted a series of events and relationships conforming to rules discoverable independently of metaphysics, Locke contended that there were no such rules, or at least that man could not discover them. According to Locke, one had to attribute such unknown rules to the *arbitrary* determination of God, and there is always the possibility that God in his mystery may from time to time act in such a way as to disrupt subordinate laws. This precludes, for Locke, anything like a Leibnizian confidence in phenomenal relations.

Leibniz, on the other hand, argued for the inherent comprehensibility of the phenomenal world. He specifically took exception to Locke's claim that "God, when it seems to him good, can put into bodies powers and modes of acting which are beyond what can be derived from our idea of body." [46] Leibniz replied:

I can only praise this modest piety of our celebrated author [Locke], who recognizes that God can do more than we can understand. . . . but I should not wish to be obliged to recur to the miracle in the ordinary course of nature and to admit powers and operations absolutely inexplicable.[47]

To the contrary, Leibniz argued that "the same force and vigour remains always in the world, and only passes from one part of matter to another, agreeably to the laws of nature, and the beautiful pre-established order." [48]

This Leibnizian response to Locke emphasizes the crucial point. Leibniz, unlike Locke, was able to restrict, with confidence, scientific knowledge to knowledge of the phenomenal world because of his metaphysical perspective. Leibniz's metaphysical position gave rise to his confidence in the orderliness of the phenomenal realm which he viewed as a series of events conforming to discoverable laws contained within the phenomenal world itself. Not only, therefore, was scientific knowledge, according to Leibniz, restricted to phenomena, but its validity as knowledge depended upon its being restricted to phenomenal relationships. Locke, on the other hand, lacked such confidence in phenomenal relationships. His metaphysics led him to interpret the phenomenal world as a series of events, the causes of which were hidden in powers beyond human comprehension. Consequently, he was convinced that scientific knowledge would have to go beyond phenomena to the internal constitutions of substances and to the necessary connections between primary and secondary qualities. As indicated, this made scientific knowledge altogether inaccessible.

Concerning that dimension of the relationship between metaphysics and science that has been emphasized here, it seems clear that Leibniz's view has prevailed. Quite to the point is Alfred Langley's observation that Leibniz's position with regard to phenomenal investigations "is also that of the modern scientist, who keeps strictly within the scientific realm and does not pass on to consider the ultimate metaphysical nature and ground of the phenomena he investigates." [49] Ironically, then, modern science has chosen the path of Leibniz rather than Locke in this matter, despite the fact that it was the latter who gave such impetus to modern science by his emphasis upon empiricism. Now one might respond to the foregoing analysis by arguing that Leibniz and Locke are not in fundamental disagreement and that what is actually involved is a verbal dispute concerning the meaning of the word "knowledge." Locke preserved this honorific term for that which is certain, while Leibniz was willing to apply it to that which is probable only. But this conclusion would overlook the significant difference between Leibniz and Locke which it has been the burden of this chapter to make explicit. Though Leibniz did not think empirical conclusions were certain (after all he did acknowledge human limitations), nevertheless he did have considerable confidence in the regularity of the laws governing phenomenal relations, a confidence growing out of his metaphysical perspective. It's precisely this latter regularity that Locke had difficulty with, a difficulty directly traceable to his metaphysical point of view. Here lies one interesting difference between Leibniz and Locke, an interesting difference because it illustrates clearly the significance of their metaphysics for their science.

NOTES

[1] Leibniz observes that "abstracts of metaphysics and such other books of this character as are commonly seen, teach only words." *New Essays Concerning Human Understanding*, trans. Alfred Gideon Langley (La Salle: The Open Court Publishing Company, 1949), p. 493. In fact, Leibniz's essay, "On the Correction of Metaphysics and the Concept of Substance," is a specific call for increased clarity in metaphysics.

[2] *Ibid.*, p. 495. Leibniz aligns himself at this point with Aristotle whom he associates with the view that "the other sciences depend upon metaphysics as the most general science and must derive from it their principles." *Ibid.*

[3] Leibniz, "The Monodology," *Leibniz Selections*, ed. Philip P. Wiener (New York: Charles Scribners' Sons, 1951), p. 538.

[4] Leroy E. Loemker (ed. and trans.), *Gottfried Wilhelm Leibniz: Philosophical Papers and Letters,* I (Chicago: University of Chicago Press, 1956), p. 56.

[5] "Specimen Dynamicum," *Leibniz Selections,* pp. 122-126.

[6] *Ibid.,* p. 133. Leibniz observes that he elsewhere worked out the same calculation of forces a priorily "by the simplest consideration of space, time and action." *Ibid.*

[7] What Leibniz called 'force' would today normally be called 'work' or 'energy.'

[8] This definition of force was contrary to the Cartesian position which defined motion as mass times velocity and then equated this with the quantity of force.

[9] "Specimen Dynamicum," p. 131.

[10] Leibniz, *New Essays Concerning Human Understanding,* p. 67.

[11] *Ibid.,* p. 80.

[12] At least truths of fact cannot be reduced to an identity by finite man. For God, truths of fact can be so reduced. For God, all truth constitutes a grand deductive system.

[13] Leibniz's view of scientific knowledge as truths of fact *supported by* truths of reason makes a simple identification of science with truths of fact somewhat misleading.

[14] *New Essays Concerning Human Understanding,* p. 417. See also p. 420.

[15] Loemker, *Leibniz: Philosophical Papers,* Vol. I, p. 37.

[16] Leibniz, *New Essays Concerning Human Understanding,* p. 422.

[17] *Ibid.,* p. 455.   [18] *Ibid.,* pp. 266-267.

[19] *Ibid.,* p. 267.   [20] *Ibid.,* p. 432.

[21] *Ibid.,* p. 446.   [22] *Ibid.,* p. 432.

[23] Leibniz, "On the Supersensible Element in Knowledge, and On the Immaterial in Nature," *Leibniz Selections,* p. 362.

[24] *New Essays Concerning Human Understanding,* p. 530.

[25] Leibniz, "Specimen Dynamicum," p. 132.

[26] *Ibid.*   [27] *Ibid.*

[28] *Ibid.,* p. 133.

[29] *John Locke* (New York: The Macmillan Co., 1957), p. 76.

[30] In his historical prolegomena to Locke's *An Essay Concerning Human Understanding,* A. C. Fraser notes that "the *Essay* starts, even in the Second Book, with the presupposition of two 'real existences,' to one or other of which all the simple ideas of men are assumed to be originally referable. The growth of our experience accordingly consists in the increased variety of simple and complex ideas gradually attributed to those two sorts of realities. Whence, he [Locke] asks, has the mind of man . . . Ideas . . . ? 'Our observation,' . . . [Locke] replies, 'employed either about external objects, or about the operations of our own minds, is what supplies the understanding with all its attainable materials of positive knowledge.' Here 'external sensible objects,' and 'our own minds,' are presupposed to exist. . . ." Locke, *An Essay Concerning Human Understanding,* (New York: Dover Publications, Inc., 1959), I, p. lxxxii.

[31] *Ibid.,* II, p. 167.   [32] *Ibid.,* I, p. 172.

[33] *Ibid.,* pp. 178-179.   [34] *Ibid.,* p. lxxvii.

[35] *Ibid.,* II, p. 203.   [36] *Ibid.,* I, p. xcv.

[37] *John Locke and the Way of Ideas* (London: Oxford University Press, 1956), p. 85.

[38] *An Essay Concerning Human Understanding,* I. p. 169.

[39] *Ibid.,* p. 170.   [40] *Ibid.,* p. 179.

[41] *Ibid.,* II, p. 256. This claim is repeatedly advanced by Locke in the *Essay.* See also II, pp. 27, 29, 62, 64, 65, 77, 85, 91, 111, 118, 136, 140, 218, 262, 265, 299.

[42] *Ibid.,* p. 253.   [43] *Ibid.,* p. 221.

[44] *Ibid.*

[45] W. T. Jones, *Morality and Freedom in the Philosophy of Immanual Kant* (London: Oxford University Press, 1940), p. 26.

[46] This statement appeared in a letter from Locke to Edward Stillingfleet. It is quoted by Leibniz in *New Essays Concerning Human Understanding,* p. 55.

[47] *New Essays Concerning Human Understanding,* p. 55.

[48] H. G. Alexander (ed.), *The Leibniz-Clarke Correspondence* (Manchester: Manchester University Press, 1956), p. 12. E. A. Burtt describes Leibniz at this point as confining "the divine activity to the first creation alone, and . . . , [Leibniz] contemptuously criticized his English contemporaries for insulting the Deity by the insinuation that he had been unable to make a

perfect machine at the beginning, but was under the necessity of tinkering with it from time to time in order to keep it in running condition." *The Metaphysical Foundations of Modern Science* (Garden City: Doubleday & Company, Inc., 1932), p. 292.

[49] Leibniz, *New Essays Concerning Human Understanding*, translator's footnote, p. 423. It should be noted that Langley, whose translation of Leibniz's work occurred in the latter part of the nineteenth century, was scarcely in a position to evaluate Leibniz with regard to contemporary scientific development. As events have transpired, however, Langley's statement has turned out to be an unusually clear, precise, and accurate evaluation of Leibniz's position in relationship to the twentieth-century situation in the sciences.

Publications by Eric C. Rust

I. Books

The Christian Understanding of History. London: Lutterworth Press, 1947.

Nature and Man in Biblical Thought. London: Lutterworth Press, 1953.

Judges, Ruth, 1 & 2 Samuel, Volume 6 in the "Layman's Bible Commentary." Richmond: John Knox Press, 1961.

Salvation History. Richmond: John Knox Press, 1962.

Towards a Theological Understanding of History. New York: Oxford University Press, 1963.

Science and Faith. New York: Oxford University Press, 1967.

Evolutionary Philosophies and Contemporary Theology. Philadelphia: The Westminster Press, 1969.

Positive Religion in a Revolutionary Time. Philadelphia: The Westminster Press, 1970.

Nature: Garden or Desert? Waco, Texas: Word Books, 1971.

Covenant and Hope. Waco, Texas: Word Books, 1972.

II. Contributions to Edited Volumes

"The Limitations of Science" in the *Official Report of the Seventh Baptist World Congress, 1947.* London: Baptist World Alliance, 1948.

Sermon: "The Challenge of a World Fellowship" in *Younger Voices,* ed. Graham W. Hughes. London: The Carey Press, No date.

"Does Science Leave Room for God" in *Science and Religion,* ed. J. C. Monsma. New York: G. P. Putnam's Sons, 1962.

Sermon: "The Hiddenness of God" in *Professor in the Pulpit,* ed. W. Morgan Patterson and Raymond Bryan Brown. Nashville: Broadman Press, 1963.

"History and Time" in *The Teacher's Yoke,* ed. E. Jerry Vardaman, Waco, Texas: Baylor University Press, 1964.

"Science and Ethics" in *Baker's Dictionary of Christian Ethics,* ed. Carl F. H. Henry, Grand Rapids: Baker Book House, 1973.

Articles on "Prophecy," "Man," "Sin," "Creation," "Grace" in *Encyclopedia of Southern Baptists,* Nashville: Broadman Press, 1958.

III. Small Pamphlet-sized Publications

So Lives the Church. London: Edinburgh House Press, 1944.

Preaching in a Scientific Age. Birmingham: Overdale College, 1951.

Faith and the Crisis of Meaning, James Montgomery Hester Lecture for 1975. Winston-Salem: Wake Forest University, 1975.

Faith-Learning Studies: History. Nashville: Sunday School Board of Southern Baptist Convention, 1969.

[Also translated into Spanish as *El Significado De La Historia Casa Bautista De Publicaciones,* 1972.]

IV. Articles (Denominational—Southern Baptist Sunday School Board and British Baptists)

In *The Baptist Student*

"Skeptic and Apologist," Vol. 36, No. 7 April 1957.

"Bringing Facts into Focus," Vol. 38, No. 2 Nov. 1958.

"Beyond the Stratosphere," Vol. 39, No. 9 June 1960.

"Isms that Threaten Man," Vol. 40, No. 8 May 1961.

"The Story of Philosophy," Vol. 42, No. 1 Oct. 1962.

"War and Peace," Vol. 46, No. 7 April 1967.

"Being the Truth," Vol. 48, No. 1 Oct. 1968.

"The Faith and Learning Conflict—Science," Vol. On To College, 1970.

"From the Garden to the Desert: The Quest for a Theology of Ecology," Vol. 50, No. 4 Jan. 1971.

"Christ and the Universe," Vol. 58, No. 6 Dec. 1978.

In *The Baptist Training Union Magazine*

"A Theology of the Incarnation," Dec. 1967.

In *The Young People's Teacher*

"The Son of the Living God," Vol. 4, No. 2, Feb. 1959.

In *Collegiate Bible Study*

"God's Representatives in Troubled Times," 10 Chapters, Vol. 9, No. 3 April–June, 1979.

In *The Fraternal,* Journal of the Baptist Ministers' Fellowship

"The Biblical Doctrine of Creation," April 1950, No. 76.

"The Contemporary Theological Scene—Parts I & II," July and Oct., 1970, No. 157, 158.

V. Journals and Magazines

3 articles on "The Bible and Revelation" In *Community, a Journal of Christian Interpretation,* magazine of the Christian Auxiliary Movement, London: Vol. XIV, Nos. 5, 6, 7, Nov. 1950, Jan. 1951, April 1951.

Articles in *The Review and Expositor,* Louisville, KY: Southern Baptist Theological Seminary.
"The Nature and Problems of Biblical Theology," Oct. 1953, Vol. 50, No. 4.
"Theology and Preaching,"April 1955, Vol. 52, No. 2.
"The Apologetic Task in the Modern Scene," April 1959, Vol. 56, No. 2.
"The Destiny of the Individual in the Thought of the Old Testament," July 1961, Vol. 58, No. 3.
"The Atoning Act of God in Christ," Jan. 1962, Vol. 59, No. 1.
"Creation and Evolution," April 1962, Vol. 59, No. 2.
"The 'God is Dead' Theology," Summer 1967, Vol. 64, No. 3.
"The Theology of the Lord's Supper," Winter 1969, Vol. 66, No. 1.
"The Church in the 1970's," Winter 1970, Vol. 67, No. 1.
"The Contemporary Theological Scene," Summer 1970, Vol. 67, No. 3.
"A Theology of Stewardship," Spring 1973, Vol. 70, No. 2.
"The Biblical Faith and Modern Science," Spring 1974, Vol. 71, No. 2.

A large number of book reviews across 26 years

Articles in *Theology Today,* Princeton, NJ
"Time and Eternity in Biblical Thought," Oct. 1953, Vol. 10, No. 3.
Review of *The Fulness of Time* by John Marsh, Oct. 1954, Vol. 11, No. 3.
Review of *History, Sacred and Profane* by Alan Richardson, Jan. 1966, Vol. 22, No. 4.

Articles in *The Journal of Bible and Religion*
"The Possible Lines of Development of Demythologising," Jan. 1959, Vol. 27, No. 1.
"Interpreting the Resurrection," Jan. 1961, Vol. 29, No. 1.

Article in *Philosophy Today,* Celina, OH: Society of the Precious Blood
"Christian Faith and Scientific Knowledge," Winter 1965, Vol. 9, No. 414.

Upper Rooms Discipline, 1973
Contributor of 7 Meditations for June 3-9.

Science, faith, and
revelation : an approach to
Christian philosophy